UNIX
IN A NUTSHELL

*A Desktop Quick Reference
for System V Release 4
and Solaris 7*

UNIX
IN A NUTSHELL

A Desktop Quick Reference
for System V Release 4
and Solaris 7

Third Edition

Arnold Robbins

O'REILLY®

Beijing · Cambridge · Farnham · Köln · Paris · Sebastopol · Taipei · Tokyo

Unix in a Nutshell, Third Edition

by Arnold Robbins

Copyright © 1999, 1992, 1989 O'Reilly & Associates, Inc. All rights reserved.

Published by O'Reilly & Associates, Inc., 101 Morris Street, Sebastopol, CA 95472.

Editors: Mike Loukides and Gigi Estabrook

Production Editor: Mary Anne Weeks Mayo

Printing History:

May 1989:	First Edition.
June 1992:	Second Edition.
August 1999:	Third Edition.

ISBN: 1-56592-427-4

[M]

[1/00]

To my wife, Miriam. May our dreams continue to come true.

To my children, Chana, Rivka, Nachum, and Malka.

Table of Contents

Part III: Text Formatting

Part IV: Software Development

Part V: Appendixes

Preface

The third edition of *Unix in a Nutshell* (for System V) generally follows the dictum that "if it's not broken, don't fix it." This edition has the following new features:

- Many mistakes and typographical errors have been fixed.

- Covers Solaris 7, the latest version of the SVR4-based operating system from Sun Microsystems.*

- Sixty new commands have been added, mostly in Chapter 2, *Unix Commands*.

- Chapter 4, *The Bourne Shell and Korn Shell*, now covers both the 1988 and the 1993 versions of ksh.

- Chapter 7, *The Emacs Editor*, now covers GNU emacs Version 20.

- A new chapter, Chapter 16, *man Macros*, describes the troff *man* macros.

- Chapter 13, *mm Macros*, through Chapter 16, which cover the troff macro packages, come with simple example documents showing the order in which to use the macros.

- Chapter 17, *troff Preprocessors*, now covers refer and its related programs.

- Chapter 19, *The Revision Control System*, now covers Version 5.7 of RCS.

- Commands that are no longer generally useful but that still come with SVR4 or Solaris have been moved to Appendix B, *Obsolete Commands*.

- The *Bibliography* lists books that every Unix wizard should have on his or her bookshelf. All books that are referred to in the text are listed here.

---

* The version used for this book was for Intel x86-based systems.

Audience

This book should be of interest to Unix users and Unix programmers, as well as to anyone (such as a system administrator) who might offer direct support to users and programmers. The presentation is geared mainly toward people who are *already* familiar with the Unix system; that is, you know what you want to do, and you even have some idea how to do it. You just need a reminder about the details. For example, if you want to remove the third field from a database, you might think, "*I know I can use the* cut *command, but what are the options?*" In many cases, specific examples are provided to show how a command is used.

This reference might also help people who are familiar with some aspects of Unix but not with others. Many chapters include an overview of the particular topic. While this isn't meant to be comprehensive, it's usually sufficient to get you started in unfamiliar territory.

And some of you may be coming from a Unix system that runs the BSD or SunOS 4.1 version. To help with such a transition, SVR4 and Solaris include a group of "compatibility" commands, many of which are presented in this guide.

Finally, if you're new to the Unix operating system, and you're feeling bold, you might appreciate this book as a quick tour of what Unix has to offer. The section "Beginner's Guide," in Chapter 1, *Introduction*, can point you to the most useful commands, and you'll find brief examples of how to use them, but take note: this book should not be used in place of a good beginner's tutorial on Unix. (You might try O'Reilly's *Learning the Unix Operating System* for that.) This reference should be a *supplement*, not a substitute. (There are references throughout the text to other relevant O'Reilly books that will help you learn the subject matter under discussion; you may be better off detouring to those books first.)

Scope of This Book

Unix in a Nutshell, Third Edition, is divided into five parts:

- Part I (Chapters 1 through 5) describes the syntax and options for Unix commands and for the Bourne, Korn, and C shells.

- Part II (Chapters 6 through 11) presents various editing tools and describes their command sets (alphabetically and by group). Part II begins with a review of pattern matching, including examples geared toward specific editors.

- Part III (Chapters 12 through 17) describes the nroff and troff text formatting programs, related macro packages, and the preprocessors tbl, eqn, pic, and refer.

- Part IV (Chapters 18 through 20) summarizes the Unix utilities for software development—SCCS, RCS, and make.

- Part V (Appendixes A and B, Bibliography) contains a table of ASCII characters and equivalent values (Appendix A), obsolete commands that are still part of SVR4 and/or Solaris (Appendix B), and a bibliography of Unix books.

Conventions

This book follows certain typographic conventions, outlined below:

Constant width
: is used for directory names, filenames, commands, program names, functions, and options. All terms shown in constant width are typed literally. It is also used to show the contents of files or the output from commands.

Constant width italic
: is used in syntax and command summaries to show generic text; these should be replaced with user-supplied values.

Constant width bold
: is used in examples to show text that should be typed literally by the user.

Italic
: is used to show generic arguments and options; these should be replaced with user-supplied values. Italic is also used to indicate URLs, macro package names, comments in examples, and the first mention of terms.

%, $, #
: are used in some examples as the C shell prompt (%) and as the Bourne shell or Korn shell prompt ($). # is the prompt for the root user.

?, >
: are used in some examples as the C shell secondary prompt (?) and as the Bourne shell or Korn shell secondary prompt (>).

program(N)
: indicates the "manpage" for *program* in section *N* of the online manual. For example, *echo*(1) means the entry for the echo command.

[ ]
: surround optional elements in a description of syntax. (The brackets themselves should never be typed.) Note that many commands show the argument [*files*]. If a filename is omitted, standard input (usually the keyboard) is assumed. End keyboard input with an end-of-file character.

EOF
: indicates the end-of-file character (normally CTRL-D).

^*x*, CTRL-*x*
: indicates a "control character," typed by holding down the Control key and the *x* key for any key *x*.

|
: is used in syntax descriptions to separate items for which only one alternative may be chosen at a time.

→
: is used at the bottom of a right-hand page to show that the current entry continues on the next page. The continuation is marked by a ←.

A final word about syntax. In many cases, the space between an option and its argument can be omitted. In other cases, the spacing (or lack of spacing) must be followed strictly. For example, -wn (no intervening space) might be interpreted differently from -w n. It's important to notice the spacing used in option syntax.

How to Contact Us

We have tested and verified all of the information in this book to the best of our ability, but you may find that features have changed (or even that we have made mistakes!). Please let us know about any errors you find, as well as your suggestions for future editions, by writing:

O'Reilly & Associates, Inc.
101 Morris Street
Sebastopol, CA 95472
1-800-998-9938 (in the United States or Canada)
1-707-829-0515 (international/local)
1-707-829-0104 (fax)

You can also send us messages electronically. To be put on the mailing list or request a catalog, send email to:

info@oreilly.com

To ask technical questions or comment on the book, send email to:

bookquestions@oreilly.com

We have a web site for the book, where we'll list examples, errata, and any plans for future editions. You can access this page at:

http://www.oreilly.com/catalog/unixnut3/

Acknowledgments

Thanks to Yosef Gold for letting me share his office, allowing me to work efficiently and productively. Deb Cameron revised Chapter 7. Thanks to Gigi Estabrook at O'Reilly & Associates for her help and support. Thanks also to Frank Willison for managing the project.

Good reviewers make for good books, even though they also make for more work for the author. I would like to thank Glenn Barry (Sun Microsystems) for a number of helpful comments. Nelson H. F. Beebe (University of Utah Department of Mathematics) went through the book with a fine-tooth comb; it is greatly improved for his efforts. A special thanks to Brian Kernighan (Bell Labs) for his review and comments. The troff-related chapters in particular benefited from his authority and expertise, as did the rest of the book (not to mention much of Unix!). Nelson H. F. Beebe, Dennis Ritchie (Bell Labs), and Peter H. Salus (Unix historian and author) provided considerable help in putting together the Bibliography.

Finally, much thanks to my wonderful wife Miriam; without her love and support this project would not have been possible.

Arnold Robbins
Nof Ayalon, ISRAEL
April 1999

PART I

Commands and Shells

Part I presents a summary of Unix commands of interest to users and programmers. It also describes the three major Unix shells, including special syntax and built-in commands.

CHAPTER 1

Introduction

The Unix operating system originated at AT&T Bell Labs in the early 1970s. System V Release 4 came from USL (Unix System Laboratories) in the late 1980s. Unix source code is currently owned by SCO (the Santa Cruz Operation). Because Unix was able to run on different hardware from different vendors, developers were encouraged to modify Unix and distribute it as their own value-added version. Separate Unix traditions evolved as a result: USL's System V, Berkeley Software Distribution (BSD, from the University of California, Berkeley), Xenix, etc.

Merging the Traditions

Today, Unix developers have blended the different traditions into a more standard version. (The ongoing work on POSIX, an international standard based on System V and BSD, is influencing this movement.) This quick reference describes two systems that offer what many people consider to be a "more standard" version of Unix: System V Release 4 (SVR4) and Solaris 7.*

SVR4, which was developed jointly by USL (then a division of AT&T) and Sun Microsystems, merged features from BSD and SVR3. This added about two dozen BSD commands (plus some new SVR4 commands) to the basic Unix command set. In addition, SVR4 provides a BSD Compatibility Package, a kind of "second string" command group. This package includes some of the most fundamental BSD commands, and its purpose is to help users of BSD-derived systems make the transition to SVR4.

Solaris 7 is a distributed computing environment from Sun Microsystems. The history of Solaris 7 is more complicated.

---

* Many other Unix-like systems, such as Linux and those based on 4.4BSD-Lite, also offer standards compliance and compatibility with SVR4 and earlier versions of BSD. Covering them, though, is outside the scope of this book.

Solaris 7 includes the SunOS 5.7 operating system, plus additional features such as the Common Desktop Environment and Java tools. SunOS 5.7, in turn, merges SunOS 4.1 and SVR4. In addition, the kernel has received significant enhancement to support multiprocessor CPUs, multithreaded processes, kernel-level threads, and dynamic loading of device drivers and other kernel modules. Most of the user-level (and system administration) content comes from SVR4. As a result, Solaris 7 is based on SVR4 but contains additional BSD/SunOS features. To help in the transition from the old (largely BSD-based) SunOS, Solaris provides the BSD/SunOS Compatibility Package and the Binary Compatibility Package.

Sun has made binary versions of Solaris for the SPARC and Intel architectures available for "free," for noncommercial use. You pay only for the media, shipping, and handling. To find out more, see *http://www.sun.com/developer.*

Bundling

Another issue affecting Unix systems is the idea of *bundling*. Unix has many features—sometimes more than you need to use. Nowadays, Unix systems are often split, or bundled, into various component packages. Some components are included automatically in the system you buy; others are optional; you get them only if you pay extra. Bundling allows you to select only the components you need. Typical bundling includes the following:

Basic system
  Basic commands and utilities

Programming
  Compilers, debuggers, and libraries

Text processing
  troff, macros, and related tools

Windowing
  Graphical user interfaces such as OPEN LOOK, Motif, and CDE—the Common Desktop Environment

Bundling depends on the vendor. For example, Solaris comes with text-processing tools. For others, they are an extra-cost option. Similarly, some vendors ship compilers, and others don't.

Solaris Installation Levels and Bundling

When you (or your system administrator) first install Solaris, you have the choice of three levels of installation:

End User System Support
  This is the simplest system.

Developer System Support
  This adds libraries and header files for software development.

Entire Distribution

This adds many optional facilities, including support for many non-English languages and character sets.

Note that many commands discussed in this book (such as make and the SCCS suite) won't be on your system if all you've done is an *end user* install. If you can afford the disk space, do at least a *developer* install.

For support issues and publicly released patches to Solaris, the web starting point is *http://sunsolve.sun.com*.

Solaris does not come with C or C++ compilers; these are available at extra cost from Sun. The GNU C compiler (which includes C++), and other free software compiled specifically for Solaris, can be downloaded from *http://www.sunfree-ware.com*. Although it does not come with pic, Solaris does include a modern version of troff and its companion tools.

What's in the Quick Reference

This guide presents the major features of generic SVR4, plus a few extras from the compatibility packages and from Solaris 7. In addition, this guide presents chapters on emacs and RCS. Although they are not part of the standard SVR4 distribution, they are found on many Unix systems because they are useful add-ons.

But keep in mind: if your system doesn't include all the component packages, there will be commands in this book you won't find on your system.

The summary of Unix commands in Chapter 2, *Unix Commands*, makes up a large part of this book. Only user/programmer commands are included; administrative commands are ignored. Chapter 2 describes the following set:

* Commands and options in SVR4

* Selected commands from the compatibility packages and from Solaris 7, such as the Java-related tools

* "Essential" tools for which source and/or binaries are available via the Internet

Solaris users should note that the following commands are either unbundled or unavailable:

```
cb        cc       cflow   cof2elf
cscope    ctrace   cxref   lprof
pic
```

Appendix B, *Obsolete Commands*, describes SVR4 commands that are obsolete. These commands still ship with SVR4 or Solaris, but their functionality has been superseded by other commands or technologies.

Beginner's Guide

If you're just beginning to work on a Unix system, the abundance of commands might prove daunting. To help orient you, the following lists present a small sampling of commands on various topics.

Communication

ftp	File transfer protocol.
login	Sign on to Unix.
mailx	Read or send mail.
rlogin	Sign on to remote Unix.
talk	Write to other terminals.
telnet	Connect to another system.
vacation	Respond to mail automatically.

Comparisons

cmp	Compare two files, byte by byte.
comm	Compare items in two sorted files.
diff	Compare two files, line by line.
diff3	Compare three files.
dircmp	Compare directories.
sdiff	Compare two files, side by side.

File Management

cat	Concatenate files or display them.
cd	Change directory.
chmod	Change access modes on files.
cp	Copy files.
csplit	Break files at specific locations.
file	Determine a file's type.
head	Show the first few lines of a file.
ln	Create filename aliases.
ls	List files or directories.
mkdir	Create a directory.
more	Display files by screenful.
mv	Move or rename files or directories.
pwd	Print working directory.
rcp	Copy files to remote system.
rm	Remove files.
rmdir	Remove directories.
split	Split files evenly.

`tail`	Show the last few lines of a file.
`wc`	Count lines, words, and characters.

Miscellaneous

`banner`	Make posters from words.
`bc`	Arbitrary precision calculator.
`cal`	Display calendar.
`calendar`	Check for reminders.
`clear`	Clear the screen.
`man`	Get information on a command.
`nice`	Reduce a job's priority.
`nohup`	Preserve a running job after logging out.
`passwd`	Set your login password.
`script`	Produce a transcript of your login session.
`spell`	Report misspelled words.
`su`	Become a superuser.

Printing

`cancel`	Cancel a printer request.
`lp`	Send to the printer.
`lpstat`	Get printer status.
`pr`	Format and paginate for printing.

Programming

`cb`	C source code "beautifier."
`cc`	C compiler.
`cflow`	C function flowchart.
`ctags`	C function references (for `vi`).
`ctrace`	C debugger using function call tracing.
`cxref`	C cross-references.
`lint`	C program analyzer.
`ld`	Loader.
`lex`	Lexical analyzer generator.
`make`	Execute commands in a specified order.
`od`	Dump input in various formats.
`strip`	Remove data from an object file.
`truss`	Trace signals and system calls.
`yacc`	Parser generator. Can be used with `lex`.

Searching

egrep	Extended version of grep.
fgrep	Search files for literal words.
find	Search the system for filenames.
grep	Search files for text patterns.
strings	Search binary files for text patterns.

Shell Programming

echo	Repeat command-line arguments on the output.
expr	Perform arithmetic and comparisons.
line	Read a line of input.
printf	Format and print command-line arguments.
sleep	Pause during processing.
test	Test a condition.

Storage

compress	Compress files to free up space.
cpio	Copy archives in or out.
gunzip	Expand compressed (.gz and .z) files (preferred).
gzcat	Display contents of compressed files (may be linked to zcat).
gzip	Compress files to free up space (preferred).
tar	Tape archiver.
uncompress	Expand compressed (.z) files.
zcat	Display contents of compressed files.

System Status

at	Execute commands later.
chgrp	Change file group.
chown	Change file owner.
crontab	Automate commands.
date	Display or set date.
df	Show free disk space.
du	Show disk usage.
env	Show environment variables.
finger	Display information about users.
kill	Terminate a running command.
ps	Show processes.
stty	Set or display terminal settings.
who	Show who is logged on.

Text Processing

cut	Select columns for display.
ex	Line editor underlying vi.
fmt	Produce roughly uniform line lengths.
join	Merge different columns into a database.
nawk	New version of awk (pattern-matching language for textual database files).
paste	Merge columns or switch order.
sed	Noninteractive text editor.
sort	Sort or merge files.
tr	Translate (redefine) characters.
uniq	Find repeated or unique lines in a file.
vi	Visual text editor.
xargs	Process many arguments in manageable portions.

nroff and troff

In SVR4, all but deroff are in the compatibility packages. Solaris comes bundled with a modern version of troff and its preprocessors (pic isn't included).

deroff	Remove troff codes.
eqn	Preprocessor for equations.
nroff	Formatter for terminal display.
pic	Preprocessor for line graphics.
refer	Preprocessor for bibliographic references.
tbl	Preprocessor for tables.
troff	Formatter for typesetting (including PostScript printers).

Guide for Users of BSD-Derived Systems

Those of you making a transition to SVR4 from a BSD-derived system should note that BSD commands reside in your system's /usr/ucb directory. This is especially important when using certain commands, because the compatibility packages include several commands that have an existing counterpart in SVR4, and the two versions usually work differently. If your PATH variable specifies /usr/ucb before the SVR4 command directories (e.g., /usr/bin), you'll end up running the BSD version of the command. Check your PATH variable (use echo $PATH) to make sure you get what you want. The commands that have both BSD and SVR4 variants are:

basename	du	ls	tr
cc	echo	ps	vacation
chown	groups	stty	
deroff	ld	sum	
df	ln	test	

This book describes the SVR4 version of these commands. (Often, the standard Solaris version of a command includes features or options from the BSD version as well.)

Solaris: Standard Compliant Programs

There are a number of different standards that specify the behavior of portable programs in a Unix-like environment. POSIX 1003.2 and XPG4 are two of the more widely known ones. Where the behavior specified by a standard differs from the historical behavior provided by a command, Solaris provides a different version of the command in /usr/xpg4/bin. These commands are listed here, but not otherwise covered in this book, as most users typically do not have /usr/xpg4/bin in their search paths. The manual entries for each command discuss the differences between the /usr/bin version and the /usr/xpg4/bin version.

ar	ed	make	rm
awk	edit	more	sccs
basename	env	nice	sed
cp	expr	nl	sort
ctags	get	nm	stty
date	grep	nohup	tail
delta	id	od	tr
df	ls	pr	who
du	m4		

CHAPTER 2

Unix Commands

This chapter presents the Unix commands of interest to users and programmers. Most of these commands appear in the "Commands" section of the *User's Reference Manual* and *Programmer's Reference Manual* for Unix System V Release 4 (SVR4). This chapter describes additional commands from the compatibility packages; these commands are prefixed with /usr/ucb, the name of the directory in which they reside. Also included here are commands specific to Solaris 7, such as those for using Java and the occasional absolutely essential program available from the Internet.

Particularly on Solaris, useful commands are spread across a number of different "bin" directories, such as /usr/ccs/bin, /usr/dt/bin, /usr/java/bin, and /usr/openwin/bin, and not just /usr/bin and /usr/ucb. In such cases, this book provides the full pathname, e.g., /usr/ccs/bin/make. In some instances, a symbolic link for a command exists in /usr/bin to the actual command elsewhere.

Each entry is labeled with the command name on the outer edge of the page. The syntax line is followed by a brief description and a list of all available options. Many commands come with examples at the end of the entry. If you need only a quick reminder or suggestion about a command, you can skip directly to the examples.

Some options can be invoked only by a user with special system privileges. Such a person is often called a "superuser." This book uses the term *privileged user* instead.

Typographic conventions for describing command syntax are listed in the Preface. For additional help in locating commands, see the Index.

Alphabetical Summary of Commands

addbib	`addbib [options] database`
	Part of the refer suite of programs. See Chapter 17, *troff Prepro-cessors.*
admin	`/usr/ccs/bin/admin [options] files`
	An SCCS command. See Chapter 18, *The Source Code Control System.*
appletviewer	`/usr/java/bin/appletviewer [options] urls`
	Solaris only. Connect to the specified *urls* and run any Java applets they specify in their own windows, outside the context of a web browser.
	Options
	`-debug` Run the applet viewer from within the Java debugger, `jdb`.
	`-encoding name` Specify the input HTML file encoding.
	`-J opt` Pass *opt* on to the `java` command. *opt* should not contain spaces; use multiple `-J` options if necessary.
apropos	`apropos keywords`
	Look up one or more *keywords* in the online manpages. Same as `man -k`. See also **whatis**.
ar	`/usr/ccs/bin/ar [-V] key [args] [posname] archive [files]`
	Maintain a group of *files* that are combined into a file *archive.* Used most commonly to create and update library files as used by the loader (`ld`). Only one key letter may be used, but each can be combined with additional *args* (with no separations between). *posname* is the name of a file in *archive.* When moving or replac-ing *files,* you can specify that they be placed before or after *pos-name.* See **lorder** in Appendix B, *Obsolete Commands,* for another example. `-V` prints the version number of `ar` on standard error.

On Solaris, *key* and *args* can be preceded with a -, as though
they were regular options.

Key

d   Delete *files* from *archive*.

m   Move *files* to end of *archive*.

p   Print *files* in *archive*.

q   Append *files* to *archive*.

r   Replace *files* in *archive*.

t   List the contents of *archive* or list the named *files*.

x   Extract contents from *archive* or only the named *files*.

Args

a   Use with r or m to place *files* in the archive after *posname*.

b   Same as a but before *posname*.

c   Create *archive* silently.

C   Don't replace existing files of the same name with the one extracted from the archive. Useful with T. Solaris only.

i   Same as b.

s   Force regeneration of *archive* symbol table (useful after running strip or mcs).

T   Truncate long filenames when extracting onto filesystems that don't support long filenames. Without this operation, extracting files with long filenames is an error. Solaris only.

u   Use with r to replace only *files* that have changed since being put in *archive*.

v   Verbose; print a description.

Example

Update the versions of object files in mylib.a with the ones in the
current directory. Any files in mylib.a that are not in the current
directory are not replaced.

```
ar r mylib.a *.o
```

/usr/ccs/bin/as [*options*] *files*

Generate an object file from each specified assembly language
source *file*. Object files have the same root name as source files
but replace the .s suffix with .o. There may be additional system-
specific options. See also **dis**.

→

Unix
Commands

as
←

Options

-m   Run m4 on *file*.

-n   Turn off optimization of long/short addresses.

-o *objfile*
    Place output in object file *objfile* (default is *file*.o).

-Qc Put the assembler's version number in the object file (when *c* = y); default is not to put it (*c* = n).

-R   Remove *file* upon completion.

-T   Force obsolete assembler directives to be obeyed.

-V   Display the version number of the assembler.

-Y [*key,*] *dir*
    Search directory *dir* for the m4 preprocessor (if *key* is m), for the file containing predefined macros (if *key* is d), or for both (if *key* is omitted).

---

at

at *options1 time* [*date*] [+ *increment*]
at *options2* [*jobs*]

Execute commands entered on standard input at a specified *time* and optional *date*. (See also **batch** and **crontab**.) End input with *EOF*. *time* can be formed either as a numeric hour (with optional minutes and modifiers) or as a keyword. *date* can be formed either as a month and date, as a day of the week, or as a special keyword. *increment* is a positive integer followed by a keyword. See the following lists for details.

Options1

-c   Use the C shell to execute the job. Solaris only.

-f *file*
    Execute commands listed in *file*.

-k   Use the Korn shell to execute the job. Solaris only.

-m   Send mail to user after job is completed.

-q *queuename*
    Schedule the job in *queuename*. Values for *queuename* are the lowercase letters a through z. Queue a is the default queue for at jobs. Queue b is the queue for batch jobs. Queue c is the queue for cron jobs. Solaris only.

-s   Use the Bourne shell to execute the job. Solaris only.

-t *time*
    Run the job at *time*, which is in the same format as allowed
    by touch. Solaris only.

Options2

-l   Report all jobs that are scheduled for the invoking user or, if
    jobs are specified, report only for those. See also **atq**.

-r   Remove specified *jobs* that were previously scheduled. To
    remove a job, you must be a privileged user or the owner of
    the job. Use -l first to see the list of scheduled jobs. See also
    atrm.

Time

hh:mm [*modifiers*]
    Hours can have one or two digits (a 24-hour clock is
    assumed by default); optional minutes can be given as one
    or two digits; the colon can be omitted if the format is *h*, *hh*,
    or *hhmm*; e.g., valid times are 5, 5:30, 0530, 19:45. If modi-
    fier am or pm is added, *time* is based on a 12-hour clock. If
    the keyword zulu is added, times correspond to Greenwich
    Mean Time (UTC).

midnight | noon | now
    Use any one of these keywords in place of a numeric time.
    now must be followed by an *increment.*

Date

month num[, *year*]
    month is one of the 12 months, spelled out or abbreviated to
    their first three letters; *num* is the calendar day of the month;
    year is the four-digit year. If the given *month* occurs before
    the current month, at schedules that month next year.

day One of the seven days of the week, spelled out or abbrevi-
    ated to their first three letters.

today | tomorrow
    Indicate the current day or the next day. If *date* is omitted,
    at schedules today when the specified *time* occurs later than
    the current time; otherwise, at schedules tomorrow.

Increment

Supply a numeric increment if you want to specify an execution
time or day *relative* to the current time. The number should precede any of the keywords minute, hour, day, week, month, or year
(or their plural forms). The keyword next can be used as a syn-
onym of + 1.

$\rightarrow$

at ←	*Examples* Note that the first two commands are equivalent: ``` at 1945 pm December 9 at 7:45pm Dec 9 at 3 am Saturday at now + 5 hours at noon next day ```
atq	atq [*options*] [*users*] List jobs created by the at command that are still in the queue. Normally, jobs are sorted by the order in which they execute. Specify the *users* whose jobs you want to check. If no *users* are specified, the default is to display all jobs if you're a privileged user; otherwise, only your jobs are displayed. *Options* -c Sort the queue according to the time the at command was given. -n Print only the total number of jobs in queue.
atrm	atrm [*options*] [*users* | *jobIDs*] Remove jobs queued with at that match the specified *jobIDs*. A privileged user may also specify the *users* whose jobs are to be removed. *Options* -a Remove all jobs belonging to the current user. (A privileged user can remove *all* jobs.) -f Remove jobs unconditionally, suppressing all information regarding removal. -i Prompt for y (remove the job) or n (do not remove).
awk	awk [*options*] [*program*] [*var=value* ...] [*files*] Use the pattern-matching *program* to process the specified *files*. awk has been replaced by nawk (there's also a GNU version called gawk). *program* instructions have the general form: ``` pattern { procedure } ```

pattern and *procedure* are optional. When specified on the command line, *program* must be enclosed in single quotes to prevent the shell from interpreting its special symbols. Any variables specified in *program* can be assigned an initial value by using command-line arguments of the form var=value. See Chapter 11, *The awk Programming Language*, for more information (including examples) on awk.

Options

-f *file*
> Use program instructions contained in *file*, instead of specifying *program* on the command line.

-F*c* Treat input *file* as fields separated by character *c*. By default, input fields are separated by runs of spaces and/or tabs.

---

banner *characters*

Print *characters* as a poster on the standard output. Each word supplied must contain ten characters or less.

---

basename *pathname* [*suffix*]

Given a *pathname*, strip the path prefix and leave just the filename, which is printed on standard output. If specified, a filename *suffix* (e.g., .c) is removed also. basename is typically invoked via command substitution ('...') to generate a filename. See also **dirname**.

The Solaris version of basename allows the suffix to be a pattern of the form accepted by expr. See the entry for **expr** for more details.

Example

Given the following fragment from a Bourne shell script:

```
ofile=output_file
myname="`basename $0`"
echo "$myname: QUITTING: can't open $ofile" 1>&2
exit 1
```

If the script is called do_it, the following message would be printed on standard error:

```
do_it: QUITTING: can't open output_file
```

batch

batch

Execute commands entered on standard input. End with *EOF.* Unlike at, which executes commands at a specific time, batch executes commands one after another (waiting for each one to complete). This avoids the potentially high system load caused by running several background jobs at once. See also **at**.

batch is equivalent to at -q b -m now.

Example

```
$ batch
sort in > out
troff -ms bigfile > bigfile.ps
EOF
```

bc

bc [*options*] [*files*]

Interactively perform arbitrary-precision arithmetic or convert numbers from one base to another. Input can be taken from *files* or read from the standard input. To exit, type quit or *EOF.*

Options

-c Do not invoke dc; compile only. (Since bc is a preprocessor for dc, bc normally invokes dc.)

-l Make available functions from the math library.

bc is a language (and compiler) whose syntax resembles that of C. bc consists of identifiers, keywords, and symbols, which are briefly described here. Examples follow at the end.

Identifiers

An identifier is a single character, consisting of the lowercase letters a–z. Identifiers are used as names for variables, arrays, and functions. Within the same program you may name a variable, an array, and a function using the same letter. The following identifiers would not conflict:

x   Variable x.

x[*i*]   Element *i* of array x. *i* can range from 0 to 2047 and can also be an expression.

x(y,z)   Call function x with parameters y and z.

Input/Output Keywords

ibase, obase, and scale each store a value. Typing them on a line by themselves displays their current value. More commonly, you would change their values through assignment. Letters A–F are treated as digits whose values are 10–15.

ibase = *n*

> Numbers that are input (e.g., typed) are read as base *n* (default is 10).

obase = *n*

> Numbers displayed are in base *n* (default is 10). Note: once ibase has been changed from 10, use digit "A" to restore ibase or obase to decimal.

scale = *n*

> Display computations using *n* decimal places (default is 0, meaning that results are truncated to integers). scale is normally used only for base-10 computations.

Statement Keywords

A semicolon or a newline separates one statement from another. Curly braces are needed only when grouping multiple statements.

if (*rel-expr*) {*statements*}

> Do one or more *statements* if relational expression *rel-expr* is true; for example:

>   **if (x == y) i = i + 1**

while (*rel-expr*) {*statements*}

> Repeat one or more *statements* while *rel-expr* is true; for example:

>   **while (i > 0) {p = p*n; q = a/b; i = i-1}**

for (*expr1*; *rel-expr*; *expr2*) {*statements*}

> Similar to while; for example, to print the first 10 multiples of 5, you could type:

>   **for (i = 1; i <= 10; i++) i*5**

break

> Terminate a while or for statement.

quit

> Exit bc.

Function Keywords

define *j*(*k*) {

> Begin the definition of function *j* having a single argument *k*. Additional arguments are allowed, separated by commas. Statements follow on successive lines. End with a }.

$\rightarrow$

auto *x, y*

> Set up *x* and *y* as variables local to a function definition, initialized to 0 and meaningless outside the function. Must appear first.

return(*expr*)

> Pass the value of expression *expr* back to the program. Return 0 if (*expr*) is left off. Used in function definitions.

sqrt(*expr*)

> Compute the square root of expression *expr.*

length(*expr*)

> Compute how many digits are in *expr.*

scale(*expr*)

> Same, but count only digits to the right of the decimal point.

Math Library Functions

These are available when bc is invoked with -l. Library functions set scale to 20.

s(*angle*)

> Compute the sine of *angle*, a constant or expression in radians.

c(*angle*)

> Compute the cosine of *angle*, a constant or expression in radians.

a(*n*)

> Compute the arctangent of *n*, returning an angle in radians.

e(*expr*)

> Compute *e* to the power of *expr.*

l(*expr*)

> Compute natural log of *expr.*

j(*n, x*)

> Compute Bessel function of integer order *n.*

Operators

These consist of operators and other symbols. Operators can be arithmetic, unary, assignment, or relational.

Arithmetic	+	-	*	/	%	^
Unary	-	++	--			
Assignment	=+	=-	=*	=/	=%	=^ =
Relational	<	<=	>	>=	==	!=

Other Symbols

/* */
> Enclose comments.

( ) Control the evaluation of expressions (change precedence). Can also be used around assignment statements to force the result to print.

{ } Used to group statements.

[ ] Array index.

"text"
> Use as a statement to print *text*.

Examples

Note that when you type some quantity (a number or expression), it is evaluated and printed, but assignment statements produce no display:

```
ibase = 8          Octal input
20                 Evaluate this octal number
16                 Terminal displays decimal value
obase = 2          Display output in base 2 instead of base 10
20                 Octal input
10000              Terminal now displays binary value
ibase = A          Restore base 10 input
scale = 3          Truncate results to three places
8/7                Evaluate a division
1.001001000        Oops! Forgot to reset output base to 10
obase = 10         Input is decimal now, so "A" isn't needed
8/7
1.142              Terminal displays result (truncated)
```

The following lines show the use of functions:

```
define p(r,n){     Function p uses two arguments
  auto v           v is a local variable
  v = r^n          r raised to the n power
  return(v)}       Value returned
scale = 5
x = p(2.5,2)       x = 2.5 ^ 2
x                  Print value of x
6.25
length(x)          Number of digits
3
scale(x)           Number of places to right of decimal point
2
```

---

bdiff *file1 file2* [*options*]

Compare *file1* with *file2* and report the differing lines. bdiff splits the files and then runs diff, allowing it to act on files that would

→

Unix
Commands

bdiff
←

normally be too large to handle. `bdiff` reads standard input if one of the files is –. See also **diff**.

Options

n   Split each file into *n*-line segments (default is 3500). This option must be listed first.

-s   Suppress error messages from `bdiff` (but not from `diff`).

biff

/usr/ucb/biff [y | n]

Turn mail notification on or off. With no arguments, `biff` indicates the current status.

When mail notification is turned on, each time you get incoming mail, the bell rings, and the first few lines of each message are displayed.

cal

cal [[*month*] *year*]

With no arguments, print a calendar for the current month. Otherwise, print either a 12-month calendar (beginning with January) for the given *year* or a one-month calendar of the given *month* and *year*. *month* ranges from 1 to 12; *year* ranges from 1 to 9999.

Examples

```
cal 12 1999
cal 1999 > year_file
```

calendar

calendar [*option*]

Read your `calendar` file and display all lines that contain the current date. The `calendar` file is like a memo board. You create the file and add entries like the following:

```
5/4     meeting with design group at 2 pm
may 6   pick up anniversary card on way home
```

When you run `calendar` on May 4, the first line is displayed. `calendar` can be automated by using `crontab` or `at`, or by including it in your startup files .profile or .login.

Option

–   Allow a privileged user to invoke `calendar` for all users, searching each user's login directory for a file named `calendar`. Entries that match are sent to a user via mail. This feature is intended for use via cron. It is not recommended in networked environments with large user bases.

---

cancel [*options*] [*printer*]

Cancel print requests made with lp. The request can be specified by its ID, by the *printer* on which it is currently printing, or by the username associated with the request (only privileged users can cancel another user's print requests). Use lpstat to determine either the *id* or the *printer* to cancel.

Options

id   Cancel print request *id*.

-u *user*
    Cancel request associated with *user*.

---

cat [*options*] [*files*]

Read one or more *files* and print them on standard output. Read standard input if no *files* are specified or if – is specified as one of the files; end input with *EOF*. Use the > shell operator to combine several files into a new file; >> appends files to an existing file.

Options

-b   Like -n, but don't number blank lines. Solaris only.

-e   Print a $ to mark the end of each line. Must be used with -v.

-n   Number lines. Solaris only.

-s   Suppress messages about nonexistent files. (Note: On some systems, -s squeezes out extra blank lines.)

-t   Print each tab as ^I and each form feed as ^L. Must be used with -v.

-u   Print output as unbuffered (default is buffered in blocks or screen lines).

-v   Display control characters and other nonprinting characters.

Examples

```
cat ch1                    Display a file
cat ch1 ch2 ch3 > all      Combine files
cat note5 >> notes         Append to a file
cat > temp1                Create file at terminal; end with EOF
cat > temp2 << STOP        Create file at terminal; end with STOP
```

cb	cb [*options*] [*files*] C program "beautifier" that formats *files* using proper C programming structure. **Options** -j Join split lines. -l *length* Split lines longer than *length*. -s Standardize code to style of Kernighan and Ritchie in *The C Programming Language*. -V Print the version of cb on standard error. *Example* `cb -l 70 calc.c > calc_new.c`
cc	/usr/ccs/bin/cc [*options*] *files* Compile one or more C source files (*file*.c), assembler source files (*file*.s), or preprocessed C source files (*file*.i). cc automatically invokes the loader ld (unless -c is supplied). In some cases, cc generates an object file having a .o suffix and a corresponding root name. By default, output is placed in a.out. cc accepts additional system-specific options. *Notes* • Add /usr/ccs/bin to your PATH to use the C compiler and other C Compilation System tools. This command runs the ANSI C compiler; use /usr/bin/cc if you want to run the compiler for pre-ANSI C. • Solaris 7 does not come with a C compiler. You must purchase one separately from Sun, or download the GNU C Compiler (GCC) from *http://www.sunfreeware.com*. • Options for cc vary wildly across Unix systems. We have chosen here to document only those options that are commonly available. You will need to check your local documentation for complete information. • Usually, cc passes any unrecognized options to the loader, ld.

-c　Suppress loading and keep any object files that were produced.

-D*name*[=*def*]
　　Supply a #define directive, defining *name* to be *def* or, if no
　　def is given, the value 1.

-E　Run only the macro preprocessor, sending results to standard
output.

-g　Generate more symbol-table information needed for debuggers.

-I*dir*
　　Search for include files in directory *dir* (in addition to stan-
　　dard locations). Supply a -I for each new *dir* to be searched.

-l*name*
　　Link source *file* with library files lib*name*.so or lib*name*.a.

-L*dir*
　　Like -I, but search *dir* for library archives.

-o *file*
　　Send object output to *file* instead of to a.out.

-O　Optimize object code (produced from .c or .i files).

-p　Generate benchmark code to count the times each routine is
called. File mon.out is created, so prof can be used later to
produce an execution profile.

-P　Run only the preprocessor and place the result in *file*.i.

-S　Compile (and optimize, if -O is supplied), but don't assemble
or load; assembler output is placed in *file*.s.

-U*name*
　　Remove definition of name, as if through an #undef directive.

Example

Compile xpop.c and load it with the X libraries:

```
cc -o xpop xpop.c -lXaw -lXmu -lXt -lX11
```

---

cd [*dir*]　　　　　　　　　　　　　　　　　　　　　　　　　cd

Change directory. cd is a built-in shell command. See Chapter 4,
The Bourne Shell and Korn Shell, and Chapter 5, *The C Shell*.

cdc	`/usr/ccs/bin/cdc -rsid [option] files` An SCCS command. See Chapter 18.
cde	**Common Desktop Environment** Solaris only. The Common Desktop Environment (CDE) is the default graphical user interface (GUI) on Solaris systems. Solaris 7 users may choose between CDE and OpenWindows, but OpenWindows is marked as obsolete and not supported past Solaris 7. Documenting CDE would require its own book and is beyond the scope of this one. Instead, listed here are some of the more useful individual CDE commands, which are kept in `/usr/dt/bin`. (Commands for the Desktop.) In addition, a number of OpenWindows commands are still useful. See the listing under **openwin** in Appendix B.

Useful CDE Programs

The following CDE and Sun Desktop commands may be of interest. Check the manpages for more information.

answerbook2	Sun hypertext documentation viewer.
dtaction	Invoke CDE actions from within shell scripts.
dtbuilder	CDE applications builder.
dtcalc	Onscreen scientific, logical, and financial calculator.
dtcm	Calendar manager.
dterror.ds	dtksh script for error notices and dialogues.
dtfile_error	dtksh script for error dialogues.
dticon	Icon editor.
dtksh	The "Desktop Korn shell," a version of ksh93.
dtmail	Mail reader.
dtpad	Simple text editor.
dtprintinfo	Print job manager.
dtscreen	Screen savers.
dtterm	Terminal emulator.
fdl	Font downloader utility for PostScript printers.
hotjava	Java-based web browser.
sdtconvtool	GUI for iconv.
sdtfind	File finder.
sdtimage	Image viewer (PostScript, GIF, JPEG, etc.).
sdtperfmeter	System performance meter.
sdtprocess	Process manager.

`cflow [options] files`

Produce an outline (or flowchart) of external function calls for the C, lex, yacc, assembler, or object *files*. cflow also accepts the cc options -D, -I, and -U.

Options

-d*n* Stop outlining when nesting level *n* is reached.

-i_ Include functions whose names begin with _.

-ix Include external and static data symbols.

-r Invert the listing; show the callers of each function and sort in lexicographical order by callee.

`checkeq [files]`

Solaris only. Check nroff/troff input files for missing or unbalanced eqn delimiters. checkeq checks both .EQ/.EN pairs and inline delimiters as indicated by the delim statement.

`checknr [options] [files]`

Solaris only. Check nroff/troff source files for mismatched delimiters and unknown commands. It also checks for macros that come in open/close pairs, such as .TS and .TE. With no *files*, checks the standard input.

checknr works best when input is designed for its conventions: \fP always ends a font change, and \s0 always restores a point-size change. checknr knows about the *me* and *ms* macros.

Options

-a*macros*
    Add new pairs of macros that come in open/close pairs. The six characters representing the new macros must immediately follow the -a, e.g., -a.PS.PE for the pic macros.

-c*commands*
    Don't complain that the given *commands* are undefined. String the command names together, as in -a. Useful if you have your own macro package.

-f Ignore inline font changes (\f).

$\rightarrow$

checknr ←	-s Ignore inline point-size changes (\s).
chgrp	chgrp [*options*] *newgroup files* Change the ownership of one or more *files* to *newgroup*. *newgroup* is either a group ID number or a group name located in /etc/group. You must own the file or be a privileged user to succeed with this command. ***Options*** -f Force error messages to be suppressed. -h Change the group on symbolic links. Normally, chgrp acts on the file *referenced* by a symbolic link, not on the link itself. (This option is not necessarily available on all Unix systems.) -R Recursively descend through the directory, including subdirectories and symbolic links, setting the specified group ID as it proceeds.

chkey	chkey [*options*]
	
	Solaris only. Prompt for login password and use it to encrypt a new key. See also **keylogin** and **keylogout**.
	
	Options
	
	-p Reencrypt the existing secret key with the user's login password.
	
	-m *mechanism*
	    Change or reencrypt the secret key for the specified mechanism. (Mechanisms are those allowed by *nisauthconf*(1).)
	
	-s *database*
	    Update the given database, which is one of files, nis, or nisplus.

chmod	chmod [*option*] *mode files* Change the access *mode* of one or more *files*. Only the owner of a file or a privileged user may change its mode. Create *mode* by concatenating the characters from *who, opcode*, and *permission*. *who* is optional (if omitted, default is a); choose only one *opcode*.

Options

-f Suppress error message upon failure to change a file's mode.

-R Recursively descend directory arguments while setting modes.

Who

u   User
g   Group
o   Other
a   All (default)

Opcode

+   Add permission
-   Remove permission
=   Assign permission (and remove permission of the unspecified fields)

Permission

r   Read
w   Write
x   Execute
s   Set user (or group) ID
t   Sticky bit; save text mode (file) or prevent removal of files by nonowners (directory)
u   User's present permission
g   Group's present permission
o   Other's present permission
l   Mandatory locking

Alternatively, specify permissions by a three-digit sequence. The first digit designates owner permission; the second, group permission; and the third, others permission. Permissions are calculated by adding the following octal values:

4   Read
2   Write
1   Execute

→

chmod
←

Note: a fourth digit may precede this sequence. This digit assigns the following modes:

4   Set user ID on execution
2   Set group ID on execution or set mandatory locking
1   Sticky bit

Examples

Add execute-by-user permission to *file*:

```
chmod u+x file
```

Either of the following assigns read-write-execute permission by owner (7), read-execute permission by group (5), and execute-only permission by others (1) to *file*:

```
chmod 751 file
chmod u=rwx,g=rx,o=x file
```

Any one of the following assigns read-only permission to *file* for everyone:

```
chmod =r file
chmod 444 file
chmod a-wx,a+r file
```

Set the user ID, assign read-write-execute permission by owner, and assign read-execute permission by group and others:

```
chmod 4755 file
```

---

chown

```
chown [options] newowner[:newgroup] files
```

Change the ownership of one or more *files* to *newowner*. *newowner* is either a user ID number or a login name located in /etc/passwd. The optional *newgroup* is either a group ID number (GID) or a group name located in the /etc/group file. When *newgroup* is supplied, the behavior is to change the ownership of one or more *files* to *newowner* and make it belong to *newgroup*.

Note: some systems accept a period as well as the colon for separating *newowner* and *newgroup*. The colon is mandated by POSIX; the period is accepted for compatibility with older BSD systems.

Options

-f   Force error messages to be suppressed.

-h Change the owner on symbolic links. Normally, chown acts on the file *referenced* by a symbolic link, not on the link itself. (This option is not necessarily available on all Unix systems.)

-R Recursively descend through the directory, including subdirectories and symbolic links, resetting the ownership ID.

---

cksum [*files*]

Solaris only. Calculate and print a cyclic redundancy check (CRC) for each file. The CRC algorithm is based on the polynomial used for Ethernet packets. For each file, cksum prints a line of the form:

    sum count filename

Here, *sum* is the CRC, *count* is the number of bytes in the file, and *filename* is the file's name. The name is omitted if standard input is used.

---

clear

Clear the terminal display.

---

cmp [*options*] *file1 file2*

Compare *file1* with *file2*. Use standard input if *file1* or *file2* is -. See also **comm** and **diff**. The exit codes are as follows:

0 Files are identical.
1 Files are different.
2 Files are inaccessible.

Options

-l For each difference, print the byte number in decimal and the differing bytes in octal.

-s Work silently; print nothing, but return exit codes.

Example

Print a message if two files are the same (exit code is 0):

    cmp -s old new && echo 'no changes'

col	col [*options*]
	
	A postprocessing filter that handles reverse linefeeds and escape characters, allowing output from tbl (or nroff, occasionally) to appear in reasonable form on a terminal.
	
	Options
	
	-b Ignore backspace characters; helpful when printing manpages.
	
	-f Process half-line vertical motions, but not reverse line motion. (Normally, half-line input motion is displayed on the next full line.)
	
	-p Print unknown escape sequences (normally ignored) as regular characters. This option can garble output, so its use is not recommended.
	
	-x Normally, col saves printing time by converting sequences of spaces to tabs. Use -x to suppress this conversion.
	
	Examples
	
	Run *file* through tbl and nroff, then capture output on screen by filtering through col and more:
	
	    tbl *file* | **nroff** | **col** | **more**
	
	Save manpage output in *file*.print, stripping out backspaces (which would otherwise appear as ^H):
	
	    man *file* | **col -b** > *file*.**print**

comb	/usr/ccs/bin/comb [*options*] *files* An SCCS command. See Chapter 18.
comm	comm [*options*] *file1 file2* Compare lines common to the sorted files *file1* and *file2*. Three-column output is produced: lines unique to *file1*, lines unique to *file2*, and lines common to both *files*. comm is similar to diff in that both commands compare two files. In addition, comm can be used like uniq; that is, comm selects duplicate or unique lines between *two* sorted files, whereas uniq selects duplicate or unique lines within the *same* sorted file.

Options

- Read the standard input.

-1 Suppress printing of Column 1.

-2 Suppress printing of Column 2.

-3 Suppress printing of Column 3.

-12 Print only lines in Column 3 (lines common to *file1* and *file2*).

-13 Print only lines in Column 2 (lines unique to *file2*).

-23 Print only lines in Column 1 (lines unique to *file1*).

Example

Compare two lists of top-10 movies and display items that appear in both lists:

```
comm -12 shalit_top10 maltin_top10
```

---

compress [*options*] [*files*]

Reduce the size of one or more *files* using adaptive Lempel-Ziv coding and move to *file*.z. Restore with uncompress or zcat.

With a filename of -, or with no *files*, compress reads standard input.

Note: Unisys claims a patent on the algorithm used by compress. Today, gzip is generally preferred for file compression.

Options

-b*n* Limit the number of bits in coding to *n*; *n* is 9–16, and 16 is the default. A lower *n* produces a larger, less densely compressed file.

-c Write to the standard output (do not change files).

-f Compress unconditionally; i.e., do not prompt before overwriting files. Also, compress files even if the resulting file would actually be larger.

-v Print the resulting percentage of reduction for *files*.

cp

cp [*options*] *file1 file2*
cp [*options*] *files directory*

Copy *file1* to *file2*, or copy one or more *files* to the same names under *directory*. If the destination is an existing file, the file is overwritten; if the destination is an existing directory, the file is copied into the directory (the directory is *not* overwritten). If one of the inputs is a directory, use the -r option.

Options

-i   Prompt for confirmation (y for yes) before overwriting an existing file.

-p   Preserve the modification time and permission modes for the copied file. (Normally cp supplies the permissions of the invoking user.)

-r   Recursively copy a directory, its files, and its subdirectories to a destination *directory*, duplicating the tree structure. (This option is used with the second command-line format when at least one of the source *file* arguments is a directory.) Bear in mind that both symbolic and hard links are copied as real files; the linking structure of the original tree is *not* preserved.

Example

Copy two files to their parent directory (keep the same names):

    cp outline memo ..

---

cpio

cpio *control_options* [*options*]

Copy file archives in from, or out to, tape or disk, or to another location on the local machine. Each of the three control options, -i, -o, or -p accepts different options. (See also **pax** and **tar**.)

cpio -i [*options*] [*patterns*]
    Copy in (extract) files whose names match selected *patterns*. Each pattern can include filename metacharacters from the Bourne shell. (Patterns should be quoted or escaped so they are interpreted by cpio, not by the shell.) If no pattern is used, all files are copied in. During extraction, existing files are not overwritten by older versions in the archive (unless -u is specified).

cpio -o [*options*]
    Copy out a list of files whose names are given on the standard input.

cpio -p [*options*] *directory*

> Copy files to another directory on the same system. Destination pathnames are interpreted relative to the named *directory*.

Comparison of Valid Options

Options available to the -i, -o, and -p options are shown respectively in the first, second, and third row below. (The - is omitted for clarity.)

```
i: 6  b B c C d E f H I k  m M  r R s S t u v V
o: a A   B c C      H   L  M O        v V
p: a        d      l L m  P R    u v V
```

Options

-a   Reset access times of input files.

-A   Append files to an archive (must use with -o).

-b   Swap bytes and half-words. Words are 4 bytes.

-B   Block input or output using 5120 bytes per record (default is 512 bytes per record).

-c   Read or write header information as ASCII characters; useful when source and destination machines are different types.

-C *n*
> Like -B, but block size can be any positive integer *n*.

-d   Create directories as needed.

-E *file*
> Extract filenames listed in *file* from the archive.

-f   Reverse the sense of copying; copy all files *except* those that match *patterns*.

-H *format*
> Read or write header information according to *format*. Values for format are bar (bar format header and file, read-only, Solaris only), crc (ASCII header containing expanded device numbers), odc (ASCII header containing small device numbers), ustar (IEEE/P1003 Data Interchange Standard header), or tar (tar header). Solaris also allows CRC, TAR, and USTAR.

-I *file*
> Read *file* as an input archive.

-k   Skip corrupted file headers and I/O errors.

cpio
←

-l   Link files instead of copying. Can be used only with -p.

-L   Follow symbolic links.

-m   Retain previous file-modification time.

-M *msg*

Print *msg* when switching media. Use variable %d in the message as a numeric ID for the next medium. -M is valid only with -I or -O.

-O *file*

Direct the output to *file*.

-P   Preserve ACLs. Can be used only with -p. Solaris only.

-r   Rename files interactively.

-R *ID*

Reassign file ownership and group information of extracted files to the user whose login ID is *ID* (privileged users only).

-s   Swap bytes.

-S   Swap half-words.

-t   Print a table of contents of the input (create no files). When used with the -v option, resembles output of ls -l.

-u   Unconditional copy; old files can overwrite new ones.

-v   Print a list of filenames.

-V   Print a dot for each file read or written (this shows cpio at work without cluttering the screen).

-6   Process a PWB Unix 6th Edition archive format file. Useful only with the -i option, mutually exclusive with -c and -H.

Examples

Generate a list of old files using find; use list as input to cpio:

```
find . -name "*.old" -print | cpio -ocBv > /dev/rmt/0
```

Restore from a tape drive all files whose name contains "save" (subdirectories are created if needed):

```
cpio -icdv "*save*" < /dev/rmt/0
```

To move a directory tree:

```
find . -depth -print | cpio -padml /mydir
```

crontab [*file*]
crontab *options* [*user*]

Run crontab on your current crontab file, or specify a crontab *file* to add to the crontab directory. A privileged user can run crontab for another user by supplying a *user* after any of the options.

A crontab file is a list of commands, one per line, that will execute automatically at a given time. Numbers are supplied before each command to specify the execution time. The numbers appear in five fields, as follows:

```
Minute          0-59
Hour            0-23
Day of month    1-31
Month           1-12
Day of week     0-6, with 0 = Sunday
```

Use a comma between multiple values, a hyphen to indicate a range, and an asterisk to indicate all possible values. For example, assuming the crontab entries below:

```
59 3 * * 5        find / -print | backup_program
0 0 1,15 * *      echo "Timesheets due" | mail user
```

The first command backs up the system files every Friday at 3:59 a.m., and the second command mails a reminder on the 1st and 15th of each month.

Options

-e   Edit the user's current crontab file (or create one).

-l   List the user's file in the crontab directory.

-r   Delete the user's file in the crontab directory.

cscope [*options*] *files*

Interactive utility for finding code fragments in one or more C, lex, or yacc source *files*. cscope builds a symbol cross reference (named cscope.out by default) and then calls up a menu. The menu prompts the user to search for functions, macros, variables, preprocessor directives, etc. Type ? to list interactive commands. Subsequent calls to cscope rebuild the cross reference if needed (i.e., if filenames or file contents have changed). Source filenames can be stored in a file cscope.files. This file can then be specified instead of *files*. Options -I, -p, and -T are also recognized when placed in cscope.files.

→

cscope
←

Options

-b   Build the symbol cross reference only.

-c   Create output in ASCII (don't compress data).

-C   Ignore uppercase/lowercase differences in searches.

-d   Don't update the cross reference.

-e   Don't show the ^E prompt between files.

-f *out*
     Name the cross-reference file out instead of cscope.*out*.

-i *in*
     Check source files whose names are listed in *in* rather than in cscope.files.

-I *dir*
     Search for include files in *dir* before searching the default (/usr/include). cscope searches the current directory, then *dir*, then the default.

-l   Run in line mode; useful from within a screen editor.

-L   Use with -*n pat* to do a single search.

-p *n*
     Show the last *n* parts of the filename path. Default is 1 (filename); use 0 to suppress the filename.

-P *path*
     Use with -d to prepend *path* to filenames in existing cross reference. This lets you run cscope without changing to the directory where the cross reference was built.

-s *dir*
     Look for source files in directory *dir* instead of in current directory.

-T   Match only the first eight characters of C symbols.

-u   Build cross reference unconditionally (assume all files changed).

-U   Ignore file timestamps (assume no files changed).

-V   Print the cscope version on first line of screen.

-n *pat*
     Go to field *n* of input (starting at 0), then find *pat*.

csh [*options*] [*arguments*]

Command interpreter that uses syntax resembling C. csh (the C
shell) executes commands from a terminal or a file. See Chapter 5
for information on the C shell, including command-line options.

csplit [*options*] *file arguments*

Separate *file* into sections and place sections in files named xx00
through xx*n* (*n* < 100), breaking *file* at each pattern specified in
arguments. See also **split**.

Options

-f *file*

> Name new files *file*00 through *fileN* (default is xx00 through
> xx*n*).

-k Keep newly created files, even when an error occurs (which
would normally remove these files). This is useful when you
need to specify an arbitrarily large repeat argument, {*n*}, and
you don't want the "out of range" error to remove the new
files.

-s Suppress all character counts.

Arguments

Any one or a combination of the following expressions. Arguments containing blanks or other special characters should be
surrounded by single quotes.

/*expr*/

> Create file from the current line up to the line containing the
> regular expression *expr*. This argument takes an optional suf-
> fix of the form +*n* or -*n*, where *n* is the number of lines
> below or above *expr*.

%*expr*%

> Same as /*expr*/, except no file is created for lines previous to
> line containing *expr*.

num Create file from current line up to line number *num*.

{*n*} Repeat argument *n* times. May follow any of the above arguments. Files will split at instances of *expr* or in blocks of
num lines.

Examples

Create up to 20 chapter files from the file novel:

$\rightarrow$

csplit
←

```
csplit -k -f chap. novel '%CHAPTER%' '{20}'
```

Create up to 100 address files (xx00 through xx99), each four lines long, from a database named address_list:

```
csplit -k address_list 4 {99}
```

---

ctags

ctags [*options*] *files*

Create a list of function and macro names that are defined in the specified C, Pascal, FORTRAN, yacc, or lex source *files*. Solaris ctags can also process C++ source files. The output list (named tags by default) contains lines of the form:

> *name*   *file*   *context*

where *name* is the function or macro name, *file* is the source file in which *name* is defined, and *context* is a search pattern that shows the line of code containing *name*. After the list of tags is created, you can invoke vi on any file and type:

```
:set tags=tagsfile
:tag name
```

This switches the vi editor to the source file associated with the *name* listed in *tagsfile* (which you specify with -f).

Options

-a   Append tag output to existing list of tags.

-B   *context* uses backward search patterns.

-f*tagsfile*
     Place output in *tagsfile* (default is tags).

-F   *context* uses forward search patterns (default).

-t   Include C typedefs as tags.

-u   Update tags file to reflect new locations of functions (e.g., when functions are moved to a different source file). Old tags are deleted; new tags are appended.

-v   Produce a listing (index) of each function, source file, and page number (1 page = 64 lines). -v is intended to create a file for use with vgrind.

-w   Suppress warning messages.

-x   Produce a listing of each function, its line number, source file, and context.

Examples

Store tags in Taglist for all C programs:

```
ctags -f Taglist *.c
```

Update tags and store in Newlist:

```
ctags -u -f Newlist *.c
```

---

ctrace [*options*] [*file*]

Debug a C program. ctrace reads the C source *file* and writes a modified version to standard output. Common options are -f and -v. ctrace also accepts the cc options -D, -I, and -U.

Options

-e   Print variables as floating point.

-f *functions*
       Trace only the specified *functions*.

-l *n*
       Follow a statement loop *n* times (default is 20).

-o   Print variables in octal.

-p *s*
       Print trace output via function *s* (default is printf).

-P   Run the C preprocessor before tracing.

-Q*c* Print information about ctrace in output (if *c* = y) or suppress information (if *c* = n, the default).

-r*file*
       Change the trace function package to *file* (default is run-time.c).

-s   Suppress certain redundant code.

-t*n* Trace *n* variables per statement (default is 10; maximum is 20).

-u   Print variables as unsigned.

-v *functions*
       Do not trace the specified *functions*.

-V   Print version information on standard error.

-x   Print variables as floating point.

cut

cut *options* [*files*]

Select a list of columns or fields from one or more *files*. Either -c or -f must be specified. *list* is a sequence of integers. Use a comma between separate values and a hyphen to specify a range (e.g., 1-10,15,20 or 50-). See also **paste** and join.

Options

-b *list*
> This *list* specifies byte positions, not character positions. This is important when multibyte characters are used. With this option, lines should be 1023 bytes or less in size. Solaris only.

-c*list*
> Cut the character positions identified in *list*.

-d*c* Use with -f to specify field delimiter as character *c* (default is tab); special characters (e.g., a space) must be quoted.

-f*list*
> Cut the fields identified in *list*.

-n Do not split characters. When used with -b, cut doesn't split multibyte characters. Solaris only.

-s Use with -f to suppress lines without delimiters.

Examples

Extract usernames and real names from /etc/passwd:

    cut -d: -f1,5 /etc/passwd

Find out who is logged on, but list only login names:

    who | cut -d" " -f1

Cut characters in the fourth column of *file*, and paste them back as the first column in the same file. Send the results to standard output:

    cut -c4 file | paste - file

---

cxref

cxref [*options*] *files*

Build a cross-reference table for each of the C source *files*. The table lists all symbols, providing columns for the name and the associated function, file, and line. In the table, symbols are marked by = if assigned, - if declared, or * if defined. cxref also accepts the cc options -D, -I, and -U.

-c   Report on all files in a single table.

-C   Don't execute the second pass of cxref; save output from first pass in .cx files. (Like -c in lint and cc.)

-d   Simplify report by omitting print declarations.

-F   Print files using full pathname, not just the filename.

-l   Don't print local variables.

-L[*n*]
Limit the LINE field to *n* columns (default is 5).

-o *file*
Send output to *file*.

-s   Silent mode; don't print input filenames.

-t   Format for 80-column listing.

-V   Print version information on standard error.

-w[*n*]
Format for maximum width of *n* columns (default is 80; *n* must be more than 50).

-W*n1,n2,n3,n4*
Set the width of each (or any) column to *n1, n2, n3,* or *n4* (respective defaults are 15, 13, 15, and 20). Column headings are NAME, FILE, FUNCTION, and LINE, respectively.

---

date [*option*] [+*format*]   date
date [*options*] [*string*]

In the first form, print the current date and time, specifying an optional display *format*. In the second form, a privileged user can set the current date by supplying a numeric *string*. *format* can consist of literal text strings (blanks must be quoted) as well as field descriptors, whose values will appear as described below (the listing shows some logical groupings).

Format

%n   Insert a newline.
%t   Insert a tab.

%m   Month of year (01–12).
%d   Day of month (01–31).

→

%y	Last two digits of year (00–99).
%D	Date in %m/%d/%y format.
%b	Abbreviated month name.
%e	Day of month (1–31); pad single digits with a space.
%Y	Four-digit year (e.g., 1996).
%g	Week-based year within century (00–99). Solaris only.
%G	Week-based year, including the century (0000–9999). Solaris only.
%h	Same as %b.
%B	Full month name.
%H	Hour in 24-hour format (00–23).
%M	Minute (00–59).
%S	Second (00–61); 61 permits leap seconds and double leap seconds.
%R	Time in %H:%M format.
%T	Time in %H:%M:%S format.
%k	Hour (24-hour clock, 0–23); single digits are preceded by a space. Solaris only.
%l	Hour (12-hour clock, 1–12); single digits are preceded by a space. Solaris only.
%I	Hour in 12-hour format (01–12).
%p	String to indicate a.m. or p.m. (default is AM or PM).
%r	Time in %I:%M:%S %p format.
%a	Abbreviated weekday.
%A	Full weekday.
%w	Day of week (Sunday = 0).
%u	Weekday as a decimal number (1–7), Sunday = 1. Solaris only.
%U	Week number in year (00–53); start week on Sunday.
%W	Week number in year (00–53); start week on Monday.
%V	The ISO-8601 week number (01–53). In ISO-8601, weeks begin on a Monday, and week 1 of the year is the one that includes both January 4th and the first Thursday of the year. If the first Monday of January is the 2nd, 3rd, or 4th, the preceding days are part of the last week of the previous year. Solaris only.
%j	Julian day of year (001–366).
%Z	Time-zone name.
%x	Country-specific date format.
%X	Country-specific time format.

%c   Country-specific date and time format (default is %a %b %e %T %Z %Y; e.g., Mon Feb 1 14:30:59 EST 1993).

The actual formatting is done by the *strftime*(3) library routine. On Solaris, the country-specific formats depend on the setting of the LC_CTYPE, LC_TIME, LC_MESSAGES, and NLSPATH environment variables.

Options

-a *s.f*

> (Privileged user only.) Gradually adjust the system clock until it drifts *s* seconds away from what it thinks is the "current" time. (This allows continuous micro-adjustment of the clock while the system is running.) *f* is the fraction of seconds by which time drifts. By default, the clock speeds up; precede *s* by a − to slow down.

-u   Display or set the time using Greenwich Mean Time (UTC) .

Strings for Setting the Date

A privileged user can set the date by supplying a numeric *string*. *string* consists of time, day, and year concatenated in one of three ways: *time* or [*day*]*time* or [*day*]*time*[*year*]. Note: don't type the brackets.

time

> A two-digit hour and two-digit minute (*HHMM*); *HH* uses 24-hour format.

day   A two-digit month and two-digit day of month (*mmdd*); default is current day and month.

year

> The year specified as either the full four digits or just the last two digits; default is current year.

Examples

Set the date to July 1 (0701), 4 a.m. (0400), 1999 (99):

    date 0701040099

The command:

    date +"Hello%t Date is %D %n%t Time is %T"

produces a formatted date as follows:

    Hello   Date is 05/09/93
              Time is 17:53:39

dc

dc [*file*]

An interactive desk calculator program that performs arbitrary-precision integer arithmetic (input may be taken from a *file*). Normally you don't run dc directly, since it's invoked by bc (see **bc**). dc provides a variety of one-character commands and operators that perform arithmetic; dc works like a Reverse Polish calculator; therefore, operators and commands follow the numbers they affect. Operators include + - / * % ^ (as in C, although ^ means exponentiation); some simple commands include:

p   Print current result.

q   Quit dc.

c   Clear all values on the stack.

v   Take square root.

i   Change input base; similar to bc's ibase.

o   Change output base; similar to bc's obase.

k   Set scale factor (number of digits after decimal); similar to bc's scale.

!   Remainder of line is a Unix command.

Examples

3 2 ^ p	*Evaluate 3 squared, then print result*
9	
8 * p	*Current value (9) times 8, then print result*
72	
47 - p	*Subtract 47 from 72, then print result*
25	
v p	*Square root of 25, then print result*
5	
2 o p	*Display current result in base 2*
101	

Note: spaces are not needed except between numbers.

---

dd

dd [*option=value*]

Make a copy of an input file (if=), or standard input if no named input file, using the specified conditions, and send the results to the output file (or standard output if of is not specified). Any number of options can be supplied, although if and of are the most common and are usually specified first. Because dd can handle arbitrary block sizes, it is useful when converting between raw physical devices.

bs=*n*

> Set input and output block size to *n* bytes; this option supersedes ibs and obs.

cbs=*n*

> Set the size of the conversion buffer (logical record length) to *n* bytes. Use only if the conversion *flag* is ascii, asciib, ebcdic, ebcdicb, ibm, ibmb, block, or unblock.

conv=*flags*

> Convert the input according to one or more (comma-separated) *flags* listed below. The first six *flags* are mutually exclusive. The next two are mutually exclusive with each other, as are the following two.

ascii	EBCDIC to ASCII.
asciib	EBCDIC to ASCII, using BSD-compatible conversions. Solaris only.
ebcdic	ASCII to EBCDIC.
ebcdicb	ASCII to EBCDIC, using BSD-compatible conversions. Solaris only.
ibm	ASCII to EBCDIC with IBM conventions.
ibmb	ASCII to EBCDIC with IBM conventions, using BSD-compatible conversions. Solaris only.
block	Variable-length records (i.e., those terminated by a newline) to fixed-length records.
unblock	Fixed-length records to variable-length.
lcase	Uppercase to lowercase.
ucase	Lowercase to uppercase.
noerror	Continue processing when errors occur (up to five in a row).
notrunc	Do not truncate the output file. This preserves blocks in the output file that this invocation of dd did not write. Solaris only.
swab	Swap all pairs of bytes.
sync	Pad input blocks to ibs.

count=*n*

> Copy only *n* input blocks.

files=*n*

> Copy *n* input files (e.g., from magnetic tape), then quit.

ibs=*n*

> Set input block size to *n* bytes (default is 512).

$\rightarrow$

dd
←

if=*file*
> Read input from *file* (default is standard input).

obs=*n*
> Set output block size to *n* bytes (default is 512).

of=*file*
> Write output to *file* (default is standard output).

iseek=*n*
> Seek *n* blocks from start of input file (like skip but more efficient for disk file input).

oseek=*n*
> Seek *n* blocks from start of output file.

seek=*n*
> Same as oseek (retained for compatibility).

skip=*n*
> Skip *n* input blocks; useful with magnetic tape.

You can multiply size values (*n*) by a factor of 1024, 512, or 2 by appending the letters k, b, or w, respectively. You can use the letter x as a multiplication operator between two numbers.

Examples

Convert an input file to all lowercase:

```
dd if=caps_file of=small_file conv=lcase
```

Retrieve variable-length data; write it as fixed-length to out:

```
data_retrieval_cmd | dd of=out conv=sync,block
```

---

delta

```
/usr/ccs/bin/delta [options] files
```

An SCCS command. See Chapter 18.

---

deroff

```
deroff [options] [files]
```

Remove all nroff/troff requests and macros, backslash escape sequences, and tbl and eqn constructs from the named *files*.

Options

-i Ignore .so and .nx requests. Solaris only.

-mm Suppress text that appears on *mm* macro lines (i.e., paragraphs print but headings might be stripped).

-ml Same as -mm, but also deletes lists created by *mm* macros; e.g., .BL/.LE, .VL/.LE constructs. (Nested lists are handled poorly.)

-ms Suppress text that appears on *ms* macro lines (i.e., paragraphs print but headings might be stripped). Solaris only.

-w Output the text as a list, one word per line. See also the example under **xargs**.

---

df [*options*] [*name*]

Report the number of free disk blocks and inodes available on all mounted filesystems or on the given *name*. (Unmounted filesystems are checked with -F.) *name* can be a device name (e.g., /dev/dsk/0s9), the directory name of a mount point (e.g., /usr), a directory name, or a remote filesystem name (e.g., an NFS filesystem). Besides the options listed, there are additional options specific to different filesystem types or df modules.

Options

-a Provide information about all filesystems, even ones usually marked in /etc/mnttab to be ignored. Solaris only.

-b Print only the number of free kilobytes.

-e Print only the number of free files.

-F *type*
Report on an unmounted filesystem specified by *type*. Available *types* can be seen in the file /etc/vfstab.

-g Print the whole statvfs structure (overriding other print options).

-i /usr/ucb/df only. Show the number of used and available inodes in a format similar to df -k.

-k Print allocation in kilobytes (typically used without other options). This option produces output in the format traditionally used by the BSD version of df.

-l Report only on local filesystems.

-n Print only the filesystem *type* name; with no other arguments, -n lists the types for all mounted filesystems.

-o *suboptions*
Supply a comma-separated list of *type*-specific *suboptions*.

df ←	-t Report total allocated space as well as free space. -v Echo command line but do not execute command.

diff	diff [*options*] [*diroptions*] *file1 file2*

diff reports lines that differ between *file1* and *file2*. Output consists of lines of context from each file, with *file1* text flagged by a < symbol and *file2* text by a > symbol. Context lines are preceded by the ed command (a, c, or d) that converts *file1* to *file2*. If one of the files is -, standard input is read. If one of the files is a directory, diff locates the filename in that directory corresponding to the other argument (e.g., diff my_dir junk is the same as diff my_dir/junk junk). If both arguments are directories, diff reports lines that differ between all pairs of files having equivalent names (e.g., olddir/program and newdir/program); in addition, diff lists filenames unique to one directory, as well as subdirectories common to both. See also **bdiff**, **cmp**, **comm**, **diff3**, **dircmp**, and **sdiff**.

Options

Options -c, -C, -D, -e, -f, -h, and -n cannot be combined with each other (they are mutually exclusive).

-b Ignore repeating blanks and end-of-line blanks; treat successive blanks as one.

-c Produce output in alternate format, with three lines of context. (This is called a "context diff.")

-C*n* Like -c, but produce *n* lines of context.

-D *def*
  Merge *file1* and *file2* into a single file containing conditional C preprocessor directives (#ifdef). Defining *def* and then compiling yields *file2*; compiling without defining *def* yields *file1*.

-e Produce a script of commands (a, c, d) to recreate *file2* from *file1* using the ed editor.

-f Produce a script to recreate *file1* from *file2*; the script is in the opposite order, so it isn't useful to ed.

-h Do a half-hearted (but hopefully faster) comparison; complex differences (e.g., long stretches of many changes) may not show up; -e and -f are disabled.

-i   Ignore uppercase and lowercase distinctions.

-n   Like -f, but counts changed lines. rcsdiff works this way.

-t   Expand tabs in output lines; useful for preserving indentation changed by -c format.

-w   Like -b, but ignores all spaces and tabs; e.g., a + b is the same as a+b.

The following *diroptions* are valid only when both file arguments are directories.

Diroptions

-1   Long format; output is paginated by pr so that diff listings for each file begin on a new page; other comparisons are listed afterward.

-r   Run diff recursively for files in common subdirectories.

-s   Report files that are identical.

-S*file*
Begin directory comparisons with *file*, skipping files whose names alphabetically precede *file*.

---

diff3 [*options*] *file1 file2 file3*   **diff3**

Compare three files and report the differences with the following codes:

====	All three files differ.
====1	*file1* is different.
====2	*file2* is different.
====3	*file3* is different.

Options

-e   Create an ed script to incorporate into *file1* all differences between *file2* and *file3*.

-E   Same as -e, but mark with angle brackets any lines that differ between all three files.

-x   Create an ed script to incorporate into *file1* all differences between all three files.

-X   Same as -x, but mark with angle brackets any lines that differ between all three files.

→

diff3 ←	-3 Create an ed script to incorporate into *file1* differences between *file1* and *file3*.

diffmk	`diffmk oldfile newfile markedfile`
	
	A useful program for reviewing changes between drafts of a document. diffmk compares two versions of a file (*oldfile* and *newfile*) and creates a third file (*markedfile*) that contains troff "change mark" requests. When *markedfile* is formatted with nroff or troff, the differences between the two files are marked in the margin (via the .mc request). diffmk uses a | to mark changed lines and a * to mark deleted lines. Note that change marks are produced even if the changes are inconsequential (e.g., extra blanks, different input line lengths).
	
	Example
	
	To run diffmk on multiple files, it's convenient to set up directories in which to keep the old and new versions of your files, and to create a directory in which to store the marked files:
	
	`$ mkdir OLD NEW CHANGED`
	
	Move your old files to OLD and your new files to NEW. Then use this rudimentary Bourne shell script:
	
	``$ cat do.mark
	for file
	do
	    echo "Running diffmk on $file ..."
	    diffmk ../OLD/$file $file ../CHANGED/$file
	done```
	
	You must run the script in the directory of new files:
	
	``$ cd NEW
	$ do.mark Ch*```

dircmp	`dircmp [options] dir1 dir2` Compare the contents of *dir1* and *dir2*. See also **diff** and **cmp**. *Options* -d Execute diff on files that differ. -s Don't report files that are identical. -w*n* Change the output line length to *n* (default is 72).

`dirname pathname`	**dirname**

Print *pathname*, excluding last level. Useful for stripping the actual filename from a pathname. See also **basename**.

`/usr/ccs/bin/dis [options] files`	**dis**

Disassemble the object or archive *files*. See also **as**.

Options

-C   Display demangled C++ symbol names. Solaris only.

-d *section*
  Disassemble only the specified *section* of data, printing its offset.

-D *section*
  Same as -d, but print the data's actual address.

-F *func*
  Disassemble only the specified function; reuse -F for additional functions.

-l *string*
  Disassemble only the library file *string* (e.g., *string* would be malloc for libmalloc.a).

-L   Look for C source labels in files containing debug information (e.g., files compiled with cc -g).

-o   Print octal output (default is hexadecimal).

-t *section*
  Same as -d, but print text output.

-V   Print version information on standard error.

`dos2unix [options] dosfile unixfile`	**dos2unix**

Solaris only. Convert files using the DOS extended character set to their ISO standard counterparts. If *dosfile* and *unixfile* are the same, the file is overwritten after the conversion is done. See also **unix2dos**.

Options

-ascii
  Remove extra carriage returns and convert (remove) DOS end-of-file characters for use under Unix.

$\rightarrow$

dos2unix ←	`-iso` Same as the default action. `-7` Convert 8-bit DOS graphics characters to space characters.

download	`/usr/lib/lp/postscript/download [options] [files]`
	
	Add a font to the beginning of one or more PostScript *files*. By adding a font name directly to a PostScript specification, this command can make additional fonts available when printing a PostScript file. download determines which fonts to add by processing PostScript comments that begin with %%DocumentFonts:, followed by a list of PostScript font names. download loads the fonts whose names are listed in a map table. This table links PostScript names with the system file that contains the font definition. A map table for the Times font family might look like:
	
	      Times-Bold times/bold
	      Times-Italic times/italic
	      Times-Roman times/roman
	
	Filenames that begin with a slash are used verbatim. Otherwise, they are taken to be relative to the host font directory.
	
	Options
	
	`-` Read the standard input.
	
	`-f` Search the entire PostScript file instead of just the header comments. Header comments such as %%DocumentFonts: (atend) redirect download to the end of the file. Use this option when such comments aren't present.
	
	`-H` *fontdir*
	    Use *fontdir* as the directory in which font-definition files are searched (default is /usr/lib/lp/postscript).
	
	`-m` *table*
	    Use map table specified by file *table*. A leading / in *table* indicates an absolute pathname; otherwise (as in the previous option), the filename is appended to the *fontdir* specified by -H. Without -H, the default is /usr/lib/lp/ postscript.
	
	`-p` *printer*
	    Normally, download loads fonts that reside on the host machine. With this option, download first checks for fonts that reside on *printer* (by looking at /etc/lp/printers/ *printer*/residentfonts).

/usr/lib/lp/postscript/dpost [*options*] [*files*]   **dpost**

A postprocessor that translates troff-formatted *files* into
PostScript for printing.

Options

-       Read the standard input.

-c *n*
        Print *n* copies of each page (default is 1).

-e 0 | 1 | 2
        Set text encoding to 0 (default), 1, or 2. Higher encoding
        reduces the output size and speeds printing, but may be less
        reliable.

-F *dir*
        Set the font directory to *dir* (default is /usr/lib/font).

-H *dir*
        Set the host-resident font directory to *dir*. Files there must
        describe PostScript fonts and have filenames corresponding
        to a two-character troff font.

-L *file*
        Set the PostScript prologue to *file* (default is /usr/lib/
        postscript/dpost.ps, /usr/lib/lp/postscript/dpost.ps on
        Solaris).

-m *scale*
        Increase (multiply) the size of logical pages by factor *scale*
        (default is 1.0).

-n *n*
        Print *n* logical pages on each sheet of output (default is 1).

-o *list*
        Print only pages contained in comma-separated *list*. A page
        range is specified by *n-m*.

-O   Omit PostScript pictures from output. Useful when running
        in a networked environment.

-p *layout*
        Specify *layout* to be either portrait (long side is vertical;
        also the default) or landscape (long side is horizontal). *layout*
        can be abbreviated to p or l.

-T *device*
        Use *device* to best describe available PostScript fonts.
        Default is post, with dpost reading binary files in /usr/lib/
        font/devpost. Use of -T is discouraged; usually the system
        PostScript fonts are best, if they are available.

→

dpost
←

-w *n*

    Draw troff graphics (e.g., pic, tbl) using lines that are *n* points thick (default is 0.3).

-x *n*

    Offset the x-coordinate of the origin *n* inches to the right (if *n* is positive).

-y *n*

    Offset the y-coordinate of the origin *n* inches down (if *n* is positive). Default origin is the upper-left corner of the page.

Example

```
pic file | tbl | eqn | troff
-ms -Tpost | dpost -c2 | lp
```

du

du [*options*] [*directories*]

Print disk usage, i.e., the number of 512-byte blocks used by each named directory and its subdirectories (default is current directory).

Options

-a   Print usage for all files, not just subdirectories.

-d   Do not cross filesystem boundaries. Solaris only.

-k   Print information in units of kilobytes.

-L   For symbolic links, process the file or directory to which the link refers, not the link itself. Solaris only.

-o   Do not add child-directory statistics to the parent directory's total. No effect if -s is also used. Solaris only.

-r   Print a "cannot open" message if a file or directory is inaccessible.

-s   Print only the grand total for each named directory.

echo

echo [-n] [*string*]

Echo arguments to standard output. Often used for producing prompts from shell scripts. This is the /bin/echo command. echo also exists in /usr/ucb, and as a command built into the Bourne, C, and Korn shells (see Chapter 4 and Chapter 5).

Although echo is conceptually the simplest of all Unix commands, using it in practice is complicated, because of portability and version differences. (Consider using `printf` instead.) The following sections summarize the differences.

Version Differences

`/bin/echo`
> Does not accept the -n option. Interprets the escape sequences described next.

`/usr/ucb/echo`
> Accepts the -n option if it's first. Does not interpret escape sequences.

Bourne shell `echo`
> Does not accept the -n option. Interprets the escape sequences described next, except \a.

C shell `echo`
> Accepts the -n option if it's first. Does not interpret escape sequences.

Korn shell `echo`
> Searches $PATH and behaves like the first version of `echo` that it finds.

Escape Sequences

\a	Alert (ASCII BEL). (Not in /bin/sh's echo.)
\b	Backspace.
\c	Suppress the terminating newline (same as -n).
\f	Formfeed.
\n	Newline.
\r	Carriage return.
\t	Tab character.
\v	Vertical-tab character.
\\	Backslash.
\0*nnn*	ASCII character represented by octal number *nnn*, where *nnn* is 1, 2, or 3 digits and is preceded by a 0.

Examples

```
echo "testing printer" | lp
echo "TITLE\nTITLE" > file ; cat doc1 doc2 >> file
echo "Warning: ringing bell \07"
```

---

ed [*options*] [*file*]

The standard text editor. If the named *file* does not exist, `ed` creates it; otherwise, the existing *file* is opened for editing. As a line editor, `ed` is generally no longer used because `vi` and `ex` have superseded it. Some utilities, such as `diff`, continue to make use

→

ed ←	of ed command syntax. Encryption (with -x) can be used only in the United States.
	Options
	-C Same as -x, but assume *file* began in encrypted form.
	-p *string* Set *string* as the prompt for commands (default is *). The P command turns the prompt display on and off.
	-s Suppress character counts, diagnostics, and the ! prompt for shell commands. Earlier versions of ed used plain -; this is still accepted.
	-x Supply a key to encrypt or decrypt *file* using crypt.
edit	edit [*options*] [*files*] A line-oriented text editor that runs a simplified version of ex for novice users. The set variables report, showmode, and magic are preset to report editing changes, to display edit modes (when in :vi mode), and to require literal search patterns (no metacharacters allowed), respectively. (Encryption is not supported outside the United States.) edit accepts the same options as ex; see **ex** for a listing. See Chapter 8, *The vi Editor*, and Chapter 9, *The ex Editor*, for more information.
egrep	egrep [*options*] [*regexp*] [*files*] Search one or more *files* for lines that match a regular expression *regexp*. egrep doesn't support the metacharacters \(, \), \n, \<, \>, \{, or \}, but does support the other metacharacters, as well as the extended set +, ?, |, and ( ). Remember to enclose these characters in quotes. Regular expressions are described in Chapter 6, *Pattern Matching*. Exit status is 0 if any lines match, 1 if not, and 2 for errors. See also **grep** and **fgrep**.
	Options
	-b Precede each line with its block number. (Not terribly useful.)
	-c Print only a count of matched lines.
	-e *regexp* Use this if *regexp* begins with -.

-f *file*
    Take expression from *file*.

-h List matched lines but not filenames (inverse of -1).

-i Ignore uppercase and lowercase distinctions.

-1 List filenames but not matched lines.

-n Print lines and their line numbers.

-s Silent mode: print only error messages, and return the exit status. Not on SVR4, but common on most commercial Unix systems.

-v Print all lines that *don't* match *regexp*.

Examples

Search for occurrences of *Victor* or *Victoria* in *file*:

```
egrep 'Victor(ia)?' file
egrep '(Victor|Victoria)' file
```

Find and print strings such as *old.doc1* or *new.doc2* in *files*, and include their line numbers:

```
egrep -n '(old|new)\.doc?' files
```

eject [*options*] [*media*]

Solaris only. Eject removable media, such as a floppy disk or CD-ROM. Necessary for media being managed by vold, or for media without an eject button, such as the floppy drives on Sun SPARC systems. *media* is either a device name or a nickname, such as floppy or cdrom.

With volume management available, eject unmounts any filesystems mounted on the named *media*. In this case, it also displays a pop-up dialog if a window system is running. Without volume management, it simply sends an "eject" command to the given device.

Options

-d Print the name of the default device to be ejected.

-f When volume management is not in effect, force the eject, even if the device is busy.

-n Display the list of nicknames and their corresponding real devices.

→

eject ←	-p Do not use a windowing pop-up dialog.
	-q Query to see if the device has media. Use the exit status to determine the answer.

elfdump	elfdump [*options*] *filename* ...
	Solaris only. Symbolically dump parts of an object file. *files* may be individual files, or ar archives (libraries) of object files.
	Options
	-c Print section headers.
	-d Print the .dynamic section.
	-e Print the ELF header.
	-i Print the .interp section.
	-G Print the .got section.
	-h Print the .hash section.
	-n Print the .note section.
	-N *name*
	Qualify an option with the specific name *name* (e.g., to choose a specific symbol table with -s).
	-p Print program headers.
	-r Print the relocation sections.
	-s Print the symbol table sections.
	-v Print the version sections.
	-w *file*
	Write the specified section to *file*.

env	env [*options*] [*variable=value* ...] [*command*]
	Display the current environment or, if environment *variables* are specified, set them to a new *value* and display the modified environment. If *command* is specified, execute it under the modified environment.

Options

env

\- Ignore current environment entirely.

\-i Same as \-. Solaris only.

---

eqn [*options*] [*files*]

eqn

Equation preprocessor for troff. See Chapter 17.

/usr/ccs/bin/error [*options*] [*files*]

error

Read compiler error messages, and insert them into the source files that generated them. This makes it easier to work during the typical edit-compile-debug cycle. Typical usage would be:

```
cc -O -c files 2>&1 | error
```

Options

\-n Do not edit any files; print errors on standard output.

\-q Query. error prompts for a y or n response before inserting error messages into a file.

\-s Print statistics about the different kinds of errors.

\-v After inserting error messages into the source files, run vi on the files.

\-t *list*
    Only process files whose suffixes appear in *list*. Suffixes are dot-separated, and wildcards are allowed, but should be quoted to prevent interpretation by the shell.

---

ex [*options*] *files*

ex

A line-oriented text editor; a superset of ed and the root of vi. See Chapter 8 and Chapter 9 for more information.

Options

\-c *command*
    Begin edit session by executing the given ex *command* (usually a search pattern or line address). If *command* contains spaces or special characters, enclose it in single quotes to protect it from the shell. For example, *command* could be ':set list' (show tabs and newlines) or /*word* (search for *word*) or '$' (show last line). (Note: \-c *command* was formerly +*command*. The old version still works.)

→

ex	
←	

-l   Run in LISP mode for editing LISP programs.

-L   List filenames saved due to an editor or system crash.

-r *file*
> Recover and edit *file* after an editor or system crash.

-R   Edit in read-only mode to prevent accidental changing of files.

-s   Suppress status messages (e.g., errors, prompts); useful when running an ex script. (-s was formerly the - option; the old version still works.)

-t *tag*
> Edit the file containing *tag* and position the editor at its definition (see **ctags** for more information).

-v   Invoke vi. Running vi directly is simpler.

-V   Verbose; print nonterminal input on standard error. Useful for tracking shell scripts running ex.

-w*n* Set the window size to *n*. Useful over slow dial-up (or slow Internet) connections.

-x   Supply a key to encrypt or decrypt *file* using crypt.

-C   Same as -x, but assume that *file* began in encrypted form.

Examples

Either of the following examples applies the ex commands in exscript to text file doc :

```
ex -s doc < exscript
cat exscript | ex -s doc
```

---

expand	

expand [*options*] [*files*]

Expand tab characters into appropriate number of spaces. expand reads the named *files* or standard input if no *files* are provided. See also **unexpand**.

Options

-t *tablist*
> Interpret tabs according to *tablist*, a space- or comma-separated list of numbers in ascending order, that describe the "tabstops" for the input data.

-*n*   Set the tabstops every *n* characters. The default is 8.

-*tablist*
> Interpret tabs according to *tablist*, a space- or comma-separated list of numbers in ascending order, that describe the "tabstops" for the input data.

Example

Cut columns 10–12 of the input data, even when tabs are used:

```
expand data | cut -c 10-12 > data.col2
```

---

expr *arg1 operator arg2* [*operator arg3* ...]

Evaluate arguments as expressions and print the result. Strings can be compared and searched. Arguments and operators must be separated by spaces. In most cases, an argument is an integer, typed literally or represented by a shell variable. There are three types of operators: arithmetic, relational, and logical. Exit status for expr is 0 (expression is nonzero and nonnull), 1 (expression is 0 or null), or 2 (expression is invalid).

expr is typically used in shell scripts to perform simple mathematics, such as addition or subtraction. It is made obsolete in the Korn shell by that program's built-in arithmetic capabilities.

Arithmetic Operators

Use the following operators to produce mathematical expressions whose results are printed:

+   Add *arg2* to *arg1*.
-   Subtract *arg2* from *arg1*.
*   Multiply the arguments.
/   Divide *arg1* by *arg2*.
%   Take the remainder when *arg1* is divided by *arg2*.

Addition and subtraction are evaluated last, unless they are grouped inside parentheses. The symbols *, (, and) have meaning to the shell, so they must be escaped (preceded by a backslash or enclosed in single or double quotes).

Relational Operators

Use relational operators to compare two arguments. Arguments can also be words, in which case comparisons assume a < z and A < z. If the comparison statement is true, the result is 1; if false, the result is 0. Symbols < and > must be escaped.

$\rightarrow$

expr
←

=	Are the arguments equal?
!=	Are the arguments different?
>	Is *arg1* greater than *arg2*?
>=	Is *arg1* greater than or equal to *arg2*?
<	Is *arg1* less than *arg2*?
<=	Is *arg1* less than or equal to *arg2*?

Logical Operators

Use logical operators to compare two arguments. Depending on the values, the result can be *arg1* (or some portion of it), *arg2*, or 0. Symbols | and & must be escaped.

| | Logical OR; if *arg1* has a nonzero (and nonnull) value, the result is *arg1*; otherwise, the result is *arg2*.

& Logical AND; if both *arg1* and *arg2* have a nonzero (and nonnull) value, the result is *arg1*; otherwise, the result is 0.

: Similar to grep; *arg2* is a pattern to search for in *arg1*. *arg2* must be a regular expression in this case. If the *arg2* pattern is enclosed in \(\), the result is the portion of *arg1* that matches; otherwise, the result is simply the number of characters that match. By default, a pattern match always applies to the beginning of the first argument (the search string implicitly begins with a ^). To match other parts of the string, start the search string with .*.

Examples

Division happens first; result is 10:

    expr 5 + 10 / 2

Addition happens first; result is 7 (truncated from 7.5):

    expr \(5 + 10 \) / 2

Add 1 to variable i; this is how variables are incremented in shell scripts:

    i=`expr $i + 1`

Print 1 (true) if variable a is the string "hello":

    expr $a = hello

Print 1 (true) if variable b plus 5 equals 10 or more:

    expr $b + 5 \>= 10

In the following examples, variable p is the string "version.100".

This command prints the number of characters in p:

   expr $p : '.*'   *Result is 11*

Match all characters and print them:

   expr $p : '\(.*\)'   *Result is "version.100"*

Print the number of lowercase letters at the beginning of p:

   expr $p : '[a-z]*'   *Result is 7*

Match the lowercase letters at the beginning of p:

   expr $p : '\([a-z]*\)' *Result is "version"*

Truncate $x if it contains five or more characters; if not, just print $x. (Logical OR uses the second argument when the first one is 0 or null; i.e., when the match fails.) Double-quoting is a good idea, in case $x contains whitespace characters.

   expr "$x" : '\(.....\)' \| "$x"

In a shell script, rename files to their first five letters:

   mv "$x" `expr "$x" : '\(.....\)' \| "$x"`

(To avoid overwriting files with similar names, use mv -i.)

---

exstr [*options*] *file*

Extract strings from C source files, so that they can be stored in a database and retrieved at application runtime using the gettxt library function. With no options, exstr produces a grep-type list showing only filename and strings. exstr is one of several commands to use when customizing applications for international use.

Typical use involves three steps:

1. Specify -e and the C source file, and redirect the output to a file. This creates a database of text strings and identifying information.

2. Edit this database by adding information that was previously returned by the mkmsgs command.

3. Specify -r and the C source file, using the edited database as input. This replaces hardcoded text strings with calls to gettxt. gettxt lets you access translated versions of text strings. (The strings reside in a directory specified by environment variable LC_MESSAGES.)

→

exstr
←

Options

-d Use with -r to give the gettxt call a second argument, the original text string. This string is printed as the fallback in case the gettxt call fails.

-e Extract text strings from *file*. (-e is not used with other options.) The information appears in this format:

file:*line*:*field*:*msg_file*:*msg_num*:*string*

file	C source file from the command line.
line	Line number on which the string is found in *file*.
field	Inline numerical position of the string's beginning.
msg_file	Initially null, but later filled in when you edit the database. *msg_file* is the name of the list of message strings you create by running the mkmsgs command.
msg_num	Initially null but filled in later. It corresponds to the order of the strings in *msg_file*.

-r Replace strings in the source file with calls to gettxt.

Example

Assume a C source file named proverbs.c:

```
main() {
    printf("Haste makes waste\n");
    printf("A stitch in time\n");
}
```

1. First issue the command:

    exstr -e proverbs.c > proverb.list

    proverb.list might look something like this:

    ```
    proverbs.c:3:8:::Haste makes waste\n
    proverbs.c:4:8:::A stitch in time\n
    ```

2. Run mkmsgs to create a message file (e.g., prov.US) that can be read by the gettxt call. If the two previous proverb strings are listed ninth and tenth in prov.US, you would edit proverb.list as follows:

    ```
    proverbs.c:3:8:prov.US:9:Haste makes waste\n
    proverbs.c:4:8:prov.US:10:A stitch in time\n
    ```

3. Finally, specify -r to insert gettxt calls:

    exstr -rd proverbs.c < proverb.list > Prov.c

The internationalized version of your program, Prov.c, now looks like this:

```
extern char *gettxt();
main() {
  printf(gettxt("prov.US:9",
      "Haste makes waste\n"));
  printf(gettxt("prov.US:10",
      "A stitch in time\n"));
  }
```

factor [*num*]

Produce the prime factors of *num* or read numbers from input.

false

A do-nothing command that returns an unsuccessful (nonzero) exit status. Normally used in Bourne shell scripts. See also **true**.

Examples

```
# This loop never executes
while false
do
        commands
done

 # This loop executes forever
until false
do
        commands
done
```

fdformat [*options*] [*device*]

Solaris only. Format floppy disks and PCMCIA memory cards. *device* is the name of the appropriate device to format, and varies considerably based on the density of the media, the capability of the disk drive, and whether or not volume management is in effect.

Options

-b *label*
    Apply the *label* to the media. SunOS labels may be up to eight characters; DOS labels may be up to eleven uppercase characters.

$\rightarrow$

fdformat ←	-B *file* Install bootloader in *file* on an MS-DOS diskette. Can only be used with -d or -t dos. -D Format a 720KB (3.5 inch) or 360KB (5.25 inch) double-density diskette (same as -1 or -L). Use on high- or extended-density drives. -e Eject floppy disk when done. -E Format a 2.88MB (3.5 inch) extended-density diskette. -f Force. Do not prompt for confirmation before formatting. -H Format a 1.44MB (3.5 inch) or 1.2MB (5.25 inch) high-density diskette. Use on extended-density drive. -M Use a 1.2MB (3.5 inch) medium-density format on a high-density diskette. Use only with the -t nec option. Identical to -m. -U Unmount any filesystems on the media, and then format. -q Quiet mode. Don't print status messages. -v Verify each block on the media after formatting. -x Don't format, just write a SunOS label or MS-DOS filesystem. -t dos Install an MS-DOS filesystem and boot sector formatting. Same as DOS format or -d. -t nec Install an NEC-DOS filesystem and boot sector after formatting. Use only with -M. ***Compatibility Options*** These options are for compatibility with previous versions of fdformat. Their use is discouraged. -d Same as -t dos. -1 Same as -D or -L. -L Same as -1 or -D. -m Same as -M.
fgrep	fgrep [*options*] [*pattern*] [*files*] Search one or more *files* for lines that match a literal, text-string *pattern*. Because fgrep does not support regular expressions, it is

faster than grep (hence fgrep, for fast grep). Exit status is 0 if any lines match, 1 if not, and 2 for errors. See also **egrep** and **grep**.

Options

-b   Precede each line with its block number. (Not terribly useful.)

-c   Print only a count of matched lines.

-e *pat*
Use this if *pat* begins with **-**.

-f*file*
Take a list of patterns from *file*.

-h   Print matched lines but not filenames (inverse of -1).

-i   Ignore uppercase and lowercase distinctions.

-1   List filenames but not matched lines.

-n   Print lines and their line numbers.

-s   Silent mode: print only error messages, and return the exit status. Not on SVR4, but common on most commercial Unix systems.

-v   Print all lines that don't match *pattern*.

-x   Print lines only if *pattern* matches the entire line.

Examples

Print lines in *file* that don't contain any spaces:

    fgrep -v ' ' *file*

Print lines in *file* that contain the words in spell_list:

    fgrep -f spell_list *file*

---

file [*options*] *files*

Classify the named *files* according to the type of data they contain. file checks the magic file (usually /etc/magic) to identify many common file types.

Options

-c   Check the format of the magic file (*files* argument is invalid with -c).

→

file ←	`-f`*list*
	    Run `file` on the filenames in *list*.
	
	`-h` Do not follow symbolic links.
	
	`-m`*file*
	    Use *file* as the magic file instead of `/etc/magic`.
	
	Many file types are understood. Output lists each filename, followed by a brief classification such as:
	
	``` ascii text c program text c-shell commands data empty iAPX 386 executable directory [nt]roff, tbl, or eqn input text shell commands symbolic link to ../usr/etc/arp ```
	
	Example
	
	List all files that are deemed to be `nroff`/`troff` input:
	
	**file *
		grep roff**

find	`find `*pathname(s)*` `*condition(s)* An extremely useful command for finding particular groups of files (numerous examples follow this description). `find` descends the directory tree beginning at each *pathname* and locates files that meet the specified *conditions*. At least one *pathname* and one *condition* must be specified. The most useful conditions include `-print` (which must be explicitly given to display any output), `-name` and `-type` (for general use), `-exec` and `-size` (for advanced users), and `-mtime` and `-user` (for administrators). On Solaris (and other recent Unix systems), `-print` is the default condition if none are provided. Conditions may be grouped by enclosing them in `\( \)` (escaped parentheses), negated with `!` (use `\!` in the C shell), given as alternatives by separating them with `-o`, or repeated (adding restrictions to the match; usually only for `-name`, `-type`, and `-perm`). The `find` command can often be combined with the `xargs` command when there are too many files for naming on the command line. (See **xargs**.)

-atime +*n* | -*n* | *n*

   Find files that were last accessed more than *n* (+*n*), less than
   n (-*n*), or exactly *n* days ago. Note that find will change the
   access time of directories supplied as *pathnames*.

-cpio *dev*

   Take matching files and write them on device *dev*, using
   cpio. Obsolete.

-ctime +*n* | -*n* | *n*

   Find files that were changed more than *n* (+*n*), less than *n*
   (-*n*), or exactly *n* days ago. Change refers to modification,
   permission or ownership changes, etc.; therefore, -ctime is
   more inclusive than -atime or -mtime.

-depth

   Descend the directory tree, skipping directories and working
   on actual files first (and *then* the parent directories). Useful
   when files reside in unwritable directories (e.g., when using
   find with cpio).

-exec *command* {} \;

   Run the Unix *command* on each file matched by find, provided *command* executes successfully on that file; i.e.,
   returns a 0 exit status. When *command* runs, the argument
   {} substitutes the current file. Follow the entire sequence
   with an escaped semicolon (\;).

-follow

   Follow symbolic links and track the directories visited (don't
   use this with -type 1).

-fstype *type*

   Find files that reside on filesystems of type *type*.

-group *gname*

   Find files belonging to group *gname*. *gname* can be a group
   name or a group ID number.

-inum *n*

   Find files whose inode number is *n*.

-links *n*

   Find files having *n* links.

-local

   Find files that physically reside on the local system.

-ls Display matching files with associated statistics (as if run
   through ls -lids).

→

-mount

Search for files that reside only on the same filesystem as *pathname*.

-mtime +n | -n | n

Find files that were last modified more than *n* (+*n*), less than *n* (-*n*), or exactly *n* days ago.

-name *pattern*

Find files whose names match *pattern*. Filename metacharacters may be used, but should be escaped or quoted.

-ncpio *dev*

Take matching files and write them on device *dev*, using cpio -c. Obsolete.

-newer *file*

Find files that have been modified more recently than *file*; similar to -mtime.

-nogroup

Find files belonging to a group *not* in /etc/group.

-nouser

Find files owned by a user *not* in /etc/passwd.

-ok *command* {} \;

Same as -exec, but user must respond (with a y) before *command* is executed.

-perm *nnn*

Find files whose permission settings (e.g., rwx) match octal number *nnn* exactly (e.g., 664 matches -rw-rw-r--). Use a minus sign to make a wildcard match of any specified bit (e.g., -perm -600 matches -rw******, where * can be any mode). Some systems also allow +*nnn* for this purpose.

Solaris allows *nnn* to be a symbolic mode in the same form as allowed by chmod.

-print

Print the matching files and directories, using their full pathnames. On Solaris, this is the default.

-prune

"Prune" the directory tree of unwanted directory searches; that is, skip the directory most recently matched.

-size *n*[c]

Find files containing *n* blocks, or, if c is specified, files that are *n* characters (bytes) long. (One block = 512 bytes).

-type *c*
> Find files whose type is *c*. *c* can be:

    b   Block special file

    c   Character special file

    d   Directory

    D   Door special file, Solaris only

    f   Plain file

    l   Symbolic link

    p   Fifo or named pipe

    s   Socket

-user *user*
> Find files belonging to a *user* name or ID.

-xdev
> Same as -mount. Solaris (and some BSD systems) only.

Examples

List all files (and subdirectories) in your home directory:

```
find $HOME -print
```

List all files named chapter1 underneath the /work directory:

```
find /work -name chapter1 -print
```

List "memo" files owned by ann (note the use of multiple starting paths):

```
find /work /usr -name 'memo*' -user ann -print
```

Search the filesystem (begin at root) for manpage directories:

```
find / -type d -name 'man*' -print
```

Search the current directory, look for filenames that don't begin with a capital letter, and send them to the printer:

```
find . \! -name '[A-Z]*' -exec lp {} \;
```

Find and compress files whose names don't end with .z :

```
compress `find . -type f \! -name '*.Z' -print`
```

Remove all empty files on the system (prompting first):

```
find / -size 0 -ok rm {} \;
```

Skip RCS directories, but list remaining read-only files:

```
find . -name RCS -prune -o -perm 444 -print
```

→

find ←	Search the system for files that were modified within the last two days (good candidates for backing up): `find / -mtime -2 -print` Recursively grep for a pattern down a directory tree: `find /book -print	xargs grep '[Nn]utshell'`
finger	`finger [options] users` Display data about one or more *users*, including information listed in the files .plan and .project in *user*'s home directory. You can specify each *user* either as a login name (exact match) or as a first or last name (display information on all matching names). Networked environments recognize arguments of the form *user@host* and *@host*. (Today, many systems on the Internet disallow connections from finger requests.) **Options** -b Omit user's home directory and shell from display. -f Used with -s to omit heading that normally displays in short format. -h Omit .project file from display. -i Show "idle" format, a terse format (like -s). -l Force long format (default). -m *users* must match usernames exactly, instead of also searching for a match of first or last names. -p Omit .plan file from display. -q Show "quick" format, the tersest of all (requires an exact match of username). -s Show short format. -w Used with -s to omit user's full name that normally displays in short format.
fmt	`fmt [options] [files]` Fill and join text, producing lines of roughly the same length. (Unlike nroff, the lines are not justified.) fmt ignores blank lines and lines beginning with a dot (.) or with "From:". The emacs editor uses ESC-q to join paragraphs, so fmt is useful for other edi-

tors, such as vi. The following vi command fills and joins the
remainder of the current paragraph:

    !}fmt

Options

-c Don't adjust the first two lines; align subsequent lines with
    the second line. Useful for paragraphs that begin with a
    hanging tag.

-s Split long lines but leave short lines alone. Useful for pre-
    serving partial lines of code.

-w *n*
    Create lines no longer than *n* columns wide. Default is 72.
    (Can also be invoked as -*n* for compatibility with BSD.)

---

ftp [*options*] [*hostname*]

Transfer files to and from remote network site *hostname*. ftp
prompts the user for a command. Type help to see a list of
known commands.

Options

-d Enable debugging.

-g Disable filename expansion (*globbing*).

-i Turn off interactive prompting.

-n No auto-login upon initial connection.

-v Verbose on. Show all responses from remote server.

---

gcore [*option*] *process_ids*

Create ("get") a core image of each running process specified.
The core image can be used with a debugger. You must own the
running process or be a privileged user to use this command.

Option

-o *file*
    Create core file named *file.process_id* (default is
    core.*process_id*).

gencat	gencat [*option*] `database msgfiles`

Append (or merge) messages contained in one or more *msgfiles* with the formatted message *database* file. If *database* doesn't exist, it is created. Each message in *msgfile* is preceded by a numerical identifier. Comment lines can be added by using a dollar sign at the beginning of a line, followed by a space or tab. See also **genmsg** and **mkmsgs**.

Option

-m   Build a single *database* that is backward-compatible with databases created by earlier versions of gencat. SVR4 only.

---

genmsg	genmsg [*options*] `files` ...

Solaris only. Extract messages strings from source code that uses *catgets*(3C) for further processing with genmsg. The purpose of this command is to create the initial data for use by a translator when internationalizing an application. See also **gencat** and **mkmsgs**.

Options

-a   Append (merge) the output into the file specified by -o.

-b   Place extracted comments after the corresponding message, instead of before it.

-c *tag*
   Extract messages containing *tag* and write them, prefixed by $, in a comment in the output file.

-d   Also add the original messages as comments in the output file.

-f   With -r, overwrite the original input files. With -l, also overwrite the project files.

-g *file*
   Create *file* as a project file, listing set numbers and their maximum message numbers.

-l *file*
   Use information in *file* as a project file to calculate new message numbers.

-m *prefix*
   Fill in the message with *prefix*. Intended for testing.

-M *suffix*
> Fill in the message with *suffix*. Intended for testing.

-n Add comments in the output indicating the original file's name and line number for the message.

-o *msgfile*
> Put the output in *msgfile*.

-p *preprocessor*
> Run the source files through *preprocessor* before extracting messages.

-r Replace message numbers with -1 (negative one). Reverse action of -1.

-s *tag*
> Extract comments of the form /* SET *tag* */ from the source files. Write them to the output as comments, prefixed with $. Only the first matching comment for *tag* is extracted.

-t Triple the lengths of extracted messages. Intended for testing.

-x Don't warn about message and set number range checks and conflicts.

/usr/ccs/bin/get [*options*] *files*

An SCCS command. See Chapter 18.

---

getconf [-v *spec*] *system_var*
getconf [-v *spec*] *path_var path*
getconf -a

Solaris only. This command is specified by POSIX as a portable way of determining system limits. In the first form, print the value of system configuration variables. In the second, print the value of filesystem-related parameters. In the third, print the values of all system configuration variables.

Options

-a Print the names and values of all system configuration variables.

-v *spec*
> Use *spec* to govern the selection of values for configuration variables.

getopts	getopts *string name* [*arg*]
	Same as built-in Bourne shell command getopts. See Chapter 4.

gettext	gettext [*domain*] *string*
	Solaris only. Retrieve and print the translated version of *string*. This provides shell-level access to the facilities of *gettext*(3C). Translations are looked up in /usr/lib/locale/*lang*/LC_MESSAGES/ *domain*.mo. *lang* is the current locale (e.g., en_US). If *domain* is not supplied, the value of $TEXTDOMAIN is used instead. Without a domain, or if no translation can be found, gettext simply prints *string*. If $TEXTDOMAINDR exists, its value is used instead of /usr/lib/locale/.

gettxt	gettxt *msgfile:msgnum* [*default_message*]
	Obtain the message that resides in file *msgfile* and whose message ID is *msgnum*. *msgnum* is a number from 1 to *n*, where *n* is the number of messages in *msgfile*. gettxt searches for *msgfile* in directory /usr/lib/locale/*locale*/LC_MESSAGES, where *locale* is the language in which the message strings have been written. The value of *locale* is set by the environment variable LC_MESSAGES, or failing that, the LANG environment variable. If neither is set, *locale* defaults to a directory named C. If gettxt fails, it displays *default_message* or (if none is specified) the string, "Message not found!!"

gprof	/usr/ccs/bin/gprof [*options*] [*objfile* [*pfile*]]
	Solaris only. (Many other modern Unix systems also have it.) Display call-graph profile data of C programs. Programs compiled with the -xpg option of cc (-pg on other compilers) produce a call-graph profile file *pfile*, whose default name is gmon.out. The specified object file *objfile* (a.out by default) contains a symbol table that is read and correlated with *pfile*. See also **prof** and **lprof**.
	Options
	-a Don't print statically declared functions.
	-b Brief; don't print field descriptions in the profile.
	-c Find the program's static call-graph. Call counts of 0 indicate static-only parents or children.

-c Demangle C++ symbol names before printing them out.

-D With this option, you supply one or more existing *pfiles*. Process the information in all specified profile files and produce profile file called gmon.sum that shows the difference between the runs. See also the -s option below.

-e *name*
    Don't print the graph profile entry for the routine *name*. -e may be repeated.

-E *name*
    Like -e above. In addition, during time computations, omit the time spent in *name*.

-f *name*
    Print the graph profile entry only for routine *name*. -f may be repeated.

-F *name*
    Like -f above. In addition, during time computations, use only the times of the printed routines. -F may be repeated, and it overrides -E.

-l Don't print entries for local symbols.

-s With this option, you supply one or more existing *pfiles*. Sum the information in all specified profile files and send it to a profile file called gmon.sum. Useful for accumulating data across several runs.

-z Show routines that have zero usage. Useful with -c to find out which routines were never called.

-n Only print the top *n* functions.

grep [*options*] *regexp* [*files*]

Search one or more *files* for lines that match a regular expression *regexp*. Regular expressions are described in Chapter 6. Exit status is 0 if any lines match, 1 if not, and 2 for errors. See also **egrep** and **fgrep**.

Options

-b Precede each line with its block number. (Not terribly useful.)

-c Print only a count of matched lines.

→

grep
←
	-e *pat*
	    Use this if *pat* begins with -. Solaris: this option is only available in /usr/xpg4/bin/grep, not /usr/bin/grep. It is common, though, on many modern Unix systems.
	
	-h Print matched lines but not filenames (inverse of -1).
	
	-i Ignore uppercase and lowercase distinctions.
	
	-1 List filenames but not matched lines.
	
	-n Print lines and their line numbers.
	
	-s Suppress error messages for nonexistent or unreadable files.
	
	-v Print all lines that *don't* match *regexp*.
	
	-w Restrict *regexp* to matching a whole word (like using \< and \> in vi). Not on SVR4, but common on many commercial Unix systems.
	
	Examples
	
	List the number of users who use the C shell:
	
	    grep -c /bin/csh /etc/passwd
	
	List header files that have at least one #include directive:
	
	    grep -1 '^#include' /usr/include/*
	
	List files that don't contain *pattern*:
	
	    grep -c *pattern files* **| grep :0**

groups	groups [*user*] Show the groups that *user* belongs to (default is your groups). Groups are listed in /etc/passwd and /etc/group.
gunzip	gunzip [*gzip options*] [*files*] Identical to gzip -d. Typically provided as a hard link to gzip. The -1 ... -9 and corresponding long-form options are not available with gunzip; all other gzip options are accepted. See **gzip** for more information.
gzcat	gzcat [*gzip options*] [*files*] A link to gzip instead of using the name zcat, which preserves zcat's original link to compress. Its action is identical to gunzip -c.

May be installed as zcat on some systems. See **gzip** for more information.

---

gzip [*options*] [*files*]

GNU Zip. Reduce the size of one or more *files* using Lempel-Ziv (L Z 7 7) coding, and move to *file*.gz. Restore with gunzip. With a filename of -, or with no *files*, gzip reads standard input. Usually, compression is considerably better than that provided by compress. Furthermore, the algorithm is patent-free.

gzip ignores symbolic links. The original file's name, permissions, and modification time are stored in the compressed file, and restored when the file is uncompressed. gzip is capable of uncompressing files that were compressed with compress, pack, or the BSD compact. Default options may be placed in the environment variable GZIP.

gunzip is equivalent to gzip -d. It is typically a hard link to the gzip command. gzcat and zcat are equivalent to gunzip -c, and are also often hard links to gzip.

Note: while not distributed with SVR4 or Solaris, gzip is the de facto standard file compression program for files available over the Internet. Source code can be obtained from the Free Software Foundation (*http://www.gnu.org*). Precompiled binaries for Solaris can be obtained from *http://www.sunfreeware.com.* gzip also has its own web site: see *http://www.gzip.org.*

Options

Like most GNU programs, gzip has both short and long versions of its command-line options:

-a, --ascii
    ASCII text mode: convert end-of-lines using local conventions. Not supported on all systems.

-c, --stdout, --to-stdout
    Write output on standard output; keep original files unchanged. Individual input files are compressed separately; for better compression, concatenate all the input files first.

-d, --decompress, --uncompress
    Decompress.

-f, --force
    Force. The file is compressed or decompressed, even if the target file exists or if the file has multiple links.

→

gzip
←

-h, --help
　　Display a help screen and exit.

-l, --list
　　List the compressed and uncompressed sizes, the compres-
　　sion ratio, and the original name of the file for each com-
　　pressed file. With --verbose, also list the compression
　　method, the 32-bit CRC, and the original file's last-modifica-
　　tion time. With --quiet, the title and totals lines are not dis-
　　played.

-L, --license
　　Display the gzip license and quit.

-n, --no-name
　　For gzip, do not save the original filename and modification
　　time in the compressed file. For gunzip, do not restore the
　　original name and modification time; use those of the com-
　　pressed file (this is the default).

-N, --name
　　For gzip, save the original filename and modification time in
　　the compressed file (this is the default). For gunzip, restore
　　the original filename and modification time based on the
　　information in the compressed file.

-q, --quiet
　　Suppress all warnings.

-r, --recursive
　　Recursively walk the current directory tree and compress (for
　　gunzip, uncompress) all files found.

-S .suf, --suffix .suf
　　Use .suf as the suffix instead of .gz. A null suffix makes
　　gunzip attempt decompression on all named files, no matter
　　what their suffix.

-t, --test
　　Check the compressed file integrity.

-v, --verbose
　　Display the name and percentage reduction for each file
　　compressed or decompressed.

-V, --version
　　Display the version number and compilation options, and
　　then quit.

-n, --fast, --best
　　Control the compression method. n is a number between 1
　　and 9. -1 (same as --fast) gives the fastest, but least com-
　　pressed method. -9 (same as --best) gives the best

compression, but is slower. Values between 1 and 9 vary the tradeoff in compression method. The default compression level is -6, which gives better compression at some expense in speed. In practice, the default is excellent, and you should not need to use these options.

---

head [*options*] [*files*]

Print the first few lines of one or more *files* (default is 10).

Options

-*n*   Print the first *n* lines of the file.

-n *n*
      Print the first *n* lines of the file. Solaris only.

Examples

Display the first 20 lines of phone_list:

    head -20 phone_list

Display the first 10 phone numbers having a 202 area code:

    grep '(202)' phone_list | head

/usr/ccs/bin/help [*commands* | *error_codes*]

An SCCS command. See Chapter 18.

---

hostid

Print the hexadecimal ID number of the host machine.

---

hostname [*newhost*]

Print the name of the host machine. Often the same as uname. A privileged user can change the hostname to *newhost.*

---

iconv -f *from_encoding* -t *to_encoding* [*file*]

Convert the contents of *file* from one character set (*from_encoding*) to another (*to_encoding*). If the destination character set provides no equivalent for a character, it is con-

→

iconv ←	verted to an underscore (_). Supported conversion sets are listed in the directory /usr/lib/iconv.
id	id [-a] List user and group IDs; list all groups with -a. When you're running an su session as another user, id displays this user's information.
indxbib	indxbib *files* Part of the refer suite of programs. See Chapter 17.

ipcrm	ipcrm [*options*]
	
	Remove a message queue, semaphore set, or shared memory identifier as specified by the *options*. ipcrm is useful for freeing shared memory left behind by programs that failed to deallocate the space. Use ipcs first to list items to remove.
	
	Options
	
	-m *shmid*
	    Remove shared memory identifier *shmid*.
	
	-M *shmkey*
	    Remove *shmid* created with key *shmkey*.
	
	-q *msqid*
	    Remove message queue identifier *msqid*.
	
	-Q *msgkey*
	    Remove *msqid* created with key *msgkey*.
	
	-s *semid*
	    Remove semaphore identifier *semid*.
	
	-S *semkey*
	    Remove *semid* created with key *semkey*.

ipcs	ipcs [*options*] Print data about active interprocess communication facilities.

-m   Report on active shared memory segments.

-q   Report on active message queues.

-s   Report on active semaphores.

With the -m, -q, or -s options, only the specified interprocess facility is reported on. Otherwise, information about all three is printed.

-a   Use almost all the print options (short for -bcopt).

-A   Use all of the print options (short for -bciopt). Solaris only.

-b   Report maximum allowed number of message bytes, segment sizes, and number of semaphores.

-c   Report the creator's login name and group.

-C*file*
    Read status from *file* instead of from /dev/kmem.

-i   Report the number of shared-memory attaches to the segment. Solaris only.

-N*list*
    Use the argument for the kernel "name list" (the list of functions and variables in the kernel) instead of /stand/unix (Solaris: /dev/ksyms).

-o   Report outstanding usage.

-p   Report process numbers.

-t   Report time information.

/usr/java/bin/jar [*options*] [*manifest*] dest files   **jar**

Solaris only. Java archive tool. All the named objects and directory trees (if directories are given) are combined into a single Java archive, presumably for downloading. jar is based on the ZIP and ZLIB compression formats; zip and unzip can process .jar files with no trouble. If a *manifest* is not provided, jar creates one automatically. The manifest becomes the first entry in the archive, and it contains any needed metainformation about the archive.

Usage is similar to tar, in that the leading - may be omitted from the options.

$\rightarrow$

jar ←	**Options** -c Create a new or empty archive to standard output. -f The second argument, *dest*, is the archive to process. -M Use specified *manifest* instead of creating a manifest file. -m Don't create a manifest file. -o Don't compress the files with ZIP compression. -t Print a table of contents for the archive on standard output. -v Produce verbose output to standard error. -x[*file*] Extract named *file*, or all files if no *file* given.

java	/usr/java/bin/java [*options*] *classname* [*args*]
	
	Solaris only. Compile and then run Java bytecode class files. By default, the compiler uses the JIT ("Just In Time") compiler for the current system. *args* are passed on to the Java program's main method. See also **java_g**.
	
	Options
	
	-cs, -checksource
	    Compare the source code file's modification time to that of the compiled class file, and recompile if it is newer.
	
	-classpath *path*
	    Use *path* as the search path for class files, overriding $CLASSPATH. *path* is a colon-separated list of directories.
	
	-debug
	    Print a password that must be used for debugging and allow jdb to attach itself to the session. (See **jdb**.)
	
	-D*prop*=*val*
	    Redefine the value of *prop* to be *val*. This option may be used any number of times.
	
	-fullversion
	    Print full version information.
	
	-help
	    Print a usage message.
	
	-ms *size*
	    Set the initial size of the heap to *size*, which is in bytes. Append k or m to specify kilobytes or megabytes, respectively. The default heap size is 4MB.

-mx *size*

    Set the maximum size of the heap to *size*, which is in bytes. Append k or m to specify kilobytes or megabytes, respectively. The default maximum size is 16MB. The value must be greater than 1000 bytes and greater than or equal to the initial heap size.

-noasyncgc

    Disable asynchronous garbage collection.

-noclassgc

    Disable garbage collection of Java classes.

-noverify

    Disable verification.

-oss *size*

    Set the maximum stack size of Java code in a Java thread. Append k or m to specify kilobytes or megabytes, respectively. The default maximum size is 400KB.

-prof[:*file*]

    java_g only. Enable Java runtime profiling. Place the trace in the named *file*, if supplied. Otherwise, use ./java.prof.

-ss *size*

    Set the maximum stack size of C code in a Java thread. Append k or m to specify kilobytes or megabytes, respectively. The default maximum size is 128KB.

-t   java_g only. Trace the executed instructions.

-v, -verbose

    Print a message to standard output each time a class file is loaded.

-verbosegc

    Print a message every time the garbage collector frees memory.

-verify

    Run the byte-code verifier on all code.

-verifyremote

    Run the verifier on all code loaded via a classloader. This is the default when interpreting.

-version

    Display version information for java.

java_g	`/usr/java/bin/java_g [`*`options`*`]` *`classname`* `[`*`args`*`]` Solaris only. `java_g` is the nonoptimizing version of the Java interpreter. It is intended for use with a Java debugger, such as `jdb`. Otherwise, it accepts the same options and works the same as `java`. See the entry for **java** for more information.

javac	`javac [`*`options`*`]` *`files`*
	
	Solaris only. Compile Java source code into Java bytecode, for execution with `java`. Java source files must have a `.java` suffix and must be named for the class whose code they contain. The generated bytecode files have a `.class` suffix. By default, class files are created in the same directory as the corresponding source files. Use the CLASSPATH variable to list directories and/or ZIP files that `javac` will search to find your classes.
	
	Options
	
	`-classpath` *`path`*
	　　Use the colon-separated list of directories in *path* instead of CLASSPATH to find class files. It is usually a good idea to have the current directory (".") on the search path.
	
	`-d` *`dir`*
	　　Specify where to create generated class files.
	
	`-depend`
	　　Recompile missing or out-of-date class files referenced from other class files, not just from source code.
	
	`-deprecation`
	　　Warn about every use or override of a deprecated member or class, instead of warning at the end.
	
	`-encoding` *`encoding`*
	　　The source file is encoded using *encoding*. Without this option, the system's default converter is used.
	
	`-g`　Generate debugging tables with line numbers. With -O, also generate information about local variables.
	
	`-J`*`option`*
	　　Pass *option* to `java`. *option* should not contain spaces; use multiple -J options if necessary.
	
	`-nowarn`
	　　Disable all warnings.

-o   Perform optimizations that may produce faster but larger class files. It may also slow down compilation. This option should be used with discretion.

-verbose
    Print messages as files are compiled and loaded.

javac

/usr/java/bin/javadoc [*options*] *files | classes*

Solaris only. Process declaration and documentation comments in Java source files and produce HTML pages describing the public and protected classes, interfaces, constructors, methods, and fields. javadoc also produces a class hierarchy in tree.html and an index of members in Allnames.html.

Options

-author
    Include @author tags.

-classpath *path*
    Use *path* as the search path for class files, overriding $CLASSPATH. *path* is a colon-separated list of directories. It is better to use -sourcepath instead of -classpath.

-d *dir*
    Create the generated HTML files in *dir*.

-docencoding *encoding*
    Use *encoding* for the generated HTML file.

-encoding *encoding*
    The Java source file is encoded using *encoding*.

-J *opt*
    Pass *opt* to the runtime system. See **java** for more information.

-nodeprecated
    Exclude paragraphs marked with @deprecated.

-noindex
    Don't generate the package index.

-notree
    Don't generate the class and interface hierarchy.

-package
    Include only package, protected and public classes and members.

javadoc

$\rightarrow$

javadoc
←
	`-private`
	    Include all classes and members.
	
	`-protected`
	    Include only protected and public classes and members. This is the default.
	
	`-public`
	    Include only public classes and members.
	
	`-sourcepath` *path*
	    Use *path* as the search path for class source files. *path* is a colon-separated list of directories. If not specified, it defaults to the current `-classpath` directory. Running `javadoc` in the directory with the sources allows you to omit this option.
	
	`-verbose`
	    Print additional messages about time spent parsing source files.
	
	`-version`
	    Include `@version` tags.
	
	The `-doctype` option is no longer available. Only HTML documentation may be produced.

javah	`/usr/java/bin/javah [`*options*`]` *classes* | *files*
	
	Solaris only. Generate C header and/or source files for implementing `native` methods. The generated `.h` file defines a structure whose members parallel those of the corresponding Java class.
	
	The header filename is derived from the corresponding Java class. If the class is inside a package, the package name is prepended to the filename and the structure name, separated by an underscore.
	
	Note: the Java Native Interface (JNI) does not require header or stub files. Use the `-jni` option to create function prototypes for JNI native methods.
	
	Options
	
	`-classpath` *path*
	    Use *path* as the search path for class files, overriding $CLASSPATH. *path* is a colon-separated list of directories.
	
	`-d` *dir*
	    Place generated files in *dir*.

-help
> Print a help message.

-jni
> Produce JNI native method function prototypes.

-o *file*
> Concatenate all generated header or source files for all the classes and write them to *file*.

-stubs
> Generate C declarations, not headers.

-td *dir*
> Use *dir* as the directory for temporary files, instead of /tmp.

-trace
> Add tracing information to the generated stubs.

-v Verbose.

-version
> Print the version of javah.

/usr/java/bin/javakey [*options*]

Solaris only. Java security tool. Use javakey to generate digital signatures for archive files, and to build and manage a database of entities, their keys and certificates, and indications of their "trusted" (or nontrusted) status.

The leading – on options may be omitted. Only one option may be specified per javakey invocation.

Options

In the option arguments below, an *id_or_signer* is either a secure ID or a secure signer already in the database.

-c *identity* [true | false]
> Create a new database identity named *identity*. The optional true or false is an indication as to whether the *identity* can be trusted. The default is false.

-cs *signer* [true | false]
> Create a new signer in the database named *signer*. The optional true or false is an indication of whether the *signer* can be trusted. The default is false.

-dc *file*
> Display the certificate in *file*.

→

-ec *id_or_signer cnum cfile*
 Export certificate *cnum* from *id* or *signer* to *cfile*. The number must be one previously created by javakey.

-ek *id_or_signer public [private]*
 Export the public key for *id* or *signer* to file *public*. Optionally, export the private key to file *private*. The keys must be in X.509 format.

-g *signer algorithm ksize [public] [private]*
 Shortcut for -gk to generate a key pair for *signer*.

-gc *file*
 Generate a certificate according to the directives in *file*.

-gk *signer algorithm ksize [public] [private]*
 Generate a key pair for *signer* using standard algorithm *algorithm*, with a key-size of *ksize* bits. The public key is placed in the file *public*, and the private key in file *private*. Exporting *private* keys should be done with caution.

-gs *dfile jarfile*
 Sign the Java Archive file *jarfile* according to directives in *dfile*.

-ic *id_or_signer csrcfile*
 Associate the public key certificate in *csrcfile* with the named *id* or *signer*. This certificate must match a preexisting one, if there is one. Otherwise, this certificate is assigned to the *id* or *signer*.

-ii *id_or_signer*
 Supply information about the *id* or *signer*. javakey reads information typed interactively. End the information with a line containing a single dot.

-ik *identity ksrcfile*
 Associate the public key in *ksrcfile* with *identity*. The key must be in X.509 format.

-ikp *signer public private*
 Import the key pair from files *public* and *private* and associate them with *signer*. The keys must be in X.509 format.

-l List the usernames of all identities and signers in the database.

-ld Like -l, but provide detailed information.

-li *id_or_signer*
 Provide detailed information just about the named *id* or *signer*.

-r *id_or_signer*
    Remove the *id* or *signer* from the database.

-t *id_or_signer* [true | false]
    Set or reset the trust level for *id* or *signer*.

Examples

Create a new identity, arnold, who is to be trusted:

```
javakey -c arnold true
```

List detailed information about arnold:

```
javakey -li arnold
```

/usr/java/bin/javald [*options*] *class*

Solaris only. Create a wrapper for Java applications. javald creates a program that, when executed, runs the specified Java program in the proper environment. This hides knowledge of the proper CLASSPATH environment variable, and so on, from the user who just wishes to run the application.

Options

-C *path*
    Add path to the CLASSPATH that runs the application. This option may be provided multiple times.

-H *dir*
    Set the JAVA_HOME environment variable to *dir*.

-j *list*
    Pass *list* on to java. Multiple options should be quoted.

-o *wrapper*
    Place the generated wrapper in file *wrapper*.

-R *path*
    Add *path* to the LD_LIBRARY_PATH environment variable that is used when the application runs. This allows java to find native methods.

/usr/java/bin/javap [*options*] *classfiles*

Solaris only. Disassemble Java class files and print the results. By default, javap prints the public fields and methods of the named classes.

→

javap ←	*Options*
	-b Ignored. For backward compatibility with the JDK 1.1 javap.
	-c Print out the disassembled byte-codes for each method in the given classes.
	-classpath *path* Use *path* as the search path for class files, overriding $CLASSPATH. *path* is a colon-separated list of directories.
	-h Generate code that can be used in a C header file.
	-J *option* Pass *option* directly to java.
	-l Display line number and local variable information.
	-package Only disassemble package, protected and public classes and members. This is the default.
	-private Disassemble all classes and members.
	-protected Only disassemble protected and public classes and members.
	-public Only disassemble public classes and members.
	-s Display the internal type signatures.
	-verbose For each method, print the stack size, number of arguments, and number of local variables.
	-verify Run the Java verifier.
	-version Print the version of javap.

jdb	/usr/java/bin/jdb [*options*] [*class*]
	Solaris only. jdb is the Java Debugger. It is a line-oriented debugger, similar to traditional Unix debuggers, providing inspection and debugging of local or remote Java interpreters.
	jdb can be used in place of java, in which case the program to be run is already started in the debugger. Or, it may be used to attach to an already running java session. In the latter case, java must have been started with the -debug option. This option generates a password you then supply on the jdb command line.

-host *host*
> Attach to the running Java interpreter on *host.*

-password *password*
> Use *password* to connect to the already running Java inter-
> preter. This password is supplied by java -debug.

---

join [*options*] *file1 file2*

Join the common lines of sorted *file1* and sorted *file2*. Read standard input if *file1* is -. The output contains the common field and
the remainder of each line from *file1* and *file2*. In the options
below, *n* can be 1 or 2, referring to *file1* or *file2*.

Options

-a[*n*]
> List unpairable lines in file *n* (or both if *n* is omitted). Solaris
> does not allow omission of *n*.

-e *s*
> Replace any empty output field with the string *s.*

-j*n m*
> Join on the *m*th field of file *n* (or both files if *n* is omitted).

-o *n.m*
> Each output line contains fields specified by file number *n*
> and field number *m*. The common field is suppressed unless
> requested.

-t*c*   Use character *c* as field separator for input and output.

-v *n*
> Print only the unpairable lines in file *n*. With both -v 1 and
> -v 2, all unpairable lines are printed. Solaris only.

-1 *m*
> Join on field *m* of file 1. Fields start with 1. Solaris only.

-2 *m*
> Join on field *m* of file 2. Fields start with 1. Solaris only.

Examples

Assuming the following input files:

```
$ cat score
olga    81    91
rene    82    92
zack    83    93
```

$\rightarrow$

join
←

```
$ cat grade
olga    B       A
rene    B       A
```

List scores followed by grades, including unmatched lines:

```
$ join -a1 score grade
olga 81 91 B A
rene 82 92 B A
zack 83 93
```

Pair each score with its grade:

```
$ join -o 1.1 1.2 2.2 1.3 2.3 score grade
olga 81 B 91 A
rene 82 B 92 A
```

---

jre

/usr/java/bin/jre [*options*] *class* [*arguments*]

Solaris only. Java Runtime Environment. This program actually executes compiled Java files.

Options

-classpath *path*
> Use *path* as the search path for class files, overriding $CLASSPATH. *path* is a colon-separated list of directories.

-cp *pathlist*
> Prepend one or more paths to the value of $CLASSPATH. Use a colon-separated list when supplying multiple paths. Components may be either directories or full pathnames to files to be executed.

-D*prop=val*
> Redefine the value of *prop* to be *val*. This option may be used any number of times.

-help
> Print a usage message.

-ms *size*
> Set the initial size of the heap to *size*, which is in bytes. Append k or m to specify kilobytes or megabytes, respectively.

-mx *size*
> Set the maximum size of the heap to *size*, which is in bytes. Append k or m to specify kilobytes or megabytes, respectively.

-noasyncgc
> Disable asynchronous garbage collection.

-noclassgc
> Disable garbage collection of Java classes.

-nojit
> Don't do JIT ("just in time") compilation; use the default interpreter instead.

-noverify.
> Disable verification.

-oss *size*
> Set the maximum stack size of Java code in a Java thread. Append k or m to specify kilobytes or megabytes, respectively. The default maximum size is 400KB.

-ss *size*
> Set the maximum stack size of C code in a Java thread. Append k or m to specify kilobytes or megabytes, respectively. The default maximum size is 128KB.

-v, -verbose
> Print a message to standard output each time a class file is loaded.

-verbosegc
> Print a message every time the garbage collector frees memory.

-verify
> Run the byte-code verifier on all code. Note that this only verifies byte-codes that are actually executed.

-verifyremote
> Run the verifier on all code loaded via a classloader. This is the default when interpreting.

---

jsh [*options*] [*arguments*]

Job control version of sh (the Bourne shell). This provides control of background and foreground processes for the standard shell. See Chapter 4.

---

keylogin [-r]

Solaris only. Prompt user for a password, then use it to decrypt the person's secret key. This key is used by secure network services (e.g., Secure NFS, NIS+). keylogin is needed only if the user

→

keylogin ←	isn't prompted for a password when logging in. The -r option updates /etc/.rootkey. Only a privileged user may use this option. See also **chkey** and **keylogout**.
keylogout	`keylogout [option]` Solaris only. Revoke access to (delete) the secret key used by secure network services (e.g., Secure NFS, NIS+). See also **chkey** and **keylogin**. *Option* -f Forget the root key. If specified on a server, NFS security is broken. Use with care.

kill	`kill [options] IDs`
	
	Terminate one or more process *IDs*. You must own the process or be a privileged user. This command is similar to the `kill` command that is built in to the Bourne, Korn, and C shells. A minus sign before an *ID* specifies a process group ID. (The built-in version doesn't allow process group IDs, but it does allow job IDs.)
	
	Options
	
	-l List the signal names. (Used by itself.)
	
	-s *signal*
	    Send signal *signal* to the given process or process group. The signal number (from /usr/include/sys/signal.h) or name (from `kill -l`). With a signal number of 9, the kill is absolute. Solaris only.
	
	-*signal*
	    Send signal *signal* to the given process or process group.

ksh	`ksh [options] [arguments]` Korn shell command interpreter. See Chapter 4 for more information, including command-line options.
ld	`/usr/ccs/bin/ld [options] objfiles` Combine several *objfiles*, in the specified order, into a single executable object module (a.out by default). ld is the loader and is usually invoked automatically by compiler commands such as cc.

-a   Force default behavior for static linking (generate an object
     file and list undefined references). Do not use with -r.

-b   Ignore special processing for shared reference symbols
     (dynamic linking only); output becomes more efficient but
     less sharable.

-B *directive*
     Obey one of the following directives:

dynamic   When loading, use both dynamic (*lib*.so) and
             static (*lib*.a) libraries to resolve unknown
             symbols.

eliminate   Remove symbols not assigned a version defi-
             nition. Solaris only.

group   Treat a shared object and its dependencies as
             a group. Implies -z defs. Solaris only.

local   Treat any global symbols that are not
             assigned a version definition as local symbols.
             Solaris only.

reduce   Perform the reduction of symbolic informa-
             tion specified by version definitions. Solaris
             only.

static   When loading, use only static (*lib*.a) libraries
             to resolve unknown symbols.

symbolic   In dynamic linking, bind a symbol to its local
             definition, not to its global definition.

-d[*c*]
     Link dynamically (*c* is y) or statically (*c* is n); dynamic linking
     is the default.

-D*token*,...
     Print debugging information as specified by *token*; use help
     to get a list of possible values. Solaris only.

-e *symbol*
     Set *symbol* as the address of the output file's entry point.

-f *obj*
     Use the symbol table of the shared object being built as an
     auxiliary filter on shared object *obj*. Do not use with -F.
     Solaris only.

-F *obj*
     Use the symbol table of the shared object being built as a fil-
     ter on shared object *obj*. Do not use with -f. Solaris only.

→

-G   In dynamic linking, create a shared object and allow unde-
     fined symbols.

-h *name*

    Use *name* as the shared object file to search for during
     dynamic linking (default is Unix object file).

-i   Ignore LD_LIBRARY_PATH. Useful for avoiding unwanted
     effects on the runtime search of the executable being built.
     Solaris only.

-I *name*

    Use *name* as the pathname of the loader (interpreter) to
     write into the program header. Default is none (static) or
     /usr/lib/libc.so.1 (dynamic).

-l*x* Search a library named lib*x*.so or lib*x*.a (the placement of
     this option on the line affects when the library is searched).

-L *dir*

    Search directory *dir* before standard search directories (this
     option must precede -1).

-m   List a memory profile for input/output sections.

-M *mapfile*

    Invoke ld directives from *mapfile* (-M messes up the output
     and is discouraged).

-N*string*

    Add a DT_NEEDED entry with the value *string* to the .dynamic
     section of the object being built. Solaris only.

-o *file*

    Send the output to *file* (default is a.out).

-Q*c* List version information about ld in the output (*c* = y, the
     default) or do not list (*c* = n).

-r   Allow output to be subject to another ld. (Retain relocation
     information.)

-R *path*

    Record the colon-separated list of directories in *path* in the
     object file for use by the runtime loader. Multiple instances
     may be supplied; the values are concatenated together.

-s   Remove (strip) symbol table and relocation entries.

-t   Suppress warnings about multiply defined symbols of
     unequal size.

-u *symbol*

    Enter *symbol* in symbol table; useful when loading from an archive library. *symbol* must precede the library that defines it (so -u must precede -l).

-V   Print the version of ld.

-YP, *dirlist*

    Specify a comma-separated list of directories to use in place of the default search directories (see also -L).

-z defs | nodefs | text

    Specify nodefs to allow undefined symbols. The default, defs, treats undefined symbols as a fatal error. Use text to produce an error when there are nonwritable relocations.

-z *directive*

    Solaris only. Obey one of the following directives:

allextract	Extract all archive members.
combreloc	Combine multiple relocation sections.
defaultextract	Return to the default archive extraction rules.
ignore	Ignore dynamic dependencies that are not referenced as part of the linking.
initfirst	Shared objects only. This object's initialization runs before that of others added to the process at the same time. Similarly, its "finalization" runs after that of other objects.
lazyload	Mark dynamic dependencies for lazy loading. Lazily loaded objects are loaded when the first binding to the object is made, not at process startup.
loadfltr	Mark the filter object for immediate processing at runtime, instead of at the first binding.
muldefs	Allow multiple symbol definitions, using the first one that occurs. Otherwise, multiple symbol definitions are a fatal error.
nodefs	Allow undefined symbols. This is the default for shared objects. The behavior is undefined for executables.
nodelete	Mark the object as not being deletable at runtime.
nodlopen	Shared objects only. The object is not available from *dlopen*(3x).

→

ld ←	nolazyload	Don't mark dynamic dependencies for lazy loading. Lazily loaded objects are loaded when the first binding to the object is made, not at process startup.
	nopartial	Expand partially initialized symbols in input relocatable objects into the generated output file.
	noversion	Do not include any versioning sections.
	now	Force nonlazy runtime binding for the object.
	origin	The object requires immediate $ORIGIN processing at runtime.
	record	Record dynamic dependencies that are not referenced as part of the linking. This is the default.
	redlocsym	Remove all local symbols except for the SECT symbols from the SHT_SYMTAB symbol table.
	textoff	In dynamic mode, allow relocations against all sections, including those that are not writable. This is the default for shared objects.
	textwarn	Dynamic mode only. Warn if there remain any relocations against non-writable, allocatable sections. This is the default for executables.
	weakextract	Allow "weak" definitions to trigger archive extraction.

---

ldd

ldd [*option*] *file*

List dynamic dependencies; that is, list shared objects that would be loaded if *file* were executed. (If a valid *file* needs no shared objects, ldd succeeds but produces no output.) In addition, ldd's options can show unresolved symbol references that result from running *file*.

Options

Specify only one of these options:

-d   Check references to data objects only.

-r   Check references to data objects and to functions.

Solaris Options

The following additional options are specific to Solaris:

-f   Force checking of nonsecure executables. This option is dangerous if running as a privileged user.

-i   Print the execution order of initialization sections.

-l   Do immediate processing of any filters, to list all "filtees" and their dependencies.

-s   Display the search path for shared object dependencies.

-v   Display all dependency relationships and version requirements.

/usr/ccs/bin/lex [*options*] [*files*]

Generate a lexical analysis program (named lex.yy.c) based on the regular expressions and C statements contained in one or more input *files*. See also **yacc** and *lex & yacc*, which is listed in the Bibliography.

Options

-c   *file*'s program statements are in C (default).

-e   Handle EUC (Extended Unix Code, i.e., 8-bit) characters. Mutually exclusive with -w. This gives yytext[] type unsigned char. Solaris only.

-n   Suppress the output summary.

-Q*c*   Print version information in lex.yy.c (if *c* = y) or suppress information (if *c* = n, the default).

-t   Write program to standard output, not lex.yy.c.

-v   Print a summary of machine-generated statistics.

-V   Print version information on standard error.

-w   Handle EUC (8-bit or wider) characters. Mutually exclusive with -e. This gives yytext[] type wchar_t. Solaris only.

---

line

Read the next line from standard input and write it to standard output. Exit status is 1 upon *EOF*. Typically used in csh scripts to read from the terminal.

→

line	*Example*
←	Print the first two lines of output from who:
	`who	(line ; line)`

lint	`/usr/ccs/bin/lint [options] files`

Detect bugs, portability problems, and other possible errors in the specified C programs. By default, lint uses definitions in the C library llib-lc.ln. If desired, output from .c files can be saved in "object files" having a .ln suffix. A second lint pass can be invoked on .ln files and libraries for further checking. lint also accepts the cc options -D, -I, and -U. It may accept additional cc options that are system-specific. See also *Checking C Programs with lint*, which is listed in the Bibliography. Note: this command checks programs written in ANSI C; use /usr/ucb/lint if you want to check programs written in pre-ANSI C. Note also that options -a, -b, -h, and -x have exactly the opposite meaning in the versions for BSD and System V.

Options

-a Ignore long values assigned to variables that aren't long.

-b Ignore break statements that cannot be reached.

-c Don't execute the second pass of lint; save output from first pass in .ln files. (Same as BSD -i option.)

-F Print files using full pathname, not just the filename.

-h Don't test for bugs, bad style, or extraneous information.

-k Reenable warnings that are normally suppressed by directive /* LINTED [*message*] */, and print the additional *message* (if specified).

-L*dir*
  Search for lint libraries in directory *dir* before searching standard directories.

-l*x* Use library llib-l*x*.ln in addition to llib-lc.ln.

-m Ignore extern declarations that could be static.

-n Do not check for compatibility.

-o *lib*
  Create a lint library named llib-1.*lib*.ln from the output of the first pass of lint.

-p   Check for portability to variants of C.

-R*file*
    Place .ln output (from a .c file) in *file*, for use by cxref.

-s   Produce short (one-line) diagnostics.

-u   Ignore functions or external variables that are undefined or unused.

-v   Ignore unused arguments within functions; same as specifying the directive /* ARGSUSED */.

-V   Print product name and release on standard error.

-W*file*
    Same as -R, except *file* is prepared for cflow.

-x   Ignore unused variables referred to by extern declarations.

-y   Same as using the directive /* LINTLIBRARY */, which is the same as supplying options -v and -x.

---

listusers [*options*]

Solaris only. List all users, optionally just by group, or by specific users.

Options

-g *grouplist*
    List all users in the comma-separated list of groups *grouplist*.

-l *users*
    List just the named *users*, sorted by login. A comma-separated list may also be provided.

---

ln [*options*] *file1 file2*
ln [*options*] *files directory*

Create pseudonyms (links) for files, allowing them to be accessed by different names. In the first form, link *file1* to *file2*, where *file2* is usually a new filename. If *file2* is an existing file, it is removed first; if *file2* is an existing directory, a link named *file1* is created in that directory. In the second form, create links in *directory*, each link having the same name as the file specified.

$\rightarrow$

ln ←	*Options* -f Force the link to occur (don't prompt for overwrite permission). -n Do not overwrite existing files. -s Create a symbolic link. This lets you link across filesystems and also see the name of the link when you run ls -l. (Otherwise, you have to use find -inum to find any other names a file is linked to.)
locale	locale [*options*] [*name* ...] Solaris only. Print locale-specific information. With no arguments, locale summarizes the current locale. Depending on the arguments, locale prints information about entire locale categories or the value of specific items within a locale. A *public* locale is one an application can access. See also **localedef**. *Options* -a Print information about all available public locales. The POSIX locale should always be available. -c Provide information about the locale category *name*. Useful with or without -k. -k Print the names and values of the given locale keywords. -m Print the names of the available charmaps.
localedef	localedef [*options*] *localename* Solaris only. localedef reads a locale definition either on standard input or from the file named with the -i option. The format is documented in the *locale*(5) manpage. It generates a temporary C source file that is compiled into a shared-object library. This library file can then be used by programs that pay attention to the settings of the locale-specific environment variables in order to return the correct values for the given locale. The generated file has the name *localename.so.version*. The default 32-bit version should be moved to /usr/lib/locale/*localename*/*localename.so.version*. The 64-bit environment on SPARC systems should use /usr/lib/locale/*localename*/sparcv9/*localename.so.version*.

Options

-c Create the shared object file, even if there are warnings.

-C *options*

> Pass *options* to the C compiler. This option is deprecated in favor of -W cc.

-f *mapfile*

> The file *mapfile* provides a mapping of character symbols and collating element symbols to actual character encodings. This option must be used if the locale definition uses symbolic names.

-i *localefile*

> Read the locale definitions from *localefile* instead of from standard input.

-L *options*

> Pass *options* to the C compiler, *after* the name of the C source file. This option is deprecated in favor of -W cc.

-m *model*

> Specify -m ilp32 to generate 32-bit object files (this is the default). Use -m lp64 to generate 64-bit object files (SPARC only).

-W cc, *args*

> Pass *args* on to the C compiler. Each argument is separated from the previous by a comma.

-x *exfile*

> Read additional options from the extension file *exfile*.

Example

Generate a 64-bit shared object locale file for Klingonese; ignore any warning messages:

```
localedef -c -m lp64 -i klingon.def klingon
```

---

logger [*options*] [*messages*]

Solaris only. Log messages to the system log. Command-line messages are logged if provided. Otherwise, messages are read and logged, line-by-line, from the file provided via -f. If no such file is given, logger reads messages from standard input.

Unix Commands

logger
←
	Options
	
	-f *file*
	    Read and log messages from *file.*
	
	-i Log the process ID of the `logger` process with each message.
	
	-p *priority*
	    Log each message with the given *priority.* Priorities have the
	    form *facility.level.* The default is `user.notice.` See *syslog*(3)
	    for more information.
	
	-t *tag*
	    Add *tag* to each message line.
	
	Example
	
	Warn about upcoming trouble:
	
	`logger -p user.emerg 'Incoming Klingon battleship!'`

---

login	`login [options]`
	
	Sign on and identify yourself to the system. At the beginning of each terminal session, the system prompts you for your username and, if relevant, a password. The options aren't normally used.
	
	The Korn shell and the C shell have their own, built-in versions of `login`. See Chapter 4 and Chapter 5 for more information.
	
	Options
	
	user
	    Sign on as *user* (instead of being prompted).
	
	-d*tty*
	    Specify the pathname of the *tty* that serves as the login port.
	
	-h *host* [*term*]
	    Used for remote logins via `telnet` to indicate the login is
	    from host *host* and that the user's terminal type is *term.*
	    Solaris only.
	
	-p Pass the current environment to the new login session.
	    Solaris only.
	
	-r *host*
	    Used for remote logins via `rlogin` to indicate the login is
	    from host *host.* Solaris only.
	
	var=value
	    When specified after the username, assign a *value* to one or
	    more environment variables. PATH and SHELL can't be
	    changed.

`value`
>   Pass values into the environment. Each value that does not
>   contain an = is assigned to a variable of the form L*n*, where
>   *n* starts at 0 and increments. Solaris only.

`logname`

Display your login name. SVR4 prints the value of the LOGNAME
environment variable located in /etc/profile. Solaris looks the
user up in /var/adm/utmp, which is where information is kept
about logged-in users. See also **whoami**.

`look [options] string [file]`

Solaris only. Look through a sorted file and print all lines that
begin with *string*. Words may be up to 256 characters long. This
program is potentially faster than fgrep because it relies on the
file being already sorted, and can thus do a binary search through
the file, instead of reading it sequentially from beginning to end.

With no *file*, look searches /usr/share/lib/dict/words (the
spelling dictionary) with options -df.

Options

-d   Use dictionary order. Only letters, digits, space, and tab are
     used in comparisons.

-f   Fold case; ignore case distinctions in comparisons.

-t *char*
>   Use *char* as the termination character, i.e., ignore all charac-
>   ters to the right of *char*.

`lookbib database`

Part of the refer suite of programs. See Chapter 17.

`lp [options] [files]`

Send *files* to the printer. With no arguments, prints standard input.
To print standard input along with other files, specify - as one of
the *files*.

→

Options

-c Copy *files* to print spooler; if changes are made to *file* while
    it is still queued for printing, the printout is unaffected.

-d *dest*
    Send output to destination printer named *dest*.

-d any
    Used after -f or -s to print the request on any printer that
    supports the given form or character set.

-f *name*
    Print request on preprinted form *name*. *name* references
    printer attributes set by the administrative command lpforms.

-H *action*
    Print according to the named *action*: hold (notify before
    printing), resume (resume a held request), immediate (print
    next; privileged users only).

-i *IDs*
    Override lp options used for request *IDs* currently in the
    queue; specify new lp options after -i. For example, change
    the number of copies sent.

-m Send mail after *files* are printed.

-n *number*
    Specify the *number* of copies to print.

-o *options*
    Set one or more printer-specific *options*. Standard options
    include:

cpi=*n*	Print *n* characters per inch. *n* can also be pica, elite, or compressed.
lpi=*n*	Print *n* lines per inch.
length=*n*	Print pages *n* units long; e.g., 11i (inches), 66 (lines).
nobanner	Omit banner page (separator) from request.
nofilebreak	Suppress formfeeds between files.
width=*n*	Print pages *n* units wide; e.g., 8.5i (inches), 72 (columns).
stty=*list*	Specify a quoted *list* of stty options.

-p Enable notification of completion of the print job. Solaris
    only.

-P *list*
    Print only the page numbers specified in *list*.

-q *n*
> Print request with priority level *n* (39 = lowest).

-r Don't adapt request if *content* isn't suitable; reject instead. (Obscure; used only with -T.)

-s Suppress messages.

-S *name*
> Use the named print wheel or character set for printing.

-t *title*
> Use *title* on the printout's banner page.

-T *content*
> Send request to a printer that supports *content* (default is simple; an administrator sets *content* via lpadmin -I).

-w Write a message on the user's terminal after *files* are printed (same as -m if user isn't logged on).

-y *modes*
> Print according to locally defined *modes*.

Examples

Send mail after printing five copies of report :

    lp -n 5 -m report

Format and print thesis; print title too:

    nroff -ms thesis | lp - title

/usr/ucb/lpq [*options*] [*job#s*] [*users*]   **lpq**

Show the printer queue. Standard SVR4 uses lpstat.

/usr/ucb/lpr [*options*] [*files*]   **lpr**

Send *files* to the printer. Standard SVR4 uses lp.

/usr/ucb/lprm [*options*] [*job#s*] [*users*]   **lprm**

Remove requests from printer queue. Standard SVR4 uses cancel.

lprof	lprof [*options*] lprof -m *files* [-T] -d *out*

	SVR4 only. Display a program's profile data on a line-by-line basis. Data includes a list of source files, each source-code line (with line numbers), and the number of times each line was executed. By default, lprof interprets the profile file *prog*.cnt. This file is generated by specifying cc -ql when compiling a program or when creating a shared object named *prog* (default is a.out). The PROFOPTS environment variable can control profiling at run-time. See also **prof** and **gprof**.
	
	Options
	
	-c *file*
	    Read input profile *file* instead of *prog*.cnt.
	
	-d *out*
	    Store merged profile data in file *out*. Must be used with -m.
	
	-I *dir*
	    Search for include files in *dir* as well as in the default place (/usr/include).
	
	-m *files*
	    Merge several profile *files* and total the execution counts. *files* are of the form *f1*.cnt, *f2*.cnt, *f3*.cnt, etc., where each file contains the profile data from a different run of the same program. Used with -d.
	
	-o *prog*
	    Look in the profile file for a program named *prog* instead of the name used when the profile file was created. -o is needed when files have been renamed or moved.
	
	-p Print the default listing; useful with -r and -s.
	
	-r *list*
	    Used with -p to print only the source files given in *list*.
	
	-s For each function, print the percentage of code lines that are executed.
	
	-T Ignore timestamp of executable files being profiled. Normally, times are checked to insure that the various profiles were made from the same version of an executable.
	
	-V Print the version of lprof on standard error.
	
	-x Omit execution counts. For lines that executed, show only the line numbers; for lines that didn't execute, print the line number, the symbol [U], and the source line.

Print the lp print queue status. With options that take a *list* argument, omitting the list produces all information for that option. *list* can be separated by commas or, if enclosed in double quotes, by spaces.

Options

-a [*list*]

Show whether the *list* of printer or class names is accepting requests.

-c [*list*]

Show information about printer classes named in *list*.

-d   Show the default printer destination.

-D   Use after -p to show a brief printer description.

-f [*list*]

Verify that the *list* of forms is known to lp.

-l   Use after -f to describe available forms, after -p to show printer configurations, or after -s to describe printers appropriate for the specified character set or print wheel.

-o [*list*]

Show the status of output requests. *list* contains printer names, class names, or request IDs.

-p [*list*]

Show the status of printers named in *list*.

-r   Show whether the print scheduler is on or off.

-R   Show the job's position in the print queue.

-s   Summarize the print status (shows almost everything).

-S [*list*]

Verify that the *list* of character sets or print wheels is known to lp.

-t   Show all status information (reports everything).

-u [*list*]

Show request status for users on *list*. *list* can be:

user	*user* on local machine
all	All users on all systems
host!*user*	*user* on machine *host*
host!all	All users on *host*
all!*user*	*user* on all systems

→

lpstat ←	all!all All users on all systems -v [*list*] Show device associated with each printer named in *list*.
ls	ls [*options*] [*names*] If no *names* are given, list the files in the current directory. With one or more *names*, list files contained in a directory *name* or that match a file *name*. The options let you display a variety of information in different formats. The most useful options include -F, -R, -a, -l, and -s. Some options don't make sense together; e.g., -u and -c. Note: the Solaris /usr/bin/ls pays attention to the LC_COLLATE environment variable. Its default value, en_US, (in the United States) causes ls to sort in dictionary order (i.e., ignoring case). Set LC_COLLATE to C to restore the traditional Unix behavior of sorting in ASCII order, or use /usr/ucb/ls. ***Options*** -a List all files, including the normally hidden . files. -A Like -a, but exclude . and .. (the current and parent directories). Solaris only. -b Show nonprinting characters in octal. -c List files by inode modification time. -C List files in columns (the default format, when displaying to a terminal device). -d List only the directory's information, not its contents. (Most useful with -l and -i.) -f Interpret each *name* as a directory (files are ignored). -F Flag filenames by appending / to directories, > to doors (Solaris only), * to executable files, | to fifos, @ to symbolic links, and = to sockets. -g Like -l, but omit owner name (show **group**). -i List the inode for each file. -l Long format listing (includes permissions, owner, size, modification time, etc.).

-L List the file or directory referenced by a symbolic link rather than the link itself.

-m Merge the list into a comma-separated series of names.

-n Like -l, but use user ID and group ID numbers instead of owner and group names.

-o Like -l, but omit group name (show owner).

-p Mark directories by appending / to them.

-q Show nonprinting characters as ?.

-r List files in reverse order (by name or by time).

-R Recursively list subdirectories as well as current directory.

-s Print sizes of the files in blocks.

-t List files according to modification time (newest first).

-u List files according to the file access time.

-x List files in rows going across the screen.

-1 Print one entry per line of output.

Examples

List all files in the current directory and their sizes; use multiple columns and mark special files:

```
ls -asCF
```

List the status of directories /bin and /etc:

```
ls -ld /bin /etc
```

List C source files in the current directory, the oldest first:

```
ls -rt *.c
```

Count the files in the current directory:

```
ls | wc -l
```

ls

/usr/ccs/bin/m4 [*options*] [*files*]   m4

Macro processor for RATFOR, C, and other program *files*.

Options

-B*n* Set push-back and argument collection buffers to *n* (default is 4096).

→

m4 ←	-D*name*[=*value*] Define *name* as *value* or, if *value* is not specified, define *name* as null.
	-e Operate interactively, ignoring interrupts.
	-H*n* Set symbol table hash array size to *n* (default is 199).
	-s Enable line-sync output for the C preprocessor.
	-S*n* Set call stack size to *n* (default is 100 slots).
	-T*n* Set token buffer size to *n* (default is 512 bytes).
	-U*name* Undefine *name*.

mail	mail [*options*] [*users*]

Read mail (if no *users* listed), or send mail to other *users*. Type ? for a summary of commands. Esoteric debugging options exist (not listed) for system administrators. See also **mailx** and **vacation**.

Options for Sending Mail

-m *type*
    Print a "Message-type:" line at the heading of the letter, followed by *type* of message.

-t Print a "To:" line at the heading of the letter, showing the names of the recipients.

-w Force mail to be sent to remote users without waiting for remote transfer program to complete.

Options for Reading Mail

-e Test for the existence of mail without printing it. Exit status is 0 if mail exists; otherwise 1.

-f *file*
    Read mail from alternate mailbox *file*.

-F *names*
    Forward all incoming mail to recipient *names*. SVR4 only. (See **vacation** in Appendix B.)

-h Display a window of messages rather than the latest message.

-p Print all messages without pausing.

-P   Print messages with all header lines displayed.

-q   Terminate on an interrupt.

-r   Print oldest messages first.

`mailx [options] [users]`

Read mail, or send mail to other *users*. For a summary of commands, type ? in command mode (e.g., when reading mail) or ~? in input mode (e.g., when sending mail). The start-up file .mailrc in the user's home directory is useful for setting display variables and for defining alias lists.

On Solaris, /usr/ucb/mail and /usr/ucb/Mail are symbolic links to mailx.

Options

-B   Do not buffer standard input or standard output. Solaris only.

-b *bcc*
> Send blind carbon copies to *bcc*. Quote the list if there are multiple recipients. Solaris only.

-c *cc*
> Send carbon copies to *cc*. Quote the list if there are multiple recipients. Solaris only.

-d   Set debugging.

-e   Test for the existence of mail without printing it. Exit status is 0 if mail exists; otherwise 1.

-f [*file*]
> Read mail in alternate *file* (default is mbox).

-F   Store message in a file named after the first recipient.

-h *n*
> Stop trying to send after making *n* network connections, or "hops" (useful for avoiding infinite loops).

-H   Print mail headers only.

-i   Ignore interrupts (useful on modems); same as **ignore** mailx option.

-I   Use with -f when displaying saved news articles; newsgroup and article-ID headers are included.

→

mailx ←	-n Do not read the system startup `mailx.rc` or `Mail.rc` file(s).
	-N Don't print mail headers.
	-r *address* Specify a return *address* for mail you send.
	-s *sub* Place string *sub* in the subject header field. *sub* must be quoted if it contains whitespace.
	-t Use `To:`, `Cc:`, and `Bcc:` headers in the input to specify recipients instead of command-line arguments. Solaris only.
	-T *file* Record message IDs and article IDs (of news articles) in *file*.
	-u *user* Read *user's* mail.
	-U Convert `uucp`-type addresses to Internet format.
	-v Invoke `sendmail` with the –v option. Solaris only.
	-V Print version number of `mailx` and exit.
	-~ Process tilde escapes, even if not reading from a terminal. Solaris only.

make	`/usr/ccs/bin/make [options] [targets]`

Update one or more *targets* according to dependency instructions in a description file in the current directory. By default, this file is called `makefile` or `Makefile`. See Chapter 20, *The make Utility*, for more information on `make`. See also *Managing Projects with make*, listed in the Bibliography.

Note: the Solaris `make` has many extensions over the standard SVR4 `make` described here. See *make*(1) for more information.

Options

-e Override `makefile` assignments with environment variables.

-f *makefile*
    Use *makefile* as the description file; a filename – denotes standard input.

-i Ignore command error codes (same as `.IGNORE`).

-k Abandon the current entry when it fails, but keep working with unrelated entries.

-n   Print commands but don't execute (used for testing).

-p   Print macro definitions and target descriptions.

-q   Query; return 0 if file is up-to-date; nonzero otherwise.

-r   Do not use "default" rules.

-s   Do not display command lines (same as .SILENT).

-t   Touch the target files, causing them to be updated.

---

man [*options*] [[*section*] *subjects*]

Display information from the online reference manual. Each *sub-ject* is usually the name of a command from Section 1 of the online manuals, unless you specify an optional *section* from 1 to 8. If you don't specify a *subject*, you must supply either a key-word (for -k) or a file (for -f). No options except -M can be used with -k or -f. The MANPATH environment variable defines the directories in which man searches for information (default is /usr/share/man). PAGER defines how output is sent to the screen (default is more -s). Note: in Solaris, *section* must be preceded by -s.

Options

-    Pipe output through cat instead of more -s.

-a   Show all pages matching *subject*. Solaris only.

-d   Debug; evaluate the man command but don't execute. Solaris only.

-f *files*
     Display a one-line summary of one or more reference *files*. Same as whatis.

-F   Search MANPATH directories, not windex database. Solaris only.

-k *keywords*
     Display any header line that contains one of the specified *keywords*. Same as apropos.

-l   Like -a, but list only the pages. Solaris only.

-M *path*
     Search for online descriptions in directory *path* instead of default directory. -M overrides MANPATH.

$\rightarrow$

man ←	-r Reformat but don't display manpage. Same as man - -t. Solaris only. -s *section* Specify the section of the manpage to search in. Required on Solaris for anything that isn't a command. -t Format the manpages with troff. -T *mac* Display information using macro package *mac* instead of tmac.an (the *man* macros). ***Examples*** Save documentation on the mv command (strip backspaces): `man mv	col -b > mv.txt`  Display commands related to linking and compiling:      `man -k link compile	more`  Display a summary of all intro files:      `man -f intro`  Look up the intro page from Section 3M (the math library):      `man 3m intro`          *In SVR4*     `man -s 3m intro` *In Solaris*
mcs	/usr/ccs/bin/mcs [*options*] *files* Manipulate the comment section. mcs adds to, compresses, deletes, or prints a section of one or more ELF object *files*. The default section is .comment. If any input file is an archive, mcs acts on each component file and removes the archive symbol table (unless -p was the only option specified). Use ar s to regenerate the symbol table. Use of mcs -d can significantly decrease the size of large executables, often saving considerable disk space. At least one option must be supplied. ***Options*** -a *string* Append *string* to the comment section of *files*. -c Compress the comment section of *files* and remove duplicate entries. -d Delete the comment section (including header).

-n *name*
>   Act on section *name* instead of .comment.

-p   Print the comment section on standard output.

-V   Print the version of mcs on standard error.

Example

>   **mcs -p kernel.o**   *Print the comment section of kernel.o*

---

mesg [*options*]

Change the ability of other users to use talk, or to send write messages to your terminal. With no options, display the permission status.

Options

-n   Forbid write messages.

-y   Allow write messages (the default).

Both options may be provided without the leading –, for compatibility with BSD.

---

mkdir [*options*] *directories*

Create one or more *directories*. You must have write permission in the parent directory in order to create a directory. See also **rmdir**.

Options

-m *mode*
>   Set the access *mode* for new directories.

-p   Create intervening parent directories if they don't exist.

Examples

Create a read/execute-only directory named personal:

>   **mkdir -m 555 personal**

The following sequence:

>   **mkdir work; cd work**
>   **mkdir junk; cd junk**
>   **mkdir questions; cd ../..**

could be accomplished by typing this:

>   **mkdir -p work/junk/questions**

mkmsgs	mkmsgs [*options*] *string_file msg_file*

Convert *string_file* (a list of text strings) into *msg_file* (the file whose format is readable by gettxt). The created *msg_file* is also used by the commands exstr and srchtxt.

Options

-i *locale*
> Create *msg_file* in directory: /usr/lib/locale/*locale*/LC_MES-SAGES. For example, if *string_file* is a collection of error messages in German, you might specify *locale* as german.

-o Overwrite existing *msg_file*.

more	more [*options*] [*files*]

Display the named *files* on a terminal, one screenful at a time. After each screen is displayed, press the Return key to display the next line or press the spacebar to display the next screenful. Press h for help with additional commands, q to quit, / to search, or :n to go to the next file. more can also be invoked using the name page.

Options

-c Page through the file by clearing the screen instead of scrolling. This is often faster and is much easier to read.

-d Display the prompt Press space to continue, 'q' to quit.

-f Count logical rather than screen lines. Useful when long lines wrap past the width of the screen.

-l Ignore formfeed (^L) characters.

-r Force display of control characters, in the form ^*x*.

-s Squeeze; display multiple blank lines as one.

-u Suppress underline characters and backspace (^H).

-w Wait for a user keystroke before exiting.

-*n* Use *n* lines for each "window" (default is a full screen).

+*num*
> Begin displaying at line number *num*.

+/*pattern*
> Begin displaying two lines before *pattern*.

Examples

Page through *file* in "clear" mode, and display prompts:

```
more -cd file
```

Format doc to the screen, removing underlines:

```
nroff doc | more -u
```

View the manpage for the grep command; begin near the word "BUGS" and compress extra whitespace:

```
man grep | more +/BUGS -s
```

---

msgfmt [*options*] *pofiles*

Solaris only. msgfmt translates "portable object files" (*file*.po) into loadable message files that can be used by a running application via the *gettext*(3C) and *dgettext*(3C) library functions.

Portable object files are created using xgettext from the original C source code files. A translator then edits the .po file, providing translations of each string (or "message") in the source program. The format is described in the *msgfmt*(1) manpage.

Once compiled by msgfmt, the running program uses the translations for its output when the locale is set up appropriately.

Options

-o *file*
> Place the output in *file*. This option ignores domain directives and duplicate msgids.

-v Be verbose. Duplicate message identifiers are listed, but message strings are not redefined.

---

mv [*options*] *sources target*

Basic command to move files and directories around on the system or to rename them. mv works as the following table shows.

Source	Target	Result
File	*name*	Rename file as *name*.
File	Existing file	Overwrite existing file with source file.

→

	Source	Target	Result
mv ←	Directory	*name*	Rename directory as *name*.
	Directory	Existing directory	Move directory to be a subdirectory of existing directory.
	One or more files	Existing directory	Move files to directory.

Options

-- Use this when one of the names begins with a −. For compatibility with old programs, a plain − also works.

-f Force the move, even if *target* file exists; suppress messages about restricted access modes.

-i Inquire; prompt for a y (yes) response before overwriting an existing target.

---

native2ascii

/usr/java/bin/native2ascii [*options*] [*input* [*output*]]

Solaris only. Convert files encoded in the native character encoding to Latin-1 or Unicode encoded files. By default, native2ascii reads standard input and writes standard output. Supply filenames for *input* and *output* to read/write named files, instead.

A large number of encodings are supported; see the manpage for the complete list.

Options

-encoding *encoding*
  Use *encoding* for the translation. The default *encoding* is the value of the system property file.encoding.

-reverse
  Perform the reverse operation: translate from Latin-1 or Unicode to a native encoding.

---

nawk

nawk [*options*] ['*program*'] [*files*] [*variable=value*]

New version of awk, with additional capabilities. nawk is a pattern-matching language useful for manipulating data. See Chapter 11 for more information on nawk.

Options

-f *file*
> Read program instructions from *file* instead of supplying *program* instructions on command line. This option may be specified multiple times; each *file* is concatenated with the others to make up the program source code.

-F *regexp*
> Separate fields using regular expression *regexp*.

-v *variable=value*
> Assign *value* to *variable* before executing '*program*'.

variable=value
> Assign *value* to *variable*. When specified intermixed with *files*, the assignment occurs at that point in the processing.

---

neqn [*options*] [*files*]

Equation preprocessor for nroff. See Chapter 17.

---

nice [*options*] *command* [*arguments*]

Execute a *command* and *arguments* with lower priority (i.e., be "nice" to other users). Also built-in to the C shell, with a different command syntax (see Chapter 5).

Options

-n   Run *command* with a niceness of *n* (1-19); default is 10. Higher *n* means lower priority. A privileged user can raise priority by specifying a negative *n* (e.g., −5). nice works differently in the C shell (see Chapter 5). +*n* raises priority, -*n* lowers it, and 4 is the default.

-n *n*
> Same as -*n*. Solaris only.

---

nl [*options*] [*file*]

Number the lines of *file* in logical page segments. Numbering resets to 1 at the start of each logical page. Pages consist of a header, body, and footer; each section may be empty. It is the body that gets numbered. The sections are delimited by special standalone lines as indicated next; the delimiter lines are copied to the output as empty lines.

→

Section Delimiters

\:\:\:	Start of header
\:\:	Start of body
\:	Start of footer

Options

−b*type*

   Number lines according to *type*. Values are:

a	All lines.
n	No lines.
t	Text lines only (the default).
p"*exp*"	Lines matching the regular expression *exp* only.

−d*xy*

   Use characters *xy* to delimit logical pages (default is \:).

−f*type*

   Like −b, but number footer (default *type* is n).

−h*type*

   Like −b, but number header (default *type* is n).

−i*n* Increment each line number by *n* (default is 1).

−l*n* Count *n* consecutive blank lines as one line.

−n*format*

   Set line number *format*. Values are:

ln	Left-justify, omit leading zeros.
rn	Right-justify, omit leading zeros (default).
rz	Right-justify.

−p Do not reset numbering at start of pages.

−s*c* Separate text from line number with character(s) *c* (default is a tab).

−v*n* Number each page starting at *n* (default is 1).

−w*n* Use *n* columns to show line number (default is 6).

Examples

List the current directory, numbering files as 1), 2), etc.:

```
ls | nl -w3 -s') '
```

Number C source code and save it:

```
nl prog.c > print_prog
```

Number only lines that begin with #include:

```
nl -bp"^#include" prog.c
```

/usr/ccs/bin/nm [*options*] *objfiles*

Print the symbol table (name list) in alphabetical order for one or more object files (usually ELF or COFF files), shared or static libraries, or binary executable programs. Output includes each symbol's value, type, size, name, etc. A key letter categorizing the symbol can also be displayed. You must supply at least one object file.

Options

-A   Write the full pathname or library name on each line. Solaris only.

-C   Print demangled C++ symbol names. Solaris only.

-D   Display the SHT_DYNSYM symbol information. Solaris only.

-e   Report only external and static symbols; obsolete.

-f   Report all information; obsolete.

-g   Write only external (global) symbol information. Solaris only.

-h   Suppress the header.

-l   Use with -p; indicate WEAK symbols by appending an asterisk (*) to key letters.

-n   Sort the external symbols by name.

-o   Report values in octal.

-p   Precede each symbol with its key letter (used for parsing).

-r   Report the object file's name on each line.

-R   Print the archive name (if present), followed by the object file and symbol name. -r overrides this option. Solaris only.

-s   Print section name instead of section index. Solaris only.

-t *format*
     Write numeric values in the specified *format*: d for decimal, o for octal, and x for hexadecimal. Solaris only.

→

Alphabetical Summary of Commands — nm   127

nm ←	-T Truncate the symbol name in the display; obsolete. -u Report only the undefined symbols. -v Sort the external symbols by value. -V Print nm's version number on standard error. -x Report values in hexadecimal. ***Key Letters*** A Absolute symbol. B BSS (uninitialized data space). C Common symbol. SVR4 only. D Data object symbol. F File symbol. N Symbol with no type. S Section symbol. T Text symbol. U Undefined symbol.
nohup	nohup *command* [*arguments*] & Continue to execute the named *command* and optional command *arguments* after you log out (make command immune to hangups; i.e., **no hangup**). In the C shell, nohup is built in. In the Bourne shell, nohup allows output redirection; output goes to nohup.out by default. In the Korn shell, nohup is an alias that allows the command it runs to also be aliased. (See Chapter 4 and Chapter 5.)
nroff	nroff [*options*] [*files*] Format documents to line printer or to screen. See Chapter 12, *nroff and troff.*
od	od [*options*] [*file*] [[+] *offset*[. | b]] Octal dump; produce a dump (normally octal) of the named *file.* *file* is displayed from its beginning, unless you specify an *offset* (normally in octal bytes). In the following options, a "word" is a 16-bit unit.

-A *base*
>   Indicate how the offset should be written. Values for *base* are d for decimal, o for octal, x for hexadecimal, or n for no offset. Solaris only.

-b   Display bytes as octal.

-c   Display bytes as ASCII.

-C   Interpret bytes as characters based on the setting of LC_CTYPE. Solaris only.

-d   Display words as unsigned decimal.

-D   Display 32-bit words as unsigned decimal.

-f   Display 32-bit words as floating point.

-F   Display 64-bit words as extended precision.

-j *skip*
>   Jump over *skip* bytes from the beginning of the input. *skip* can have a leading 0 or 0x for it to be treated as an octal or hexadecimal value. It can have a trailing b, k, or m to be treated as a multiple of 512, 1024, or 1,048,576 bytes. Solaris only.

-N *count*
>   Process up to *count* input bytes. Solaris only.

-o   Display words as unsigned octal (the default).

-O   Display 32-bit words as unsigned octal.

-s   Display words as signed decimal.

-S   Display 32-bit words as signed decimal.

-t *type_string*
>   Specify one or more output types. See the section "Type Strings." Solaris only.

-v   Verbose; show all data. Duplicate lines print as *.

-x   Display words as hexadecimal.

-X   Display 32-bit words as hexadecimal.

+   Required before *offset* if *file* isn't specified.

Modifiers for offset

.   *offset* value is decimal.

→

Unix
Commands

od ←	b *offset* value is 512-byte blocks. ***Type Strings*** Type strings can be followed by a decimal number indicating how many bytes to process. a ASCII named characters (e.g., BEL for \007) c Single- or multibyte characters d, o, u, x Signed decimal, unsigned octal, decimal, and hexadecimal f Floating point
page	page [*options*] [*files*] Same as more.

passwd	passwd [*options*] [*user*]
	
	Create or change a password associated with a *user* name. Only the owner or a privileged user may change a password. Owners need not specify their *user* name.
	
	Options
	
	Normal users may change the so-called *gecos* information (user's full name, office, etc.) and login shell when using NIS or NIS+; otherwise only privileged users may change the following:
	
	-D *domain*
	    Use the passwd.org_dir database in *domain*, instead of in the local domain. Solaris only.
	
	-e Change the login shell. Solaris only.
	
	-g Change the gecos information. Solaris only.
	
	-r *db*
	    Change the password in password database *db*, which is one of files, nis, or nisplus. Only a privileged user may use files. Solaris only.
	
	-s Display password information:
	
	    1. *user* name.
	
	    2. Password status (NP for no password, PS for password, LK for locked).
	
	    3. The last time the password was changed (in *mm/dd/yy* format).

4. Number of days that must pass before *user* can rechange the password.

5. Number of days before the password expires.

6. Number of days prior to expiration that *user* is warned of impending expiration.

Options (privileged users only)

-a Use with -s to display password information for all users. *user* should not be supplied.

-d Delete password; *user* is no longer prompted for one.

-f Force expiration of *user*'s password; *user* must change password at next login.

-h Change the home (login) directory. Solaris only.

-l Lock *user*'s password; mutually exclusive with -d.

-n Set Item 4 of *user*'s password information. Usually used with -x.

-w Set Item 6 for *user*.

-x Set Item 5 for *user*. Use −1 to disable password aging, 0 to force expiration like -f.

---

paste [*options*] *files*

Merge corresponding lines of one or more *files* into vertical columns, separated by a tab. See also **cut**, **join**, and **pr**.

Options

-   Replace a filename with the standard input.

-d'*char*'
    Separate columns with *char* instead of a tab. *char* can be any regular character or the following escape sequences:

    \n Newline
    \t Tab
    \   Backslash
    \0 Empty string

    Note: you can separate columns with different characters by supplying more than one *char*.

$\rightarrow$

paste
←
	-s Merge subsequent lines from one file.
	
	Examples
	
	Create a three-column *file* from files *x*, *y*, and *z*:
	
	    paste x y z > *file*
	
	List users in two columns:
	
	    who
		paste - -
		
		Merge each pair of lines into one line:
		
		    paste -s -d"\t\n" list

patch	patch [*options*] [*sourcefile* [*patchfile*]]
	
	Solaris only. patch reads a "patch" containing the output of diff in normal, ed-script, or context format, and applies the changes contained therein to the original version of *sourcefile*. Multiple files can be patched, but it must be possible to determine the name of the original file from the contents of the patch. Distributing patches is an easy way to provide upgrades to source file distributions where the changes are small relative to the size of the entire distribution.
	
	Note: this entry documents the Solaris version, which is a somewhat older version of Larry Wall's original patch program. The Free Software Foundation now maintains patch. Newer, more capable versions are available from them and are recommended; see *http://www.gnu.org.*
	
	Options
	
	-b Make a backup of each file, in *file*.orig. An existing *file*.orig is overwritten.
	
	-c The *patchfile* is a context diff (from diff -c or diff -C).
	
	-d *dir*
	    Change directory to *dir* before applying the patch.
	
	-D *identifier*
	    Bracket changes with C preprocessor #ifdef.
	
	        #ifdef identifier
	          ...
	        #endif
	
	-e The *patchfile* is an ed script (from diff -e).

-i *file*
> Read the patch from *file* instead of from standard input.

-l   Patch loosely. Any sequence of whitespace characters in the patch may match any sequence of whitespace in *sourcefile*. Other characters must match exactly.

-n   The *patchfile* is a normal diff (from diff with no special options).

-N   Ignore patches that have already been applied. Normally, such patches are rejected.

-o *newfile*
> Instead of updating each source file in place, write the full contents of the modified file(s) to *newfile*. If a file is updated multiple times, *newfile* will contain a copy of each intermediate version.

-p*N* Remove *N* leading pathname components from the filename used in the patch. The leading / of a full pathname counts as one component. Without this option, only the final filename part of the filename is used.

-r *rejfile*
> Use *rejfile* to contain patches that could not be applied, instead of *file*.rej. Rejected patches are always in context diff format.

-R   Reverse the sense of the patch. In other words, assume that the patch was created using diff *new old*, instead of diff *old new*.

Example

Update a software distribution:

```
$ cd whizprog-1.1
$ patch -p1 < whizprog-1.1-1.2.diff
Lots of messages here as patch works
$ find . -name '*.orig' -print | xargs rm
$ cd ..
$ mv whizprog-1.1 whizprog-1.2
```

---

pathchk [-p] *pathnames*

Solaris only. Check pathnames. This command verifies that the file(s) named by *pathnames* do not violate any constraints of the underlying filesystem (such as a name that might be too long), and that the files could be accessed (e.g., if an intermediate direc-

$\rightarrow$

tory lacks search permission, it is a problem). The -p option provides additional portability checks for the *pathnames*.

pax

pax [*options*] [*patterns*]

Solaris only. Portable Archive Exchange program. When members
of the POSIX 1003.2 working group could not standardize on
either tar or cpio, they invented this program.* (See also **cpio**
and **tar**.)

pax operates in four modes, depending on the combinations of -r
and -w:

List mode
　　No -r and no -w. List the contents of a pax archive. Option-
　　ally, restrict the output to filenames and/or directories that
　　match a given pattern.

Extract mode
　　-r only. Extract files from a pax archive. Intermediate direc-
　　tories are created as needed.

Archive mode
　　-w only. Archive files to a new or existing pax archive. The
　　archive is written to standard output; it may be redirected to
　　an appropriate tape device if needed for backups.

Pass-through mode
　　-r and -w. Copy a directory tree from one location to
　　another, analogous to cpio -p.

Options

Here are the options available in the four modes:

```
None:      c d f      n   s    v
-r:        c d f i k  n o p s  u v
-w:    a b d f i        o   s t u v x X
-rw:       d   i k l n  p   s t u v   X
```

-a　Append files to the archive. This may not work on some
　　tape devices.

-b *size*
　　Use *size* as the blocksize, in bytes, of blocks to be written to
　　the archive.

---

* This period in Unix history is known as the "tar wars." ☺

-c Complement. Match all file or archive members that do *not* match the patterns.

-d For files or archive members that are directories, extract or archive only the directory itself, not the tree it contains.

-f *archive*
    Use *archive* instead of standard input or standard output.

-i Interactively rename files. For each file, pax writes a prompt to /dev/tty and reads a one-line response from /dev/tty. The responses are as follows:

Return	Skip the file.
A period	Take the file as is.
new name	Anything else is taken as the new name to use for the file.
EOF	Exit immediately with a nonzero exit status.

-k Do not overwrite existing files.

-l Make hard links. When copying a directory tree (-rw), make hard links between the source and destination hierarchies wherever possible.

-n Choose the first archive member that matches each pattern. No more than one archive member will match for each pattern.

-o *options*
    Reserved for format-specific options. (Apparently unused in Solaris.)

-p *privs*
    Specify one or more privileges for the extracted file. *privs* specify permissions or other characteristics to be preserved or ignored.

a	Do not preserve file access times.
e	Retain the user and group IDs, permissions (mode), and access and modification time.
m	Do not preserve the file modification time.
o	Retain the user and group ID.
p	Keep the permissions (mode).

-r Read an archive and extract files.

-s *replacement*
    Use *replacement* to modify file or archive member names. This is a string of the form -s/*old*/*new*/[gp]. This is similar to the substitution commands in ed, ex, and sed. *old* is a regular expression, and *new* may contain & to mean the matched

→

text and \ *n* for subpatterns. The trailing g indicates the substitution should be applied globally. A trailing p causes pax to print the resulting new filename. Multiple -s options may be supplied. The first one that works is applied. Any delimiter may be used, not just /, but in all cases it is wise to quote the argument to prevent the shell from expanding wildcard characters.

-t   Reset the access time of archived files to what they were before being archived by pax.

-u   Ignore files older than preexisting files or archive members. The behavior varies based on the current mode.

Extract mode
> Extract the archive file if it is newer than an existing file with the same name.

Archive mode
> If an existing file with the same name as an archive member is newer than the archive member, supersede the archive member.

Pass-through mode
> Replace the file in the destination hierarchy with the file in the source hierarchy (or a link to it) if the source hierarchy's file is newer.

-v   In list mode, print a verbose table of contents. Otherwise, print archive member names on standard error.

-w   Write files to standard output in the given archive format.

-x *format*
> Use the given *format* for the archive. The value of *format* is either cpio or ustar. The details of both formats are provided in the IEEE 1003.1 (1990) POSIX standard. The two formats are mutually incompatible; attempting to append using one format to an archive using the other is an error.

-X   When traversing directory trees, do not cross into a directory on a different device (the st_dev field in the stat structure, see *stat*(2); similar to the -mount option of find).

Examples

Copy the current directory to tape:

```
pax -x ustar -w -f /dev/rmt/0m .
```

Copy a home directory to a different directory (presumably on a bigger disk).

```
# cd /home
# pax -r -w arnold /newhome
```

perl [*options*] [*programfile*] [*files*]

perl is the interpreter for the Perl programming language (the Swiss Army knife of Unix programming tools). The Perl program is provided via one or more -e options. If no -e options are used, the first file named on the command line is used for the program.

For more information about Perl, see *Learning Perl, Programming Perl*, and *Advanced Perl Programming*, all listed in the Bibliography.

Note: while not distributed with SVR4 or Solaris, perl is widely used for the Web, CGI, and system-administration tasks, and many other things. The starting point for All Things Perl is *http://www.perl.com*.

Options

This option list is for perl Version 5.005 patchlevel 2. See *perlrun*(1) for more details.

-a   Turn on autosplit mode when used with -n or -p. Splits to
     @F.

-c   Check syntax but does not execute.

-d   Run the script under the debugger. Use -de 0 to start the
     debugger without a script.

-d:*module*
     Run the script under control of the module installed as
     Devel:*module*.

-D*flags*
     Set debugging flags. *flags* may be a string of letters, or the
     sum of their numerical equivalents. See "Debugging Flags."
     perl must be compiled with -DDEBUGGING for these flags to
     take effect.

-e '*commandline*'
     May be used to enter a single line of script. Multiple -e commands may be given to build up a multiline script.

-F *regexp*
     Specify a regular expression to split on if -a is in effect.

→

-h   Print a summary of the options.

-i[*ext*]

Files processed by the <> construct are to be edited in place. The old copy is renamed, and the processed copy is written to the original filename. The optional *ext* indicates an extension to use for the renamed copy. Various rules apply to how this is done; see *perlrun*(1).

-I*dir*

With -P, tells the C preprocessor where to look for include files. The directory is also prepended to @INC.

-l[*octnum*]

Enables automatic line-end processing, e.g., -l013.

-m[-]*module*

Equivalent to use *module*();. With a - after -m, it is equivalent to no *module*();.

-m[-]'*module=arg[,arg]*', -M[-]'*module=arg[,arg]*',

Shorthand for -M'module qw(arg ...)'. This avoids the need for quoting inside the argument.

-M[-]'*module* [...]'

Equivalent to use *module*...;. With a - after -M, it is equivalent to no *module*...;. The "..." represents additional code you might wish to supply, for example:

        -M'mymodule qw(whizfunc wimpfunc)'

-n   Assume an input loop around your script. Input lines are not printed. (Like sed -n or awk.)

-p   Assume an input loop around your script. Input lines are printed. (Like sed.)

-P   Run the C preprocessor on the script before compilation by perl.

-s   Interpret -*xxx* on the command line as a switch and sets the corresponding variable $*xxx* in the script.

-S   Use the PATH environment variable to search for the script.

-T   Force taint checking.

-u   Dump core after compiling the script. For use with the *undump*(1) program (where available). Largely superseded by the Perl-to-C compiler that comes with perl.

-U   Allow perl to perform unsafe operations.

-v   Print the version and patchlevel of the `perl` executable.

-V   Print the configuration information and the value of `@INC`.

-V:*var*
> Print the value of configuration variable *var* to standard output.

-w   Print warnings about possible spelling errors and other error-prone constructs in the script.

-x [*dir*]
> Extract the Perl program from the input stream. If *dir* is specified, `perl` switches to it before running the program.

-0*val*
> (That's the number zero.) Designate an initial value for the record separator `$/`. See also -1.

Debugging Flags

Value	Letter	Debugs
1	p	Tokenizing and parsing
2	s	Stack snapshots
4	l	Context (loop) stack processing
8	t	Trace execution
16	o	Method and overloading resolution
32	c	String/numeric conversions
64	P	Print preprocessor command for -P
128	m	Memory allocation
256	f	Format processing
512	r	Regular expression parsing and execution
1024	x	Syntax tree dump
2048	u	Tainting checks
4096	L	Memory leaks (needs -DLEAKTEST when compiling `perl`)
8192	H	Hash dump; usurps `values()`
16384	X	Scratch-pad allocation
32768	D	Cleaning up
65536	S	Thread synchronization

---

pic [*options*] [*files*]

Preprocessor for `nroff`/`troff` line pictures. See Chapter 17.

pr [*options*] [*files*]

Format one or more *files* according to *options* to standard output. Each page includes a heading that consists of the page number, filename, date, and time. When files are named directly, the date and time are those of the file's modification time. Otherwise, the current date and time are used.

Options

-a   Multicolumn format; list items in rows going across.

-d   Double-spaced format.

-e[*cn*]
> Set input tabs to every *n*th position (default is 8), and use *c* as field delimiter (default is a tab).

-f   Separate pages using formfeed character (^L) instead of a series of blank lines.

-F   Fold input lines (avoids truncation by -a or -m).

-h*str*
> Replace default header with string *str*.

-i*cn*
> For output, replace whitespace with field delimiter *c* (default is a tab) every *n*th position (default is 8).

-l*n* Set page length to *n* lines (default is 66).

-m   Merge files, printing one in each column (can't be used with -*n* and -a). Text is chopped to fit. See also **paste**.

-n[*cn*]
> Number lines with numbers *n* digits in length (default is 5), followed by field separator *c* (default is a tab). See also **nl**.

-o*n* Offset each line *n* spaces (default is 0).

-p   Pause before each page.

-r   Suppress messages for files that can't be found.

-s*c* Separate columns with *c* (default is a tab).

-t   Omit the page header and trailing blank lines.

-w*n* Set line width to *n* (default is 72).

+*num*
> Begin printing at page *num* (default is 1).

−*n*   Produce output having *n* columns (default is 1); tabs are expanded as with −i.

Examples

Print a side-by-side list, omitting heading and extra lines:

```
pr -m -t list.1 list.2 list.3
```

Alphabetize a list of states; number the lines in five columns:

```
sort states_50 | pr -n -5
```

/usr/ucb/printenv [*variable*]

Print values of all environment variables or, optionally, only the specified *variable*. The SVR4 alternative, env, doesn't let you view just one variable, but it lets you redefine them.

---

printf *formats* [*strings*]

Print *strings* using the specified *formats*. *formats* can be ordinary text characters, C-language escape characters, *printf*(3S) format conversion specifiers, or, more commonly, a set of conversion *arguments* listed next.

Arguments

%b   Process a string argument for backslash escapes (not in *printf*(3S)). See the description of allowed escapes under **echo**.

%s   Print the next *string*.

%*n*$s
      Print the *n*th *string*.

%[−]*m*[.*n*]s
      Print the next *string*, using a field that is *m* characters wide. Optionally limit the field to print only the first *n* characters of *string*. Strings are right-adjusted unless the left-adjustment flag − is specified.

Examples

```
$ printf '%s %s\n' "My files are in" $HOME
My files are in /home/arnold
$ printf '%-25.15s %s\n' "My files are in" $HOME
My files are in           /home/arnold
```

prof	/usr/ccs/bin/prof [*options*] [*object_file*]

Display the profile data for an object file. The file's symbol table is compared with profile file mon.out (created by programs compiled with cc -p). Choose only one of the sort options -a, -c, -n, or -t . See also **gprof** and **lprof**.

Options

-a	List output by symbol address.
-c	List output by decreasing number of calls.
-C	Demangle C++ symbol names. Solaris only.
-g	Include nonglobal (static) function symbols (invalid with -1).
-h	Suppress the report heading.
-1	Exclude nonglobal function symbols (the default). Invalid with -g.
-m*pf*	Use *pf* as the input profile file instead of mon.out.
-n	List by symbol name.
-o	Show addresses in octal (invalid with -x).
-s	Print a summary on standard error.
-t	List by decreasing total time percentage (the default).
-V	Print version information on standard error.
-x	Show addresses in hexadecimal (invalid with -o).
-z	Include zero usage calls.

prs	/usr/ccs/bin/prs [*options*] *files*

An SCCS command. See Chapter 18.

prt	/usr/ccs/bin/prt [*options*] *files*

Solaris only. An SCCS command. See Chapter 18.

ps	ps [*options*]

Report on active processes. In options, *list* arguments should either be separated by commas or put in double quotes. In comparing the amount of output produced, note that -e > -d > -a and -1 > -f. In the BSD version, options work much differently; you can also display data for a single process.

-a   List all processes except group leaders and processes not associated with a terminal.

-A   Same as -e. Solaris only.

-c   List scheduler data set by priocntl (an administrative command).

-d   List all processes except session leaders.

-e   List all processes.

-f   Produce a full listing.

-g*list*
     List data only for specified *list* of group leader ID numbers (i.e., processes with same ID and group ID).

-G *list*
     Show information for processes whose real group ID is found in *list*. Solaris only.

-j   Print the process group ID and session ID.

-l   Produce a long listing.

-n*file*
     Use the alternate *file* for the list of function names in the running kernel (default is /unix); obsolete as of SVR4.

-o *format*
     Customize information according to *format*. Rarely used. Solaris only.

-p*list*
     List data only for process IDs in *list*.

-s*list*
     List data only for session leader IDs in *list*.

-t*list*
     List data only for terminals in *list* (e.g., tty1).

-u*list*
     List data only for usernames in *list*.

-U *uidlist*
     Show information for processes whose real user ID is found in *list*. Solaris only.

-y   With -l, omit the F and ADDR columns and use kilobytes instead of pages for the RSS and SZ columns. Solaris only.

pwd	pwd
	Print the full pathname of the current directory. (Command name stands for "print working directory.") Note: the built-in versions, pwd (Bourne and Korn shells) and dirs (C shell), are faster, so you might want to define the following C shell alias:

```
alias pwd dirs -1
```

rcp	rcp [*options*] *sources target*

Copy files between machines. Both *sources* and *target* are file-name specifications of the form *host*:*pathname*, where *host*: can be omitted for a file on the local machine. If no *pathname* is included in *target*, source files are placed in your home directory. If you have a different username on the remote host, specify the form *username@hostname:file*. See also **ssh**.

Options

-p Preserve in copies the modification times, access times, and modes of the source files.

-r If *target* and *sources* are both directories, copy each subtree rooted at *source*. Bear in mind that both symbolic and hard links are copied as real files; the linking structure of the original tree is *not* preserved.

Examples

Copy the local files junk and test to your home directory on machine hermes :

```
rcp junk test hermes:
```

Copy the local bin directory and all subdirectories to the /usr/tools directory on machine diana :

```
rcp -r /bin diana:/usr/tools
```

Copy all files in your home directory on machine hera, and put them in local directory /home/daniel with times and modes unchanged:

```
rcp -p "hera:*" /home/daniel
```

Quote the first argument to prevent filename expansion from occurring on the local machine.

`/usr/ccs/bin/regcmp [-] files`	**regcmp**

Stands for "regular expression compile." Compile the regular expressions in one or more *files* and place output in *file*.i (or in *file*.c if - is specified). The output is C source code, while the input entries in *files* are of the form:

```
C variable     "regular expression"
```

The purpose of this program is to precompile regular expressions for use with the *regex*(3C) library routine, avoiding the overhead of the *regcmp*(3C) function.

`refer [options] files`	**refer**

Bibliographic references preprocessor for troff. See Chapter 17.

`/usr/ucb/reset [options] [type]`	**reset**

Clear terminal settings. reset disables CBREAK mode, RAW mode, output delays, and parity checking. reset also restores undefined special characters and enables processing of newlines, tabs, and echoing. This command is useful when a program aborts in a way that leaves the terminal confused (e.g., keyboard input might not echo on the screen). To enter reset at the keyboard, you may need to use a linefeed (^J) instead of a carriage return. reset uses the same command-line arguments as tset.

`rksh [options] [arguments]`	**rksh**

Restricted version of ksh (the Korn shell), used in secure environments. rksh prevents you from changing out of the directory or from redirecting output. See Chapter 4.

`rlogin [options] host`	**rlogin**

Connect terminal on current local host system (i.e., log in) to a remote *host* system. The .rhosts file in your home directory (on the remote host) lists the hostnames (and optionally, the usernames on those hosts) you're allowed to connect from without giving a password. See also **ssh**.

Options

-8   Allow 8-bit data to pass instead of 7-bit data.

$\rightarrow$

rlogin
←
	-e c
	    Use escape character *c* (default is ~). You can type ~. to disconnect from remote host, though you'll exit more "cleanly" by logging out.
	
	-E Do not have any escape character. Solaris only.
	
	-l *user*
	    Log in to remote host as *user*, instead of using the name on the local host.
	
	-L Allow `rlogin` to run in LITOUT mode (8-bit data may pass in output only).

---

rm

rm [*options*] *files*

Delete one or more *files*. To remove a file, you must have write permission in the directory that contains the file, but you need not have permission on the file itself. If you do not have write permission on the file, you are prompted (y or n) to override.

Options

-f Force. Remove write-protected files without prompting.

-i Prompt for y (remove the file) or n (do not remove the file). Overrides -f.

-r If *file* is a directory, remove the entire directory and all its contents, including subdirectories. Be forewarned: use of this option can be dangerous.

-R Same as -r. Solaris only.

-- Mark the end of options (rm still accepts -, the old form). Use this when supplying a filename beginning with -.

---

rmdel

/usr/ccs/bin/rmdel -rsid *files*

An SCCS command. See Chapter 18.

---

rmdir

rmdir [*options*] *directories*

Delete the named *directories* (the directory itself, not the contents). *directories* are deleted from the parent directory and must be empty (if not, rm -r can be used instead). See also **mkdir**.

-p   Remove *directories* and any intervening parent directories
      that become empty as a result; useful for removing subdirec-
      tory trees.

-s   Suppress standard error messages caused by -p.

Solaris only. Remote Method Invocation compiler for Java. rmic
takes the fully package-qualified class names and generates skeleton and stub class files to provide remote method invocation. The
class must have previously been successfully compiled with java.

For a method WhizImpl in class whiz, rmic creates two files, Whiz-
Impl_Skel.class and WhizImpl_Stub.class. The "skeleton" file
implements the server side of the RMI; the "stub" file implements
the client side.

Options

-classpath *path*
      Use *path* as the search path for class files, overriding
      $CLASSPATH. *path* is a colon-separated list of directories.

-d *dir*
      Place the generated files in *dir*.

-depend
      Recompile missing or out-of-date class files referenced from
      other class files, not just from source code.

-g   Generate debugging tables with line numbers. With -o, also
      generate information about local variables.

-keepgenerated
      Keep the generated .java source files for the skeletons and
      the stubs.

-nowarn
      Disable all warnings.

-o   Perform optimizations that may produce faster but larger
      class files. It may also slow down compilation. This option
      should be used with discretion.

-show
      Use the GUI for the RMI compiler to enter class names.

→

rmic ←	-verbose 　　Print messages as files are compiled and loaded.
rmiregistry	/usr/java/bin/rmiregistry [*port*] Solaris only. Create and start a remote object registry on the specified *port*. The default *port* is 1099. The registry provides naming services for RMI (Remote Method Invocation) servers and clients.
roffbib	roffbib [*options*] [*files*] Part of the refer suite of programs. See Chapter 17.
rsh	/usr/lib/rsh Restricted version of sh (the Bourne shell) that is intended to be used where security is important. rsh prevents you from changing out of the directory or from redirecting output. See Chapter 4.
rsh	rsh [*options*] *host* [*command*] A BSD-derived command to invoke a remote shell. This command is often found in /usr/ucb and should not be confused with rsh, the restricted shell. On Solaris, it is in /usr/bin. rsh connects to *host* and executes *command*. If *command* is not specified, rsh allows you to rlogin to *host*. If shell metacharacters need to be interpreted on the remote machine, enclose them in quotes. This command is sometimes called remsh. See also **ssh**. *Options* -l *user* 　　Connect to *host* with a login name of *user*. -n　Divert input to /dev/null. Sometimes useful when piping rsh to a command that reads standard input but that might terminate before rsh.
sact	/usr/ccs/bin/sact *files* An SCCS command. See Chapter 18.

/usr/ccs/bin/sccs [options] command [SCCS_options] [files]

A user-friendly interface to SCCS. See Chapter 18.

sccs

/usr/ccs/bin/sccsdiff -rsid1 -rsid2 [options] files

An SCCS command. See Chapter 18.

sccsdiff

script [option] [file]

Create a record of your login session, storing in *file* everything that displays on your screen. The default file is called typescript. script records non-printing characters as control characters and includes prompts. This command is useful for beginners or for saving output from a time-consuming command.

Option

-a   Append the script record to *file*.

script

sdiff [options] file1 file2

Produce a side-by-side comparison of *file1* with *file2*. Output is:

text   *text*
    Identical lines.

text <
    Line that exists only in *file1*.

> *text*
    Line that exists only in *file2*.

text | *text*
    Lines that are different.

Options

-1   List only lines of *file1* that are identical.

-o *outfile*
    Send identical lines of *file1* and *file2* to *outfile*; print line differences and edit *outfile* by entering, when prompted, the following commands:

sdiff

→

sdiff ←	e Edit an empty file. e b Edit both left and right columns. e l Edit left column. e r Edit right column. l Append left column to outfile. q Exit the editor. r Append right column to outfile. s Silent mode; do not print identical lines. v Turn off "silent mode." -s Do not print identical lines. -wn Set line length to *n* (default is 130). *Example* Show differences using 80 columns and ignore identical lines: `sdiff -s -w80 list.1 list.2`

sed	sed [*options*] [*files*]
	
	Stream editor. Edit one or more *files* without user interaction. See Chapter 10, *The sed Editor*, for more information on sed. The -e and -f options may be provided multiple times, and they may be used with each other.
	
	Options
	
	-e '*instruction*'
	    Apply the editing *instruction* to the files.
	
	-f *script*
	    Apply the set of instructions from the editing *script*.
	
	-n Suppress default output.

serialver	/usr/java/bin/serialver [-show | *classname*] Solaris only. Print the serialVersionUID for *classname* in a form suitable for copying into an evolving class. The -show option starts a simple GUI in which you enter the full classname.
sh	sh [*options*] [*arguments*] The standard command interpreter (or Bourne shell) that executes commands from a terminal or a file. See Chapter 4 for more

information on the Bourne shell, including command-line options.

/usr/ccs/bin/size [*options*] [*objfile* ...]

Print the (decimal) number of bytes of each section of *objfile*. If *objfile* is not specified, a.out is used.

Options

-f   Print sizes, names, and total size for allocatable sections.

-F   Print sizes, permission flags, and total size for loadable segments.

-n   Print sizes for nonallocatable sections or for nonloadable segments.

-o   Print output in octal.

-V   Report the size program version number.

-x   Print output in hexadecimal.

---

sleep *seconds*

Wait a specified number of *seconds* before executing another command. Often used in shell scripts. sleep is built in to ksh93.

---

soelim [*files*]

A preprocessor that reads nroff/troff input *files*, resolving and then eliminating .so requests. That is, input lines such as:

```
.so header
```

are replaced by the contents of the file header. Normally, .so requests are resolved by nroff or troff. Use soelim whenever you are preprocessing the input (e.g., passing it through tbl or sed), and the complete text is needed prior to formatting.

Example

Run a sed script on (all) input before formatting:

```
soelim file | sed -e 's/--/\\(em/g' | nroff -mm - | lp
```

sort	sort [*options*] [*files*]

Sort the lines of the named *files*, typically in alphabetical order. See also **uniq**, **comm**, and **join**.

Options

-b Ignore leading spaces and tabs.

-c Check whether *files* are already sorted, and if so, produce no output.

-d Sort in dictionary order (ignore punctuation).

-f "Fold"; ignore uppercase/lowercase differences.

-i Ignore nonprinting characters (those outside ASCII range 040-176).

-k *fieldspec*
    Specify significance of input fields for sorting. See the fuller description below. Solaris only.

-m Merge sorted input files.

-M Compare first three characters as months.

-n Sort in arithmetic (numerical) order.

-o *file*
    Put output in *file*.

-r Reverse the order of the sort.

-t*c* Fields are separated with *c* (default is any whitespace).

-T *dir*
    Use *dir* for temporary files. Solaris only.

-u Identical lines in input file appear only one (*u*nique) time in output.

-y[*kmem*]
    Adjust the amount of memory (in kilobytes) sort uses. If *kmem* is not specified, allocate the maximum memory.

-z*recsz*
    Provide the maximum number of bytes for any one line in the file. This option prevents abnormal termination of sort in certain cases. Solaris sort accepts but otherwise ignores this option.

+*n* [-*m*]
    Skip *n* fields before sorting, and sort up to field position *m*. If *m* is missing, sort to end of line. Positions take the form *a.b*, which means character *b* of field *a*. If .*b* is missing, sort

at the first character of the field. Counting starts at zero. Solaris allows fields to have optional trailing modifiers, as in the -k option.

Field Specifications for -k

A *fieldspec* has the form *fieldstart*[*type*][,*fieldend*[*type*]].

fieldstart
> A field number and optional starting character of the form *fnum*[.*schar*]. *fnum* is the field number, starting from 1. *schar*, if present, is the starting character within the field, also counting from 1.

fieldend
> A field number and optional ending character of the form *fnum*[.*echar*]. *fnum* is the field number, starting from 1. *echar*, if present, is the last significant character within the field, also counting from 1.

type
> A modifier, one of the letters b, d, f, i, M, n, or r. The effect is the same as the corresponding option, except that the b modifier only applies to the fields, not the whole line.

Examples

List files by decreasing number of lines:

```
wc -l * | sort -rn
```

Alphabetize a list of words, remove duplicates, and print the frequency of each word:

```
sort -fd wordlist | uniq -c
```

Sort the password file numerically by the third field (user ID):

```
sort +2n -t: /etc/passwd
```

Find the top 20 disk hogs on a system:

```
cd /home; du -sk * | sort -nr | head -20
```

---

sortbib [*option*] *files*

Part of the refer suite of programs. See Chapter 17.

---

sotruss [*options*] *program* [*args* ...]

Solaris only. Shared object library version of truss. sotruss executes *program*, passing it *args*, if any. It then traces calls into and/ or out of shared object libraries that are loaded dynamically.

$\rightarrow$

Unix Commands

sotruss
←

Options

-f Follow children created by *fork*(2) and print output for each
child. Each output line contains the process's process ID.

-F *fromlist*
Only trace calls from the libraries named in *fromlist*, which is
a colon-separated list of libraries. The default is to trace only
calls from the main executable.

-o *file*
Send output to *file*. If used with -f, the process ID of the
running program is appended to the filename.

-T *tolist*
Only trace calls to routines in the libraries named in *tolist*,
which is a colon-separated list of libraries. The default is to
trace all calls.

spell

spell [*options*] [*files*]

Compare the words of one or more named *files* with the system
dictionary and report all misspelled words. System files for spell
reside in /usr/lib/spell.

Options

-b Check for British spelling.

-i Ignore files included with the nroff or troff .so request. No
effect if deroff is unavailable.

-l Follow *all* included files (files named in .so or .nx requests);
default is to ignore files that begin with /usr/lib.

-v Include words that are derived from dictionary list but are
not literal entries.

-x Show every possible word stem (on standard error).

+*wordlist*
Use the sorted *wordlist* file as a local dictionary to add to the
system dictionary; words in *wordlist* are not treated as misspelled.

Example

Run the first pass of spell:

```
spell file1 file2 > jargon
```

After editing the `jargon` file, use it as a list of special terms. The second pass of `spell` produces genuine misspellings:

```
spell +jargon file[12] > typos
```

`split` [*options*] [*infile*] [*outfile*]

Split *infile* into several files of equal length. *infile* remains unchanged, and the results are written to *outfile*aa, *outfile*ab, etc. (default is xaa, xab, etc.). If *infile* is – (or missing), standard input is read. See also **csplit**.

Option

-*n*   Split *infile* into files, each *n* lines long (default is 1000).

Solaris Options

These options are unique to Solaris:

-a *slen*
   Use *slen* characters for the filename suffix. Default is 2.

-b *n*[*m*]
   Split into pieces of size *n* bytes. An optional multiplier *m* may be supplied: k for kilobytes and m for megabytes. Mutually exclusive with -l.

-l*n* Same as -*n*. Mutually exclusive with -b.

Examples

Break *bigfile* into 1000-line segments:

```
split bigfile
```

Join four files, then split them into ten-line files named new.aa, new.ab, etc. Note that without the –, new. would be treated as a nonexistent input file:

```
cat list[1-4] | split -10 - new.
```

`srchtxt` [*options*] [*regexp*]

A grep-like utility to search message files for text strings that match regular expression *regexp*. srchtxt is one of the message manipulation commands like gettxt and mkmsgs. If no *regexp* is used, srchtxt displays all message strings from the specified files.

→

srchtxt
←
	Options
	
	-l *locale*
	    Search files that reside in the directory /usr/lib/locale/
	    locale/LC_MESSAGES, where *locale* is the language in which
	    the message strings have been written. The default *locale* is
	    set by environment variables LC_MESSAGES or LANG. If nei-
	    ther is set, srchtxt searches directory /usr/lib/locale/C/
	    LC_MESSAGES.
	
	-m *msgfiles*
	    Search for strings in one or more comma-separated *msgfiles*.
	    Specifying a pathname for *msgfiles* overrides the -l option.
	
	-s Don't print message numbers for strings.

ssh	ssh2 [-l *user*] *host* [*commands*] ssh2 [*options*] [*user*@]*host* Secure shell. This is a secure replacement for the rsh, rlogin, and rcp programs. ssh uses strong public-key encryption technologies to provide end-to-end encryption of data. There may be licens- ing/patent issues restricting the use of the software in some coun- tries. Note: ssh2 is not distributed with SVR4 or Solaris. Source code for the noncommercial version for Unix can be downloaded from *ftp://ftp.cs.hut.fi/pub/ssh*. More information can be found at *http://www.ssh.fi* and *http://www.ipsec.com*.

strings	strings [*options*] *files*
	
	Search object or binary *files* for sequences of four or more print-
	able characters that end with a newline or null. See also **od**.
	
	Options
	
	-a Search entire *file*, not just the initialized data portion of
	    object files. Can also specify this option as -.
	
	-o Display the string's offset position before the string.
	
	-n *n*
	    Minimum string length is *n* (default is 4). Can also specify
	    this option as -*n*.
	
	-t *format*
	    Specify how to print string offsets. *format* is one of d, o, or x
	    for decimal, octal, or hexadecimal, respectively. Solaris only.

`/usr/ccs/bin/strip` [*options*] *files*

Remove information from ELF object *files* or archive *files*, thereby reducing file sizes and freeing disk space. The following items can be removed:

1. Symbol table

2. Debugging information

3. Line number information

4. Static symbol information

5. External symbol information

6. Block delimiters

7. Relocation bits

ELF versions of strip provide facilities for removing only the first three items.

Options

The following options refer to the previous list:

-b   Strip only Items 1, 2, and 3. This is the default.

-l   Strip only Item 3 (line number information).

-r   Strip Items 1, 2, 3, and 6. (Solaris: same as the default action: strip Items 1, 2, and 3.)

-V   Print the version number of strip on standard error.

-x   Strip only Items 2 and 3.

---

stty [*options*] [*modes*]

Set terminal I/O options for the current device. Without options, stty reports the terminal settings, where a ^ indicates the Control key, and ^` indicates a null value. Most modes can be switched using an optional preceding – (shown in brackets). The corresponding description is also shown in brackets. As a privileged user, you can set or read settings from another device using the syntax:

   stty [*options*] [*modes*] < *device*

stty is one of the most complicated Unix commands. The complexity stems from the need to deal with a large range of conflicting, incompatible, and nonstandardized terminal devices—everything from printing teletypes to CRTs to pseudo-terminals

$\rightarrow$

for windowing systems. Only a few of the options are really needed for day-to-day use. stty sane is a particularly valuable one to remember.

Options

-a   Report all option settings.

-g   Report current settings.

Control Modes

0   Hang up connection (set the baud rate to zero).

n   Set terminal baud rate to n (e.g., 19200).

[-]clocal
:   [Enable] disable modem control.

[-]cread
:   [Disable] enable the receiver.

[-]crtscts
:   [Disable] enable output hardware flow control using RTS/CTS.

[-]crtsxoff
:   [Disable] enable input hardware flow control using RTS.

csn   Select character size in bits ($5 \leq n \leq 8$).

[-]cstopb
:   [One] two stop bits per character.

defeucw
:   Set the width in bytes per character and screen display columns per character, for EUC (Extended Unix Code) characters. Solaris only.

[-]hup
:   [Do not] hang up connection on last close.

[-]hupcl
:   Same as [-]hup.

ispeed n
:   Set terminal input baud rate to n.

[-]loblk
:   [Do not] block layer output. For use with shl; obsolete.

ospeed n
:   Set terminal output baud rate to n.

[-]parenb
> [Disable] enable parity generation and detection.

[-]parext
> [Disable] enable extended parity generation and detection for mark and space parity.

[-]parodd
> Use [even] odd parity.

Input Modes

[-]brkint
> [Do not] signal INTR on break.

[-]icrnl
> [Do not] map carriage return (^M) to newline (^J) on input.

[-]ignbrk
> [Do not] ignore break on input.

[-]igncr
> [Do not] ignore carriage return on input.

[-]ignpar
> [Do not] ignore parity errors.

[-]imaxbel
> [Do not] echo BEL when input line is too long.

[-]inlcr
> [Do not] map newline to carriage return on input.

[-]inpck
> [Disable] enable input parity checking.

[-]istrip
> [Do not] strip input characters to 7 bits.

[-]iuclc
> [Do not] map uppercase to lowercase on input.

[-]ixany
> Allow [only XON] any character to restart output.

[-]ixoff
> [Do not] send START/STOP characters when the queue is nearly empty/full.

[-]ixon
> [Disable] enable START/STOP output control.

[-]parmrk
> [Do not] mark parity errors.

→

Output Modes

bs*n* Select style of delay for backspaces (*n* = 0 or 1).

cr*n* Select style of delay for carriage returns (0 ≤ *n* ≤ 3).

ff*n* Select style of delay for formfeeds (*n* = 0 or 1).

nl*n* Select style of delay for linefeeds (*n* = 0 or 1).

[-]ocrnl
   [Do not] map carriage return to newline on output.

[-]ofdel
   Set fill character to [NULL] DEL.

[-]ofill
   Delay output with [timing] fill characters.

[-]olcuc
   [Do not] map lowercase to uppercase on output.

[-]onlcr
   [Do not] map newline to carriage return-newline on output.

[-]onlret
   [Do not] perform carriage return after newline.

[-]onocr
   [Do not] output carriage returns at column zero.

[-]opost
   [Do not] postprocess output; ignore all other output modes.

tab*n*
   Select style of delay for horizontal tabs (0 ≤ *n* ≤ 3).

vt*n* Select style of delay for vertical tabs (*n* = 0 or 1).

Local Modes

[-]echo
   [Do not] echo every character typed.

[-]echoctl
   [Do not] echo control characters as ^*char*, DEL as ^?.

[-]echoe
   [Do not] echo ERASE character as BS-space-BS string.

[-]echok
   [Do not] echo newline after KILL character.

[-]echoke
   [Do not] BS-SP-BS erase entire line on line kill.

[-]echonl
> [Do not] echo newline (^J).

[-]echoprt
> [Do not] echo erase character as character is "erased."

[-]flusho
> Output is [not] being flushed.

[-]icanon
> [Disable] enable canonical input (ERASE and KILL processing).

[-]iexten
> [Disable] enable extended functions for input data.

[-]isig
> [Disable] enable checking of characters against INTR, QUIT, and SWITCH.

[-]lfkc
> Same as [-]echok. Obsolete.

[-]noflsh
> [Enable] disable flush after INTR, QUIT, or SWITCH.

[-]pendin
> [Do not] retype pending input at next read or input character.

[-]stappl
> [Line] application mode on a synchronous line.

[-]stflush
> [Disable] enable flush on synchronous line.

[-]stwrap
> [Enable] disable truncation on synchronous line.

[-]tostop
> [Do not] send SIGTTOU when background processes write to the terminal.

[-]xcase
> [Do not] change case on local output.

Control Assignments

ctrl-char c
> Set control character to c. ctrl-char is: ctab, discard, dsusp, eof, eol, eol2, erase, intr, kill, lnext, quit, reprint, start, stop, susp, swtch, werase.

→

min *n*

> With –icanon, *n* is the minimum number of characters that will satisfy the read system call until the timeout set with time expires.

time *n*

> With –icanon, *n* is the number of tenths of seconds to wait before a read system call times out. If the minimum number of characters set with min has been read, the read can return before the timeout expires.

line *i*

> Set line discipline to *i* ($1 \leq i \leq 126$).

Combination Modes

async

> Set normal asynchronous communications.

cooked

> Same as –raw.

[–]evenp

> Same as [–]parenb and cs7[8].

ek Reset ERASE and KILL characters to # and @.

[–]lcase

> [Un] set xcase, iuclc, and olcuc.

[–]LCASE

> Same as [–]lcase.

[–]markp

> [Disable] enable parenb, parodd, and parext, and set cs7[8].

[–]nl

> [Un] set icrnl and onlcr. –nl also unsets inlcr, igncr, ocrnl, and onlret.

[–]oddp

> Same as [–]parenb, [–]parodd, and cs7[8].

[–]parity

> Same as [–]parenb and cs7[8].

[–]raw

> [Disable] enable raw input and output (no ERASE, KILL, INTR, QUIT, EOT, SWITCH, or output postprocessing).

sane

> Reset all modes to reasonable values.

[-]spacep
> [Disable] enable parenb and parext, and set cs7[8].

[-]tabs
> [Expand to spaces] preserve output tabs.

term
> Set all modes suitable for terminal type *term* (tty33, tty37, vt05, tn300, ti700, or tek). (These predefined names are all so obsolete as to be useless.)

Hardware Flow Control Modes

[-]cdxon
> [Disable] enable CD on output.

[-]ctsxon
> [Disable] enable CTS on output.

[-]dtrxoff
> [Disable] enable DTR on input.

[-]isxoff
> [Disable] enable isochronous hardware flow control on input.

[-]rtsxoff
> [Disable] enable RTS on input.

Clock Modes

These options may not be supported on all hardware:

[x|r]cibrg
> Get the transmit|receive clock from internal baud rate generator.

[x|r]ctset
> Get the transmit|receive clock from transmitter timing-lead, CCITT V.24 circuit 114, EIA-232-D pin 15.

[x|r]crset
> Get the transmit|receive clock from receiver timing-lead, CCITT V.24 circuit 115, EIA-232-D pin 17.

For modes beginning with t, *pin* is transmitter timing-lead, V.24 circuit 113, EIA-232-D pin 24. For modes beginning with r, *pin* is receiver timing-lead, V.24 circuit 128, no EIA-232-D pin.

[t|r]setcoff
> No transmitter|receiver timing clock.

[t|r]setcrbrg
> Send receive baud rate generator to *pin*.

→

stty
←
	[t|r]setctbrg
	    Send transmit baud rate generator to *pin*.
	
	[t|r]setctset
	    Send transmitter timing to *pin*.
	
	[t|r]setcrset
	    Send receiver timing to *pin*.
	
	Window size
	
	columns *n*
	    Set size to *n* columns. Can also be given as cols.
	
	rows *n*
	    Set size to *n* rows.
	
	xpixels *n*
	    Set size to *n* pixels across.
	
	ypixels *n*
	    Set size to *n* pixels up and down.

---

su	su [*option*] [*user*] [*shell_args*] Create a shell with the effective user ID of another *user* (that is, login as *user*). If no *user* is specified, create a shell for a privileged user (that is, become a superuser). Enter *EOF* to terminate. You can run the shell with particular options by passing them as *shell_args* (e.g., if the shell runs sh, you can specify -c *command* to execute *command* via sh, or -r to create a restricted shell). su will inherit your environment settings. Administrators wishing to switch to a user's setup (perhaps to help them solve a problem) may wish to consider using this sequence:

```
me$ su              Switch to root
Password:           Enter root password
# su - user         Switch to other user
user$
```

Option

-    Go through the entire login sequence (i.e., change to *user*'s environment).

---

tail	tail [*options*] [*file*] Print the last ten lines of the named *file*. Use only one of -f or -r.

Options

-f Don't quit at the end of file; "follow" file as it grows. End with an INTR (usually ^c).

-r Copy lines in reverse order.

-n[k]

Begin printing at nth item from end of file. k specifies the item to count: 1 (lines, the default), b (blocks), or c (characters).

-k Same as previous, but use the default count of 10.

+n[k]

Like -n, but start at nth item from beginning of file.

+k Like -k, but count from beginning of file.

Examples

Show the last 20 lines containing instances of .Ah:

```
grep '\.Ah' file | tail -20
```

Continually track the latest uucp activity:

```
tail -f /var/spool/uucp/LOGFILE
```

Show the last 10 characters of variable name:

```
echo "$name" | tail -c
```

Reverse all lines in list:

```
tail -r list
```

talk *user* [@*hostname*] [*tty*]

Exchange typed communication with another *user* who is on the local machine or on machine *hostname*. talk might be useful when you're logged in via modem and need something quickly, making it inconvenient to telephone or send email. talk splits your screen into two windows. When connection is established, you type in the top half while *user*'s typing appears in the bottom half. Type ^L to redraw the screen and ^c (or interrupt) to exit. If *user* is logged in more than once, use *tty* to specify the terminal line. The *user* needs to have used mesg y.

Notes

• There are different versions of talk that use different protocols; interoperability across different Unix systems is very limited.

→

talk ←	• talk is also not very useful if the remote user you are "calling" is using a windowing environment, since there is no way for you to know which *tty* to use to get their attention. The connection request could easily show up in an iconified window! Even if you know the remote *tty*, the called party must have done a mesg y to accept the request.
tar	tar [*options*] [*files*] Copy *files* to or restore *files* from tape (**tape archive**). If any *files* are directories, tar acts on the entire subtree. (See also **cpio** and **pax**.) Options are supplied as one group, with any arguments placed afterward in corresponding order. Originally, tar did not even accept a leading – on its options. Although the Solaris version allows one, it does not require it. On many other Unix systems, you may use conventional option notation, with each option preceded by a dash and separated from the other options with whitespace. Some systems actually require the use of separate options. Check your local documentation for the final word. *Notes* For the following reasons, tar is best used as a way to exchange file or source code archives over a network. A system administrator performing system backups is advised to use the vendor-supplied backup program (typically called dump or backup; see your local documentation) for backups instead of tar. (Many of these same points apply to cpio and to pax as well.) • Most Unix versions of tar preserve the leading / from an absolute filename in the archive. This makes it difficult or impossible to extract the files on a different system. • The tar archive format was designed when Unix file and directory names were short (14 characters maximum). Modern Unix systems allow individual filenames to be up to 255 characters in length, but the tar archive header has a limit of 100 characters for the entire pathname. This makes it difficult or impossible in practice to archive a typical Unix filesystem. • In general, Unix versions of tar cannot recover from data errors, which are particularly common with tapes. An early tape error can render an entire tar tape useless. • While tar does checksum the header information describing each archived file, it does not checksum the actual data

blocks. Thus, if a data block becomes corrupted on a tape, tar will never notice.

The GNU version of tar has extensions to get around many of these problems, at the cost of portability of the archive format to non-GNU versions. Source code can be obtained from the Free Software Foundation (*http://www.gnu.org*).

Control Options (Solaris)

-C *dir files*
> Change directory to *dir* before adding *files* to the archive. Use relative pathnames. This option makes it possible to archive files that don't share a common ancestor directory.

-I *file*
> Read a list of filenames to be archived, one filename per line, from file. Useful when there are too many files to name on the command line.

-X
> Exclude files. The corresponding file argument is read for a list of relative pathnames, one per line, of files that should not be archived. This option may be provided multiple times with multiple files. Filenames that appear here are excluded even if the same name was provided in a file used with -I.

Function Options (choose one)

c
> Create a new archive.

r
> Append *files* to archive.

t
> Table of contents. Print the names of *files* if they are stored on the archive (if *files* not specified, print names of all files).

u
> Update. Add files if not in archive or if modified.

x
> Extract *files* from archive (if *files* not specified, extract all files).

Options

b *n*
> Use blocking factor *n* (default is 1; maximum is 20). Different Unix systems often allow larger blocking factors.

B
> Continue reading until logical blocks are full. For use across Ethernet connections with rsh. On by default when reading standard input. Solaris only, but also common on many other Unix systems.

e
> Exit immediately upon unexpected errors. Solaris only.

$\rightarrow$

E   Use an extended header that allows longer filenames, larger files, and other extensions. Not portable. Solaris only.

f *arch*
> Store files in or extract files from archive *arch*; *arch* is usually a device name (default varies from system to system). If *arch* is -, standard input or output is used as appropriate (e.g., when piping a tar archive to a remote host).

F, FF
> With F, do not archive SCCS and RCS directories. With FF, also exclude files named a.out, core, errs, and all .o files. Solaris only.

i   Ignore directory checksum errors. Solaris only.

k *size*
> Specify the archive size in kilobytes. Archives that are larger than *size* are split across volumes. Useful for fixed-size media, such as floppy disks. Solaris only.

l   Print error messages about links that can't be found.

L   Follow symbolic links. SVR4 only.

m   Do not restore file modification times; update them to the time of extraction.

n   Archive is not a tape device. This allows tar to seek, instead of doing sequential reads, which is faster. Solaris only.

o   Change ownership of extracted files to that of user running program. This is the default for nonprivileged users.

p   Preserve permissions of extracted files. Solaris ACLs are restored if recorded in the archive and are added to the archive when used with c.

P   Do not add a trailing / to directory names in the archive. Solaris only.

v   Print function letter (x for extraction or a for archive) and name of files. With t, print a listing similar to that of ls -l.

w   Wait for user confirmation (y).

n[c] Select tape drive *n* and use speed *c*. *n* is 0–7 (default is 0); *c* is l (low), h (high), or m (medium, the default). Used to modify *arch*. (These are highly system-specific and nonportable: it is much better to always just specify the *arch* explicitly.)

Examples

Create an archive of /bin and /usr/bin (c), show the command working (v), and write on the tape in /dev/rmt/0:

```
tar cvf /dev/rmt/0 /bin /usr/bin
```

List the archive's contents in a format like ls -l:

```
tar tvf /dev/rmt/0
```

Extract the /bin directory:

```
tar xvf /dev/rmt/0 /bin
```

Create an archive of the current directory, and store it in a file /tmp/backup.tar on the system. (Backing up a directory into a file in that directory almost never works.)

```
tar cvf /tmp/backup.tar .
```

Similar, but compress the archive file:

```
tar cvf - . | compress > /tmp/backup.tar.Z
```

(The - tells tar to store the directory on standard output, which is then redirected through the pipe.)

Copy a directory tree from one location to another:

```
# cd olddir; tar cf - . | (cd newdir; tar xvpf -)
```

---

tbl [options] [files]

Preprocessor for nroff/troff tables. See Chapter 17.

---

tee [options] [files]

Duplicate the standard input; send one copy to standard output and another copy to *files*.

Options

-a   Append output to *files*.

-i   Ignore all interrupts.

Examples

Display a who listing on the screen and store it in two files:

```
who | tee userlist ttylist
```

$\rightarrow$

tee ←	Display misspelled words and add them to existing typos:
	``spell ch02	tee -a typos```

---

telnet

```
telnet [options] [host [port]]
```

Communicate with another *host* using the Telnet protocol. *host* may be either a name or a numeric Internet address (dot format). telnet has a command mode (indicated by the telnet> prompt) and an input mode (usually a login session on the *host* system). If no *host* is given, telnet defaults to command mode. You can also enter command mode from input mode by typing the escape character ^]. In command mode, type ? or help to list the available commands.

Solaris Options

Solaris telnet provides these options:

-8   Use an 8-bit data path. This negotiates the BINARY option for input and output.

-c   Don't read $HOME/.telnetrc at startup.

-d   Set the debug option to true.

-e *c*
   Use *c* as the escape character. The default is ^]. A null value disables the escape character mechanism.

-E   Don't have an escape character.

-l *user*
   Use the ENVIRON option to pass the value of the USER environment variable.

-L   Use an 8-bit data path on output. This negotiates the BINARY option only for output.

-n *file*
   Record trace information in *file*.

-r   Provide an rlogin-style interface, in which the escape character is ~ and is only recognized after a carriage return. The regular telnet escape character must still be used before a telnet command. "~. Return" and "~ ^z" terminates or stops a session, respectively. This feature may change in future versions of Solaris.

test *expression*
or
[*expression*]

Evaluate an *expression* and, if its value is true, return a zero exit status; otherwise, return a nonzero exit status. In shell scripts, you can use the alternate form [*expression*]. The brackets are typed literally and must be separated from *expression*. Generally, this command is used with conditional constructs in shell programs. See Chapter 4 for more information on test.

time [*option*] *command* [*arguments*]

Execute a *command* with optional *arguments* and print the total elapsed time, execution time, process execution time, and system time of the process (all in seconds). Times are printed on standard error.

Option

This option is available only on Solaris:

-p   Print the real, user, and system times with a single space separating the title and the value, instead of a tab.

timex [*options*] *command* [*arguments*]

Execute a *command* with optional *arguments* and print information specified by the time command. Report process data with various options.

Options

-o   Show total number of blocks and characters used.

-p *suboptions*
     Show process accounting data with possible *suboptions*.

-s   Show total system activity.

Suboptions for -p

-f   Include fork/exec flag and system exit status.

-h   Show "hog" factor (fraction of CPU time used) instead of mean memory size.

-k   Show total kcore-minutes instead of memory size.

$\rightarrow$

timex ←	-m Show mean core size (this is the default behavior). -r Show CPU use percentage (user time / (system time + user time)). -t Show user and system CPU times.

touch	touch [*options*] [*date*] *files*
	
	For one or more *files*, update the access time and modification timestamp to the current time and date, or update to the optional *date*. *date* is a date and time in the format *mmddhhmm*[*yy*]. touch is useful in forcing other commands to handle files a certain way; e.g., the operation of make, and sometimes find, relies on a file's access and modification times.
	
	Options
	
	-a Update only the access time.
	
	-c Do not create nonexistent files.
	
	-m Update only the modification time.
	
	-r *file*
	    Use the access and/or modification times of *file* instead of the current time. Solaris only.
	
	-t *time*
	    Use the time as provided by *time*, which has the form [[*cc*]*yy*]*mmddhhmm*[.*ss*]. Solaris only.

tput	tput [*options*] *capname* [*arguments*] Print the value of the terminal capability *capname* (and its associated numeric or string *arguments*) from the terminfo database. *capname* is a terminfo capability such as clear or col. (See *termcap & terminfo*, which is listed in the Bibliography.) The last five options are mutually exclusive and are not used when specifying a *capname*. Exit statuses are: 0 When a Boolean *capname* is set to true or when a string *capname* is defined 1 When a Boolean is false or when a string is undefined

2   For usage errors

3   For unknown terminal *type*

4   For unknown *capname*

Options

-T*type*
  Print the capabilities of terminal *type* (default is the terminal in use).

-s   Read *capname* from standard input (this allows tput to evaluate more than one *capname*).

clear
  Print the clear-screen sequence. Solaris only.

init
  Print initialization strings and expand tabs.

reset
  Print reset strings if present; act like init if not.

longname
  Print the terminal's long name.

Examples

Show the number of columns for the xterm terminal type:

```
tput -Txterm cols
```

Define shell variable restart to reset terminal characteristics:

```
restart='tput reset'
```

---

tr [*options*] [*string1* [*string2*]]

Copy standard input to standard output, performing substitution of characters from *string1* to *string2* or deletion of characters in *string1*. System V requires that *string1* and *string2* be enclosed in square brackets. BSD versions do not have this requirement.

Options

-c   Complement characters in *string1* with characters in the current character set. The complement is the set of all characters not in *string1*.

-d   Delete characters in *string1* from output.

$\rightarrow$

tr
←
	-s Squeeze out repeated output characters in *string2*.
	
	Examples
	
	Change uppercase to lowercase in a file:
	
	    `tr '[A-Z]' '[a-z]' < file`
	
	Solaris allows the use of character classes:
	
	    `tr '[:upper:]' '[:lower:]' < file`
	
	Turn spaces into newlines (ASCII code 012):
	
	    `tr ' ' '\012' < file`
	
	Strip blank lines from `file` and save in `new.file` (or use `\011` to change successive tabs into one tab):
	
	    `tr -s "" "\012" < file > new.file`
	
	Delete colons from `file`; save result in `new.file`:
	
	    `tr -d : < file > new.file`
	
	Make long search path more readable:
	
	    `echo $PATH
		tr ':' '\n'`

troff	`troff [options] [files]` Document formatter for laser printer or typesetter. See Chapter 12.
true	`true` A do-nothing command that returns a successful (zero) exit status. Normally used in Bourne shell scripts. See also **false**.
truss	`truss [options] arguments` Trace system calls, signals, and machine faults while executing *arguments*. *arguments* is either a Unix command to run or, if -p is specified, a list of process IDs representing the already running processes to trace. The options -m, -r, -s, -t, -v, -w, and -x accept a comma-separated list of arguments. A ! reverses the sense of the list, telling `truss` to ignore those elements of the list during the trace. (In the C shell, use a backslash before !.) The keyword `all` can include/exclude all possible elements for the list. The optional ! and corresponding description are shown in brackets.

The Solaris truss also provides tracing of user-level function calls in dynamically loaded shared libraries.

This command is particularly useful for finding missing files when a third-party application fails. By watching the access and open system calls, you can find where, and which, files the application program expected to find, but did not.

Many systems have similar programs named trace or strace. These programs are worth learning how to use.

Options

-a Display parameters passed by each *exec*(2) call.

-c Count the traced items and print a summary rather than listing them as they happen.

-d Print a timestamp in the output, of the form *seconds.fraction*, indicating the time relative to the start of the trace. Times are when the system call completes, not starts. Solaris only.

-D Print a delta timestamp in the output, of the form *seconds.fraction*, indicating the time between events (i.e., the time *not* inside system calls). Solaris only.

-e Display values of environment variables passed by each *exec*(2) call.

-f Follow child processes. Useful for tracing shell scripts.

-i List sleeping system calls only once, upon completion.

-m[!]*faults*
    Trace [exclude from trace] the list of machine *faults. faults* are names or numbers, as listed in <sys/fault.h> (default is -mall -m!fltpage).

-M[!]*faults*
    When the traced process receives one of the named faults, truss leaves the process in a stopped state and detaches from it (default is -M!all). The process can subsequently be attached to with a debugger, or with another invocation of truss using different options. Solaris only.

-l Show the lightweight process ID for a multithreaded process. Solaris only.

-o *outfile*
    Send trace output to *outfile*, not standard error.

→

-p   Trace one or more running processes instead of a command.

-r[!]*file_descriptors*

Display [don't display] the full I/O buffer of read system calls for *file_descriptors* (default is -r!all).

-s[!]*signals*

Trace [exclude from trace] the list of *signals*. *signals* are names or numbers, as listed in <sys/signal.h> (default is -sall).

-S[!]*signals*

When the traced process receives one of the named signals, truss leaves the process in a stopped state and detaches from it (see -M) (default is -S!all). Solaris only.

-t[!]*system_calls*

Trace [exclude from trace] the list of *system_calls*. *system_calls* are names or numbers, as listed in Section 2, "System Calls," of the *UNIX Programmer's Reference Manual* (see Bibliography); default is -tall.

-T[!]*system_calls*

When the traced process executes one of the named system calls, truss leaves the process in a stopped state and detaches from it (see -M) (default is -T!all). Solaris only.

-u[!]*lib*,...:[:][!]*func*,...

Trace user-level function calls, not just system calls. *lib* is a comma-separated list of dynamic library names, without the .so.*n* suffix. *func* is a comma-separated list of names. Shell wildcard syntax may be used to specify many names. (Such use should be quoted to protect it from expansion by the shell.) The leading ! indicates libraries and/or functions to exclude. With :, only calls into the library from outside it are traced; with ::, all calls are traced. Solaris only.

-U[!]*lib*,...:[:][!]*func*,...

When the traced process executes one of the named user-level functions, truss leaves the process in a stopped state and detaches from it (see -M). Solaris only.

-v[!]*system_calls*

Verbose mode. Same as -t, but also list the contents of any structures passed to *system_calls* (default is -v!all).

-w[!]*file_descriptors*

Display [don't display] the full I/O buffer of write system calls for *file_descriptors* (default is -w!all).

-x[!]*system_calls*
　　Same as -t, but display the system call arguments as raw
　　code (hexadecimal) (default is -x!all).

Examples

Trace system calls access, open, and close for the lp command:

```
truss -t access,open,close lp files > truss.out
```

Trace the make command, including its child processes, and store
the output in make.trace:

```
truss -f -o make.trace make target
```

/usr/ucb/tset [*options*] [*type*]

Set terminal modes. Without arguments, the terminal is reinitial-
ized according to the TERM environment variable. tset is typically used in startup scripts (.profile or .login). *type* is the
terminal type; if preceded by a ?, tset prompts the user to enter
a different type, if needed. Press the Return key to use the default
value, *type*. See also **reset**.

Options

-　　Print terminal name on standard output; useful for passing
　　this value to TERM.

-e*c*　Set erase character to *c*; default is ^H (backspace).

-i*c*　Set interrupt character to *c* (default is ^C).

-I　　Do not output terminal initialization setting.

-k *c*
　　Set line-kill character to *c* (default is ^U).

-m[*port*[*baudrate*]:*type*]
　　Declare terminal specifications. *port* is the port type (usually
　　dialup or plugboard). *tty* is the terminal type; it can be pre-
　　ceded by ? as above. *baudrate* checks the port speed and
　　can be preceded by any of these characters:

　　>　Port must be greater than *baudrate*.
　　<　Port must be less than *baudrate*.
　　@　Port must transmit at *baudrate*.
　　!　Negate a subsequent >, <, or @ character.
　　?　Prompt for the terminal type. With no response, use
　　　the given *type*.

$\rightarrow$

tset ←	-n Initialize "new" tty driver modes. Useless because of redundancy with the default stty settings in SVR4 that incorporate the functionality of the BSD "new" tty driver.
	-Q Do not print "Erase set to" and "Kill set to" messages.
	-r Report the terminal type.
	-s Return the values of TERM assignments to shell environment. This is a commonly done via eval \`tset -s\` (in the C shell, you would surround this with the commands set noglob and unset noglob).

tset (continued)

Examples

Set TERM to wy50:

```
eval `tset -s wy50`
```

Prompt user for terminal type (default is vt100):

```
eval `tset -Qs -m '?vt100'`
```

Similar to above, but the baudrate must exceed 1200:

```
eval `tset -Qs -m '>1200:?xterm'`
```

Set terminal via modem. If not on a dial-in line, the ?$TERM causes tset to prompt with the value of $TERM as the default terminal type:

```
eval `tset -s -m dialup:'?vt100' "?$TERM"`
```

---

tty

tty [*options*]

Print the device name of your terminal. This is useful for shell scripts and often for commands that need device information.

Options

-l   Print the synchronous line number, if on an active synchronous line.

-s   Return only the codes: 0 (a terminal), 1 (not a terminal), 2 (invalid options used).

---

type

type *program* ...

Print a description of *program*, i.e., whether it is a shell built in, a function, or an external command. type is built-in to the Bourne and Korn shells. See Chapter 4 and also see **which**.

Example

Describe cd and ls:

```
$ type cd ls
cd is a shell builtin
ls is /usr/bin/ls
```

umask [*value*]

Print the current value of the file creation mode mask, or set it to *value*, a three-digit octal code specifying the read-write-execute permissions to be turned off. This is the opposite of chmod. Normally used in .login or .profile. umask is a built-in command in the Bourne, Korn, and C shells (see Chapter 4 and Chapter 5).

umask Number	File Permission	Directory Permission
0	rw-	rwx
1	rw-	rw-
2	r--	r-x
3	r--	r--
4	-w-	-wx
5	-w-	-w-
6	---	--x
7	---	---

Examples

Turn off write permission for others:

    umask 002   *Produces file permission* -rw-rw-r--

Turn off all permissions for group and others:

    umask 077   *Produces file permission* -rw-------

Note that you can omit leading zeroes.

uname [*options*]

Print the current Unix system name.

Options

-a   Report the information supplied by all the other options.

-i   The hardware platform name. (For example, i86pc; compare to i386 from -p.) Solaris only.

$\rightarrow$

uname ←	-m The hardware name.
	-n The node name.
	-p The host's processor type.
	-r The operating system release.
	-s The system name. This is the default action when no options are provided.
	-v The operating system version.
	-S *name*
	Change the nodename to *name*. Privileged users only. Solaris only.
	-X Print expanded information as expected by SCO Unix systems. Solaris only.

uncompress	uncompress [*option*] [*files*]
	Restore the original file compressed by compress. The .z extension is implied, so it can be omitted when specifying *files*.
	The -f and -v options from compress are also allowed. See **compress** for more information.
	Option
	-c Same as zcat (write to standard output without changing *files*).

unexpand	unexpand [*options*] [*files*]
	Convert spaces back into an appropriate number of tab characters. unexpand reads the named *files*, or standard input if no *files* are provided. See also **expand**.
	Options
	-a Replace spaces with tabs everywhere possible, not just leading spaces and tabs.
	-t *tablist*
	Interpret tabs according to *tablist*, a space- or comma-separated list of numbers in ascending order that describe the "tabstops" for the input data.

/usr/ccs/bin/unget [*options*] *files*	**unget**

An SCCS command. See Chapter 18.

uniq [*options*] [*file1* [*file2*]]	**uniq**

Remove duplicate adjacent lines from sorted *file1*, sending one copy of each line to *file2* (or to standard output). Often used as a filter. Specify only one of –c, –d, or –u. See also **comm** and **sort**.

Options

–c Print each line once, counting instances of each.

–d Print duplicate lines once, but no unique lines.

–f *n*
    Ignore first *n* fields of a line. Fields are separated by spaces or by tabs. Solaris only.

–s *n*
    Ignore first *n* characters of a field. Solaris only.

–u Print only unique lines (no copy of duplicate entries is kept).

–*n* Ignore first *n* fields of a line. Fields are separated by spaces or by tabs.

+*n* Ignore first *n* characters of a field.

Examples

Send one copy of each line from list to output file list.new (list must be sorted):

    uniq list list.new

Show which names appear more than once:

    sort names | uniq -d

Show which lines appear exactly three times:

    sort names | uniq -c | awk '$1 == 3'

units	**units**

Interactively supply a formula to convert a number from one unit to another. /usr/lib/units (Solaris: /usr/share/lib/unittab) gives a complete list of the units. Use *EOF* to exit.

unix2dos	`unix2dos [options] unixfile dosfile`
	Solaris only. Convert files using the ISO standard characters to their DOS counterparts. If *unixfile* and *dosfile* are the same, the file is overwritten after the conversion is done. See also **dos2unix**.
	Options
	`-ascii`
	Add extra carriage returns for use under DOS.
	`-iso`
	Same as the default action.
	`-7` Convert 8-bit Solaris characters to 7-bit DOS characters.
unzip	`unzip [options[modifiers]] zipfile ... [extraction options]`
	`unzip -Z [zipinfo options] zipfile...`
	Solaris only. (Many other modern Unix systems also have it.) unzip prints information about or extracts files from ZIP format archives. The *zipfile* is a ZIP archive whose filename ends in `.zip`. The `.zip` can be omitted from the command line; unzip supplies it. *zipfile* may also be a shell-style wildcard pattern (which should be quoted); all matching files in the ZIP archive will be acted upon. The behavior of *options* is affected by the various *modifiers*.
	In the second form, the *options* are taken to be zipinfo options, and unzip performs like that command. See **zipinfo** for more information.
	Options may also be included in the UNZIP environment variable, to set a default behavior. Options on the command line can override settings in $UNZIP by preceding them with an extra minus. See the Examples.
	When extracting files, if a file exists already, unzip prompts for an action. You may to choose to overwrite or skip the existing file, overwrite or skip all files, or rename the current file.
	Notes
	• unzip and its companion program zip (which is not included with Solaris) are part of the InfoZIP project. InfoZIP is an open collaborative compressed archive format, and implementations exist for Unix, Amiga, Atari, DEC VAX and Alpha VMS and OpenVMS, MS-DOS, Macintosh, Minix, OS/2, Windows NT, and many others. It is the *only* similar format one can expect to port to all of these systems without difficulty.

The web home page is *http://www.cdrom.com/pub/infozip.*

- Unlike most Unix tar implementations, zip removes leading slashes when it creates a ZIP archive, so there is never any problem unbundling it at another site.

- The Java Archive format (.jar) is based on ZIP; zip and unzip can process .jar files with no trouble.

Extraction Options

-d *dir*
   Extract files in *dir* instead of in the current directory. This option need not appear at the end of the command line.

-x *files*
   Exclude. Do not extract archive members that match *files.*

Options

-A   Print help for the shared library programming interface (API).

-c   Print files to standard output (the CRT). Similar to -p, but a header line is printed for each file, it allows -a, and automatically does ASCII to EBCDIC conversion. Not in the unzip usage message.

-f   Freshen existing files. Only files in the archive that are newer than existing disk files are extracted. unzip queries before overwriting, unless -o is used.

-l   List archived files, in short format (name, full size, modification time, and totals).

-p   Extract files to standard output (for piping). Only the file data is printed. No conversions are done.

-t   Test the archived files. Each file is extracted in memory, and the extracted file's CRC is compared to the stored CRC.

-T   Set the timestamp on the archive itself to be that of the newest file in the archive.

-u   Same as -f, but also extract any files that don't exist on disk yet.

-v   Be verbose or print diagnostic information. -v is both an option and a modifier, depending upon the other options. By itself, it prints the unzip ftp site information, information about how it was compiled, and what environment variable settings are in effect. With a *zipfile*, it adds compression information to that provided by -l.

→

-z   Only print the archive comment.

-Z   Run as zipinfo. Remaining options are zipinfo options. See **zipinfo** for more information.

Modifiers

-a[a]
Convert text files. Normally, files are extracted as binary files. This option causes text files to be converted to the native format (e.g., adding or removing CR characters in front of LF characters). EBCDIC-to-ASCII conversion is also done as needed. Use -aa to force all files to be extracted as text.

-b   Treat all files as binary.

-B   Save a backup copy of each overwritten file in *file~*. Only available if compiled with UNIXBACKUP defined.

-C   Ignore case when matching filenames. Useful on non-Unix systems where filesystems are not case-sensitive.

-j   "Junk" paths. Extract all files in the current extraction directory, instead of reproducing the directory tree structure stored in the archive.

-L   Convert filenames to lowercase from archives created on uppercase-only systems. By default, filenames are extracted exactly as stored in the archive.

-M   Pipe output through the internal pager, which is similar to more. Press the Return key or spacebar at the --More-- prompt to see the next screenful.

-n   Never overwrite existing files. If a file already exists, don't extract it, just continue on without prompting. Normally, unzip prompts for an action.

-o   Overwrite existing files without prompting. Often used together with -f. Use with care.

Examples

List the contents of a ZIP archive:

```
unzip -lv whizprog.zip
```

Extract C source files in the main directory, but not in subdirectories:

```
unzip whizprog.zip '*.[ch]' -x '*/*'
```

uptime | **uptime**

Print the current time, amount of time the system has been up, number of users logged in, and the system-load averages. This output is also produced by the first line of the w command.

/usr/ucb/users [*file*] | **users**

Display the currently logged-in users as a space-separated list. Same as who -q. Information is read from a system *file* (default is /var/adm/utmp).

---

uudecode [-p] [*file*] | **uudecode**

Read a uuencoded file and recreate the original file with the same mode and name (see **uuencode**).

Solaris provides the -p option, which decodes the file to standard output. This allows you to use uudecode in a pipeline.

---

uuencode [*file*] *name* | mail *remoteuser* | **uuencode**

Convert a binary *file* to a form which can be sent to *remoteuser* via mail. The encoding uses only printing ASCII characters and includes the mode and *name* of the file. When *file* is reconverted via uudecode on the remote system, output is sent to *name*. (Therefore, when saving the encoded mail message to a file on the remote system, don't store it in a file called *name*, or you'll overwrite it!) Note that uuencode can take standard input, so a single argument is the name given to the file when it is decoded.

The Solaris version does local character set translation of the encoded characters.

Note: the uuencode format does not provide any kind of checksumming or other data integrity checking. It is advisable to first package files into an archive that does provide checksumming of the data (such as a .zip file), and then uuencode the archive for sending in electronic mail.

---

vacation
vacation [*options*] [*user*] | **vacation**

Automatically return a mail message to the sender announcing that you are on vacation. Solaris version, for use with sendmail. (The SVR4 version is described in Appendix B.)

→

vacation

←

Use vacation with no options to initialize the vacation mechanism. The process performs several steps.

1. Create a .forward file in your home directory. The .forward file contains:

   ```
   \user, "|/usr/bin/vacation user"
   ```

   user is your login name. The action of this file is to actually deliver the mail to *user* (i.e., you), and to run the incoming mail through vacation.

2. Create the .vacation.pag and .vacation.dir files. These files keep track of who has sent you messages, so that they only receive one "I'm on vacation" message from you per week.

3. Start an editor to edit the contents of .vacation.msg. The contents of this file are mailed back to whoever sends you mail. Within its body, $SUBJECT is replaced with the contents of the incoming message's Subject: line.

Remove or rename the .forward file to disable vacation processing.

Options

The -a, -j, and -t options are used within a .forward file; see the Example.

-a *alias*
　　Mail addressed to *alias* is actually mail for the *user* and should produce an automatic reply.

-I　Reinitialize the .vacation.pag and .vacation.dir files. Use this right before leaving for your next vacation.

-j　Do not verify that *user* appears in the To: or Cc: headers.

-t *interval*
　　By default, no more than one message per week is sent to any sender. This option changes that interval. *interval* is a number with a trailing s, m, h, d, or w indicating seconds, minutes, hours, days, or weeks, respectively.

Example

Send no more than one reply every three weeks to any given sender:

```
$ cd
$ vacation -I
$ cat .forward
\jp, "|/usr/bin/vacation -t3w jp"
$ cat .vacation.msg
From: jp@wizard-corp.com (J. Programmer, via the vacation program)
Subject: I'm out of the office ...
```

```
Hi. I'm off on a well-deserved vacation after finishing
up whizprog 1.0. I will read and reply to your mail
regarding "$SUBJECT" when I return.

Have a nice day.
```

`/usr/ccs/bin/val [options] file ...`

An SCCS command. See Chapter 18.

`vedit [options] [files]`

Same as running vi, but with the showmode and novice flags set, the report flag set to 1, and magic turned off (metacharacters have no special meaning). Intended for beginners.

`vgrind [options] files`

Solaris only (from the BSD command). Produce nicely formatted source code listings for use with troff. vgrind formats program source code so that it looks good when typeset with troff. Comments are in italic, keywords in bold, and each function's name is printed in the margin of the page where it is defined. Definitions for each language are kept in /usr/lib/vgrindefs. vgrind can format a number of languages; see -1 below.

vgrind has two modes of operation:

Filter mode
> Similar to eqn, pic, and tbl. Lines are passed through unchanged, except for those bracketed by .vS and .vE. In this mode, vgrind can be used in a pipeline with other preprocessors.

Regular mode
> vgrind processes all files named on the command line and then invokes troff to print them. Use - as a filename to mean the standard input. Otherwise, vgrind will not read standard input.

Options

Spacing between option characters and option arguments is specific. Use the options exactly as shown here:

-2   Produce two-column output. Implies -s8 and the -L (landscape) option for $TROFF. (This option was specific to troff at UCB.)

$\rightarrow$

-d *definitions*
> Use *definitions* as the file with language definitions, instead of the default file.

-f Run in filter mode.

-h *header*
> Place *header* in the top center of every output page.

-l*lang*
> Supported languages are:

> | | |
> |---|---|
> | Bourne shell | -lsh |
> | C | -lc |
> | C++ | -lc++ |
> | C shell | -lcsh |
> | emacs MLisp | -lml |
> | FORTRAN | -lf |
> | Icon | -lI |
> | ISP | -li |
> | LDL | -lLDL |
> | Model | -lm |
> | Modula-2 | -lm2 |
> | Pascal | -lp |
> | RATFOR | -lr |
> | Russel | -lrussell |
> | YACC | -lyacc |

> The default is -lc (for C).

-n Do not use bold for keywords.

-s*size*
> Use point size *size* (same as troff's .ps request).

-w Use a tab stop of four columns, instead of the default eight.

-x Print the index. If a file named index exists in the current directory, vgrind writes the index into it. This file can then be formatted and printed separately using vgrind -x index.

Typesetter Options

The following options are passed to the program named by $TROFF, or to troff if that environment variable is not set:

-o*list*
> Output only the pages in *list*; same as -o in troff.

-P*printer*
> Send the output to *printer*.

-t   Same as -t for troff; send formatted text to standard output.

-T*device*
     Format output for *device*.

-W   Use the wide Versatec printer instead of the narrow Varian. (These refer to printers that existed at one time at the University of California at Berkeley. This option likely has no real effect under Solaris.)

---

vi [*options*] [*files*]

A screen-oriented text editor based on ex. See Chapter 8 and Chapter 9 for more information on vi and ex. Options -c, -C, -L, -r, -R, and -t are the same as in ex.

Options

-c *command*
     Enter vi and execute the given vi *command*.

-l   Run in LISP mode for editing LISP programs.

-L   List filenames that were saved due to an editor or system crash.

-r *file*
     Recover and edit *file* after an editor or system crash.

-R   Read-only mode. Files can't be changed.

-s   Use with -t to indicate that the tag file may not be sorted and to use a linear search. Solaris only.

-t *tag*
     Edit the file containing *tag*, and position the editor at its definition (see **ctags** for more information).

-w*n* Set default window size to *n*; useful when editing via a slow dial-up line.

-x   Supply a key to encrypt or decrypt *file* using crypt. (Note that the supplied key is visible to other users via the ps command.)

-C   Same as -x, but assume *file* began in encrypted form.

+   Start vi on last line of file.

+*n* Start vi on line *n* of file.

→

vi ←	`+/pat` Start vi on line containing pattern *pat*. This option fails if nowrapscan is set in your .exrc file.
view	`view [options] [files]` Same as vi -R.

volcheck	`volcheck [options] [pathnames]`
	
	Solaris only. Check one or more devices named by *pathnames* to see if removable media has been inserted. The default is to check every device being managed by volume management. Most often used with floppies; volume management usually notices when CD-ROMs have been inserted.
	
	Note: use of the −i and −t options, particularly with short intervals, is not recommended for floppy-disk drives.
	
	Options
	
	−i *nsec*
	    Check the device(s) every *nsec* seconds. The default is every two seconds.
	
	−t *nsecs*
	    Keep checking over the next *nsecs* seconds. Maximum *nsecs* is 28,800 (eight hours).
	
	−v Be verbose.

w	`w [options] [user]` Print summaries of system usage, currently logged-in users, and what they are doing. w is essentially a combination of uptime, who, and ps −a. Display output for one user by specifying *user*. *Options* −h Suppress headings and uptime information. −l Display in long format (the default). −s Display in short format.

-u   Print just the heading line. Equivalent to uptime. Solaris only.

-w   Same as -1. Solaris only.

wait [n]

Wait for all background processes to complete and report their termination status. Used in shell scripts. If *n* is specified, wait only for the process with process ID *n*. wait is a built-in command in the Bourne, Korn, and C shells. See Chapter 4 and Chapter 5 for more information.

wc [options] [files]

Word count. Print a character, word, and line count for *files*. If multiple files, print totals as well. If no *files* are given, read standard input. See other examples under **ls** and **sort**.

Options

-c   Print byte count only.

-C   Print character count only. This will be different than -c in a multibyte character environment. Solaris only.

-l   Print line count only.

-m   Same as -C. Solaris only.

-w   Print word count only.

Examples

Count the number of users logged in:

```
who | wc -l
```

Count the words in three essay files:

```
wc -w essay.[123]
```

Count lines in file named by $file (don't display filename):

```
wc -l < $file
```

what	/usr/ccs/bin/what [*option*] *files*
	An SCCS command. See Chapter 18.
whatis	whatis *commands*
	Look up one or more *commands* in the online manpages, and display a brief description. Same as man -f. The MANPATH environment variable can affect the results obtained with this command. See also **apropos**.
which	which [*commands*]
	List which files are executed if the named *commands* are run as a command. which reads the user's .cshrc file (using the source built-in command), checking aliases and searching the path variable. Users of the Bourne or Korn shells can use the built-in type command as an alternative. (See **type**, Chapter 4 and Chapter 5.)
	Example

```
$ which file ls
/usr/bin/file
ls:      aliased to ls -sFC
```

who	who [*options*] [*file*]
	Display information about the current status of the system. With no options, list the names of users currently logged in to the system. An optional system *file* (default is /var/adm/utmp) can be supplied to give additional information. who is usually invoked without options, but useful options include am i and -u. For more examples, see **cut**, **line**, **paste**, **tee**, and **wc**.
	Options
	-a Use the -b, -d, -l, -p, -r, -t, -T, and -u options.
	-b Report information about the last reboot.
	-d Report expired processes.
	-H Print headings.
	-l Report inactive terminal lines.
	-m Report only about the current terminal. Solaris only.

-n *x*
> Display *x* users per line (works only with -q).

-p   Report previously spawned processes.

-q   "Quick." Display only the usernames.

-r   Report the run level.

-s   List the name, line, and time fields (the default behavior).

-t   Report the last change of the system clock (via date).

-T   Report whether terminals are writable (+), not writable (-), or unknown (?).

-u   Report terminal usage (idle time). A dot (.) means less than one minute idle; old means more than 24 hours idle.

am i
> Print the username of the invoking user. (Similar to results from id.)

Example

This sample output was produced at 8 a.m. on April 17:

```
$ who -uH
NAME    LINE   TIME         IDLE   PID   COMMENTS
martha  ttyp3  Apr 16 08:14 16:25  2240
george  ttyp0  Apr 17 07:33   .    15182
```

Since martha has been idle since yesterday afternoon (16 hours), it appears that Martha isn't at work yet. She simply left herself logged in. George's terminal is currently in use. (He likes to beat the traffic.)

/usr/ucb/whoami

Print the username based on effective user ID. This is usually the same as the standard SVR4 command logname. However, when you're running an su session as another user, whoami displays this user's name, but logname still displays your name.

---

xargs [*options*] [*command*]

Execute *command* (with any initial arguments), but read remaining arguments from standard input instead of specifying them directly. xargs passes these arguments in several bundles to *command*, allowing *command* to process more arguments than it could normally handle at once. The arguments are typically a long list of filenames (generated by ls or find, for example) that get passed to xargs via a pipe.

→

xargs
←

Without a *command*, xargs behaves similarly to echo, simply bundling the input lines into output lines and printing them to standard output.

Options

-e[*string*]
> Stop passing arguments when argument *string* is encountered (default is underscore). An omitted *string* disables the logical EOF capability.

-E *string*
> Use *string* instead of underscore as the default logical EOF string. Solaris only.

-i[*string*]
> Pass arguments to *command*, replacing instances of {} on the command line with the current line of input. With Solaris, the optional *string* can be used instead of {}.

-I *string*
> Same as -i, but *string* is used instead of {}.

-l[*n*]
> Execute *command* for *n* lines of arguments. With Solaris, default *n* is 1 when -l is supplied.

-L *n*
> Same as -l *n*. Solaris only.

-n*n* Execute *command* with up to *n* arguments.

-p Prompt for a y to confirm each execution of *command*. Implies -t.

-s*n* Each argument list can contain up to *n* characters. (Older systems limited *n* to 470. The default is system-dependent.)

-t Echo each *command* before executing.

-x Exit if argument list exceeds *n* characters (from -s); -x takes effect automatically with -i and -l.

Examples

grep for *pattern* in all files on the system:

```
find / -print | xargs grep pattern > out &
```

Run diff on file pairs (e.g., f1.a and f1.b, f2.a and f2.b ...):

```
echo $* | xargs -n2 diff
```

The previous line could be invoked as a shell script, specifying filenames as arguments.

Display *file*, one word per line (similar to deroff -w):

```
cat file | xargs -n1
```

Move files in olddir to newdir, showing each command:

```
ls olddir | xargs -i -t mv olddir/{} newdir/{}
```

```
xgettext [options] files
xgettext -h
```

Solaris only. Extract messages (specially marked strings) from C and C++ source files. Place them in a "portable object" file (*file*.po) for translation and compilation by msgfmt. By default, xgettext only extracts strings inside calls to the *gettext*(3C) and *dgettext*(3C) functions. Source files are named on the command line. A filename of - indicates the standard input.

Options

-a   Extract all strings, not just those in calls to gettext or dgettext.

-c *tag*
    Copy source file comments marked with *tag* into the .po file as #-delimited comments.

-d *domain*
    Use *domain*.po as the output file instead of messages.po.

-h   Print a help message on the standard output.

-j   Join (merge) extracted messages with those in the current .po file. Domain directives in the existing .po file are ignored.

-m *prefix*
    Fill each msgstr with *prefix*. Intended for debugging.

-M *suffix*
    Fill each msgstr with *suffix*. Intended for debugging.

-n   Add comments to the .po file indicating the source filename and line number where each string is used.

-p *path*
    Place output files in the directory *path*.

-s   Sort the output by msgid (original string), with all duplicates removed.

→

xgettext ←	-x *exfile* *exfile* is a .po file with msgids that are not to be extracted (i.e., excluded).

yacc	/usr/ccs/bin/yacc [*options*] *file*
	
	Given a *file* containing a context-free LALR(1) grammar, convert it to tables for subsequent parsing and send output to y.tab.c. This command name stands for yet another compiler-compiler. See also lex and *lex & yacc*, which is listed in the Bibliography.
	
	Options
	
	-b *prefix*
	    Use *prefix* instead of y for the generated filenames. Solaris only.
	
	-d Generate y.tab.h, producing #define statements that relate yacc's token codes to the token names declared by the user.
	
	-l Exclude #line constructs from code produced in y.tab.c. (Use after debugging is complete.)
	
	-p *prefix*
	    Use *prefix* instead of yy for all external names in the generated parser. Solaris only.
	
	-P *parser*
	    Use *parser* instead of /usr/ccs/bin/yaccpar. Solaris only.
	
	-Q*c* Place version information about yacc in y.tab.c (if *c* = y) or suppress information (if *c* = n, the default).
	
	-t Compile runtime debugging code by default.
	
	-v Generate y.output, a file containing diagnostics and notes about the parsing tables.
	
	-V Print the version of yacc on standard error.

zcat	zcat [*files*] Uncompress one or more .z *files* to the standard output, leaving *files* unchanged. See **compress**.
zip	zip [*options*] *zipfile* [*files*] Archive files in InfoZIP format. These files can be retrieved using unzip. The files are compressed as they are added to the archive. Compression ratios of 2:1 to 3:1 are common for text files. zip

may also replace files in an existing archive. With no arguments, display the help information. See also **zipinfo** and **unzip**.

Default options may be placed in the ZIPOPT environment variable, with the exceptions of -i and -x. Multiple options may be included in ZIPOPT.

While zip is not distributed with SVR4 or Solaris, source code is readily available from *http://www.cdrom.com/pub/infozip*.

There are a number of important notes in the **unzip** entry. Go there for more information.

Options

-b *path*
> Use *path* as the location to store the temporary ZIP archive while updating an existing one. When done, copy the temporary archive over the new one. Useful primarily when there is not enough disk space on the filesystem containing the original archive.

-c
> Add one-line comments for each file. zip first performs any file operations and then prompts you for a comment describing each file.

-d
> Delete entries from a ZIP archive. Filenames to be deleted must be entered in uppercase if the archive was created by PKZIP on an MS-DOS system.

-D
> Don't create entries in the archive for directories. Usually entries are created, so that attributes for directories may be restored upon extraction.

-e
> Encrypt the archive. zip prompts on the terminal for a password and prompts twice, to avoid typing errors. If standard error is not a terminal, zip exits with an error.

-f
> Freshen (replace) an existing entry in the ZIP archive if the file has a more recent modification time than the one in the archive. This doesn't add files that are not already in the archive: use -u for that. Run this command from the same directory where the ZIP archive was created, since the archive stores relative path names.

-F, -FF
> Fix the ZIP archive. This option should be used with care; make a backup copy of the archive first. The -FF version does not trust the compressed sizes in the archive, and instead scans it for special "signatures" that identify the boundaries of different archive members. See the manpage for more information.

$\rightarrow$

zip
←

-g   Grow the archive (append files to it).

-h   Display the zip help information.

-i *files*
> Include only the specified *files*, typically specified as a quoted shell wildcard-style pattern.

-j   "Junk" the path; i.e., store just the name of the saved file, not any directory names. The default is to store complete paths, although paths are always relative.

-J   Strip any prepended data (e.g., an SFX stub, for self-extracting executables) from the archive.

-k   Create an archive that (attempts to) conform to the conventions used under MS-DOS. This makes it easier for PKUNZIP to extract the archive.

-l   For text files only, translate the Unix newline into a CR-LF pair. Primarily for archives extracted under MS-DOS.

-ll   For text files only, translate the MS-DOS CR-LF into a Unix newline.

-L   Display the zip license.

-m   "Move" the files into the ZIP archive. This actually deletes the original files and/or directories after the archive has been created successfully. This is somewhat dangerous; use -T in conjunction with this option.

-n *suffixlist*
> Do not compress files with suffixes in *suffixlist*. Useful for sound or image files that often have their own, specialized compression method.

-o   Set the modified time of the ZIP archive to be that of the youngest file (most recently modified) in the archive.

-q   Quiet mode. Don't print informational messages and comment prompts. Most useful in shell scripts.

-r   Recursively archive all files and subdirectories of the named *files*. The -i option is also useful in combination with this one.

-t *mmddyy*
> Ignore files modified prior to the date given by *mmddyy*.

-T   Test the new ZIP archive's integrity. If the test fails, an existing ZIP archive is not changed, and with -m, no files are removed.

-u   Update existing entries in the ZIP archive if the named *files*
      have modification dates that are newer than those in the
      archive. Similar to -f, except that this option adds files to
      the archive if they aren't already there.

-v   As the only argument, print help and version information, a
      pointer to the home and distribution Internet sites, and infor-
      mation about how zip was compiled. When used with other
      options, cause those options to print progress information
      and provide other diagnostic information.

-x *files*
      Exclude the specified *files*, typically specified as a quoted
      shell wildcard-style pattern.

-X   Do not save extra file attributes (extended attributes on OS/2,
      user ID/group ID, and file times on Unix).

-y   Preserve symbolic links in the ZIP archive, instead of archiv-
      ing the file the link points to.

-z   Prompt for a (possibly multiline) comment describing the
      entire ZIP archive. End the comment with line containing
      just a period, or *EOF*.

-n   Specify compression speed: *n* is a digit between 0 and 9. 0
      indicates no compression, 1 indicates fast but minimal com-
      pression, 9 indicates slowest but maximal compression.
      Default is -6.

-@   Read standard input for names of files to be archived. File-
      names containing spaces must be quoted using single
      quotes.

Examples

Archive the current directory into source.zip, including only C
source files:

    zip source -i '*.[ch]'

Archive the current directory into source.zip, excluding the
object files:

    zip source -x '*.o'

Archive files in the current directory into source.zip, but don't
compress .tiff and .snd files:

    zip source -z '.tiff:.snd' *

Recursively archive the entire directory tree into one archive:

    zip -r /tmp/dist.zip .

zipinfo

`zipinfo [options] zipfile ... [exclusion option]`

Solaris only. `zipinfo` prints information about ZIP format archives. The *zipfile* is a ZIP archive whose filename ends in `.zip`. The `.zip` can be omitted from the command line; `zipinfo` supplies it. *zipfile* may also be a shell-style wildcard pattern (which should be quoted to protect it from the shell); all matching files in the ZIP archive will be acted upon. See also **zip** and **unzip**.

Exclusion Option

`-x files`
  Exclude. Do not extract archive members that match *files*.

Options

`-1` Only list filenames, one per line. Nothing else is printed. For use in shell scripts.

`-2` Like `-1`, but also permit headers, trailers, and ZIP archive comments (`-h`, `-t`, `-z`).

`-h` Print a header line with the archive name, size in bytes, and total number of files.

`-l` Use "long" format. Like `-m`, but also print the compressed size in bytes, instead of the compression ratio.

`-m` Use "Medium" format. Like `-s`, but also include the compression factor (as a percentage).

`-M` Pipe output through the internal pager, which is similar to more. Press the Return key or spacebar at the `--More--` prompt to see the next screenful.

`-s` Use "short" format, similar to `ls -l`. This is the default.

`-t` Print totals for all files (number of files, compressed and uncompressed sizes, overall compression factor).

`-T` Print times and dates in a decimal format (*yymmdd.hhmmss*) that can be sorted.

`-v` Use verbose, multipage format.

`-z` Print the archive comment.

CHAPTER 3

The Unix Shell: An Overview

For novice users, this chapter presents basic concepts about the Unix shell. For advanced users, this chapter also summarizes the major similarities and differences between the Bourne, Korn, and C shells. Details on the three shells are provided in Chapter 4, *The Bourne Shell and Korn Shell*, and Chapter 5, *The C Shell*.

The following topics are presented:

- Introduction to the shell

- Purpose of the shell

- Shell flavors

- Common features

- Differing features

Introduction to the Shell

Let's suppose that the Unix operating system is a car. When you drive, you issue a variety of "commands": you turn the steering wheel, press the accelerator, or press the brake. But how does the car translate your commands into the action you want? The car's drive mechanism, which can be thought of as the car's user interface, is responsible. Cars can be equipped with front-wheel drive, rear-wheel drive, four-wheel drive, and sometimes combinations of these.

The shell is the user interface to Unix, and by the same token, several shells are available in Unix. Most systems provide more than one for you to choose from. Each shell has different features, but all of them affect how commands will be interpreted and provide tools to create your Unix environment.

The shell is simply a program that allows the system to understand your commands. (That's why the shell is often called a *command interpreter*.) For many users, the shell works invisibly—"behind the scenes." Your only concern is that the system does what you tell it to do; you don't care about the inner workings. In our car analogy, this is comparable to pressing the brake. Most of us don't care whether the user interface involves disk brakes or drum brakes, as long as the car stops.

Purpose of the Shell

There are three uses for the shell:

- Interactive use
- Customization of your Unix session
- Programming

Interactive Use

When the shell is used interactively, the system waits for you to type a command at the Unix prompt. Your commands can include special symbols that let you abbreviate filenames or redirect input and output.

Customization of Your Unix Session

A Unix shell defines variables to control the behavior of your Unix session. Setting these variables will tell the system, for example, which directory to use as your home directory, or the file in which to store your mail. Some variables are preset by the system; you can define others in startup files that are read when you log in. Startup files can also contain Unix commands or special shell commands. These are executed every time you log in.

Programming

Unix shells provide a set of special (or built-in) commands that let you create programs called *shell scripts*. In fact, many built-in commands can be used interactively like Unix commands, and Unix commands are frequently used in shell scripts. Scripts are useful for executing a series of individual commands. This is similar to BATCH files in MS-DOS. Scripts can also execute commands repeatedly (in a loop) or conditionally (if-else), as in many high-level programming languages.

Shell Flavors

Many different Unix shells are available. This quick reference describes the three most popular shells:

- The Bourne (or standard) shell, the most compact shell and also the simplest.

- The Korn shell, a superset of the Bourne shell that lets you edit the command line. There are in fact two commonly available versions of the Korn shell, distinguished by the year they were released, and referred to in this book as ksh88 and ksh93 respectively.

- The C shell, which uses C-like syntax and is more convenient for the interactive user than the Bourne shell.

Most systems have more than one shell, and people will often use the Bourne shell for writing shell scripts and another shell for interactive use.

The /etc/passwd file determines which shell takes effect during your interactive Unix session. When you log in, the system checks your entry in /etc/passwd. The last field of each entry names a program to run as the default shell.* For example:

If the program name is:	Your shell is the:
/bin/sh	Bourne shell
/bin/rsh	Restricted Bourne shell
/bin/jsh	Bourne shell, including job control
/bin/ksh	Korn shell
/usr/dt/bin/dtksh	The Desktop Korn shell, a version of ksh93 (Solaris only)
/bin/rksh	Restricted Korn shell
/bin/csh	C shell

You can change to another shell by typing the program name at the command line. For example, to change from the Bourne shell to the Korn shell, type:

```
$ exec ksh
```

Note that on most systems, rsh is the "remote shell" for executing commands on a remote system across a network. On some systems, though, rsh is indeed the restricted shell, and remsh is the remote shell. Check your local documentation.

Which Shell Do I Want?

If you are new to Unix, picking a shell may be a bewildering question. Before ksh was commonly available, the general advice was to use csh for interactive use (because it supported job control and had other features that made it a better interactive shell than the Bourne shell), but to use the Bourne shell for scripting (because it is a more powerful programming language, and more universally available).

Today, ksh is widely available; it is upwardly compatible with the Bourne shell as a programming language, and it has all the interactive capabilities of csh, and more. If it is available, it is probably your best choice.

---

* On Solaris or other networked Unix systems, this information may come from NIS or NIS+. Usually, your system administrator will handle this for you; just don't be surprised if your login name doesn't appear in /etc/passwd.

Common Features

The following table displays features that are common to the Bourne, Korn, and C shells. Note that the Korn shell is an enhanced version of the Bourne shell; therefore, the Korn shell includes all features of the Bourne shell, plus some others. The commands bg, fg, jobs, stop, and suspend are available only on systems that support job control. (Essentially all modern Unix systems do.)

Symbol/Command	Meaning/Action
>	Redirect output.
>>	Append to file.
<	Redirect input.
<<	"Here" document (redirect input).
|	Pipe output.
|&	Start a coprocess. Korn shell only.
&	Run process in background.
;	Separate commands on same line.
*	Match any character(s) in filename.
?	Match single character in filename.
[ ]	Match any characters enclosed.
( )	Execute in subshell.
` `	Substitute output of enclosed command.
" "	Partial quote (allows variable and command expansion).
' '	Full quote (no expansion).
\	Quote following character.
$var	Use value for variable.
$$	Process ID.
$0	Command name.
$n	nth argument ($0 \leq n \leq 9$).
$*	All arguments as simple words.
#	Begin comment.
bg	Background execution.
break	Break from loop statements.
cd	Change directory.
continue	Resume a program loop.
echo	Display output.
eval	Evaluate arguments.
exec	Execute a new shell.
fg	Foreground execution.
jobs	Show active jobs.
kill	Terminate running jobs.
shift	Shift positional parameters.
stop	Suspend a background job.
suspend	Suspend a foreground job (such as a shell created by su).
time	Time a command.

Symbol/Command	Meaning/Action
umask	Set default file permissions for new files.
unset	Erase variable or function definitions.
wait	Wait for a background job to finish.

Differing Features

The following table displays features that are different among the three shells.

sh	ksh	csh	Meaning/Action
$	$	%	Prompt.
	>|	>!	Force redirection.
		>>!	Force append.
> *file* 2>&1	> *file* 2>&1	>& *file*	Combine stdout and stderr.
		{ }	Expand elements in list.
` `	` `	` `	Substitute output of enclosed command.
	$( )		Substitute output of enclosed command. (Preferred form.)
$HOME	$HOME	$home	Home directory.
	~	~	Home directory symbol.
var=value	*var=value*	set *var=value*	Variable assignment.
export *var*	export *var=val*	setenv var val	Set environment variable.
	${*nn*}		More than nine args can be referenced.
"$@"	"$@"		All args as separate words.
$#	$#	$#argv	Number of arguments.
$?	$?	$status	Exit status.
$!	$!		Background exit status.
$-	$-		Current options.
. *file*	. *file*	source *file*	Read commands in *file*.
	alias *x=y*	alias *x y*	Name *x* stands for *y*.
case	case	switch/case	Choose alternatives.
	cd ~-	popd/pushd	Switch directories.
done	done	end	End a loop statement.
esac	esac	endsw	End case or switch.
exit [*n*]	exit [*n*]	exit [(*expr*)]	Exit with a status.
for / do	for / do	foreach	Loop through variables.
	print -r	glob	Ignore echo escapes.
hash	alias -t	hashstat	Display hashed commands (tracked aliases).
hash *cmds*	alias -t *cmds*	rehash	Remember command locations.
hash -r	PATH=$PATH	unhash	Forget command locations.

sh	ksh	csh	Meaning/Action
	history	history	List previous commands.
	r	!!	Redo previous command.
	r *str*	!*str*	Redo command that starts with *str*.
	r *x=cmd*	!*cmd*:s/*x*/*y*	Edit command, then execute.
if [$i -eq 5]	if ((i==5))	if ($i==5)	Sample if statement.
fi	fi	endif	End if statement.
ulimit	ulimit	limit	Set resource limits.
pwd	pwd	dirs	Print working directory.
read	read	$<	Read from standard input.
trap 2	trap 2	onintr	Ignore interrupts.
	unalias	unalias	Remove aliases.
until/do	until/do		Begin until loop.
while/do	while/do	while	Begin while loop.

The Bourne Shell and Korn Shell

This chapter presents the following topics:

- Overview of features
- Syntax
- Variables
- Arithmetic expressions (Korn shell only)
- Command history (Korn shell only)
- Job control
- Invoking the shell
- Restricted shells
- Built-in commands

http://www.kornshell.com provides considerable information about the Korn shell. Follow the links there for binaries of ksh93 that can be downloaded for noncommercial and educational use. See also *Learning the Korn Shell*, which is listed in the Bibliography.

Overview of Features

The Bourne shell is the standard shell and provides the following features:

- Input/output redirection
- Wildcard characters (metacharacters) for filename abbreviation

- Shell variables for customizing your environment

- A built-in command set for writing shell programs

- Job control (beginning in SVR4)

The Korn shell is a backward-compatible extension of the Bourne shell. Features that are valid only in the Korn shell are so indicated:

- Command-line editing (using the command syntax of either vi or emacs)

- Access to previous commands (command history)

- Integer arithmetic

- More ways to match patterns and substitute variables

- Arrays and arithmetic expressions

- Command-name abbreviation (aliasing)

- More built-in commands

ksh93 adds the following capabilities:

- Upwards compliance with POSIX

- Internationalization facilities

- An arithmetic for loop

- Floating-point arithmetic and built-in arithmetic functions

- Structured variable names and indirect variable references

- Associative arrays

- Even more ways to match patterns and substitute variables

- Even more built-in commands

Syntax

This section describes the many symbols peculiar to the Bourne and Korn shells. The topics are arranged as follows:

- Special files

- Filename metacharacters

- Quoting

- Command forms

- Redirection forms

- Coprocesses (Korn shell only)

Special Files

`/etc/profile`
> Executed automatically at login, first.

`$HOME/.profile`
> Executed automatically at login, second.

`$ENV`
> Specifies the name of a file to read when a new Korn shell is created. (ksh88: all shells. ksh93: interactive shells only.) The value is variable (ksh93: and command and arithmetic) substituted in order to determine the actual file name. Login shells read `$ENV` after processing `/etc/profile` and `$HOME/.pro-file`.

`/etc/passwd`
> Source of home directories for *name* abbreviations. (On networked systems, this information may come from NIS or NIS+, not your workstation password file.)

Filename Metacharacters

`*`	Match any string of zero or more characters.
`?`	Match any single character.
`[abc...]`	Match any one of the enclosed characters; a hyphen can specify a range (e.g., a–z, A–Z, 0–9).
`[!abc...]`	Match any character *not* enclosed as above.

In the Korn shell:

`?(pattern)`	Match zero or one instance of *pattern*.
`*(pattern)`	Match zero or more instances of *pattern*.
`+(pattern)`	Match one or more instances of *pattern*.
`@(pattern)`	Match exactly one instance of *pattern*.
`!(pattern)`	Match any strings that don't match *pattern*.
`\n`	Match the text matched by the *n*'th subpattern in `(...)`. ksh93 only.
`~`	Home directory of the current user.
`~name`	Home directory of user *name*.
`~+`	Current working directory ($PWD).
`~-`	Previous working directory ($OLDPWD).

This *pattern* can be a sequence of patterns separated by `|`, meaning that the match applies to any of the patterns. If `&` is used instead of `|`, all the patterns must match. `&` has higher precedence than `|`. This extended syntax resembles that available in egrep and awk.

ksh93 supports the POSIX `[[=c=]]` notation for matching characters that have the same weight, and `[[.c.]]` for specifying collating sequences. In addition, character classes, of the form `[[:class:]]`, allow you to match the following classes of characters.

Class	Characters Matched
alnum	Alphanumeric characters
alpha	Alphabetic characters
blank	Space or tab
cntrl	Control characters
digit	Decimal digits
graph	Nonspace characters
lower	Lowercase characters
print	Printable characters
space	Whitespace characters
upper	Uppercase characters
xdigit	Hexadecimal digits

Examples

```
$ ls new*              List new and new.1
$ cat ch?              Match ch9 but not ch10
$ vi [D-R]*            Match files that begin with uppercase D through R
$ pr !(*.o|core) | lp  Korn shell only; print files that are not object files or core dumps
```

Quoting

Quoting disables a character's special meaning and allows it to be used literally, as itself. The following table displays characters have special meaning to the Bourne and Korn shells.

Character	Meaning
;	Command separator
&	Background execution
( )	Command grouping
		Pipe
< > &	Redirection symbols
* ? [ ] ~ + - @ !	Filename metacharacters
" ' \	Used in quoting other characters
`	Command substitution
$	Variable substitution (or command or arithmetic substitution)
space tab newline	Word separators

These characters can be used for quoting:

" " Everything between " and " is taken literally, except for the following characters that keep their special meaning:

   $ Variable (or Korn shell command and arithmetic) substitution will occur.

`   Command substitution will occur.

"   This marks the end of the double quote.

' ' Everything between ' and ' is taken literally except for another '. You cannot embed another ' within such a quoted string.

\   The character following a \ is taken literally. Use within " " to escape ", $, and `. Often used to escape itself, spaces, or newlines.

$" "

ksh93 only. Just like " ", except that locale translation is done.

$' '

ksh93 only. Similar to ' ', but the quoted text is processed for the following escape sequences:

Sequence	Value	Sequence	Value
\a	Alert	\nnn	Octal value nnn
\b	Backspace	\xnn	Hexadecimal value nn
\f	Form feed	\'	Single quote
\n	Newline	\"	Double quote
\r	Carriage return	\\	Backslash
\t	Tab	\E	Escape
\v	Vertical tab		

Examples

```
$ echo 'Single quotes "protect" double quotes'
Single quotes "protect" double quotes
$ echo "Well, isn't that \"special\"?"
Well, isn't that "special"?
$ echo "You have `ls | wc -l` files in `pwd`"
You have      43 files in /home/bob
$ echo "The value of \$x is $x"
The value of $x is 100
```

Command Forms

cmd &	Execute *cmd* in background.
cmd1 ; cmd2	Command sequence; execute multiple *cmd*s on the same line.
{ cmd1 ; cmd2 ; }	Execute commands as a group in the current shell.
(cmd1 ; cmd2)	Execute commands as a group in a subshell.
cmd1 | cmd2	Pipe; use output from *cmd1* as input to *cmd2*.
cmd1 `cmd2`	Command substitution; use *cmd2* output as arguments to *cmd1*.
cmd1 $(cmd2)	Korn shell command substitution; nesting is allowed.
cmd $((expression))	Korn shell arithmetic substitution. Use the result of *expression* as argument to *cmd*.

`cmd1 && cmd2`	AND; execute *cmd1* and then (if *cmd1* succeeds) *cmd2*. This is a "short-circuit" operation; *cmd2* is never executed if *cmd1* fails.
`cmd1 || cmd2`	OR; execute either *cmd1* or (if *cmd1* fails) *cmd2*. This is a "short-circuit" operation; *cmd2* is never executed if *cmd1* succeeds.

Examples

`$ nroff file > file.txt &`	*Format in the background*
`$ cd; ls`	*Execute sequentially*
`$ (date; who; pwd) > logfile`	*All output is redirected*
`$ sort file	pr -3	lp`	*Sort file, page output, then print*
`$ vi `grep -l ifdef *.c``	*Edit files found by grep*
`$ egrep '(yes|no)' `cat list``	*Specify a list of files to search*
`$ egrep '(yes|no)' $(cat list)`	*Korn shell version of previous*
`$ egrep '(yes|no)' $(<list)`	*Same, but faster*
`$ grep XX file && lp file`	*Print file if it contains the pattern;*
`$ grep XX file || echo "XX not found"`	*otherwise, echo an error message*

Redirection Forms

File Descriptor	Name	Common Abbreviation	Typical Default
0	Standard input	stdin	Keyboard
1	Standard output	stdout	Terminal
2	Standard error	stderr	Terminal

The usual input source or output destination can be changed, as seen in the following sections.

Simple redirection

`cmd > file`

Send output of *cmd* to *file* (overwrite).

`cmd >> file`

Send output of *cmd* to *file* (append).

`cmd < file`

Take input for *cmd* from *file*.

`cmd << text`

The contents of the shell script up to a line identical to *text* become the standard input for *cmd* (*text* can be stored in a shell variable). This command form is sometimes called a *Here document*. Input is usually typed at the keyboard or in the shell program. Commands that typically use this syntax include cat, ex, and sed. (If `<<-` is used, leading tabs are ignored when comparing input with the end-of-input *text* marker.) If *text* is quoted, the input is passed through verbatim. Otherwise, the contents are processed for variable and command substitutions. The Korn shell also processes the input for arithmetic substitution.

cmd <> *file*

Korn shell only. Open *file* for reading *and* writing on the standard input. The contents are not destroyed.*

Redirection using file descriptors

cmd >&*n*	Send *cmd* output to file descriptor *n*.
cmd *m*>&*n*	Same, except that output that would normally go to file descriptor *m* is sent to file descriptor *n* instead.
cmd >&-	Close standard output.
cmd <&*n*	Take input for *cmd* from file descriptor *n*.
cmd *m*<&*n*	Same, except that input that would normally come from file descriptor *m* comes from file descriptor *n* instead.
cmd <&-	Close standard input.
cmd <&*n*-	Move input file descriptor *n* instead of duplicating it. ksh93 only.
cmd >&*n*-	Move output file descriptor *n* instead of duplicating it. ksh93 only.

Multiple redirection

cmd 2>*file*	Send standard error to *file*; standard output remains the same (e.g., the screen).
cmd > *file* 2>&1	Send both standard error and standard output to *file*.
cmd > *f1* 2>*f2*	Send standard output to file *f1*, standard error to file *f2*.
cmd | tee *files*	Send output of *cmd* to standard output (usually the terminal) and to *files*. (See the Example in Chapter 2, *Unix Commands*, under **tee**.)
cmd 2>&1 | tee *files*	Send standard output and error output of *cmd* to standard output (usually the terminal) and to *files*.

No space should appear between file descriptors and a redirection symbol; spacing is optional in the other cases.

Examples

```
$ cat part1 > book
$ cat part2 part3 >> book
$ mail tim < report
$ sed 's/^/XX /g' << END_ARCHIVE
> This is often how a shell archive is "wrapped",
> bundling text for distribution. You would normally
> run sed from a shell program, not from the command line.
> END_ARCHIVE
XX This is often how a shell archive is "wrapped",
XX bundling text for distribution.  You would normally
XX run sed from a shell program, not from the command line.
```

---

* With <, the file is opened read-only, and writes on the file descriptor will fail. With <>, the file is opened read-write; it is up to the application to actually take advantage of this.

To redirect standard output to standard error:

```
$ echo "Usage error: see administrator" 1>&2
```

The following command sends output (files found) to `filelist` and error messages (inaccessible files) to file no_access:

```
$ find / -print > filelist 2>no_access
```

Coprocesses

Coprocesses are a feature of the Korn shell only.

cmd1 | *cmd2* |&	Coprocess; execute the pipeline in the background. The shell sets up a two-way pipe, allowing redirection of both standard input and standard output.
read -p *var*	Read coprocess output into variable *var*.
print -p *string*	Write *string* to the coprocess.
cmd <&p	Take input for *cmd* from the coprocess.
cmd >&p	Send output of *cmd* to the coprocess.
exec *n*<&p	Move input for coprocess to file descriptor *n*.
exec *n*>&p	Move output from coprocess to file descriptor *n*.

Moving the coprocess input and output file descriptors to standard file descriptors allows you to open multiple coprocesses.

Examples

```
$ ed - memo |&              Start coprocess
$ print -p /word/           Send ed command to coprocess
$ read -p search            Read output of ed command into variable search
$ print "$search"           Show the line on standard output
A word to the wise.
```

Variables

This section describes the following:

- Variable substitution

- Built-in shell variables

- Other shell variables

- Arrays (Korn shell only)

- Discipline functions (ksh93 only)

Variable Substitution

ksh93 provides structured variables, such as pos.x and pos.y. To create either one, pos must already exist, and braces must be used to retrieve their values. Names beginning with .sh are reserved for use by ksh.

No spaces should be used in the following expressions. The colon (:) is optional; if it's included, *var* must be nonnull as well as set.

`var=value ...`	Set each variable *var* to a *value*.
`${var}`	Use value of *var*; braces are optional if *var* is separated from the following text. They are required in ksh93 if a variable name contains periods.
`${var:-value}`	Use *var* if set; otherwise, use *value*.
`${var:=value}`	Use *var* if set; otherwise, use *value* and assign *value* to *var*.
`${var:?value}`	Use *var* if set; otherwise, print *value* and exit (if not interactive). If *value* isn't supplied, print the phrase "parameter null or not set."
`${var:+value}`	Use *value* if *var* is set; otherwise, use nothing.

In the Korn shell:

`${#var}`	Use the length of *var*.
`${#*}` `${#@}`	Use the number of positional parameters.
`${var#pattern}`	Use value of *var* after removing *pattern* from the left. Remove the shortest matching piece.
`${var##pattern}`	Same as #*pattern*, but remove the longest matching piece.
`${var%pattern}`	Use value of *var* after removing *pattern* from the right. Remove the shortest matching piece.
`${var%%pattern}`	Same as %*pattern*, but remove the longest matching piece.

In ksh93:

`${!prefix*}` `${!prefix@}`	List of variables whose names begin with *prefix*.
`${var:pos}` `${var:pos:len}`	Starting at position *pos* (0-based) in variable *var*, extract *len* characters, or rest of string if no *len*. *pos* and *len* may be arithmetic expressions.
`${var/pat/repl}`	Use value of *var*, with first match of *pat* replaced with *repl*.
`${var/pat}`	Use value of *var*, with first match of *pat* deleted.
`${var//pat/repl}`	Use value of *var*, with every match of *pat* replaced with *repl*.
`${var/#pat/repl}`	Use value of *var*, with match of *pat* replaced with *repl*. Match must occur at beginning of the value.

`${var/%pat/repl}`   Use value of *var*, with match of *pat* replaced with *repl*. Match must occur at end of the value.

In `ksh93`, indirect variables allow you to "alias" one variable name to affect the value of another. This is accomplished using `typeset -n`:

```
$ greet="hello, world"                          Create initial variable
$ typeset -n friendly_message=greet             Set up alias
$ echo $friendly_message                        Access old value through new name
hello, world
$ friendly_message="don't panic"                Change the value
$ echo $greet                                   Old variable is changed
don't panic
```

Examples

```
$ u=up d=down blank=                   Assign values to three variables (last is null)
$ echo ${u}root                        Braces are needed here
uproot
$ echo ${u-$d}                         Display value of u or d; since u is set, it's printed
up
$ echo ${tmp-`date`}                   If tmp is not set, the date command is executed
Thu Feb  4 15:03:46 EST 1993
$ echo ${blank="no data"}              blank is set, so it is printed (a blank line)
$ echo ${blank:="no data"}             blank is set but null, so the string is printed
no data
$ echo $blank                          blank now has a new value
no data
```

Korn shell example

```
tail='${PWD##*/}'     Take the current directory name and remove the longest character string ending
                      with /, which removes the leading pathname and leaves the tail
```

Built-in Shell Variables

Built-in variables are automatically set by the shell and are typically used inside shell scripts. Built-in variables can make use of the variable substitution patterns shown previously. Note that the `$` is not actually part of the variable name, although the variable is always referenced this way.

`$#`   Number of command-line arguments.

`$-`   Options currently in effect (arguments supplied to `sh` or to `set`).

`$?`   Exit value of last executed command.

`$$`   Process number of current process.

`$!`   Process number of last background command.

`$0`   First word; that is, command name. This will have the full path name if it was found via a PATH search.

`$n`   Individual arguments on command line (positional parameters). The Bourne shell allows only nine parameters to be referenced directly (*n* = 1–9); the Korn shell allows *n* to be greater than 9 if specified as `${n}`.

`$*, $@` All arguments on command line (`$1 $2 ...`).

| `"$*"` | All arguments on command line as one string (`"$1 $2..."`). |
| `"$@"` | All arguments on command line, individually quoted (`"$1" "$2"` ...). |

The Korn shell automatically sets these additional variables:

`$_`	Temporary variable; initialized to pathname of script or program being executed. Later, stores the last argument of previous command. Also stores name of matching MAIL file during mail checks.
`LINENO`	Current line number within the script or function.
`OLDPWD`	Previous working directory (set by `cd`).
`OPTARG`	Name of last option processed by `getopts`.
`OPTIND`	Numerical index of OPTARG.
`PPID`	Process number of this shell's parent.
`PWD`	Current working directory (set by `cd`).
`RANDOM[=n]`	Generate a new random number with each reference; start with integer n, if given.
`REPLY`	Default reply, used by `select` and `read`.
`SECONDS[=n]`	Number of seconds since the shell was started, or, if n is given, number of seconds + n since the shell started.

ksh93 automatically sets these additional variables. Variables whose names contain "." must be enclosed in braces when referenced, e.g., `${.sh.edchar}`.

`HISTCMD`	The history number of the current command.
`.sh.edchar`	The character(s) entered when processing a KEYBD trap. Changing it replaces the characters that caused the trap.
`.sh.edcol`	The position of the cursor in the most recent KEYBD trap.
`.sh.edmode`	Will be equal to ESCAPE if in a KEYBD trap in `vi` mode, otherwise empty.
`.sh.edtext`	The characters in the input buffer during a KEYBD trap.
`.sh.name`	The name of the variable running a discipline function.
`.sh.subscript`	The subscript of the variable running a discipline function.
`.sh.value`	The value of the variable inside the `set` and `get` discipline functions.
`.sh.version`	The version of ksh93.

Other Shell Variables

The following variables are not automatically set by the shell. They are typically used in your `.profile` file, where you can define them to suit your needs. Variables can be assigned values by issuing commands of the form:

```
variable=value
```

This list includes the type of value expected when defining these variables. Those that are specific to the Korn shell are marked as (K). Those that are specific to ksh93 are marked (K93).

CDPATH=*dirs*	Directories searched by cd; allows shortcuts in changing directories; unset by default.
COLUMNS=*n*	(K) Screen's column width; used in line edit modes and select lists.
EDITOR=*file*	(K) Pathname of line edit mode to turn on (can end in emacs or vi); used when VISUAL is not set.
ENV=*file*	(K) Name of script that gets executed at startup; useful for storing alias and function definitions. For example, ENV=$HOME/.kshrc (like C shell's .cshrc).
FCEDIT=*file*	(K) Editor used by fc command (default is /bin/ed). Obsoleted in ksh93 by HISTEDIT.
FIGNORE=*pattern*	(K93) Pattern describing the set of filenames to ignore during pattern matching.
FPATH=*dirs*	(K) Directories to search for function definitions; undefined functions are set via typeset -fu; FPATH is searched when these functions are first referenced. (ksh93 also searches PATH.)
HISTEDIT=*file*	(K93) Editor used by hist command, if set. Overrides the setting of FCEDIT.
HISTFILE=*file*	(K) File in which to store command history (must be set before ksh is started); default is $HOME/.sh_history.
HISTSIZE=*n*	(K) Number of history commands available (must be set before ksh is started); default is 128.
HOME=*dir*	Home directory; set by login (from /etc/passwd file).
IFS='*chars*'	Input field separators; default is space, tab, and newline.
LANG=*dir*	Directory to use for certain language-dependent programs.
LC_ALL=*locale*	(K93) Current locale; overrides LANG and the other LC_* variables.
LC_COLLATE=*locale*	(K93) Locale to use for character collation (sorting order).
LC_CTYPE=*locale*	(K93) Locale to use for character class functions. (See the earlier section "Filename Metacharacters.")
LC_NUMERIC=*locale*	(K93) Locale to use for the decimal-point character.
LINES=*n*	(K) Screen's height; used for select lists.
MAIL=*file*	Default file in which to receive mail; set by login.
MAILCHECK=*n*	Number of seconds between mail checks; default is 600 (10 minutes).
MAILPATH=*files*	One or more files, delimited by a colon, in which to receive mail. Along with each file, you may supply an optional message that the shell prints when the file increases in size. Messages are separated from the file name by a separator character. The Korn shell separator is ?, and the default message is You have mail in $_. $_ is replaced with the name of the file. The Bourne shell separator is %, and the default message is You have mail. For example, for ksh, you might have:

```
MAILPATH="$MAIL?Ring! Candygram!:/etc/motd?New Login Message"
```

| PATH=*dirlist* | One or more pathnames, delimited by colons, in which to search for commands to execute. Default for SVR4 is /bin:/usr/bin. On Solaris, the default is /usr/bin:. However, the standard start-up scripts change it to: |
| | |

/usr/bin:/usr/ucb:/etc:.

ksh93: PATH is also searched for function definitions for undefined functions.

PS1=*string*	Primary prompt string; default is $.
PS2=*string*	Secondary prompt (used in multiline commands); default is >.
PS3=*string*	(K) Prompt string in select loops; default is #?.
PS4=*string*	(K) Prompt string for execution trace (ksh -x or set -x); default is +.
SHACCT=*file*	"Shell account"; file in which to log executed shell scripts. Not in Korn shell.
SHELL=*file*	Name of default shell (e.g., /bin/sh).
TERM=*string*	Terminal type.
TMOUT=*n*	(K) If no command is typed after *n* seconds, exit the shell.
VISUAL=*path*	(K) Same as EDITOR, but VISUAL is checked first.

Arrays

The Korn shell supports one-dimensional arrays of up to 1024 elements. The first element is numbered 0. An array *name* can be initialized as follows:

```
set -A name value0 value1 ...
```

where the specified values become elements of *name*. Declaring arrays is not required, however. Any valid reference to a subscripted variable can create an array.

When referencing arrays, use the ${ ... } syntax. This isn't needed when referencing arrays inside (( )) (the form of let that does automatic quoting). Note that [and] are typed literally (i.e., they don't stand for optional syntax).

${*name*[*i*]}	Use element *i* of array *name*. *i* can be any arithmetic expression as described under let. The expression must return a value between 0 and 1023.
${*name*}	Use element 0 of array *name*.
${*name*[*]} ${*name*[@]}	Use all elements of array *name*.
${#*name*[*]} ${#*name*[@]}	Use the number of elements in array *name*.

ksh93 provides associative arrays, where the indices are strings instead of numbers (as in awk). In this case, [and] act like double quotes. Associative arrays are created with `typeset -A`. A special syntax allows assigning to multiple elements at once:

```
data=([joe]=30 [mary]=25)
```

The values would be retrieved as `${data[joe]}` and `${data[mary]}`.

Discipline Functions (ksh93 only)

Along with structured variables, ksh93 introduces *discipline functions*. These are special functions that are called whenever a variable's value is accessed or changed. For a shell variable named x, you can define the following functions:

x.get	Called when x's value is retrieved ($x).
x.set	Called when x's value is changed (x=2).
x.unset	Called when x is unset (unset x).

Within the discipline functions, special variables provide information about the variable being changed:

.sh.name	The name of the variable being changed.
.sh.subscript	The subscript of the array element being changed.
.sh.value	The value of the variable being assigned or returned. Changing it within the discipline function changes the value that is actually assigned or returned.

Arithmetic Expressions

The Korn shell's `let` command performs arithmetic. ksh88 is restricted to integer arithmetic. ksh93 can do floating-point arithmetic as well. The Korn shell provides a way to substitute arithmetic values (for use as command arguments or in variables); base conversion is also possible:

$((*expr*))	Use the value of the enclosed arithmetic expression.
B#n	Interpret integer *n* in numeric base *B*. For example, 8#100 specifies the octal equivalent of decimal 64.

Operators

The Korn shell uses arithmetic operators from the C programming language; in decreasing order of precedence.

Operator	Description
++ --	Auto-increment and auto-decrement, both prefix and postfix. ksh93 only.
+	Unary plus. ksh93 only.
-	Unary minus.
! ~	Logical negation; binary inversion (one's complement).

Operator	Description
* / %	Multiplication; division; modulus (remainder).
+ -	Addition; subtraction.
<< >>	Bitwise left shift; bitwise right shift.
<= >=	Less than or equal to; greater than or equal to.
< >	Less than; greater than.
== !=	Equality; inequality (both evaluated left to right).
&	Bitwise AND.
^	Bitwise exclusive OR.
|	Bitwise OR.
&&	Logical AND (short-circuit).
||	Logical OR (short-circuit).
?:	Inline conditional evaluation. ksh93 only.
*= /= %= = += -= <<= >>= &= ^= |=	Assignment.
,	Sequential expression evaluation. ksh93 only.

Built-in Mathematical Functions (ksh93 only)

ksh93 provides access to the standard set of mathematical functions. They are called using C function call syntax.

Name	Function	Name	Function
abs	Absolute value	log	Natural logarithm
acos	Arc cosine	sin	Sine
asin	Arc sine	sinh	Hyperbolic sine
cos	Cosine	sqrt	Square root
cosh	Hyperbolic cosine	tan	Tangent
exp	Exponential function	tanh	Hyperbolic tangent
int	Integer part of floating-point number		

Examples

See the let command for more information and examples:

```
let "count=0" "i = i + 1"          Assign i and count
let "num % 2"                      Test for an even number
(( percent >= 0 && percent <= 100 ))   Test the range of a value
```

Command History

The Korn shell lets you display or modify previous commands. Commands in the history list can be modified using:

- Line-edit mode

- The fc and hist commands

Line-Edit Mode

Line-edit mode emulates many features of the vi and emacs editors. The history list is treated like a file. When the editor is invoked, you type editing keystrokes to move to the command line you want to execute. You can also change the line before executing it. When you're ready to issue the command, press the Return key.

Line-edit mode can be started in several ways. For example, these are equivalent:

```
$ VISUAL=vi
$ EDITOR=vi
$ set -o vi        Overrides value of VISUAL or EDITOR
```

Note that vi starts in input mode; to type a vi command, press the Escape key first.

Common editing keystrokes

vi	emacs	Result
k	CTRL-p	Get previous command.
j	CTRL-n	Get next command.
/string	CTRL-r string	Get previous command containing string.
h	CTRL-b	Move back one character.
l	CTRL-f	Move forward one character.
b	ESC-b	Move back one word.
w	ESC-f	Move forward one word.
X	DEL	Delete previous character.
x	CTRL-d	Delete character under cursor.
dw	ESC-d	Delete word forward.
db	ESC-h	Delete word backward.
xp	CTRL-t	Transpose two characters.

The fc and hist Commands

Use fc -l to list history commands and fc -e to edit them. See the entry under "Built-in Commands" for more information.

In ksh93, the fc command has been renamed hist, and alias fc=hist is predefined.

Examples

$ **history**	*List the last 16 commands*
$ **fc -l 20 30**	*List commands 20 through 30*
$ **fc -l -5**	*List the last five commands*
$ **fc -l cat**	*List the last command beginning with cat*
$ **fc -ln 5 > doit**	*Save command 5 to file doit.*
$ **fc -e vi 5 20**	*Edit commands 5 through 20 using vi*
$ **fc -e emacs**	*Edit previous command using emacs*
$ **r**	*Reexecute previous command*
$ **r cat**	*Reexecute last cat command*
$ **r doc=Doc**	*Substitute, then reexecute last command*
$ **r chap=doc c**	*Reexecute last command that begins with c, but change string chap to doc*

Job Control

Job control lets you place foreground jobs in the background, bring background jobs to the foreground, or suspend (temporarily stop) running jobs. Job control is enabled by any of the following commands:

```
jsh -i          Bourne shell

ksh -m -i       Korn shell (same as next two)
set -m
set -o monitor
```

Many job control commands take a *jobID* as an argument. This argument can be specified as follows:

%*n*   Job number *n*.

%*s*   Job whose command line starts with string *s*.

%?*s* Job whose command line contains string *s*.

%%   Current job.

%+   Current job (same as above).

%-   Previous job.

The Bourne and Korn shells provide the following job control commands. For more information on these commands, see the section "Built-in Commands" later in this chapter.

bg   Put a job in the background.

fg   Put a job in the foreground.

jobs
    List active jobs.

kill
    Terminate a job.

```
stop
```
Suspend a background job.

```
stty tostop
```
Stop background jobs if they try to send output to the terminal. (Note that stty is not a built-in command.)

```
suspend
```
Suspend a job-control shell (such as one created by su).

```
wait
```
Wait for background jobs to finish.

```
CTRL-Z
```
Suspend a foreground job. Then use bg or fg. (Your terminal may use something other than CTRL-Z as the suspend character.)

Invoking the Shell

The command interpreter for the Bourne shell (sh) or the Korn shell (ksh) can be invoked as follows:

```
sh    [options]   [arguments]

ksh   [options]   [arguments]
```

ksh and sh can execute commands from a terminal, from a file (when the first *argument* is an executable script), or from standard input (if no arguments remain or if -s is specified). ksh and sh automatically print prompts if standard input is a terminal, or if -i is given on the command line.

Arguments

Arguments are assigned in order to the positional parameters $1, $2, etc. If array assignment is in effect (-A or +A), arguments are assigned as array elements. If the first argument is an executable script, commands are read from it, and the remaining arguments are assigned to $1, $2, etc.

Options

-c *str*
Read commands from string *str.*

-D Print all $"..." strings in the program. ksh93 only.

-i Create an interactive shell (prompt for input).

-I *file*
Create a cross-reference database for variable and command definitions and references. May not be compiled in. ksh93 only.

-p Start up as a privileged user (Bourne shell: don't set the effective user and group IDs to those of the real user and group IDs. Korn shell: don't process $HOME/.profile).

-r   Create a restricted shell (same as rksh or rsh).

-s   Read commands from standard input; output from built-in commands goes to file descriptor 1; all other shell output goes to file descriptor 2.

The remaining options to sh and ksh are listed under the set built-in command.

Restricted Shells

Restricted shells can be invoked in any of the following ways:

```
rksh              Korn shell
ksh -r
set -r

/usr/lib/rsh      Bourne shell
set -r
```

Restricted shells can also be set up by supplying the full pathname to rksh or rsh in the shell field of /etc/passwd or by using them as the value for the SHELL variable.

Restricted shells act the same as their nonrestricted counterparts, except that the following are prohibited:

- Changing directory (i.e., using cd).

- Setting the PATH variable. rksh also prohibits setting ENV and SHELL.

- Specifying a / for command names or pathnames.

- Redirecting output (i.e., using > and >>). ksh also prohibits the use of <>.

- Adding new built-in commands (ksh93).

Shell scripts can still be run, since in that case the restricted shell calls ksh or sh to run the script. This includes the /etc/profile, $HOME/.profile, and $ENV files.

Restricted shells are not used much in practice, as they are difficult to set up correctly.

Built-in Commands (Bourne and Korn Shells)

Examples to be entered as a command line are shown with the $ prompt. Otherwise, examples should be treated as code fragments that might be included in a shell script. For convenience, some of the reserved words used by multiline commands are also included.

! *pipeline*   **!**

ksh93 only. Negate the sense of a pipeline. Returns an exit status of 0 if the pipeline exited nonzero, and an exit status of 1 if the pipeline exited zero. Typically used in if and while statements.

→

! ←	*Example* This code prints a message if user `jane` is not logged on: ``` if ! who	grep jane > /dev/null then echo jane is not currently logged on fi ```
#	# Ignore all text that follows on the same line. # is used in shell scripts as the comment character and is not really a command. (Take care when commenting a Bourne shell script. A file that has # as its first character is sometimes interpreted by older systems as a C shell script.)
#!*shell*	#!*shell* [*option*] Used as the first line of a script to invoke the named *shell*. Anything given on the rest of the line is passed *as a single argument* to the named *shell*. This feature is typically implemented by the kernel, but may not be supported on some older systems. Some systems have a limit of around 32 characters on the maximum length of *shell*. For example: ``` #!/bin/sh ```
:	: Null command. Returns an exit status of 0. Sometimes used on older systems as the first character in a file to denote a Bourne shell script. See this Example and under **case**. The line is still processed for side effects, such as variable and command substitutions. *Example* Check whether someone is logged in: ``` if who	grep $1 > /dev/null then : # Do nothing if pattern is found else echo "User $1 is not logged in" fi ```

. file [*arguments*]

Read and execute lines in *file*. *file* does not have to be executable but must reside in a directory searched by PATH. The Korn shell supports *arguments* that are stored in the positional parameters.

[[*expression*]]

Korn shell only. Same as test *expression* or [*expression*], except that [[ ]] allows additional operators. Word splitting and filename expansion are disabled. Note that the brackets ([ ]) are typed literally, and that they must be surrounded by whitespace.

Additional Operators

&&   Logical AND of test expressions (short circuit).
|| Logical OR of test expressions (short circuit).
<   First string is lexically "less than" the second.
>   First string is lexically "greater than" the second.

name () { *commands*; }

Define *name* as a function. Syntax can be written on one line or across many. Since the Bourne shell has no aliasing capability, simple functions can serve as aliases. The Korn shell provides the function keyword, an alternate form that works the same way.

There are semantic differences that should be kept in mind:

- In the Bourne shell, all functions share traps with the "parent" shell and may not be recursive.

- In ksh88, all functions have their own traps and local variables, and may be recursive.

- In ksh93, *name* () functions share traps with the "parent" shell and may not be recursive.

- In ksh93, function functions have their own traps and local variables, and may be recursive. Using the . command with a function function gives it Bourne shell semantics.

Example

```
$ count () {
> ls | wc -l
> }
```

name ( ) ←	When issued at the command line, count now displays the number of files in the current directory.
alias	`alias` [*options*] [*name*[=`'`*cmd*`'`]] Korn shell only. Assign a shorthand *name* as a synonym for *cmd*. If =`'`*cmd*`'` is omitted, print the alias for *name*; if *name* is also omitted, print all aliases. If the alias value contains a trailing space, the next word on the command line also becomes a candidate for alias expansion. See also **unalias**. These aliases are built into ksh88. Some use names of existing Bourne shell or C shell commands (which points out the similarities among the shells).

```
autoload='typeset -fu'
false='let 0'
functions='typeset -f'
hash='alias -t'
history='fc -l'
integer='typeset -i'
nohup='nohup '
r='fc -e -'
true=':'
type='whence -v'
```

The following aliases are built into ksh93:

```
autoload='typeset -fu'
command='command '
fc='hist'
float='typeset -E'
functions='typeset -f'
hash='alias -t --'
history='hist -l'
integer='typeset -i'
nameref='typeset -n'
nohup='nohup '
r='hist -s'
redirect='command exec'
stop='kill -s STOP'
times='{ {time;} 2>&1;}'
type='whence -v'
```

Options

-p   Print the word `alias` before each alias. ksh93 only.

-t   Create a tracked alias for a Unix command *name*. The Korn shell remembers the full pathname of the command, allowing it to be found more quickly and to be issued from any directory. If no name is supplied, current tracked aliases are listed. Tracked aliases are the similar to hashed commands in the Bourne shell.

-x Export the alias; it can now be used in shell scripts and other subshells. If no name is supplied, current exported aliases are listed.	**alias**

Example

```
alias dir='echo ${PWD##*/}'
```

---

autoload [*functions*]	**autoload**

Load (define) the *functions* only when they are first used. Korn shell alias for typeset -fu.

---

bg [*jobIDs*]	**bg**

Put current job or *jobIDs* in the background. See the earlier section "Job Control."

---

break [*n*]	**break**

Exit from a for while, select, or until loop (or break out of *n* loops).

---

builtin [-ds] [-f *library*] [*name* ...]	**builtin**

ksh93 only. This command allows you to load new built-in commands into the shell at runtime from shared library files.

If no arguments are given, builtin prints all the built-in command names. With arguments, builtin adds each *name* as a new built-in command (like cd or pwd). If the *name* contains a slash, the newly-added built-in version is used only if a path search would otherwise have found a command of the same name. (This allows replacement of system commands with faster, built-in versions.) Otherwise, the built-in command is always found.

Options

-d   Delete the built-in command *name*.

-f   Load new built-in command from *library*.

-s   Only print "special" built-ins (those designated as special by POSIX).

case

```
case value in
   pattern1) cmds1;;
   pattern2) cmds2;;

        .

        .

esac
```

Execute the first set of commands (*cmds1*) if *value* matches *pattern1*, execute the second set of commands (*cmds2*) if *value* matches *pattern2*, etc. Be sure the last command in each set ends with ;;. *value* is typically a positional parameter or other shell variable. *cmds* are typically Unix commands, shell programming commands, or variable assignments. Patterns can use file-generation metacharacters. Multiple patterns (separated by |) can be specified on the same line; in this case, the associated *cmds* are executed whenever *value* matches any of these patterns. See the Examples here and under eval.

Korn Shell Notes

* The Korn shell allows *pattern* to be preceded by an optional open parenthesis, as in (*pattern*). It's useful for balancing parentheses inside a $( ) construct.

* The Korn shell also allows a case to end with ;& instead of ;;. In such cases control "falls through" to the group of statements for the next *pattern*.

Examples

Check first command-line argument and take appropriate action:

```
case $1 in       # Match the first arg
   no|yes) response=1;;
   -[tT])   table=TRUE;;
   *)       echo "unknown option"; exit 1;;
esac
```

Read user-supplied lines until user exits:

```
while :         # Null command; always true
do
   echo "Type . to finish ==> \c"
   read line
   case "$line" in
      .) echo "Message done"
         break ;;
      *) echo "$line" >> $message ;;
   esac
done
```

cd [*dir*]
cd [-LP] [*dir*]
cd [-LP] [-]
cd [-LP] [*old new*]

With no arguments, change to home directory of user. Otherwise, change working directory to *dir*. If *dir* is a relative pathname but is not in the current directory, the CDPATH variable is searched. The last three command forms are specific to the Korn shell, where - stands for the previous directory. The fourth syntax modifies the current directory name by replacing string *old* with *new* and then switches to the resulting directory.

Options

-L Use the logical path (what the user typed, including any symbolic links) for cd .. and the value of PWD. This is the default.

-P Use the actual filesystem physical path for cd .. and the value of PWD.

Example

```
$ pwd
/var/spool/cron
$ cd cron uucp        cd prints the new directory
/var/spool/uucp
```

command [-pvV] *name* [*arg* ...]

ksh93 only. Without -v or -V, execute *name* with given arguments. This command bypasses any aliases or functions that may be defined for *name*.

Options

-p Use a predefined, default search path, not the current value of PATH.

-v Just like whence.

-V Just like whence -v.

Example

Create an alias for rm that will get the system's version, and run it with the -i option:

```
alias 'rm=command -p rm -i'
```

Bourne and Korn (side tab)

continue	continue [*n*] Skip remaining commands in a for, while, select, or until loop, resuming with the next iteration of the loop (or skipping *n* loops).
disown	disown [*job* ...] ksh93 only. When a login shell exits, do not send a SIGHUP to the given jobs. If no jobs are listed, no background jobs will receive SIGHUP.
do	do Reserved word that precedes the command sequence in a for, while, until, or select statement.
done	done Reserved word that ends a for, while, until, or select statement.
echo	echo [-n] [*string*] Write *string* to standard output; if -n is specified, the output is not terminated by a newline. If no *string* is supplied, echo a newline. In the Korn shell, echo is built-in, and it emulates the system's real echo command.* (See also **echo** in Chapter 2.) echo understands special escape characters, which must be quoted (or escaped with a \) to prevent interpretation by the shell:

\a   Alert (ASCII BEL). (Not in /bin/sh's echo.)

\b   Backspace.

\c   Suppress the terminating newline (same as -n).

\f   Formfeed.

\n   Newline.

\r   Carriage return.

\t   Tab character.

---

* But, if a path search finds /usr/bin/echo, the ksh built-in echo doesn't accept the -n option. (The situation with echo is a mess; consider using printf instead.)

\v   Vertical-tab character.

\\   Backslash.

\0*nnn*
> ASCII character represented by octal number *nnn*, where *nnn* is one, two, or three digits and is preceded by a 0.

Examples

```
$ echo "testing printer" | lp
$ echo "Warning: ringing bell \a"
```

---

esac

Reserved word that ends a case statement. Omitting esac is a common programming error.

---

eval *args*

Typically, eval is used in shell scripts, and *args* is a line of code that contains shell variables. eval forces variable expansion to happen first and then runs the resulting command. This "double-scanning" is useful any time shell variables contain input/output redirection symbols, aliases, or other shell variables. (For example, redirection normally happens before variable expansion, so a variable containing redirection symbols must be expanded first using eval; otherwise, the redirection symbols remain uninterpreted.) See the C shell eval (Chapter 5, *The C Shell*) for another example.

Example

This fragment of a Bourne shell script shows how eval constructs a command that is interpreted in the right order:

```
for option
do
   case "$option" in      Define where output goes
       save) out=' > $newfile' ;;
       show) out=' | more' ;;
   esac
done

eval sort $file $out
```

exec	exec [*command args ...*] exec [-a *name*] [-c] [*command args* ...] Execute *command* in place of the current process (instead of creating a new process). exec is also useful for opening, closing, or copying file descriptors. The second form is for ksh93 only. *Options* -a Use *name* for the value of argv[0]. -c Clear the environment before executing the program. *Examples* ```\ntrap 'exec 2>&-' 0 Close standard error when\n shell script exits (signal 0)\n$ exec /bin/csh Replace Bourne shell with C shell\n$ exec < infile Reassign standard input to infile\n```
exit	exit [*n*] Exit a shell script with status *n* (e.g., exit 1). *n* can be 0 (success) or nonzero (failure). If *n* is not given, exit status is that of the most recent command. exit can be issued at the command line to close a window (log out). Exit statuses can range in value from 0 to 255. *Example* ```\nif [$# -eq 0]\nthen\n echo "Usage: $0 [-c] [-d] file(s)" 1>&2\n exit 1 # Error status\nfi\n```
export	export [*variables*] export [*name*=[*value*] ...] export -p Pass (export) the value of one or more shell *variables*, giving global meaning to the variables (which are local by default). For example, a variable defined in one shell script must be exported if its value is used in other programs called by the script. If no *variables* are given, export lists the variables exported by the current shell. The second form is the Korn shell version, which is similar to the first form except that you can set a variable *name* to a *value* before exporting it. The third form is specific to ksh93.

-p   Print export before printing the names and values of exported variables. This allows saving a list of exported variables for rereading later.

Example

In the Bourne shell, you would type:

```
TERM=vt100
export TERM
```

In the Korn shell, you could type this instead:

```
export TERM=vt100
```

---

false   false

ksh88 alias for let 0. Built-in command in ksh93 that exits with a false return value.

---

fc [*options*] [*first* [*last*]]   fc
fc -e - [*old=new*] [*command*]

ksh88 only. Display or edit commands in the history list. (Use only one of -l or -e.) *first* and *last* are numbers or strings specifying the range of commands to display or edit. If *last* is omitted, fc applies to a single command (specified by *first*). If both *first* and *last* are omitted, fc edits the previous command or lists the last 16. The second form of fc takes a history *command*, replaces *old* string with *new* string, and executes the modified command. If no strings are specified, *command* is just reexecuted. If no *command* is given either, the previous command is reexecuted. *command* is a number or string like *first*. See the examples in the earlier section "Command History."

Options

-e [*editor*]
     Invoke *editor* to edit the specified history commands. The default *editor* is set by the shell variable FCEDIT. If that variable is not set, the default is /bin/ed.

-e -
     Execute (or redo) a history command; refer to second syntax line above.

$\rightarrow$

fc ←	-l List the specified command or range of commands, or list the last 16. -n Suppress command numbering from the -l listing. -r Reverse the order of the -l listing.
fc	`fc` ksh93 alias for hist.
fg	`fg [jobIDs]` Bring current job or *jobIDs* to the foreground. See the earlier section "Job Control."
fi	`fi` Reserved word that ends an if statement. (Don't forget to use it!)

for	`for x [in list]`
	`do`
	    `commands`
	`done`
	
	For variable *x* (in optional *list* of values) do *commands*. If in *list* is omitted, "$@" (the positional parameters) is assumed.
	
	Examples
	
	Paginate files specified on the command line; save each result:
	
	```\nfor file; do\n pr $file > $file.tmp\ndone\n```
	
	Search chapters for a list of words (like fgrep -f):
	
	```\nfor item in `cat program_list`\ndo\n echo "Checking chapters for"\n echo "references to program $item..."\n grep -c "$item.[co]" chap*\ndone\n```

Extract a one-word title from each file and use as new filename:

```
for file
do
      name=`sed -n 's/NAME: //p' $file`
      mv $file $name
done
```

```
for ((init; cond; incr))
do
   commands
done
```

ksh93 only. Arithmetic for loop, similar to C's. Evaluate *init*. While *cond* is true, execute the body of the loop. Evaluate *incr* before re-testing *cond*. Any one of the expressions may be omitted; a missing *cond* is treated as being true.

Examples

Search for a phrase in each odd chapter:

```
for ((x=1; x <= 20; x += 2))
do
        grep $1 chap$x
done
```

```
function name { commands; }
```

Korn shell only. Define *name* as a shell function. See the description of semantic issues in the *name* () entry earlier.

Example

Define a function to count files.

```
$ function fcount {
>       ls | wc -l
> }
```

```
functions
```

Korn shell alias for typeset -f. (Note the "s" in the name; function is a Korn shell keyword.) See **typeset** later in this listing.

getconf	getconf [*name* [*path*]]
	ksh93 only. Retrieve the values for parameters that can vary across systems. *name* is the parameter to retrieve; *path* is a filename to test for parameters that can vary on different filesystem types.
	The parameters are defined by the POSIX 1003.1 and 1003.2 standards. See the entry for **getconf** in Chapter 2.
	Example
	Print the maximum value that can be held in a C int.

```
$ getconf INT_MAX
2147483647
```

getopts	getopts [-a *name*] *string name* [*args*]
	Process command-line arguments (or *args*, if specified) and check for legal options. getopts is used in shell script loops and is intended to ensure standard syntax for command-line options. Standard syntax dictates that command-line options begin with a + or a -. Options can be stacked; i.e., consecutive letters can follow a single -. End processing of options by specifying -- on the command line. *string* contains the option letters to be recognized by getopts when running the shell script. Valid options are processed in turn and stored in the shell variable *name*. If an option is followed by a colon, the option must be followed by one or more arguments. (Multiple arguments must be given to the command as one shell *word*. This is done by quoting the arguments or separating them with commas. The application must be written to expect multiple arguments in this format.) getopts uses the shell variables OPTARG and OPTIND. getopts is available to non-Bourne shell users as /usr/ bin/getopts.
	Option
	-a Use *name* in error messages about invalid options. ksh93 only.

hash	hash [-r] [*commands*]
	Bourne shell version. As the shell finds commands along the search path ($PATH), it remembers the found location in an internal hash table. The next time you enter a command, the shell uses the value stored in its hash table.
	With no arguments, hash lists the current hashed commands. The display shows *hits* (the number of times the command is called by the shell) and *cost* (the level of work needed to find the command).

Commands that were found in a relative directory have an asterisk (*) added in the *hits* column.

With *commands*, the shell will add those commands to the hash table.

-r removes commands from the hash list, either all of them or just the specified *commands*. The hash table is also cleared when PATH is assigned. Use PATH=$PATH to clear the hash table without affecting your search path. This is most useful if you have installed a new version of a command in a directory that is earlier in $PATH than the current version of the command.

hash

---

hash

hash

Korn shell alias for alias -t (alias -t — in ksh93). Emulates Bourne shell's hash.

---

hist [*options*] [*first* [*last*]]
hist -s [*old=new*] [*command*]

hist

ksh93 only. Display or edit commands in the history list. (Use only one of -l or -s.) *first* and *last* are numbers or strings specifying the range of commands to display or edit. If *last* is omitted, hist applies to a single command (specified by *first*). If both *first* and *last* are omitted, hist edits the previous command or lists the last 16. The second form of hist takes a history *command*, replaces *old* string with *new* string, and executes the modified command. If no strings are specified, *command* is just reexecuted. If no *command* is given either, the previous command is reexecuted. *command* is a number or string like *first*. See the examples in the earlier section "Command History."

Options

-e [*editor*]
    Invoke *editor* to edit the specified history commands. The default *editor* is set by the shell variable HISTEDIT. If that variable is not set, FCEDIT is used. If neither is set, the default is /bin/ed.

-l List the specified command or range of commands, or list the last 16.

-n Suppress command numbering from the -l listing.

-r Reverse the order of the -l listing.

$\rightarrow$

Bourne and Korn

hist ←	-s Execute (or redo) a history command; refer to second syntax line above.
history	`history` Show the last 16 commands. `ksh88` alias for `fc -l`. `ksh93` alias for `hist -l`.
| if | ```
if condition1
then commands1
[ elif condition2
    then commands2 ]
   .
   .
   .
[ else commands3 ]
fi
```<br><br>If *condition1* is met, do *commands1*; otherwise, if *condition2* is met, do *commands2*; if neither is met, do *commands3*. Conditions are usually specified with the `test` and `[[ ]]` commands. See **test** and `[[ ]]` for a full list of conditions, and see additional Examples under **:** and **exit**.<br><br>*Examples*<br><br>Insert a 0 before numbers less than 10:<br><br>```
if [ $counter -lt 10 ]
then number=0$counter
else number=$counter
fi
```<br><br>Make a directory if it doesn't exist:<br><br>```
if [ ! -d $dir ]; then
   mkdir $dir
   chmod 775 $dir
fi
``` |
| integer | `integer`

Specify integer variables. Korn shell alias for `typeset -i`. |
| jobs | `jobs [options] [jobIDs]`

List all running or stopped jobs, or list those specified by *jobIDs*. For example, you can check whether a long compilation or text format |
```

is still running. Also useful before logging out. See the earlier section "Job Control." **jobs**

Options

-l   List job IDs and process group IDs.

-n   List only jobs whose status changed since last notification. Korn shell only.

-p   List process group IDs only.

-x *cmd*
>   Replace each job ID found in *cmd* with the associated process ID and then execute *cmd*. Not valid for Korn shell.

---

kill [*options*] *IDs* **kill**

Terminate each specified process *ID* or job *ID*. You must own the process or be a privileged user. This built-in is similar to /usr/bin/kill described in Chapter 2. See the earlier section "Job Control."

Options

-l   List the signal names. (Used by itself.)

-n *num*
>   Send the given signal number. ksh93 only.

-s *name*
>   Send the given signal name. ksh93 only.

-*signal*
>   The signal number (from /usr/include/sys/signal.h) or name (from kill -l). With a signal number of 9, the kill is absolute.

Signals

Signals are defined in /usr/include/sys/signal.h and are listed here without the SIG prefix. You probably have more signals on your system than the ones shown here.

```
HUP     1     hangup
INT     2     interrupt
QUIT    3     quit
ILL     4     illegal instruction
TRAP    5     trace trap
IOT     6     IOT instruction
EMT     7     EMT instruction
FPE     8     floating point exception
KILL    9     kill
BUS     10    bus error
SEGV    11    segmentation violation
SYS     12    bad argument to system call
PIPE    13    write to pipe, but no process to read it
```

→

kill	ALRM	14	alarm clock
←	TERM	15	software termination (the default signal)
	USR1	16	user-defined signal 1
	USR2	17	user-defined signal 2
	CLD	18	child process died
	PWR	19	restart after power failure

let

let *expressions*

    or

((*expressions*))

Korn shell only. Perform arithmetic as specified by one or more *expressions*. *expressions* consist of numbers, operators, and shell variables (which don't need a preceding $). Expressions must be quoted if they contain spaces or other special characters. The (( )) form does the quoting for you. For more information and examples, see "Arithmetic Expressions" earlier in this chapter. See also **expr** in Chapter 2.

Examples

Each of these examples adds 1 to variable i:

```
i=`expr $i + 1`       sh, ksh88, ksh93
let i=i+1             ksh88 and ksh93
let "i = i + 1"
(( i = i + 1 ))
(( i += 1 ))
(( i++ ))             ksh93 only
```

nameref

nameref *newvar=oldvar* ...

ksh93 alias for typeset -n. See the discussion of indirect variables in the section "Variables," earlier in this chapter.

newgrp

newgrp [*group*]

Change your group ID to *group*, or return to your default group. On modern Unix systems where users can be in multiple groups, this command is obsolete.

nohup

nohup

Don't terminate a command after log out. nohup is a Korn shell alias:

```
nohup='nohup '
```

The embedded space at the end lets nohup interpret the following command as an alias, if needed.

---

print [*options*] [*string* ...]

Korn shell only. Display *string* (on standard output by default). print includes the functions of echo and can be used in its place on most Unix systems.

Options

-   Ignore all subsequent options.

--   Same as -.

-f *format*
    Print like printf, using *format* as the format string. Ignores the -n, -r, and -R options. ksh93 only.

-n   Don't end output with a newline.

-p   Send *string* to the process created by |&, instead of to standard output.

-r   Ignore the escape sequences often used with echo.

-R   Same as -r and ignore subsequent options (except -n).

-s   Send *string* to the history file.

-u[*n*]
    Send *string* to file descriptor *n* (default is 1).

---

printf *format* [*val* ...]

ksh93 only.Formatted printing, like the ANSI C printf function.

Additional Format Letters

%b   Expand escape sequences in strings (e.g., \t to tab, and so on).

%d   An additional period and the output base can follow the precision (e.g., %5.3.6d to produce output in base 6).

%P   Translate egrep extended regular expression into ksh pattern.

%q   Print a quoted string that can be reread later on.

pwd	pwd pwd [-LP] Print your present working directory on standard output. The second form is specific to the Korn shell. *Options* Options give control over the use of logical versus physical treatment of the printed path. See the entry for **cd**, earlier in this section. -L Use logical path (what the user typed, including any symbolic links) and the value of PWD for the current directory. This is the default. -P Use the actual filesystem physical path for the current directory.
r	r Reexecute previous command. ksh88 alias for fc -e -. ksh93 alias for hist -s.

read	read *variable1* [*variable2* ...]
	
	Read one line of standard input and assign each word to the corresponding *variable*, with all leftover words assigned to the last variable. If only one variable is specified, the entire line will be assigned to that variable. See the Examples here and under case. The return status is 0 unless *EOF* is reached.
	
	Example
	
	<pre>$ **read first last address**
	Sarah Caldwell 123 Main Street
	$ **echo "$last, $first\n$address"**
	Caldwell, Sarah
	123 Main Street</pre>

read	read [*options*] [*variable1*[?*string*]] [*variable2* ...] Korn shell only. Same as in the Bourne shell, except that the Korn shell version supports the following options as well as the ? syntax for prompting. If the first variable is followed by ?*string*, *string* is displayed as a user prompt. If no variables are given, input is stored in the REPLY variable. Additionally, ksh93 allows you to specify a timeout.

-A *array*
 Read into indexed array *array*. ksh93 only.

-d *delim*
 Read up to first occurrence of *delim*, instead of newline. ksh93 only.

-p Read from the output of a |& coprocess.

-r Raw mode; ignore \ as a line continuation character.

-s Save input as a command in the history file.

-t *timeout*
 When reading from a terminal or pipe, if no data is entered after *timeout* seconds, return 1. This prevents an application from hanging forever, waiting for user input. ksh93 only.

-u[*n*]
 Read input from file descriptor *n* (default is 0).

Example

Prompt yourself to enter two temperatures:

```
$ read n1?"High low: " n2
High low: 65 33
```

---

readonly [*variable1 variable2* ...]
readonly -p

readonly

Prevent the specified shell variables from being assigned new values. Variables can be accessed (read) but not overwritten. In the Korn shell, the syntax *variable=value* can assign a new value that cannot be changed. The second form is specific to ksh93.

Option

-p Print readonly before printing the names and values of read-only variables. This allows saving a list of read-only variables for rereading later.

---

redirect *i/o-redirection* ...

redirect

ksh93 alias for command exec.

$\rightarrow$

redirect ←	*Example*
	Change the shell's standard error to the console:
	`$ redirect 2>/dev/console`

return	return [*n*]
	Use inside a function definition. Exit the function with status *n* or with the exit status of the previously executed command.

select	select *x* [in *list*] do *commands* done

Korn shell only. Display a list of menu items on standard error, numbered in the order they are specified in *list*. If no in *list* is given, items are taken from the command line (via `"$@"`). Following the menu is a prompt string (set by PS3). At the PS3 prompt, users select a menu item by typing its line number, or they redisplay the menu by pressing the Return key. (User input is stored in the shell variable REPLY.) If a valid line number is typed, *commands* are executed. Typing *EOF* terminates the loop.

Example

```
PS3="Select the item number: "
select event in Format Page View Exit
do
    case "$event" in
      Format) nroff $file | lp;;
      Page)   pr $file | lp;;
      View)   more $file;;
      Exit)   exit 0;;
      *  )    echo "Invalid selection";;
    esac
done
```

The output of this script looks like this:

```
1. Format
2. Page
3. View
4. Exit
Select the item number:
```

set	set [*options arg1 arg2 ...*]

With no arguments, set prints the values of all variables known to the current shell. Options can be enabled (*-option*) or disabled

(+*option*). Options can also be set when the shell is invoked, via ksh or sh. (See the earlier section "Invoking the Shell.") Arguments are assigned in order to $1, $2, etc.

Options

+A *name*
> Assign remaining arguments as elements of array *name*. Korn shell only.

-A *name*
> Same as +A, but unset *name* before making assignments. Korn shell only.

-a From now on automatically mark variables for export after defining or changing them.

-b Same as -o notify. The single-letter form is only in ksh93.

-C Same as -o noclobber. The single-letter form is only in ksh93.

-e Exit if a command yields a nonzero exit status. In the Korn shell, the ERR trap is executed before the shell exits.

-f Ignore filename metacharacters (e.g., * ? [ ]).

-h Locate commands as they are defined. The Korn shell creates tracked aliases, whereas the Bourne shell hashes command names. See **hash**.

-k Assignment of environment variables (*var=value*) takes effect regardless of where they appear on the command line. Normally, assignments must precede the command name.

-m Enable job control; background jobs execute in a separate process group. -m is usually set automatically. Korn shell only.

-n Read commands but don't execute; useful for checking syntax. The Korn shell ignores this option if it is interactive.

-o [*mode*]
> List Korn shell modes, or turn on mode *mode*. Many modes can be set by other options. Modes are:

allexport	Same as -a.
bgnice	Run background jobs at lower priority.
emacs	Set command-line editor to emacs.
errexit	Same as -e.
ignoreeof	Don't process *EOF* signals. To exit the shell, type exit.
keyword	Same as -k.
markdirs	Append / to directory names.
monitor	Same as -m.

→

set ←	noclobber	Prevent overwriting via > redirection; use >| to overwrite files.
	noexec	Same as -n.
	noglob	Same as -f.
	nolog	Omit function definitions from history file.
	notify	Print job completion messages as soon as jobs terminate; don't wait until the next prompt.
	nounset	Same as -u.
	privileged	Same as -p.
	trackall	Same as -h.
	verbose	Same as -v.
	vi	Set command-line editor to vi.
	viraw	Same as vi, but process each character when it's typed.
	xtrace	Same as -x.

-p Start up as a privileged user (i.e., don't process $HOME/.profile).

-s Sort the positional parameters. Korn shell only.

-t Exit after one command is executed.

-u In substitutions, treat unset variables as errors.

-v Show each shell command line when read.

-x Show commands and arguments when executed, preceded by a +. (Korn shell: precede with the value of PS4.) This provides step-by-step debugging of shell scripts.

- Turn off -v and -x, and turn off option processing. Included in Korn shell for compatibility with older versions of Bourne shell.

-- Used as the last option; -- turns off option processing so that arguments beginning with - are not misinterpreted as options. (For example, you can set $1 to -1.) If no arguments are given after --, unset the positional parameters.

Examples

```
set - "$num" -20 -30       Set $1 to $num, $2 to -20, $3 to -30
set -vx                    Read each command line; show it;
                           execute it; show it again (with arguments)
set +x                     Stop command tracing
set -o noclobber           Prevent file overwriting
set +o noclobber           Allow file overwriting again
```

shift	shift [n]

Shift positional arguments (e.g., $2 becomes $1). If *n* is given, shift to the left *n* places. Used in while loops to iterate through command-line arguments. In the Korn shell, *n* can be an integer expression.

shift

`sleep [n]`

ksh93 only. Sleep for *n* seconds. *n* can have a fractional part.

sleep

`stop [jobIDs]`

Suspend the background job specified by *jobIDs*; this is the complement of CTRL-Z or suspend. Not valid in ksh88. See the earlier section "Job Control."

stop

`stop [jobIDs]`

ksh93 alias for `kill -s STOP`.

stop

`suspend`

Same as CTRL-Z. Often used to stop an su command. Not valid in ksh88; in ksh93, suspend is an alias for `kill -s STOP $$`.

suspend

`test condition`
   or
`[ condition ]`

test

Evaluate a *condition* and, if its value is true, return a zero exit status; otherwise, return a nonzero exit status. An alternate form of the command uses `[ ]` rather than the word test. The Korn shell allows an additional form, `[[ ]]`. *condition* is constructed using the following expressions. Conditions are true if the description holds true. Features that are specific to the Korn shell are marked with a (K). Features that are specific to ksh93 are marked with a (K93).

File Conditions

`-a file`
   file exists. (K)

`-b file`
   file exists and is a block special file.

`-c file`
   file exists and is a character special file.

Bourne and Korn

$\rightarrow$

test
←
	-d *file*
	    file exists and is a directory.
	
	-f *file*
	    file exists and is a regular file.
	
	-g *file*
	    file exists, and its set-group-id bit is set.
	
	-G *file*
	    file exists, and its group is the effective group ID. (K)
	
	-k *file*
	    file exists, and its sticky bit is set.
	
	-L *file*
	    file exists and is a symbolic link. (K)

-o *c*
> Option *c* is on. (K)

-O *file*
> *file* exists, and its owner is the effective user ID. (K)

-p *file*
> *file* exists and is a named pipe (fifo).

-r *file*
> *file* exists and is readable.

-s *file*
> *file* exists and has a size greater than zero.

-S *file*
> *file* exists and is a socket. (K)

-t [*n*]
> The open file descriptor *n* is associated with a terminal device; default *n* is 1.

-u *file*
> *file* exists, and its set-user-id bit is set.

-w *file*
> *file* exists and is writable.

-x *file*
> *file* exists and is executable.

f1 -ef *f2*
> Files *f1* and *f2* are linked (refer to same file). (K)

f1 -nt *f2*
> File *f1* is newer than *f2*. (K)

f1 -ot *f2*
> File *f1* is older than *f2*. (K)

String Conditions

string
> *string* is not null.

-n *s1*
> String *s1* has nonzero length.

-z *s1*
> String *s1* has zero length.

s1 = *s2*
> Strings *s1* and *s2* are identical. In the Korn shell, *s2* can be a wildcard pattern. (See the section "Filename Metacharacters," earlier in this chapter.)

s1 == *s2*
> Strings *s1* and *s2* are identical. *s2* can be a wildcard pattern. Preferred over =. (K93)

s1 != *s2*
> Strings *s1* and *s2* are *not* identical. In the Korn shell, *s2* can be a wildcard pattern.

s1 < *s2*
> ASCII value of *s1* precedes that of *s2*. (Valid only within [[ ]] construct). (K)

s1 > *s2*
> ASCII value of *s1* follows that of *s2*. (Valid only within [[ ]] construct). (K)

Integer Comparisons

n1 -eq *n2*
> *n1* equals *n2*.

n1 -ge *n2*
> *n1* is greater than or equal to *n2*.

n1 -gt *n2*
> *n1* is greater than *n2*.

n1 -le *n2*
> *n1* is less than or equal to *n2*.

n1 -lt *n2*
> *n1* is less than *n2*.

→

test
←
	n1 -ne *n2*
	    n1 does not equal *n2*.
	
	Combined Forms
	
	(*condition*)
	    True if *condition* is true (used for grouping). The ( )s should be quoted by a \.
	
	! *condition*
	    True if *condition* is false.
	
	condition1 -a *condition2*
	    True if both conditions are true.
	
	condition1 && *condition2*
	    True if both conditions are true. (Valid only within [[ ]] construct.) (K)
	
	condition1 -o *condition2*
	    True if either condition is true.
	
	condition1 || *condition2*
	    True if either condition is true. (Valid only within [[ ]] construct.) (K)
	
	Examples
	
	The following examples show the first line of various statements that might use a test condition:

```
while test $# -gt 0              While there are arguments...
while [ -n "$1" ]                While there are nonempty arguments...
if [ $count -lt 10 ]            If $count is less than 10...
if [ -d RCS ]                    If the RCS directory exists...
if [ "$answer" != "y" ]          If the answer is not y...
if [ ! -r "$1" -o ! -f "$1" ]    If the first argument is not a
                                 readable file or a regular file...
```

time	time *command* time [*command*] Korn shell only. Execute *command* and print the total elapsed time, user time, and system time (in seconds). Same as the Unix command time (see Chapter 2), except that the built-in version can also time other built-in commands as well as all commands in a pipeline. The second form applies to ksh93; with no *command*, the total user and system times for the shell, and all children are printed.

`times`	**times**
Print accumulated process times for user and system.	

`times`	**times**
ksh93 alias for { {time;} 2>&1;}. See also **time**.	

`trap [ [`*`commands`*`]` *`signals`*`]` `trap -p`	**trap**

Execute *commands* if any *signals* are received. The second form is specific to ksh93; it prints the current trap settings in a form suitable for rereading later.

Common signals include 0, 1, 2, and 15. Multiple commands should be quoted as a group and separated by semicolons internally. If *commands* is the null string (i.e., `trap " "` *signals*), *signals* are ignored by the shell. If *commands* are omitted entirely, reset processing of specified signals to the default action. ksh93: if *commands* is "-", reset *signals* to their initial defaults.

If both *commands* and *signals* are omitted, list current trap assignments. See the Examples here and in **exec**.

Signals

Signals are listed along with what triggers them:

0	Exit from shell (usually when shell script finishes).
1	Hangup (usually logout).
2	Interrupt (usually CTRL-C).
3	Quit.
4	Illegal instruction.
5	Trace trap.
6	IOT instruction.
7	EMT instruction.
8	Floating-point exception.
10	Bus error.
12	Bad argument to a system call.
13	Write to a pipe without a process to read it.
14	Alarm timeout.
15	Software termination (usually via kill).
ERR	Nonzero exit status. Korn shell only.
DEBUG	Execution of any command. Korn shell only.
KEYBD	A key has been read in emacs, gmacs, or vi editing mode. ksh93 only.

$\rightarrow$

Bourne and Korn

trap ←	**Examples** ``` trap "" 2 Ignore signal 2 (interrupts) trap 2 Obey interrupts again ``` Remove a $tmp file when the shell program exits, or if the user logs out, presses CTRL-C, or does a kill: • ``` trap "rm -f $tmp; exit" 0 1 2 15 ``` Print a "clean up" message when the shell program receives signals 1, 2, or 15: ``` trap 'echo Interrupt! Cleaning up...' 1 2 15 ```
true	`true` ksh88 alias for :. ksh93 built-in command that exits with a true return value.

type	`type commands`
	
	Show whether each command name is a Unix command, a built-in command, or a defined shell function. In the Korn shell, this is simply an alias for whence -v.
	
	Example
	
	``
	$ type mv read
	mv is /bin/mv
	read is a shell builtin
	``

typeset	`typeset [options] [variable[=value ...]]`
	`typeset -p`
	
	Korn shell only. Assign a type to each variable (along with an optional initial *value*), or, if no variables are supplied, display all variables of a particular type (as determined by the options). When variables are specified, -*option* enables the type, and +*option* disables it. With no variables given, -*option* prints variable names and values; +*option* prints only the names.
	
	The second form shown is specific to ksh93.
	
	Options
	
	-A *arr*
	    arr is an associative array. ksh93 only.

-E *d*

> *variable* is a floating-point number. *d* is the number of decimal places. The value is printed using printf %g format. ksh93 only.

-F *d*

> *variable* is a floating-point number. *d* is the number of decimal places. The value is printed using printf %f format. ksh93 only.

-f[*c*]

> The named variable is a function; no assignment is allowed. If no variable is given, list current function names. Flag *c* can be t, u, or x. t turns on tracing (same as set -x). u marks the function as undefined, which causes autoloading of the function (i.e., a search of FPATH locates the function when it's first used. ksh93 also searches PATH). x exports the function. Note the aliases **autoload** and **functions**.

-H On non-Unix systems, map Unix filenames to host filenames.

-i[*n*]

> Define variables as integers of base *n*. integer is an alias for typeset -i.

-L[*n*]

> Define variables as left-justified strings, *n* characters long (truncate or pad with blanks on the right as needed). Leading blanks are stripped; leading 0s are stripped if -z is also specified. If no *n* is supplied, field width is that of the variable's first assigned value.

-l Convert uppercase to lowercase.

-n *variable* is an indirect reference to another variable (a *nameref*). ksh93 only. (See the section "Variables," earlier in this chapter.)

-p Print typeset commands to recreate the types of all the current variables. ksh93 only.

-R[*n*]

> Define variables as right-justified strings, *n* characters long (truncate or pad with blanks on the left as needed). Trailing blanks are stripped. If no *n* is supplied, field width is that of the variable's first assigned value.

-r Mark variables as read-only. See also **readonly**.

-t Mark variables with a user-definable tag.

-u Convert lowercase to uppercase.

→

| **typeset**<br>← | -x   Mark variables for automatic export.<br><br>-z[*n*]<br><br>When used with –L, strip leading 0s.  When used alone, it's similar to –R except that –z pads numeric values with 0s and pads text values with blanks.<br><br>***Examples***<br><br>```
typeset              List name, value, and type of all set variables
typeset -x           List names and values of exported variables
typeset +r PWD       End read-only status of PWD
typeset -i n1 n2 n3  Three variables are integers
typeset -R5 zipcode  zipcode is flush right, five characters wide
``` |
| **ulimit** | ulimit [*options*] [*n*]

Print the value of one or more resource limits, or, if *n* is specified, set a resource limit to *n*. Resource limits can be either hard (–H) or soft (–S). By default, ulimit sets both limits or prints the soft limit. The options determine which resource is acted on.

Options

-H   Hard limit. Anyone can lower a hard limit; only privileged users can raise it.

-S   Soft limit. Must be lower than the hard limit.

-a   Print all limits.

-c   Maximum size of core files.

-d   Maximum kilobytes of data segment or heap.

-f   Maximum size of files (the default option).

-m   Maximum kilobytes of physical memory. Korn shell only. (Not effective on all Unix systems.)

-n   Maximum file descriptor plus 1.

-p   Size of pipe buffers. Korn shell only. (Not effective on all Unix systems.)

-s   Maximum kilobytes of stack segment.

-t   Maximum CPU seconds.

-v   Maximum kilobytes of virtual memory. |
```

umask [*nnn*]
umask [-S] [*mask*]

Display file creation mask or set file creation mask to octal value *nnn*. The file creation mask determines which permission bits are turned off (e.g., umask 002 produces rw-rw-r--). See the entry in Chapter 2 for examples.

The second form is specific to ksh93. A symbolic mask is permissions to keep.

Option

-S   Print the current mask using symbolic notation. ksh93 only.

---

unalias *names*
unalias -a

Korn shell only. Remove *names* from the alias list. See also **alias**.

Option

-a   Remove all aliases. ksh93 only.

---

unset *names*

Bourne shell version. Erase definitions of functions or variables listed in *names*.

---

unset [*options*] *names*

Erase definitions of functions or variables listed in *names*. The Korn shell version supports options.

Options

-f   Unset functions in *names*.

-n   Unset indirect variable (nameref) *name*, not the variable the nameref refers to. ksh93 only.

-v   Unset variables *names* (default). ksh93 only.

until	```until condition```
	```do```
	    ```commands```
	```done```
	
	Until *condition* is met, do *commands*. *condition* is usually specified with the test command.

wait	```wait [ID]```
	
	Pause in execution until all background jobs complete (exit status 0 is returned), or pause until the specified background process *ID* or job *ID* completes (exit status of *ID* is returned). Note that the shell variable $! contains the process ID of the most recent background process. If job control is not in effect, *ID* can be only a process ID number. See the earlier section "Job Control."
	
	Example
	
	```wait $!``` *Wait for most recent background process to finish*

whence	```whence [options] commands``` Korn shell only. Show whether each command name is a Unix command, a built-in command, a defined shell function, or an alias. *Options* -a Print all interpretations of *commands*. ksh93 only. -f Skip the search for shell functions. ksh93 only. -p Search for the pathname of *commands*. -v Verbose output; same as type.

while	```while condition```
	```do```
	    ```commands```
	```done```
	
	While *condition* is met, do *commands*. *condition* is usually specified with the test command. See the Examples under **case** and **test**.

filename

Read and execute commands from executable file *filename*, or execute a binary object file.

CHAPTER 5

The C Shell

This chapter describes the C shell, so named because many of its programming constructs and symbols resemble those of the C programming language. The following topics are presented:

- Overview of features

- Syntax

- Variables

- Expressions

- Command history

- Job control

- Invoking the shell

- Built-in commands

For more information on the C shell, see *Using csh & tcsh*, which is listed in the Bibliography.

Overview of Features

Features of the C shell include:

- Input/output redirection

- Wildcard characters (metacharacters) for filename abbreviation

- Shell variables for customizing your environment

- Integer arithmetic

- Access to previous commands (command history)

- Command name abbreviation (aliasing)

- A built-in command set for writing shell programs

- Job control

- Optional filename completion

Syntax

This section describes the many symbols peculiar to the C shell. The topics are arranged as follows:

- Special files

- Filename metacharacters

- Quoting

- Command forms

- Redirection forms

Special Files

~/.cshrc	Executed at each instance of shell invocation.
~/.login	Executed by login shell after .cshrc at login.
~/.logout	Executed by login shell at logout.
~/.history	History list saved from previous login.
/etc/passwd	Source of home directories for ~*name* abbreviations. (May come from NIS or NIS+ instead.)

Filename Metacharacters

Metacharacter	Description
*	Match any string of zero or more characters.
?	Match any single character.
[*abc*...]	Match any one of the enclosed characters; a hyphen can be used to specify a range (e.g., a–z, A–Z, 0–9).
{*abc*, *xxx*, ...}	Expand each comma-separated string inside braces. The strings need not match actual filenames.
~	Home directory for the current user.
~*name*	Home directory of user *name*.

Examples

`% ls new*`	*Match new and new.1*
`% cat ch?`	*Match ch9 but not ch10*
`% vi [D-R]*`	*Match files that begin with uppercase D through R*
`% ls {ch,app}?`	*Expand, then match ch1, ch2, app1, app2*
`% mv info{,.old}`	*Expands to mv info info.old*
`% cd ~tom`	*Change to tom's home directory*

Quoting

Quoting disables a character's special meaning and allows it to be used literally, as itself. The characters in the following table have special meaning to the C shell.

Character	Meaning
;	Command separator
&	Background execution
( )	Command grouping
|	Pipe
* ? [ ] ~	Filename metacharacters
{ }	String expansion characters; usually don't require quoting
< > & !	Redirection symbols
! ^	History substitution, quick substitution
" ' \	Used in quoting other characters
`	Command substitution
$	Variable substitution
space tab newline	Word separators

These characters can be used for quoting:

" " Everything between " and " is taken literally, except for the following characters that keep their special meaning:

    $ Variable substitution will occur.

    `   Command substitution will occur.

    "   This marks the end of the double quote.

    \   Escape next character.

    !   The history character.

    newline
        The newline character.

' ' Everything between ' and ' is taken literally except for ! (history) and another ', and newline.

\ The character following a \ is taken literally. Use within "" to escape ", $, `, and newline. Use within ' ' to escape newlines. Often used to escape itself, spaces, or newlines. Always needed to escape a history character (usually !).

Examples

```
% echo 'Single quotes "protect" double quotes'
Single quotes "protect" double quotes

% echo "Don't double quotes protect single quotes too?"
Don't double quotes protect single quotes too?

% echo "You have `ls|wc -l` files in `pwd`"
You have      43 files in /home/bob

% echo The value of \$x is $x
The value of $x is 100
```

Command Forms

cmd &	Execute *cmd* in background.
cmd1 ; cmd2	Command sequence; execute multiple *cmd*s on the same line.
(cmd1 ; cmd2)	Subshell; treat *cmd1* and *cmd2* as a command group.
cmd1 | cmd2	Pipe; use output from *cmd1* as input to *cmd2*.
cmd1 `cmd2`	Command substitution; use *cmd2* output as arguments to *cmd1*.
cmd1 && cmd2	AND; execute *cmd1* and then (if *cmd1* succeeds) *cmd2*. This is a "short-circuit" operation; *cmd2* is never executed if *cmd1* fails.
cmd1 || cmd2	OR; execute either *cmd1* or (if *cmd1* fails) *cmd2*. This is a "short-circuit" operation; *cmd2* is never executed if *cmd1* succeeds.

Examples

% nroff file > file.out &	*Format in the background*
% cd; ls	*Execute sequentially*
% (date; who; pwd) > logfile	*All output is redirected*
% sort file | pr -3 | lp	*Sort file, page output, then print*
% vi `grep -l ifdef *.c`	*Edit files found by grep*
% egrep '(yes|no)' `cat list`	*Specify a list of files to search*
% grep XX file && lp file	*Print file if it contains the pattern,*
% grep XX file || echo XX not found	*otherwise, echo an error message*

Redirection Forms

File Desciptor	Name	Common Abbreviation	Typical Default
0	Standard input	stdin	Keyboard
1	Standard output	stdout	Terminal
2	Standard error	stderr	Terminal

The usual input source or output destination can be changed, as seen in the following sections.

Simple redirection

cmd > `file`
> Send output of *cmd* to *file* (overwrite).

cmd >! `file`
> Same as above, even if `noclobber` is set.

cmd >> `file`
> Send output of *cmd* to *file* (append).

cmd >>! `file`
> Same as above, but write to *file* even if `noclobber` is set.

cmd < `file`
> Take input for *cmd* from *file*.

cmd << `text`
> Read standard input up to a line identical to *text* (*text* can be stored in a shell variable). Input is usually typed at the terminal or in the shell program. Commands that typically use this syntax include cat, echo, ex, and sed. If *text* is quoted (using any of the shell-quoting mechanisms), the input is passed through verbatim.

Multiple redirection

cmd >& `file`	Send both standard output and standard error to *file*.
cmd >&! `file`	Same as above, even if `noclobber` is set.
cmd >>& `file`	Append standard output and standard error to end of *file*.
cmd >>&! `file`	Same as above, but append to or create *file* even if `noclobber` is set.
cmd1 |& *cmd2*	Pipe standard error together with standard output.
(*cmd* > `f1`) >& `f2`	Send standard output to file *f1*, standard error to file *f2*.
cmd | tee `files`	Send output of *cmd* to standard output (usually the terminal) and to *files*. (See the Example in Chapter 2, *Unix Commands*, under **tee**.)

Examples

```
% cat part1 > book
% cat part2 part3 >> book
% mail tim < report
% cc calc.c >& error_out
% cc newcalc.c >&! error_out
% grep Unix ch* |& pr
% (find / -print > filelist) >& no_access

% sed 's/^/XX /g' << "END_ARCHIVE"
This is often how a shell archive is "wrapped",
bundling text for distribution. You would normally
run sed from a shell program, not from the command line.
```

```
"END_ARCHIVE"
XX This is often how a shell archive is "wrapped",
XX bundling text for distribution.  You would normally
XX run sed from a shell program, not from the command line.
```

Variables

This section describes the following:

- Variable substitution

- Variable modifiers

- Predefined shell variables

- Example .cshrc file

- Environment variables

Variable Substitution

In the following substitutions, braces ({}) are optional, except when needed to separate a variable name from following characters that would otherwise be a part of it.

${var}	The value of variable *var*.
${var[i]}	Select word or words in position *i* of *var*. *i* can be a single number, a range *m–n*, a range *-n* (missing *m* implies 1), a range *m-* (missing *n* implies all remaining words), or * (select all words). *i* can also be a variable that expands to one of these values.
${#var}	The number of words in *var*.
${#argv}	The number of arguments.
$0	Name of the program. (Usually not set in interactive shells.)
${argv[n]}	Individual arguments on command line (positional parameters). *n* = 1–9.
${n}	Same as ${argv[n]}.
${argv[*]}	All arguments on command line.
$*	Same as $argv[*].
$argv[$#argv]	The last argument.
${?var}	Return 1 if *var* is set; 0 if *var* is not set.
$$	Process number of current shell; useful as part of a filename for creating temporary files with unique names.
$?0	Return 1 if input filename is known; 0 if not.
$<	Read a line from standard input.

C Shell

Examples

Sort the third through last arguments (files) and save the output in a unique temporary file:

```
sort $argv[3-] > tmp.$$
```

Process .cshrc commands only if the shell is interactive (i.e., the prompt variable must be set):

```
if ($?prompt) then
    set commands,
    alias commands,
    etc.
endif
```

Variable Modifiers

Except for $?*var*, $$, $?0, and $<, the previous variable substitutions may be followed by one of the following modifiers. When braces are used, the modifier goes inside them.

:r Return the variable's root.

:e Return the variable's extension.

:h Return the variable's header.

:t Return the variable's tail.

:gr Return all roots.

:ge Return all extensions.

:gh Return all headers.

:gt Return all tails.

:q Quote a wordlist variable, keeping the items separate. Useful when the variable contains filename metacharacters that should not be expanded.

:x Quote a pattern, expanding it into a wordlist.

Examples using pathname modifiers

This table shows the use of pathname modifiers on the following variable:

```
set aa=(/progs/num.c /book/chap.ps)
```

Variable Portion	Specification	Output Result
Normal variable	echo $aa	/progs/num.c /book/chap.ps
Second root	echo $aa[2]:r	/book/chap
Second header	echo $aa[2]:h	/book
Second tail	echo $aa[2]:t	chap.ps

Variable Portion	Specification	Output Result
Second extension	echo $aa[2]:e	ps
Root	echo $aa:r	/progs/num /book/chap.ps
Global root	echo $aa:gr	/progs/num /book/chap
Header	echo $aa:h	/progs /book/chap.ps
Global header	echo $aa:gh	/progs /book
Tail	echo $aa:t	num.c /book/chap.ps
Global tail	echo $aa:gt	num.c chap.ps
Extension	echo $aa:e	c /book/chap.ps
Global extension	echo $aa:ge	c ps

Examples using quoting modifiers

```
% set a="[a-z]*" A="[A-Z]*"
% echo "$a" "$A"
[a-z]* [A-Z]*

% echo $a $A
at cc m4 Book Doc

% echo $a:x $A
[a-z]* Book Doc

% set d=($a:q $A:q)
% echo $d
at cc m4 Book Doc

% echo $d:q
[a-z]* [A-Z]*

% echo $d[1] +++ $d[2]
at cc m4 +++ Book Doc

% echo $d[1]:q
[a-z]*
```

Predefined Shell Variables

Variables can be set in one of two ways, by assigning a value:

```
set var=value
```

or by simply turning them on:

```
set var
```

In the following table, variables that accept values are shown with the equals sign followed by the type of value they accept; the value is then described. (Note, however, that variables such as argv, cwd, or status are never explicitly assigned.) For variables that are turned on or off, the table describes what they do when set. The C shell automatically sets the variables argv, cwd, home, path, prompt, shell, status, term, and user.

C Shell

Variable	Description
argv=(args)	List of arguments passed to current command; default is ().
cdpath=(dirs)	List of alternate directories to search when locating arguments for cd, popd, or pushd.
cwd=dir	Full pathname of current directory.
echo	Redisplay each command line before execution; same as csh -x command.
fignore=(chars)	List of filename suffixes to ignore during filename completion (see filec).
filec	If set, a filename that is partially typed on the command line can be expanded to its full name when the Escape key is pressed. If more than one filename matches, type *EOF* to list possible completions.
hardpaths	Tell dirs to display the actual pathname of any directory that is a symbolic link.
histchars=ab	A two-character string that sets the characters to use in history-substitution and quick-substitution (default is !^).
history=n	Number of commands to save in history list.
home=dir	Home directory of user, initialized from HOME. The ~ character is shorthand for this value.
ignoreeof	Ignore an end-of-file (*EOF*) from terminals; prevents accidental logout.
mail=(n file)	One or more files checked for new mail every five minutes or (if *n* is supplied) every *n* seconds.
nobeep	Don't ring bell for ambiguous file completion (see filec).
noclobber	Don't redirect output to an existing file; prevents accidental destruction of files.
noglob	Turn off filename expansion; useful in shell scripts.
nonomatch	Treat filename metacharacters as literal characters; e.g., vi ch* creates new file ch* instead of printing "No match."
notify	Notify user of completed jobs right away, instead of waiting for the next prompt.
path=(dirs)	List of pathnames in which to search for commands to execute. Initialized from PATH. SVR4 default is (. /usr/ucb /usr/bin). On Solaris, the default path is (/usr/bin .). However, the standard start-up scripts then change it to (/bin /usr/bin /usr/ucb /etc .).
prompt='str'	String that prompts for interactive input; default is %.
savehist=n	Number of history commands to save in ~/.history upon logout; they can be accessed at the next login.
shell=file	Pathname of the shell program currently in use; default is /bin/csh.
status=n	Exit status of last command. Built-in commands return 0 (success) or 1 (failure).
term=ID	Name of terminal type, same as TERM.
time='n %c'	If command execution takes more than *n* CPU seconds, report user time, system time, elapsed time, and CPU percentage. Supply optional %c flags to show other data.

Variable	Description
user=*name*	Login name of user, initialized from USER.
verbose	Display a command after history substitution; same as the command csh -v.

Example .cshrc File

```
# PREDEFINED VARIABLES
set path=(~ ~/bin /usr/ucb /bin /usr/bin . )
set mail=(/var/mail/tom)

if ($?prompt) then            # Settings for interactive use
  set echo
  set filec
  set noclobber ignoreeof

  set cdpath=(/usr/lib /var/spool/uucp)
# Now I can type cd macros
# instead of cd /usr/lib/macros

  set fignore=.o              # Ignore object files for filec
  set history=100 savehist=25
  set prompt='tom \!% '       # Includes history number
  set time=3

# MY VARIABLES

  set man1="/usr/man/man1"    # Lets me do    cd $man1, ls $man1
  set a="[a-z]*"              # Lets me       do vi $a
  set A="[A-Z]*"              # Or            grep string $A

# ALIASES

  alias c "clear; dirs"       # Use quotes to protect ; or |
  alias h "history | more"
  alias j jobs -l
  alias ls ls -sFC            # Redefine ls command
  alias del 'mv \!* ~/tmp_dir'# A safe alternative to rm
endif
```

Environment Variables

The C shell maintains a set of *environment variables*, which are distinct from shell variables and aren't really part of the C shell. Shell variables are meaningful only within the current shell, but environment variables are automatically exported, making them available globally. For example, C shell variables are accessible only to a particular script in which they're defined, whereas environment variables can be used by any shell scripts, mail utilities, or editors you might invoke.

Environment variables are assigned as follows:

```
setenv VAR value
```

By convention, environment variable names are all uppercase. You can create your own environment variables, or you can use the following predefined environment variables.

These environment variables have a corresponding C shell variable:

HOME

Home directory; same as home. These may be changed independently of each other.

PATH

Search path for commands; same as path. Changing either one updates the value stored in the other.

TERM

Terminal type; same as term. Changing term updates TERM, but not the other way around.

USER

Username; same as user. Changing user updates USER, but not the other way around.

Other environment variables include the following:

EXINIT

A string of ex commands similar to those found in the startup .exrc file (e.g., set ai). Used by vi and ex.

LOGNAME

Another name for the USER variable.

MAIL

The file that holds mail. Used by mail programs. This is not the same as the C shell mail variable, which only checks for new mail.

PWD

The current directory; the value is copied from cwd.

SHELL

Undefined by default; once initialized to shell, the two are identical.

Expressions

Expressions are used in @ (the C shell math operator), if, and while statements to perform arithmetic, string comparisons, file testing, etc. exit and set can also specify expressions. Expressions are formed by combining variables and constants with operators that resemble those in the C programming language. Operator precedence is the same as in C. It is easiest to just remember the following precedence rules:

- ● * / %

- ● + -

- ● Group all other expressions inside ( )s; parentheses are required if the expression contains <, <, &, or |

Operators

Operators can be one of the following types.

Assignment operators

Operator	Description
=	Assign value.
+= -=	Reassign after addition/subtraction.
*= /= %=	Reassign after multiplication/division/remainder.
&= ^= |=	Reassign after bitwise AND/XOR/OR.
++	Increment.
--	Decrement.

Arithmetic operators

Operator	Description
* / %	Multiplication; integer division; modulus (remainder).
+ -	Addition; subtraction.

Bitwise and logical operators

Operator	Description
~	Binary inversion (one's complement).
!	Logical negation.
<< >>	Bitwise left shift; bitwise right shift.
&	Bitwise AND.
^	Bitwise exclusive OR.
		Bitwise OR.
&&	Logical AND (short-circuit).
||	Logical OR (short-circuit).
{ command }	Return 1 if command is successful; 0 otherwise. Note that this is the opposite of *command*'s normal return code. The $status variable may be more practical.

C Shell

Comparison operators

Operator	Description
== !=	Equality; inequality.
<= >=	Less than or equal to; greater than or equal to.
< >	Less than; greater than.
=~	String on left matches a filename pattern containing *, ?, or [...].
!~	String on left does not match a filename pattern containing *, ?, or [...].

File inquiry operators

Command substitution and filename expansion are performed on *file* before the test is performed.

Operator	Description
-d *file*	The file is a directory.
-e *file*	The file exists.
-f *file*	The file is a plain file.
-o *file*	The user owns the file.
-r *file*	The user has read permission.
-w *file*	The user has write permission.
-x *file*	The user has execute permission.
-z *file*	The file has zero size.
!	Reverse the sense of any inquiry above.

Examples

The following examples show @ commands and assume n = 4.

Expression	Value of $x
@ x = ($n > 10 || $n < 5)	1
@ x = ($n >= 0 && $n < 3)	0
@ x = ($n << 2)	16
@ x = ($n >> 2)	1
@ x = $n % 2	0
@ x = $n % 3	1

The following examples show the first line of if or while statements.

Expression	Meaning
while ($#argv != 0)	While there are arguments ...
if ($today[1] == "Fri")	If the first word is "Fri"...
if ($file !~ *.[zZ])	If the file doesn't end with .z or .Z ...

Expression	Meaning
if ($argv[1] =~ chap?)	If the first argument is chap followed by a single character ...
if (-f $argv[1])	If the first argument is a plain file ...
if (! -d $tmpdir)	If $tmpdir is not a directory ...

Command History

Previously executed commands are stored in a history list. The C shell lets you access this list so you can verify commands, repeat them, or execute modified versions of them. The history built-in command displays the history list; the predefined variables histchars, history, and savehist also affect the history mechanism. Accessing the history list involves three things:

- Making command substitutions (using ! and ^)

- Making argument substitutions (specific words within a command)

- Using modifiers to extract or replace parts of a command or word

Command Substitution

!	Begin a history substitution
!!	Previous command
!N	Command number N in history list
!-N	Nth command back from current command
!string	Most recent command that starts with string
!?string?	Most recent command that contains string
!?string?%	Most recent command argument that contains string
!$	Last argument of previous command
!!string	Previous command, then append string
!N string	Command N, then append string
!{s1}s2	Most recent command starting with string s1, then append string s2
^old^new^	Quick substitution; change string old to new in previous command; execute modified command

Command Substitution Examples

The following command is assumed:

```
3% vi cprogs/01.c ch002 ch03
```

Event Number	Command Typed	Command Executed
4	^00^0	vi cprogs/01.c ch02 ch03
5	nroff !*	nroff cprogs/01.c ch02 ch03

Event Number	Command Typed	Command Executed
6	nroff !$	nroff ch03
7	!vi	vi cprogs/01.c ch02 ch03
8	!6	nroff ch03
9	!?01	vi cprogs/01.c ch02 ch03
10	!{nr}.new	nroff ch03.new
11	!!|lp	nroff ch03.new	lp
12	more !?pr?%	more cprogs/01.c

Word Substitution

Word specifiers allow you to retrieve individual words from previous command lines. Colons may precede any word specifier. After an event number, colons are optional unless shown here.

:0	Command name
:*n*	Argument number *n*
^	First argument
$	Last argument
:*n-m*	Arguments *n* through *m*
-*m*	Words 0 through *m*; same as :0-*m*
:*n-*	Arguments *n* through next-to-last
:*n**	Arguments *n* through last; same as *n*-$
*	All arguments; same as ^-$ or 1-$
#	Current command line up to this point; fairly useless

Word Substitution Examples

The following command is assumed:

```
13% cat ch01 ch02 ch03 biblio back
```

Event Number	Command Typed	Command Executed
14	ls !13^	ls ch01
15	sort !13:*	sort ch01 ch02 ch03 biblio back
16	lp !cat:3*	lp ch03 biblio back
17	!cat:0-3	cat ch01 ch02 ch03
18	vi !-5:4	vi biblio

History Modifiers

Command and word substitutions can be modified by one or more of these:

Printing, Substitution, and Quoting

:p	Display command but don't execute.
:s/*old*/*new*	Substitute string *new* for *old*, first instance only.
:gs/*old*/*new*	Substitute string *new* for *old*, all instances.
:&	Repeat previous substitution (:s or ^ command), first instance only.
:g&	Repeat previous substitution, all instances.
:q	Quote a word list.
:x	Quote separate words.

Truncation

:r	Extract the first available pathname root.
:gr	Extract all pathname roots.
:e	Extract the first available pathname extension.
:ge	Extract all pathname extensions.
:h	Extract the first available pathname header.
:gh	Extract all pathname headers.
:t	Extract the first available pathname tail.
:gt	Extract all pathname tails.

History Modifier Examples

From the table in the section "Word Substitution Examples," command number 17 is:

    17% cat ch01 ch02 ch03

Event #	Command Typed	Command Executed
19	!17:s/ch/CH/	cat CH01 ch02 ch03
20	!:g&	cat CH01 CH02 CH03
21	!more:p	more cprogs/01.c (displayed only)
22	cd !$:h	cd cprogs
23	vi !mo:$:t	vi 01.c
24	grep stdio !$	grep stdio 01.c
25	^stdio^include stdio^:q	grep "include stdio" 01.c
26	nroff !21:t:p	nroff 01.c (is that want I wanted?)
27	!!	nroff 01.c (execute it)

Job Control

Job control lets you place foreground jobs in the background, bring background jobs to the foreground, or suspend (temporarily stop) running jobs. The C shell provides the following commands for job control. For more information on these commands, see "Built-in C Shell Commands," later in this chapter.

bg   Put a job in the background.

fg   Put a job in the foreground.

jobs
> List active jobs.

kill
> Terminate a job.

notify
> Notify when a background job finishes.

stop
> Suspend a background job.

CTRL-Z
> Suspend a foreground job.

Many job-control commands take a *jobID* as an argument. This argument can be specified as follows:

%*n*   Job number *n*

%*s*   Job whose command line starts with string *s*

%?*s*   Job whose command line contains string *s*

%%   Current job

%   Current job (same as above)

%+   Current job (same as above)

%-   Previous job

Invoking the Shell

The C shell command interpreter can be invoked as follows:

> csh [*options*] [*arguments*]

csh executes commands from a terminal or a file. Options -n, -v, and -x are useful when debugging scripts.

The following list details the options:

-b   Allow the remaining command-line options to be interpreted as options to a specified command, rather than as options to csh itself.

-c   Treat the first *argument* as a string of commands to execute. Remaining arguments are available via the argv array.

-e   Exit if a command produces errors.

-f Fast startup; start csh without executing .cshrc or .login.

-i Invoke interactive shell (prompt for input).

-n Parse commands but do not execute.

-s Read commands from the standard input.

-t Exit after executing one command.

-v Display commands before executing them; expand history substitutions but don't expand other substitutions (e.g., filename, variable, and command). Same as setting verbose.

-V Same as -v, but also display .cshrc.

-x Display commands before executing them, but expand all substitutions. Same as setting echo. -x is often combined with -v.

-X Same as -x, but also display .cshrc.

Built-in C Shell Commands

#	#
Ignore all text that follows on the same line. # is used in shell scripts as the comment character and is not really a command. In addition, a file that has # as its first character is sometimes interpreted by older systems as a C shell script.	

#!shell [option]	#!
Used as the first line of a script to invoke the named *shell*. Anything given on the rest of the line is passed *as a single argument* to the named *shell*. This feature is typically implemented by the kernel, but may not be supported on some older systems. Some systems have a limit of around 32 characters on the maximum length of *shell*. For example: `#!/bin/csh -f`	

:	:
Null (do-nothing) command. Returns an exit status of 0.	

alias [name [command]]	**alias**
Assign *name* as the shorthand name, or alias, for *command*. If *command* is omitted, print the alias for *name*; if *name* is also omitted,	

→

alias
←

print all aliases. Aliases can be defined on the command line, but they are more often stored in .cshrc so that they take effect after login. (See the section "Example .cshrc File" earlier in this chapter.) Alias definitions can reference command-line arguments, much like the history list. Use \!* to refer to all command-line arguments, \!^ for the first argument, \!$ for the last, etc. An alias *name* can be any valid Unix command; however, you lose the original command's meaning unless you type *name*. See also **unalias**.

Examples

Set the size for xterm windows under the X Window System:

```
alias R 'set noglob; eval `resize`; unset noglob'
```

Show aliases that contain the string *ls*:

```
alias | grep ls
```

Run nroff on all command-line arguments:

```
alias ms 'nroff -ms \!*'
```

Copy the file that is named as the first argument:

```
alias back 'cp \!^ \!^.old'
```

Use the regular ls, not its alias:

```
% \ls
```

---

bg

bg [*jobIDs*]

Put the current job or the *jobIDs* in the background. See the earlier section "Job Control."

Example

To place a time-consuming process in the background, you might begin with:

```
4% nroff -ms report | col > report.txt
CTRL-Z
```

and then issue any one of the following:

```
5% bg
5% bg %            Current job
5% bg %1           Job number 1
5% bg %nr          Match initial string nroff
5% % &
```

`break`	**break**
Resume execution following the `end` command of the nearest enclosing `while` or `foreach`.	

`breaksw`	**breaksw**
Break from a `switch`; continue execution after the `endsw`.	

`case pattern :`	**case**
Identify a *pattern* in a `switch`.	

`cd [dir]`	**cd**
Change working directory to *dir*; default is home directory of user. If *dir* is a relative pathname but is not in the current directory, the `cdpath` variable is searched. See the section "Example .cshrc File" earlier in this chapter.	

`chdir [dir]`	**chdir**
Same as `cd`. Useful if you are redefining `cd` as an alias.	

`continue`	**continue**
Resume execution of nearest enclosing `while` or `foreach`.	

`default:`	**default**
Label the default case (typically last) in a `switch`.	

`dirs [-l]`	**dirs**
Print the directory stack, showing the current directory first; use `-l` to expand the home directory symbol (`~`) to the actual directory name. See also **popd** and **pushd**.	

`echo [-n] string`	**echo**
Write *string* to standard output; if `-n` is specified, the output is not terminated by a newline. Unlike the Unix version (`/bin/echo`) and the Bourne shell version, the C shell's `echo` doesn't support escape char-	

$\rightarrow$

C Shell

echo ←	acters. See also **echo** in Chapter 2 and Chapter 4, *The Bourne Shell and Korn Shell.*
end	`end` Reserved word that ends a `foreach` or `while` statement.
endif	`endif` Reserved word that ends an `if` statement.
endsw	`endsw` Reserved word that ends a `switch` statement.

eval	`eval args`
	
	Typically, `eval` is used in shell scripts, and *args* is a line of code that contains shell variables. `eval` forces variable expansion to happen first and then runs the resulting command. This "double-scanning" is useful any time shell variables contain input/output redirection symbols, aliases, or other shell variables. (For example, redirection normally happens before variable expansion, so a variable containing redirection symbols must be expanded first using `eval`; otherwise, the redirection symbols remain uninterpreted.) A Bourne shell example can be found under **eval** in Chapter 4. Other uses of `eval` are shown next.
	
	Examples
	
	The following lines can be placed in the `.login` file to set up terminal characteristics:
	
	`set noglob`
	`eval 'tset -s xterm'`
	`unset noglob`
	
	The following commands show the effect of `eval`:
	
	`% set b='$a'`
	`% set a=hello`
	
	`% echo $b` *Read the command line once*
	`$a`
	`% eval echo $b` *Read the command line twice*
	`hello`

```
exec command
```

Execute *command* in place of current shell. This terminates the current shell, rather than creating a new process under it.

```
exit [(expr)]
```

Exit a shell script with the status given by *expr*. A status of 0 means success; nonzero means failure. If *expr* is not specified, the exit value is that of the status variable. exit can be issued at the command line to close a window (log out).

```
fg [jobIDs]
```

Bring the current job or the *jobIDs* to the foreground. See also the section "Job Control" earlier in this chapter.

Example

If you suspend a vi editing session (by pressing CTRL-Z), you might resume vi using any of these commands:

```
8% %
8% fg
8% fg %
8% fg %vi     Match initial string
```

```
foreach name (wordlist)
    commands
end
```

Assign variable *name* to each value in *wordlist*, and execute *commands* between foreach and end. You can use foreach as a multiline command issued at the C shell prompt (first Example), or you can use it in a shell script (second Example).

Examples

Rename all files that begin with a capital letter:

```
% foreach i ([A-Z]*)
? mv $i $i.new
? end
```

Check whether each command-line argument is an option or not:

```
foreach arg ($argv)
    # does it begin with - ?
    if ("$arg" =~ -*) then
        echo "Argument is an option"
    else
```

$\rightarrow$

foreach
←
	``
	        echo "Argument is a filename"
	    endif
	end
	``

glob	glob *wordlist* Do filename, variable, and history substitutions on *wordlist*. This expands it much like echo, except that no \ escapes are recognized, and words are delimited by null characters. glob is typically used in shell scripts to "hardcode" a value so that it remains the same for the rest of the script.
goto	goto *string* Skip to a line whose first nonblank character is *string* followed by a :, and continue execution below that line. On the goto line, *string* can be a variable or filename pattern, but the label branched to must be a literal, expanded value and must not occur within a foreach or while.
hashstat	hashstat Display statistics that show the hash table's level of success at locating commands via the path variable.
history	history [*options*] Display the list of history events. (History syntax is discussed earlier in the section "Command History.") Note: multiline compound commands such as foreach ... end are *not* saved in the history list. **Options** -h Print history list without event numbers. -r Print in reverse order; show oldest commands last. *n* Display only the last *n* history commands, instead of the number set by the history shell variable. *Example* To save and execute the last five commands: ``` history -h 5 > do_it source do_it ```

```
if                                                                          if
```

Begin a conditional statement. The simple format is:

```
if (expr) cmd
```

There are three other possible formats, shown side-by-side:

```
if (expr) then    if (expr) then    if (expr) then
    cmds              cmds1             cmds1
endif             else              else if (expr) then
                      cmds2             cmds2
                  endif             else
                                        cmds3
                                    endif
```

In the simplest form, execute *cmd* if *expr* is true; otherwise, do nothing (redirection still occurs; this is a bug). In the other forms, execute one or more commands. If *expr* is true, continue with the commands after then; if *expr* is false, branch to the commands after else (or after the else if and continue checking). For more examples, see the earlier section "Expressions," or **shift** or **while**.

Example

Take a default action if no command-line arguments are given:

```
if ($#argv == 0) then
    echo "No filename given.  Sending to Report."
    set outfile = Report
else
    set outfile = $argv[1]
endif
```

```
jobs [-l]                                                                 jobs
```

List all running or stopped jobs; -l includes process IDs. For example, you can check whether a long compilation or text format is still running. Also useful before logging out.

```
kill [options] ID                                                         kill
```

Terminate each specified process *ID* or job *ID*. You must own the process or be a privileged user. This built-in is similar to /usr/bin/ kill described in Chapter 2 but also allows symbolic job names. Stubborn processes can be killed using signal 9. See also the earlier section "Job Control."

→

kill

←

Options

-l   List the signal names. (Used by itself.)

-*signal*

The signal number (from /usr/include/sys/signal.h) or name
(from kill -1). With a signal number of 9, the kill is absolute.

Signals

Signals are defined in /usr/include/sys/signal.h and are listed here
without the SIG prefix. You probably have more signals on your system than the ones shown here.

```
HUP    1     hangup
INT    2     interrupt
QUIT   3     quit
ILL    4     illegal instruction
TRAP   5     trace trap
IOT    6     IOT instruction
EMT    7     EMT instruction
FPE    8     floating point exception
KILL   9     kill
BUS    10    bus error
SEGV   11    segmentation violation
SYS    12    bad argument to system call
PIPE   13    write to pipe, but no process to read it
ALRM   14    alarm clock
TERM   15    software termination (the default signal)
USR1   16    user-defined signal 1
USR2   17    user-defined signal 2
CLD    18    child process died
PWR    19    restart after power failure
```

Examples

If you've issued the following command:

```
44% nroff -ms report > report.txt &
[1] 19536                    csh prints job and process IDs
```

you can terminate it in any of the following ways:

```
45% kill 19536              Process ID
45% kill %                  Current job
45% kill %1                 Job number 1
45% kill %nr                Initial string
45% kill %?report           Matching string
```

limit

limit [-h] [*resource* [*limit*]]

Display limits or set a *limit* on resources used by the current process
and by each process it creates. If no *limit* is given, the current limit is
printed for *resource*. If *resource* is also omitted, all limits are printed.
By default, the current limits are shown or set; with -h, hard limits

are used. A hard limit imposes an absolute limit that can't be exceeded. Only a privileged user may raise it. See also **unlimit**.

Resource

cputime

> Maximum number of seconds the CPU can spend; can be abbreviated as cpu

filesize

> Maximum size of any one file

datasize

> Maximum size of data (including stack)

stacksize

> Maximum size of stack

coredumpsize

> Maximum size of a core dump file

Limit

A number followed by an optional character (a unit specifier).

For cputime:	nh (for n hours),
	nm (for n minutes),
	mm:ss (minutes and seconds).
For others:	nk (for n kilobytes, the default),
	nm (for n megabytes).

---

login [*user* | -p]

Replace *user*'s login shell with /bin/login. -p preserves environment variables.

---

logout

Terminate the login shell.

---

nice [±n] *command*

Change the execution priority for *command*, or, if none is given, change priority for the current shell. (See also **nice** in Chapter 2.) The priority range is −20 to 20, with a default of 4. The range is backwards from what you might expect: −20 gives the highest priority (fastest execution); 20 gives the lowest.

C Shell

→

nice ←	+*n* Add *n* to the priority value (lower job priority). -*n* Subtract *n* from the priority value (raise job priority). Privileged users only.
nohup	nohup [*command*] "No hangup signals." Do not terminate *command* after terminal line is closed (i.e., when you hang up from a phone or log out). Use without *command* in shell scripts to keep script from being terminated. (See also **nohup** in Chapter 2.)
notify	notify [*jobID*] Report immediately when a background job finishes (instead of waiting for you to exit a long editing session, for example). If no *jobID* is given, the current background job is assumed.

onintr	onintr *label*
	onintr -
	onintr
	
	"On interrupt." Used in shell scripts to handle interrupt signals (similar to the Bourne shell's trap 2 and trap "" 2 commands). The first form is like a goto *label*. The script branches to *label*: if it catches an interrupt signal (e.g., CTRL-C). The second form lets the script ignore interrupts. This is useful at the beginning of a script or before any code segment that needs to run unhindered (e.g., when moving files). The third form restores interrupt handling that was previously disabled with onintr -.
	
	Example
	
	    onintr cleanup *Go to "cleanup" on interrupt*
	      .
	      . *Shell script commands*
	      .
	    cleanup: *Label for interrupts*
	      onintr - *Ignore additional interrupts*
	      rm -f $tmpfiles *Remove any files created*
	      exit 2 *Exit with an error status*

popd	popd [+*n*] Remove the current entry from the directory stack or remove the *n*th entry from the stack. The current entry has number 0 and appears on the left. See also **dirs** and **pushd**.

pushd *name*
pushd +*n*
pushd

The first form changes the working directory to *name* and adds it to the directory stack. The second form rotates the *n*th entry to the beginning, making it the working directory. (Entry numbers begin at 0.) With no arguments, pushd switches the first two entries and changes to the new current directory. See also **dirs** and **popd**.

Examples

```
5% dirs
/home/bob /usr
6% pushd /etc          Add /etc to directory stack
/etc /home/bob /usr
7% pushd +2            Switch to third directory
/usr /etc /home/bob
8% pushd               Switch top two directories
/etc /usr /home/bob
9% popd                Discard current entry; go to next
/usr /home/bob
```

rehash

Recompute the hash table for the path variable. Use rehash whenever a new command is created during the current session. This allows the shell to locate and execute the command. (If the new command resides in a directory not listed in path, add this directory to path before rehashing.) See also **unhash**.

repeat *n* *command*

Execute *n* instances of *command*.

Examples

Generate a test file for a program by saving 25 copies of /usr/dict/words in a file:

```
% repeat 25 cat /usr/dict/words > test_file
```

Read 10 lines from the terminal and store in item_list:

```
% repeat 10 line > item_list
```

Append 50 boilerplate files to report:

```
% repeat 50 cat template >> report
```

C Shell

set	`set variable = value`
	`set variable[n] = value`
	`set`

Set *variable* to *value*, or, if multiple values are specified, set the variable to the list of words in the value list. If an index *n* is specified, set the *n*th word in the variable to *value*. (The variable must already contain at least that number of words.) With no arguments, display the names and values of all set variables. See also the section "Predefined Shell Variables" earlier in this chapter.

Examples

```
% set list=(yes no maybe)        Assign a word list
% set list[3]=maybe              Assign an item in existing word list
% set quote="Make my day"        Assign a variable
% set x=5 y=10 history=100       Assign several variables
% set blank                      Assign a null value to blank
```

setenv	`setenv [name [value]]`

Assign a *value* to an environment variable *name*. By convention, *name* should be uppercase. *value* can be a single word or a quoted string. If no *value* is given, the null value is assigned. With no arguments, display the names and values of all environment variables. setenv is not necessary for the USER, TERM, and PATH variables because they are automatically exported from user, term, and path. See also the earlier section "Environment Variables."

shift	`shift [variable]`

If *variable* is given, shift the words in a word list variable; i.e., *name*[2] becomes *name*[1]. With no argument, shift the positional parameters (command-line arguments); i.e., $2 becomes $1. shift is typically used in a while loop. See additional Example under **while**.

Example

```
while ($#argv)          While there are arguments
    if (-f $argv[1])
        wc -l $argv[1]
    else
        echo "$argv[1] is not a regular file"
    endif
    shift               Get the next argument
end
```

source [-h] *script*

Read and execute commands from a C shell script. With -h, the commands are added to the history list but aren't executed.

Example

```
source ~/.cshrc
```

stop [*jobIDs*]

Suspend the current background job or the background job specified by *jobIDs*; this is the complement of CTRL-Z or suspend.

suspend

Suspend the current foreground job; similar to CTRL-Z. Often used to stop an su command.

switch

Process commands depending on the value of a variable. When you need to handle more than three choices, switch is a useful alternative to an if-then-else statement. If the *string* variable matches *pattern1*, the first set of *commands* is executed; if *string* matches *pattern2*, the second set of *commands* is executed; and so on. If no patterns match, execute commands under the default case. *string* can be specified using command substitution, variable substitution, or file-name expansion. Patterns can be specified using pattern-matching symbols *, ?, and [ ]. breaksw exits the switch after *commands* are executed. If breaksw is omitted (which is rarely done), the switch continues to execute another set of commands until it reaches a breaksw or endsw. Here is the general syntax of switch, side-by-side with an example that processes the first command-line argument.

```
switch (string)          switch ($argv[1])
   case pattern1:            case -[nN]:
       commands                 nroff $file | lp
       breaksw                  breaksw
   case pattern2:            case -[Pp]:
       commands                 pr $file | lp
       breaksw                  breaksw
   case pattern3:            case -[Mm]:
       commands                 more $file
       breaksw                  breaksw
         .                    case -[Ss]:
         .                       sort $file
         .                       breaksw
   default:                  default:
       commands                 echo "Error-no such option"
```

C Shell

switch ←	exit 1
	\`breaksw` breaksw
	endsw endsw

time	`time [command]`
	Execute a *command* and show how much time it uses. With no argument, `time` can be used in a shell script to time it.

umask	`umask [nnn]`
	Display file-creation mask or set file creation mask to octal *nnn*. The file-creation mask determines which permission bits are turned off. See the entry in Chapter 2 for examples.

unalias	`unalias name`
	Remove *name* from the alias list. See **alias** for more information.

unhash	`unhash`
	Remove internal hash table. The C shell stops using hashed values and spends time searching the `path` directories to locate a command. See also **rehash**.

unlimit	`unlimit [resource]`
	Remove the allocation limits on *resource*. If *resource* is not specified, remove limits for all resources. See **limit** for more information.

unset	`unset variables`
	Remove one or more *variables*. Variable names may be specified as a pattern, using filename metacharacters. See **set**.

unsetenv	`unsetenv variable`
	Remove an environment variable. Filename matching is *not* valid. See **setenv**.

Pause in execution until all background jobs complete, or until an interrupt signal is received.

```
while (expression)
    commands
end
```

As long as *expression* is true (evaluates to nonzero), evaluate *commands* between while and end. break and continue can terminate or continue the loop. See also the Example under **shift**.

Example

```
set user = (alice bob carol ted)
while ($argv[1] != $user[1])
    Cycle through each user, checking for a match
  shift user
    If we cycled through with no match...
  if ($#user == 0) then
     echo "$argv[1] is not on the list of users"
     exit 1
  endif
end
```

```
@ variable = expression
@ variable[n] = expression
@
```

Assign the value of the arithmetic *expression* to *variable*, or to the *n*th element of *variable* if the index *n* is specified. With no *variable* or *expression* specified, print the values of all shell variables (same as set). Expression operators as well as examples are listed in the earlier section "Expressions." Two special forms are also valid:

```
@ variable++
```
    Increment *variable* by one.

```
@ variable--
```
    Decrement *variable* by one.

C Shell

PART II

Text Editing and Processing

Part II summarizes the command set for the text editors and related utilities in Unix. Chapter 6 reviews pattern matching, an important aspect of text editing.

CHAPTER 6

Pattern Matching

A number of Unix text-processing utilities let you search for, and in some cases change, text patterns rather than fixed strings. These utilities include the editing programs ed, ex, vi, and sed, the awk programming language, and the commands grep and egrep. Text patterns (formally called regular expressions) contain normal characters mixed with special characters (called metacharacters).

This chapter presents the following topics:

- Filenames versus patterns

- List of metacharacters available to each program

- Description of metacharacters

- Examples

For more information on regular expressions, see *Mastering Regular Expressions*, listed in the Bibliography.

Filenames Versus Patterns

Metacharacters used in pattern matching are different from metacharacters used for filename expansion (see Chapter 4, *The Bourne Shell and Korn Shell*, and Chapter 5, *The C Shell*). When you issue a command on the command line, special characters are seen first by the shell, then by the program; therefore, unquoted metacharacters are interpreted by the shell for filename expansion. The command:

```
$ grep [A-Z]* chap[12]
```

could, for example, be transformed by the shell into:

```
$ grep Array.c Bug.c Comp.c chap1 chap2
```

and would then try to find the pattern `Array.c` in files `Bug.c`, `Comp.c`, `chap1`, and `chap2`. To bypass the shell and pass the special characters to `grep`, use quotes:

```
$ grep "[A-Z]*" chap[12]
```

Double quotes suffice in most cases, but single quotes are the safest bet.

Note also that in pattern matching, ? matches zero or one instance of a regular expression; in filename expansion, ? matches a single character.

Metacharacters, Listed by Unix Program

Some metacharacters are valid for one program but not for another. Those that are available to a Unix program are marked by a bullet (•) in Table 6-1. Items marked with a "P" are specified by POSIX; double-check your system's version. (On Solaris, the versions in `/usr/xpg4/bin` accept these items.) Full descriptions are provided after the table.

Table 6–1: Unix Metacharacters

Symbol	ed	ex	vi	sed	awk	grep	egrep	Action
.	•	•	•	•	•	•	•	Match any character.
*	•	•	•	•	•	•	•	Match zero or more preceding.
^	•	•	•	•	•	•	•	Match beginning of line/string.
$	•	•	•	•	•	•	•	Match end of line/string.
\	•	•	•	•	•	•	•	Escape following character.
[ ]	•	•	•	•	•	•	•	Match one from a set.
\(\)	•	•	•	•		•		Store pattern for later replay.[a]
\n	•	•	•	•		•		Replay subpattern in match.
{ }					• P		• P	Match a range of instances.
\{ \}	•			•		•		Match a range of instances.
\< \>	•	•	•					Match word's beginning or end.
+					•		•	Match one or more preceding.
?					•		•	Match zero or one preceding.

Table 6–1: Unix Metacharacters (continued)

Symbol	ed	ex	vi	sed	awk	grep	egrep	Action
|					•		•	Separate choices to match.
( )					•		•	Group expressions to match.

a Stored subpatterns can be "replayed" during matching. See Table 6-2.

Note that in ed, ex, vi, and sed, you specify both a search pattern (on the left) and a replacement pattern (on the right). The metacharacters in Table 6-1 are meaningful only in a search pattern.

In ed, ex, vi, and sed, the metacharacters in Table 6-2 are valid only in a replacement pattern.

Table 6-2: Metacharacters in Replacement Patterns

Symbol	ex	vi	sed	ed	Action
\	•	•	•	•	Escape following character.
\n	•	•	•	•	Text matching pattern stored in \(\).
&	•	•	•	•	Text matching search pattern.
~		•	•		Reuse previous replacement pattern.
%				•	Reuse previous replacement pattern.
\u \U	•	•			Change character(s) to uppercase.
\l \L	•	•			Change character(s) to lowercase.
\E	•	•			Turn off previous \U or \L.
\e	•	•			Turn off previous \u or \l.

Metacharacters

Search Patterns

The characters in the following table have special meaning only in search patterns.

Character	Pattern
.	Match any *single* character except newline. Can match newline in awk.
*	Match any number (or none) of the single character that immediately precedes it. The preceding character can also be a regular expression; e.g., since . (dot) means any character, .* means "match any number of any character."
^	Match the following regular expression at the beginning of the line or string.

Character	Pattern
$	Match the preceding regular expression at the end of the line or string.
[ ]	Match any *one* of the enclosed characters.
	A hyphen (–) indicates a range of consecutive characters. A circumflex (^) as the first character in the brackets reverses the sense: it matches any one character *not* in the list. A hyphen or close bracket (]) as the first character is treated as a member of the list. All other metacharacters are treated as members of the list (i.e., literally).
{n,m}	Match a range of occurrences of the single character that immediately precedes it. The preceding character can also be a metacharacter. {n} matches exactly *n* occurrences, {n,} matches at least *n* occurrences, and {n,m} matches any number of occurrences between *n* and *m*. *n* and *m* must be between 0 and 255, inclusive.
\{n,m\}	Just like {n,m}, above, but with backslashes in front of the braces.
\	Turn off the special meaning of the character that follows.
\(\)	Save the pattern enclosed between \(and \) into a special holding space. Up to nine patterns can be saved on a single line. The text matched by the subpatterns can be "replayed" in substitutions by the escape sequences \1 to \9.
\n	Replay the *n*th subpattern enclosed in \(and \) into the pattern at this point. *n* is a number from 1 to 9, with 1 starting on the left. See the following Examples.
\< \>	Match characters at beginning (\<) or end (\>) of a word.
+	Match one or more instances of preceding regular expression.
?	Match zero or one instances of preceding regular expression.
|	Match the regular expression specified before or after.
( )	Apply a match to the enclosed group of regular expressions.

Many Unix systems allow the use of POSIX "character classes" within the square brackets that enclose a group of characters. These classes, listed here, are typed enclosed in [: and :]. For example, [[:alnum:]] matches a single alphanumeric character.

Class	Characters Matched
alnum	Alphanumeric characters
alpha	Alphabetic characters
blank	Space or tab
cntrl	Control characters
digit	Decimal digits
graph	Nonspace characters
lower	Lowercase characters
print	Printable characters
space	Whitespace characters
upper	Uppercase characters
xdigit	Hexadecimal digits

Replacement Patterns

The characters in this table have special meaning only in replacement patterns.

Character	Pattern
\	Turn off the special meaning of the character that follows.
\n	Restore the text matched by the *n*th pattern previously saved by \(and \). *n* is a number from 1 to 9, with 1 starting on the left.
&	Reuse the text matched by the search pattern as part of the replacement pattern.
~	Reuse the previous replacement pattern in the current replacement pattern. Must be the only character in the replacement pattern. (ex and vi)
%	Reuse the previous replacement pattern in the current replacement pattern. Must be the only character in the replacement pattern. (ed)
\u	Convert first character of replacement pattern to uppercase.
\U	Convert entire replacement pattern to uppercase.
\l	Convert first character of replacement pattern to lowercase.
\L	Convert entire replacement pattern to lowercase.
\e, \E	Turn off previous \u, \U, \l, and \L.

Examples of Searching

When used with grep or egrep, regular expressions should be surrounded by quotes. (If the pattern contains a $, you must use single quotes; e.g., *'pattern'*.) When used with ed, ex, sed, and awk, regular expressions are usually surrounded by /, although (except for awk) any delimiter works. The following tables shows some example patterns.

Pattern	What Does It Match?
bag	The string *bag*.
^bag	*bag* at the beginning of the line.
bag$	*bag* at the end of the line.
^bag$	*bag* as the only word on the line.
[Bb]ag	*Bag* or *bag*.
b[aeiou]g	Second letter is a vowel.
b[^aeiou]g	Second letter is a consonant (or uppercase or symbol).
b.g	Second letter is any character.
^...$	Any line containing exactly three characters.
^\.	Any line that begins with a dot.
^\.[a-z][a-z]	Same, followed by two lowercase letters (e.g., troff requests).
^\.[a-z]\{2\}	Same as previous; ed, grep, and sed only.
^[^.]	Any line that doesn't begin with a dot.
bugs*	*bug*, *bugs*, *bugss*, etc.
"word"	A word in quotes.
"*word"*	A word, with or without quotes.

Pattern	What Does It Match?
[A-Z][A-Z]*	One or more uppercase letters.
[A-Z]+	Same; egrep or awk only.
[[:upper:]]+	Same; POSIX egrep or awk.
[A-Z].*	An uppercase letter, followed by zero or more characters.
[A-Z]*	Zero or more uppercase letters.
[a-zA-Z]	Any letter.
[^0-9A-Za-z]	Any symbol or space (not a letter or a number).
[^[:alnum:]]	Same, using POSIX character class.

egrep or awk Pattern	What Does It Match?
[567]	One of the numbers 5, 6, or 7.
five|six|seven	One of the words *five*, *six*, or *seven*.
80[2-4]?86	*8086, 80286, 80386,* or *80486.*
80[2-4]?86|(Pentium(-II)?)	*8086, 80286, 80386, 80486, Pentium,* or *Pentium-II.*
compan(y|ies)	*company* or *companies.*

ex or vi Pattern	What Does It Match?
\\<the	Words like *theater* or *the.*
the\\>	Words like *breathe* or *the.*
\\<the\\>	The word *the.*

ed, sed or grep Pattern	What Does It Match?
0\\{5,\\}	Five or more zeros in a row.
[0-9]\\{3\\}-[0-9]\\{2\\}-[0-9]\\{4\\}	U.S. Social Security number (*nnn-nn-nnnn*).
\\(why\\).*\\1	A line with two occurrences of *why.*
\\([[:alpha:]_][[:alnum:]_.]*\\) = \\1;	C/C++ simple assignment statements.

Examples of Searching and Replacing

The examples in Table 6-3 show the metacharacters available to sed or ex. Note that ex commands begin with a colon. A space is marked by a □; a tab is marked by a ➡.

Table 6-3: Searching and Replacing

Command	Result
s/.*/(&)/	Redo the entire line, but add parentheses.
s/.*/mv & &.old/	Change a wordlist (one word per line) into mv commands.
/^$/d	Delete blank lines.

Table 6–3: Searching and Replacing (continued)

Command	Result
`:g/^$/d`	Same as previous, in ex editor.
`/^[□➞]*$/d`	Delete blank lines, plus lines containing only spaces or tabs.
`:g/^[□➞]*$/d`	Same as previous, in ex editor.
`s/□□*/□/g`	Turn one or more spaces into one space.
`:%s/□□*/□/g`	Same as previous, in ex editor.
`:s/[0-9]/Item &:/`	Turn a number into an item label (on the current line).
`:s`	Repeat the substitution on the first occurrence.
`:&`	Same as previous.
`:sg`	Same, but for all occurrences on the line.
`:&g`	Same as previous.
`:%&g`	Repeat the substitution globally (i.e., on all lines).
`:.,$s/Fortran/\U&/g`	On current line to last line, change word to uppercase.
`:%s/.*/\L&/`	Lowercase entire file.
`:s/\<./\u&/g`	Uppercase first letter of each word on current line. (Useful for titles.)
`:%s/yes/No/g`	Globally change a word to *No*.
`:%s/Yes/~/g`	Globally change a different word to *No* (previous replacement).

Finally, some sed examples for transposing words. A simple transposition of two words might look like this:

```
s/die or do/do or die/                    Transpose words
```

The real trick is to use hold buffers to transpose variable patterns. For example:

```
s/\([Dd]ie\) or \([Dd]o\)/\2 or \1/    Transpose, using hold buffers
```

CHAPTER 7

The Emacs Editor

This chapter presents the following topics:

- Introduction
- Summary of emacs commands by group
- Summary of emacs commands by key
- Summary of emacs commands by name

For more information about emacs, see *Learning GNU Emacs*, listed in the Bibliography.

Introduction

Although emacs is not part of SVR4 or Solaris,* this text editor is found on many Unix systems because it is a popular alternative to vi. This book documents GNU emacs (Version 20.3), which is available from the Free Software Foundation (*http://www.gnu.org*).

To start an emacs editing session, type:

    emacs [file]

On some systems, GNU emacs is invoked by typing gmacs instead of emacs.

---

* The Sun Workshop programming environment, available separately from Sun, does come with Xemacs, a derivative of GNU emacs.

Notes on the Tables

emacs commands use the Control key and the Meta key (Meta is usually the Escape key). In this chapter, the notation C- indicates that the Control key is pressed at the same time as the character that follows. Similarly, M- indicates the use of the Meta key. When Meta is simulated by the Escape key, it's not necessary to keep the Meta key pressed down while typing the next key. But if your keyboard actually has a Meta key, then it is just like Control or Shift, and you should press it simultaneously with the other key(s).

In the command tables that follow, the first column lists the keystroke and the last column describes it. When there is a middle column, it lists the command name. This name is accessed by typing M-x followed by the command name. If you're unsure of the name, you can type a space or a carriage return, and emacs lists possible completions of what you've typed so far.

Because emacs is such a comprehensive editor, containing literally thousands of commands, some commands must be omitted for the sake of preserving a "quick" reference. You can browse the command set by typing C-h (for help) or M-x (for command names).

Absolutely Essential Commands

If you're just getting started with emacs, here's a short list of the most important commands:

Keystrokes	Description
C-h	Enter the online help system.
C-x C-s	Save the file.
C-x C-c	Exit emacs.
C-x u	Undo last edit (can be repeated).
C-g	Get out of current command operation.
C-p C-n C-f C-b	Up/down/forward/back by line or character.
C-v M-v	Forward/backward by one screen.

Emacs

Keystrokes	Description
C-s C-r	Search forward/backward for characters.
C-d Del	Delete next/previous character.

Typical Problems

A very common problem is that the Del or Backspace key on the terminal does not delete the character before the cursor, as it should. Instead, it invokes a help prompt. This problem is caused by an incompatible terminal. A fairly robust fix is to create a file named .emacs in your home directory (or edit one that's already there) and add the following lines:

```
(keyboard-translate ?\C-h ?\C-?)
(keyboard-translate ?\C-\\ ?\C-h)
```

Now the Del or Backspace key should work, and you can invoke help by pressing C-\ (an arbitrarily chosen key sequence).

Another problem that could happen when you are logged in from a remote terminal is that C-s may cause the terminal to hang. This is caused by an old-fashioned handshake protocol between the terminal and the system. You can restart the terminal by pressing C-q, but that doesn't help you enter commands that contain the sequence C-s. The only solution (aside from using a more modern dial-in protocol) is to create new key bindings that replace C-s.

Summary of Commands by Group

Reminder: C- indicates the Control key; M- indicates the Meta key.

File-Handling Commands

Keystrokes	Command Name	Description
C-x C-f	find-file	Find file and read it.
C-x C-v	find-alternate-file	Read another file; replace the one read with C-x C-f.
C-x i	insert-file	Insert file at cursor position.
C-x C-s	save-buffer	Save file (may hang terminal; use C-q to restart).
C-x C-w	write-file	Write buffer contents to file.
C-x C-c	save-buffers-kill-emacs	Exit emacs.
C-z	suspend-emacs	Suspend emacs (use exit or fg to restart).

Cursor-Movement Commands

Keystrokes	Command Name	Description
C-f	forward-char	Move *forward* one character (right).
C-b	backward-char	Move *backward* one character (left).
C-p	previous-line	Move to *previous* line (up).
C-n	next-line	Move to *next* line (down).
M-f	forward-word	Move one word *forward*.
M-b	backward-word	Move one word *backward*.
C-a	beginning-of-line	Move to beginning of line.
C-e	end-of-line	Move to *end* of line.
M-a	backward-sentence	Move backward one sentence.
M-e	forward-sentence	Move forward one sentence.
M-{	backward-paragraph	Move backward one paragraph.
M-}	forward-paragraph	Move forward one paragraph.
C-v	scroll-up	Move forward one screen.
M-v	scroll-down	Move backward one screen.
C-x [	backward-page	Move backward one page.
C-x]	forward-page	Move forward one page.
M->	end-of-buffer	Move to end of file.
M-<	beginning-of-buffer	Move to beginning of file.
(none)	goto-line	Go to line *n* of file.
(none)	goto-char	Go to character *n* of file.
C-l	recenter	Redraw screen with current line in the center.
M-*n*	digit-argument	Repeat the next command *n* times.
C-u *n*	universal-argument	Repeat the next command *n* times.

Deletion Commands

Keystrokes	Command Name	Description
Del	backward-delete-char	Delete previous character.
C-d	delete-char	Delete character under cursor.
M-Del	backward-kill-word	Delete previous word.
M-d	kill-word	Delete the word the cursor is on.
C-k	kill-line	Delete from cursor to end of line.
M-k	kill-sentence	Delete sentence the cursor is on.
C-x Del	backward-kill-sentence	Delete previous sentence.
C-y	yank	Restore what you've deleted.
C-w	kill-region	Delete a marked region (see next section).

Keystrokes	Command Name	Description
(none)	backward-kill-para-graph	Delete previous paragraph.
(none)	kill-paragraph	Delete from the cursor to the end of the paragraph.

Paragraphs and Regions

Keystrokes	Command Name	Description
C-@	set-mark-command	Mark the beginning (or end) of a region.
C-Space	(same as above)	
C-x C-p	mark-page	Mark page.
C-x C-x	exchange-point-and-mark	Exchange location of cursor and mark.
C-x h	mark-whole-buffer	Mark buffer.
M-q	fill-paragraph	Reformat paragraph.
(none)	fill-region	Reformat individual paragraphs within a region.
M-h	mark-paragraph	Mark paragraph.

Stopping and Undoing Commands

Keystrokes	Command Name	Description
C-g	keyboard-quit	Abort current command.
C-x u	advertised-undo	Undo last edit (can be done repeatedly).
(none)	revert-buffer	Restore buffer to the state it was in when the file was last saved (or auto-saved).

Transposition Commands

Keystrokes	Command Name	Description
C-t	transpose-chars	Transpose two letters.
M-t	transpose-words	Transpose two words.
C-x C-t	transpose-lines	Transpose two lines.
(none)	transpose-sentences	Transpose two sentences.
(none)	transpose-paragraphs	Transpose two paragraphs.

Capitalization Commands

Keystrokes	Command Name	Description
M-c	capitalize-word	Capitalize first letter of word.
M-u	upcase-word	Uppercase word.
M-l	downcase-word	Lowercase word.
M--; M-c	negative-argument; capitalize-word	Capitalize previous word.
M-- M-u	negative-argument; upcase-word	Uppercase previous word.
M-- M-l	negative-argument; downcase-word	Lowercase previous word.
(none)	capitalize-region	Capitalize region.
C-x C-u	upcase-region	Uppercase region
C-x C-l	downcase-region	Lowercase region.

Word-Abbreviation Commands

Keystrokes	Command Name	Description
(none)	abbrev-mode	Enter (or exit) word abbreviation mode.
C-x a i g	inverse-add-global-abbrev	Type global abbreviation, then definition.
C-x a i l	inverse-add-local-abbrev	Type local abbreviation, then definition.
(none)	unexpand-abbrev	Undo the last word abbreviation.
(none)	write-abbrev-file	Write the word abbreviation file.
(none)	edit-abbrevs	Edit the word abbreviations.
(none)	list-abbrevs	View the word abbreviations.
(none)	kill-all-abbrevs	Kill abbreviations for this session.

Buffer-Manipulation Commands

Keystrokes	Command Name	Description
C-x b	switch-to-buffer	Move to specified buffer.
C-x C-b	list-buffers	Display buffer list.
C-x k	kill-buffer	Delete specified buffer.
(none)	kill-some-buffers	Ask about deleting each buffer.
(none)	rename-buffer	Change buffer name to specified name.
C-x s	save-some-buffers	Ask whether to save each modified buffer.

Emacs

Window Commands

Keystrokes	Command Name	Description
C-x 2	split-window-vertically	Divide the current window into two, one on top of the other.
C-x 3	split-window-horizontally	Divide the current window into two, side by side.
C-x >	scroll-right	Scroll the window right.
C-x <	scroll-left	Scroll the window left.
C-x o	other-window	Move to the other window.
C-x 0	delete-window	Delete current window.
C-x 1	delete-other-windows	Delete all windows but this one.
(none)	delete-windows-on	Delete all windows on a given buffer.
C-x ^	enlarge-window	Make window taller.
(none)	shrink-window	Make window shorter.
C-x }	enlarge-window-horizontally	Make window wider.
C-x {	shrink-window-horizontally	Make window narrower.
M-C-v	scroll-other-window	Scroll other window.
C-x 4 f	find-file-other-window	Find a file in the other window.
C-x 4 b	switch-to-buffer-other-window	Select a buffer in the other window.
C-x 5 f	find-file-other-frame	Find a file in a new frame.
C-x 5 b	switch-to-buffer-other-frame	Select a buffer in another frame.
(none)	compare-windows	Compare two buffers; show first difference.

Special Shell Characters

Keystrokes	Command Name	Description
C-c C-c	comint-interrupt-subjob	Terminate the current job.
C-c C-d	comint-send-eof	End of file character.
C-c C-u	comint-kill-input	Erase current line.
C-c C-w	backward-kill-word	Erase the previous word.
C-c C-z	comint-stop-subjob	Suspend the current job.

Indentation Commands

Keystrokes	Command Name	Description
C-x .	set-fill-prefix	Use characters from the beginning of the line up to the cursor column as the "fill prefix." This prefix is prepended to each line in the paragraph. Cancel the prefix by typing this command in column 1.
(none)	indented-text-mode	Major mode: each tab defines a new indent for subsequent lines.
(none)	text-mode	Exit indented text mode; return to text mode.
M-C-\	indent-region	Indent a region to match first line in region.
M-m	back-to-indentation	Move cursor to first character on line.
M-C-o	split-line	Split line at cursor; indent to column of cursor.
(none)	fill-individual-para-graphs	Reformat indented paragraphs, keeping indentation.

Centering Commands

Keystrokes	Command Name	Description
M-s	center-line	Center line that cursor is on.
(none)	center-paragraph	Center paragraph that cursor is on.
(none)	center-region	Center currently defined region.

Macro Commands

Keystrokes	Command Name	Description
C-x (	start-kbd-macro	Start macro definition.
C-x)	end-kbd-macro	End macro definition.
C-x e	call-last-kbd-macro	Execute last macro defined.
M-n C-x e	digit-argument and call-last-kbd-macro	Execute last macro defined n times.
C-u C-x (	universal-argument and start-kbd-macro	Execute last macro defined, then add keystrokes.
(none)	name-last-kbd-macro	Name last macro you created (before saving it).
(none)	insert-keyboard-macro	Insert the macro you named into a file.
(none)	load-file	Load macro files you've saved.
(none)	macroname	Execute a keyboard macro you've saved.
C-x q	kbd-macro-query	Insert a query in a macro definition.
C-u C-x q	(none)	Insert a recursive edit in a macro definition.
M-C-c	exit-recursive-edit	Exit a recursive edit.

Emacs

Basic Indentation Commands

Keystrokes	Command Name	Description
M-C-\	indent-region	Indent a region to match first line in region.
M-m	back-to-indentation	Move to first non-blank character on line.
M-^	delete-indentation	Join this line to the previous one.

Detail Information Help Commands

Keystrokes	Command Name	Description
C-h a	command-apropos	What commands involve this concept?
(none)	apropos	What functions and variables involve this concept?
C-h c	describe-key-briefly	What command does this keystroke sequence run?
C-h b	describe-bindings	What are all the key bindings for this buffer?
C-h k	describe-key	What command does this keystroke sequence run, and what does it do?
C-h l	view-lossage	What are the last 100 characters I typed?
C-h w	where-is	What is the key binding for this command?
C-h f	describe-function	What does this function do?
C-h v	describe-variable	What does this variable mean, and what is its value?
C-h m	describe-mode	Tell me about the mode the current buffer is in.
C-h s	describe-syntax	What is the syntax table for this buffer?

Help Commands

Keystrokes	Command Name	Description
C-h t	help-with-tutorial	Run the emacs tutorial.
C-h i	info	Start the Info documentation reader.
C-h n	view-emacs-news	View news about updates to emacs.
C-h C-c	describe-copying	View the emacs General Public License.
C-h C-d	describe-distribution	View information on ordering emacs from the FSF.
C-h C-w	describe-no-warranty	View the (non-)warranty for emacs.

Summary of Commands by Key

Emacs commands are presented below in two alphabetical lists. Reminder: C- indicates the Control key; M- indicates the Meta key.

Control-Key Sequences

Keystrokes	Command Name	Description
C-@	set-mark-command	Mark the beginning (or end) of a region.
C-Space	(same as previous)	
C-]	(none)	Exit recursive edit and exit query-replace.
C-a	beginning-of-line	Move to beginning of line.
C-b	backward-char	Move *backward* one character (left).
C-c C-c	comint-interrupt-subjob	Terminate the current job.
C-c C-d	comint-send-eof	End-of-file character.
C-c C-u	comint-kill-input	Erase current line.
C-c C-w	backward-kill-word	Erase the previous word.
C-c C-z	comint-stop-subjob	Suspend the current job.
C-d	delete-char	Delete character under cursor.
C-e	end-of-line	Move to *end* of line.
C-f	forward-char	Move *forward* one character (right).
C-g	keyboard-quit	Abort current command.
C-h	help-command	Enter the online help system.
C-h a	command-apropos	What commands involve this concept?
C-h b	describe-bindings	What are all the key bindings for this buffer?
C-h C-c	describe-copying	View the emacs General Public License.
C-h C-d	describe-distribution	View information on ordering emacs from FSF.
C-h C-w	describe-no-warranty	View the (non-)warranty for emacs.
C-h c	describe-key-briefly	What command does this keystroke sequence run?
C-h f	describe-function	What does this function do?
C-h i	info	Start the Info documentation reader.
C-h k	describe-key	What command does this keystroke sequence run, and what does it do?
C-h l	view-lossage	What are the last 100 characters I typed?
C-h m	describe-mode	Tell me about the mode the current buffer is in.
C-h n	view-emacs-news	View news about updates to emacs.
C-h s	describe-syntax	What is the syntax table for this buffer?
C-h t	help-with-tutorial	Run the emacs tutorial.
C-h v	describe-variable	What does this variable mean, and what is its value?

Keystrokes	Command Name	Description
C-h w	where-is	What is the key binding for this command?
C-k	kill-line	Delete from cursor to end of line.
C-l	recenter	Redraw screen with current line in the center.
C-n	next-line	Move to *next* line (down).
C-p	previous-line	Move to *previous* line (up).
C-r Meta	(none)	Start nonincremental search backwards.
C-r	(none)	Repeat nonincremental search backward.
C-r	(none)	Enter recursive edit (during query replace).
C-r	isearch-backward	Start incremental search backward.
C-s Meta	(none)	Start nonincremental search forward.
C-s	(none)	Repeat nonincremental search forward.
C-s	isearch-forward	Start incremental search forward.
C-t	transpose-chars	Transpose two letters.
C-u n	universal-argument	Repeat the next command n times.
C-u C-x (	universal-argument and start-kbd-macro	Execute last macro defined, then add keystrokes.
C-u C-x q	(none)	Insert recursive edit in a macro definition.
C-v	scroll-up	Move forward one screen.
C-w	kill-region	Delete a marked region.
C-x (	start-kbd-macro	Start macro definition.
C-x)	end-kbd-macro	End macro definition.
C-x [	backward-page	Move backward one page.
C-x]	forward-page	Move forward one page.
C-x ^	enlarge-window	Make window taller.
C-x {	shrink-window-horizontally	Make window narrower.
C-x }	enlarge-window-horizontally	Make window wider.
C-x <	scroll-left	Scroll the window left.
C-x >	scroll-right	Scroll the window right.
C-x .	set-fill-prefix	Use characters from the beginning of the line up to the cursor column as the "fill prefix." This prefix is prepended to each line in the paragraph. Cancel the prefix by typing this command in column 1.
C-x 0	delete-window	Delete current window.
C-x 1	delete-other-windows	Delete all windows but this one.
C-x 2	split-window-vertically	Divide the current window into two, one on top of the other.
C-x 3	split-window-horizontally	Divide the current window into two, side by side.
C-x 4 b	switch-to-buffer-other-window	Select a buffer in the other window.

Keystrokes	Command Name	Description
C-x 4 f	find-file-other-window	Find a file in the other window.
C-x 5 b	switch-to-buffer-other-frame	Select a buffer in another frame.
C-x 5 f	find-file-other-frame	Find a file in a new frame.
C-x C-b	list-buffers	Display the buffer list.
C-x C-c	save-buffers-kill-emacs	Exit emacs.
C-x C-f	find-file	Find file and read it.
C-x C-l	downcase-region	Lowercase region.
C-x C-p	mark-page	Mark page.
C-x C-q	(none)	Toggle read-only status of buffer.
C-x C-s	save-buffer	Save file (may hang terminal; use C-q to restart).
C-x C-t	transpose-lines	Transpose two lines.
C-x C-u	upcase-region	Uppercase region
C-x C-v	find-alternate-file	Read an alternate file, replacing the one read with C-x C-f.
C-x C-w	write-file	Write buffer contents to file.
C-x C-x	exchange-point-and-mark	Exchange location of cursor and mark.
C-x DEL	backward-kill-sentence	Delete previous sentence.
C-x a i g	inverse-add-global-abbrev	Type global abbreviation, then definition.
C-x a i l	inverse-add-local-abbrev	Type local abbreviation, then definition.
C-x b	switch-to-buffer	Move to the buffer specified.
C-x e	call-last-kbd-macro	Execute last macro defined.
C-x h	mark-whole-buffer	Mark buffer.
C-x i	insert-file	Insert file at cursor position.
C-x k	kill-buffer	Delete the buffer specified.
C-x o	other-window	Move to the other window.
C-x q	kbd-macro-query	Insert a query in a macro definition.
C-x s	save-some-buffers	Ask whether to save each modified buffer.
C-x u	advertised-undo	Undo last edit (can be done repeatedly).
C-y	yank	Restore what you've deleted.
C-z	suspend-emacs	Suspend emacs (use exit or fg to restart).

Meta-Key Sequences

Keystrokes	Command Name	Description
Meta	(none)	Exit a query-replace or successful search.
M-- M-c	negative-argument; capitalize-word	Capitalize previous word.
M-- M-l	negative-argument; downcase-word	Lowercase previous word.
M-- M-u	negative-argument; upcase-word	Uppercase previous word.
M-$	spell-word	Check spelling of word after cursor.
M-<	beginning-of-buffer	Move to beginning of file.
M->	end-of-buffer	Move to end of file.
M-{	backward-paragraph	Move backward one paragraph.
M-}	forward-paragraph	Move forward one paragraph.
M-^	delete-indentation	Join this line to the previous one.
M-n	digit-argument	Repeat the next command n times.
M-n C-x e	digit-argument and call-last-kbd-macro	Execute the last defined macro, n times.
M-a	backward-sentence	Move backward one sentence.
M-b	backward-word	Move one word *backward*.
M-C-\	indent-region	Indent a region to match first line in region.
M-C-c	exit-recursive-edit	Exit a recursive edit.
M-C-o	split-line	Split line at cursor; indent to column of cursor.
M-C-v	scroll-other-window	Scroll other window.
M-c	capitalize-word	Capitalize first letter of word.
M-d	kill-word	Delete word that cursor is on.
M-DEL	backward-kill-word	Delete previous word.
M-e	forward-sentence	Move forward one sentence.
M-f	forward-word	Move one word *forward*.
(none)	fill-region	Reformat individual paragraphs within a region.
M-h	mark-paragraph	Mark paragraph.
M-k	kill-sentence	Delete sentence the cursor is on.
M-l	downcase-word	Lowercase word.
M-m	back-to-indentation	Move cursor to first nonblank character on line.
M-q	fill-paragraph	Reformat paragraph.
M-s	center-line	Center line that cursor is on.
M-t	transpose-words	Transpose two words.
M-u	upcase-word	Uppercase word.
M-v	scroll-down	Move backward one screen.
M-x	(none)	Access command by command name.

Summary of Commands by Name

The emacs commands below are presented alphabetically by command name. Use M-x to access the command name. Reminder: C- indicates the Control key; M- indicates the Meta key.

Command Name	Keystrokes	Description
macroname	(none)	Execute a keyboard macro you've saved.
abbrev-mode	(none)	Enter (or exit) word abbreviation mode.
advertised-undo	C-x u	Undo last edit (can be done repeatedly).
apropos	(none)	What functions and variables involve this concept?
back-to-indentation	M-m	Move cursor to first non-blank character on line.
backward-char	C-b	Move *backward* one character (left).
backward-delete-char	Del	Delete previous character.
backward-kill-paragraph	(none)	Delete previous paragraph.
backward-kill-sentence	C-x Del	Delete previous sentence.
backward-kill-word	C-c C-w	Erase previous word.
backward-kill-word	M-Del	Delete previous word.
backward-page	C-x [	Move backward one page.
backward-paragraph	M-{	Move backward one paragraph.
backward-sentence	M-a	Move backward one sentence.
backward-word	M-b	Move backward one word.
beginning-of-buffer	M-<	Move to beginning of file.
beginning-of-line	C-a	Move to beginning of line.
call-last-kbd-macro	C-x e	Execute last macro defined.
capitalize-region	(none)	Capitalize region.
capitalize-word	M-c	Capitalize first letter of word.
center-line	M-s	Center line that cursor is on.
center-paragraph	(none)	Center paragraph that cursor is on.
center-region	(none)	Center currently defined region.
comint-interrupt-subjob	C-c C-c	Terminate the current job.
comint-kill-input	C-c C-u	Erase current line.
comint-send-eof	C-c C-d	End of file character.
comint-stop-subjob	C-c C-z	Suspend current job.
command-apropos	C-h a	What commands involve this concept?
compare-windows	(none)	Compare two buffers; show first difference.

Command Name	Keystrokes	Description
delete-char	C-d	Delete character under cursor.
delete-indentation	M-^	Join this line to previous one.
delete-other-windows	C-x 1	Delete all windows but this one.
delete-window	C-x 0	Delete current window.
delete-windows-on	(none)	Delete all windows on a given buffer.
describe-bindings	C-h b	What are all the key bindings for in this buffer?
describe-copying	C-h C-c	View the emacs General Public License.
describe-distribution	C-h C-d	View information on ordering emacs from the FSF.
describe-function	C-h f	What does this function do?
describe-key	C-h k	What command does this keystroke sequence run, and what does it do?
describe-key-briefly	C-h c	What command does this keystroke sequence run?
describe-mode	C-h m	Tell me about the mode the current buffer is in.
describe-no-warranty	C-h C-w	View the (non-)warranty for emacs.
describe-syntax	C-h s	What is the syntax table for this buffer?
describe-variable	C-h v	What does this variable mean, and what is its value?
digit-argument and call-last-kbd-macro	M-n C-x e	Execute the last defined macro, n times.
digit-argument	M-n	Repeat next command, n times.
downcase-region	C-x C-l	Lowercase region.
downcase-word	M-l	Lowercase word.
edit-abbrevs	(none)	Edit word abbreviations.
end-kbd-macro	C-x)	End macro definition.
end-of-buffer	M->	Move to end of file.
end-of-line	C-e	Move to end of line.
enlarge-window	C-x ^	Make window taller.
enlarge-window-horizontally	C-x }	Make window wider.
exchange-point-and-mark	C-x C-x	Exchange location of cursor and mark.
exit-recursive-edit	M-C-c	Exit a recursive edit.
fill-individual-paragraphs	(none)	Reformat indented paragraphs, keeping indentation.
fill-paragraph	M-q	Reformat paragraph.
fill-region	(none)	Reformat individual paragraphs within a region.

Command Name	Keystrokes	Description
find-alternate-file	C-x C-v	Read an alternate file, replacing the one read with C-x C-f.
find-file	C-x C-f	Find file and read it.
find-file-other-frame	C-x 5 f	Find a file in a new frame.
find-file-other-window	C-x 4 f	Find a file in the other window.
forward-char	C-f	Move *forward* one character (right).
forward-page	C-x]	Move forward one page.
forward-paragraph	M-}	Move forward one paragraph.
forward-sentence	M-e	Move forward one sentence.
forward-word	M-f	Move forward one word.
goto-char	(none)	Go to character *n* of file.
goto-line	(none)	Go to line *n* of file.
help-command	C-h	Enter the online help system.
help-with-tutorial	C-h t	Run the emacs tutorial.
indent-region	M-C-\	Indent a region to match first line in region.
indented-text-mode	(none)	Major mode: each tab defines a new indent for subsequent lines.
info	C-h i	Start the Info documentation reader.
insert-file	C-x i	Insert file at cursor position.
insert-keyboard-macro	(none)	Insert the macro you named into a file.
inverse-add-global-abbrev	C-x a i g	Type global abbreviation, then definition.
inverse-add-local-abbrev	C-x a i l	Type local abbreviation, then definition.
isearch-backward	C-r	Start incremental search backward.
isearch-backward-regexp	C-r	Same, but search for regular expression.
isearch-forward	C-s	Start incremental search forward.
isearch-forward-regexp	C-r	Same, but search for regular expression.
kbd-macro-query	C-x q	Insert a query in a macro definition.
keyboard-quit	C-g	Abort current command.
kill-all-abbrevs	(none)	Kill abbreviations for this session.
kill-buffer	C-x k	Delete the buffer specified.
kill-line	C-k	Delete from cursor to end of line.
kill-paragraph	(none)	Delete from cursor to end of paragraph.
kill-region	C-w	Delete a marked region.
kill-sentence	M-k	Delete sentence the cursor is on.
kill-some-buffers	(none)	Ask about deleting each buffer.
kill-word	M-d	Delete word the cursor is on.
list-abbrevs	(none)	View word abbreviations.

Command Name	Keystrokes	Description
list-buffers	C-x C-b	Display buffer list.
load-file	(none)	Load macro files you've saved.
mark-page	C-x C-p	Mark page.
mark-paragraph	M-h	Mark paragraph.
mark-whole-buffer	C-x h	Mark buffer.
name-last-kbd-macro	(none)	Name last macro you created (before saving it).
negative-argument; capitalize-word	M- - M-c	Capitalize previous word.
negative-argument; downcase-word	M- - M-l	Lowercase previous word.
negative-argument; upcase-word	M- - M-u	Uppercase previous word.
next-line	C-n	Move to *next* line (down).
other-window	C-x o	Move to the other window.
previous-line	C-p	Move to *previous* line (up).
query-replace-reg-exp	C-% Meta	Query-replace a regular expression.
recenter	C-l	Redraw screen, with current line in center.
rename-buffer	(none)	Change buffer name to specified name.
replace-regexp	(none)	Replace a regular expression uncon-ditionally.
re-search-backward	(none)	Simple regular expression search backward.
re-search-forward	(none)	Simple regular expression search forward.
revert-buffer	(none)	Restore buffer to the state it was in when the file was last saved (or auto-saved).
save-buffer	C-x C-s	Save file (may hang terminal; use C-q to restart).
save-buffers-kill-emacs	C-x C-c	Exit emacs.
save-some-buffers	C-x s	Ask whether to save each modified buffer.
scroll-down	M-v	Move backward one screen.
scroll-left	C-x <	Scroll the window left.
scroll-other-window	M-C-v	Scroll other window.
scroll-right	C-x >	Scroll the window right.
scroll-up	C-v	Move forward one screen.

Command Name	Keystrokes	Description
set-fill-prefix	C-x .	Use characters from the beginning of the line up to the cursor column as the "fill prefix." This prefix is prepended to each line in the paragraph. Cancel the prefix by typing this command in column 1.
set-mark-command	C-@ or C-Space	Mark the beginning (or end) of a region.
shrink-window	(none)	Make window shorter.
shrink-window-horizontally	C-x {	Make window narrower.
spell-buffer	(none)	Check spelling of current buffer.
spell-region	(none)	Check spelling of current region.
spell-string	(none)	Check spelling of string typed in minibuffer.
spell-word	M-$	Check spelling of word after cursor.
split-line	M-C-o	Split line at cursor; indent to column of cursor.
split-window-vertically	C-x 2	Divide the current window into two, one on top of the other.
split-window-horizontally	C-x 3	Divide the current window into two, side by side.
start-kbd-macro	C-x (	Start macro definition.
suspend-emacs	C-z	Suspend emacs (use exit or fg to restart).
switch-to-buffer	C-x b	Move to the buffer specified.
switch-to-buffer-other-frame	C-x 5 b	Select a buffer in another frame.
switch-to-buffer-other-window	C-x 4 b	Select a buffer in the other window.
text-mode	(none)	Exit indented text mode; return to text mode.
transpose-chars	C-t	Transpose two letters.
transpose-lines	C-x C-t	Transpose two lines.
transpose-paragraphs	(none)	Transpose two paragraphs.
transpose-sentences	(none)	Transpose two sentences.
transpose-words	M-t	Transpose two words.
unexpand-abbrev	(none)	Undo the last word abbreviation.
universal-argument	C-u *n*	Repeat the next command *n* times.
universal-argument and start-kbd-macro	C-u C-x (	Execute last macro defined, then add keystrokes to it.
upcase-region	C-x C-u	Uppercase region.
upcase-word	M-u	Uppercase word.
view-emacs-news	C-h n	View news about updates to emacs.

Emacs

Command Name	Keystrokes	Description
view-lossage	C-h l	What are the last 100 characters I typed?
where-is	C-h w	What is the key binding for this command?
write-abbrev-file	(none)	Write the word abbreviation file.
write-file	C-x C-w	Write buffer contents to file.
yank	C-y	Restore what you've deleted.

CHAPTER 8

The vi Editor

This chapter presents the following topics:

- Review of vi operations
- Movement commands
- Edit commands
- Saving and exiting
- Accessing multiple files
- Interacting with Unix
- Macros
- Miscellaneous commands
- Alphabetical list of keys
- Setting up vi

vi is pronounced "vee eye."

Besides the original Unix vi, there are a number of freely available vi clones. Both the original vi and the clones are covered in *Learning the vi Editor*, listed in the Bibliography.

Review of vi Operations

This section provides a review of the following:

- Command-line syntax

321

- vi modes
- Syntax of vi commands
- Status-line commands

Command-Line Syntax

The three most common ways of starting a vi session are:

```
vi file
vi +n file
vi +/pattern file
```

You can open *file* for editing, optionally at line *n* or at the first line matching *pattern*. If no *file* is specified, vi opens with an empty buffer. See Chapter 2, *Unix Commands*, for more information on command-line options for vi.

Note that vi and ex are actually the same program; thus it is worthwhile to review the material in Chapter 9, *The ex Editor*, as well, in order to become familiar with the ex command set.

Command Mode

Once the file is opened, you are in command mode. From command mode, you can:

- Invoke insert mode
- Issue editing commands
- Move the cursor to a different position in the file
- Invoke ex commands
- Invoke a Unix shell
- Save or exit the current version of the file

Insert Mode

In insert mode, you can enter new text in the file. Press the Escape key to exit insert mode and return to command mode. The following commands invoke insert mode:

a   Append after cursor.
A   Append at end of line.
c   Begin change operation.
C   Change to end of line.
i   Insert before cursor.
I   Insert at beginning of line.
o   Open a line below current line.
O   Open a line above current line.

R	Begin overwriting text.
s	Substitute a character.
S	Substitute entire line.

Syntax of vi Commands

In vi, commands have the following general form:

[n] operator [m] object

The basic editing *operators* are:

c	Begin a change.
d	Begin a deletion.
y	Begin a yank (or copy).

If the current line is the object of the operation, the object is the same as the operator: cc, dd, yy. Otherwise, the editing operators act on objects specified by cursor-movement commands or pattern-matching commands. *n* and *m* are the number of times the operation is performed, or the number of objects the operation is performed on. If both *n* and *m* are specified, the effect is $n \times m$.

An object can represent any of the following text blocks:

word	Includes characters up to a whitespace character (space or tab) or punctuation mark. A capitalized object is a variant form that recognizes only whitespace.
sentence	Is up to ., !, or ?, followed by two spaces.
paragraph	Is up to next blank line or paragraph macro defined by the para= option.
section	Is up to next section heading defined by the sect= option.

Examples

2cw	Change the next two words.
d}	Delete up to next paragraph.
d^	Delete back to beginning of line.
5yy	Copy the next five lines.
y]]	Copy up to the next section.

Status-Line Commands

Most commands are not echoed on the screen as you input them. However, the status line at the bottom of the screen is used to echo input for these commands:

/	Search forward for a pattern.
?	Search backward for a pattern.
:	Invoke an ex command.

! Invoke a Unix command that takes as its input an object in the buffer and replaces it with output from the command.

Commands that are input on the status line must be entered by pressing the Return key. In addition, error messages and output from the CTRL-G command are displayed on the status line.

Movement Commands

A number preceding a command repeats the movement. Movement commands are also objects for change, delete, and yank operations.

Character

h, j, k, l	Left, down, up, right ($\leftarrow$, $\downarrow$, $\uparrow$, $\rightarrow$).
Spacebar	Right.

Text

w, W, b, B	Forward, backward by word.
e, E	End of word.
), (	Beginning of next, current sentence.
}, {	Beginning of next, current paragraph.
]], [[	Beginning of next, current section.

Lines

0, $	First, last position of current line.
^	First nonblank character of current line.
+, -	First character of next, previous line.
Return	First character of next line.
n|	Column n of current line.
H	Top line of screen.
M	Middle line of screen.
L	Last line of screen.
nH	n lines after top line.
nL	n lines before last line.

Screens

CTRL-F CTRL-B	Scroll forward, backward one screen.
CTRL-D CTRL-U	Scroll down, up one-half screen.
CTRL-E CTRL-Y	Show one more line at bottom, top of window.
z Return	Reposition line with cursor to top of screen.
z.	Reposition line with cursor to middle of screen.
z-	Reposition line with cursor to bottom of screen.
CTRL-L CTRL-R	Redraw screen (without scrolling).

Searches

/text	Search forward for *text*.
n	Repeat previous search.
N	Repeat search in opposite direction.
/	Repeat forward search.
?	Repeat previous search backward.
?text	Search backward for *text*.
/text/+n	Go to line *n* after *text*.
?text?-n	Go to line *n* before *text*.
%	Find match of current parenthesis, brace, or bracket.
fx	Move search forward to *x* on current line.
Fx	Move search backward to *x* on current line.
tx	Search forward to character before *x* in current line.
Tx	Search backward to character after *x* in current line.
,	Reverse search direction of last f, F, t, or T.
;	Repeat last character search (f, F, t, or T).

Line Numbering

CTRL-G	Display current line number.
nG	Move to line number *n*.
G	Move to last line in file.
:n	Move to line number *n*.

Marking Position

mx	Mark current position with character *x*.
`x	Move cursor to mark *x*.
'x	Move to start of line containing *x*.
` `	Return to previous mark (or to location prior to a search).
' '	Like above, but return to start of line.

Edit Commands

Recall that c, d, and y are the basic editing operators.

Inserting New Text

a	Append after cursor.
A	Append to end of line.
i	Insert before cursor.
I	Insert at beginning of line.
o	Open a line below cursor.
O	Open a line above cursor.
Esc	Terminate insert mode.
CTRL-J	Move down one line.
Return	Move down one line.
CTRL-I	Insert a tab.
CTRL-T	Move to next tab setting.
Backspace	Move back one character.
CTRL-H	Move back one character.
CTRL-U	Delete current line.
CTRL-V	Quote next character.
CTRL-W	Move back one word.

Changing and Deleting Text

cw	Change word.
cc	Change line.
C	Change text from current position to end of line.
dd	Delete current line.
*n*dd	Delete *n* lines.
D	Delete remainder of line.
dw	Delete a word.
d}	Delete up to next paragraph.
d^	Delete back to beginning of line.
d/pat	Delete up to first occurrence of pattern.
dn	Delete up to next occurrence of pattern.

dfa	Delete up to and including *a* on current line.
dta	Delete up to (but not including) *a* on current line.
dL	Delete up to last line on screen.
dG	Delete to end of file.
p	Insert last deleted text after cursor.
P	Insert last deleted text before cursor.
rx	Replace character with *x*.
Rtext	Replace with new *text* (overwrite), beginning at cursor.
s	Substitute character.
4s	Substitute four characters.
S	Substitute entire line.
u	Undo last change.
U	Restore current line.
x	Delete current cursor position.
X	Delete back one character.
5X	Delete previous five characters.
.	Repeat last change.
~	Reverse case.

Copying and Moving

Y	Copy current line to new buffer.
yy	Copy current line.
"xyy	Yank current line to buffer *x*.
"xd	Delete into buffer *x*.
"Xd	Delete and append into buffer *x*.
"xp	Put contents of buffer *x*.
y]]	Copy up to next section heading.
ye	Copy to end of word.

Buffer names are the letters a–z. Uppercase names append text to the specified buffer.

Saving and Exiting

Writing a file means saving the edits and updating the file's modification time.

ZZ	Quit vi, writing the file only if changes were made.
:x	Same as ZZ.
:wq	Write and quit file.
:w	Write file.
:w *file*	Save copy to *file*.
:*n,m*w *file*	Write lines *n* to *m* to new *file*.
:*n,m*w >> *file*	Append lines *n* to *m* to existing *file*.
:w!	Write file (overriding protection).

:w! *file*	Overwrite *file* with current buffer.
:w %.*new*	Write current buffer named *file* as *file.new*.
:q	Quit vi.
:q!	Quit vi (discarding edits).
Q	Quit vi and invoke ex.
:vi	Return to vi after Q command.
:e *file2*	Edit *file2* without leaving vi.
:n	Edit next file.
:e!	Return to version of current file at time of last write.
:e #	Edit alternate file.
%	Current filename.
#	Alternate filename.

Accessing Multiple Files

:e *file*	Edit another *file*; current file becomes alternate.
:e!	Return to version of current file at time of last write.
:e + *file*	Begin editing at end of *file*.
:e +*n file*	Open *file* at line *n*.
:e #	Open to previous position in alternate file.
:ta *tag*	Edit file at location *tag*.
:n	Edit next file.
:n!	Forces next file.
:n *files*	Specify new list of *files*.
CTRL-G	Show current file and line number.
:args	Display multiple files to be edited.
:rew	Rewind list of multiple files to top.

Interacting with Unix

:r *file*	Read in contents of *file* after cursor.
:r !*command*	Read in output from *command* after current line.
:*nr* !*command*	Like above, but place after line *n* (0 for top of file).
:!*command*	Run *command*, then return.
!*object command*	Send buffer *object* to Unix *command*; replace with output.
:*n,m*! *command*	Send lines *n–m* to *command*; replace with output.
n!!*command*	Send *n* lines to Unix *command*; replace with output.
!!	Repeat last system command.
:sh	Create subshell; return to file with *EOF*.
CTRL-Z	Suspend editor, resume with fg.
:so *file*	Read and execute ex commands from *file*.

Macros

`:ab` *in out*	Use *in* as abbreviation for *out*.
`:unab` *in*	Remove abbreviation for *in*.
`:ab`	List abbreviations.
`:map` *c sequence*	Map character *c* as *sequence* of commands.
`:unmap` *c*	Remove map for character *c*.
`:map`	List characters that are mapped.
`:map!` *c sequence*	Map character *c* to input mode *sequence*.
`:unmap!` *c*	Remove input mode map (you may need to quote the character with CTRL-V).
`:map!`	List characters that are mapped for input mode.

The following characters are unused in command mode and can be mapped as user-defined commands:

Letters

  g K q V v

Control keys

  ^A ^K ^O ^W ^X

Symbols

  _ * \ =

(Note: the = is used by vi if Lisp mode is set. Different versions of vi may use some of these characters, so test them before using.)

Miscellaneous Commands

`J`	Join two lines.
`:j!`	Join two lines, preserving whitespace.
`<<`	Shift this line left one shift width (default is eight spaces).
`>>`	Shift this line right one shift width (default is eight spaces).
`>}`	Shift right to end of paragraph.
`<%`	Shift left until matching parenthesis, brace, or bracket. (Cursor must be on the matching symbol.)

Alphabetical List of Keys

For brevity, control characters are marked by ^.

`^]`	Perform a tag look-up on the text under the cursor.
`a`	Append text after cursor.
`A`	Append text at end of line.
`^A`	Unused.

b	Back up to beginning of word in current line.
B	Back up to beginning of word, ignoring punctuation.
^B	Scroll backward one window.

c	Change operator.
C	Change to end of current line.
^C	Unused in command mode; ends insert mode (stty interrupt character).

d	Delete operator.
D	Delete to end of current line.
^D	Scroll down half-window (command mode). Move backward one tab-stop (insert mode).

e	Move to end of word.
E	Move to end of word, ignoring punctuation.
^E	Show one more line at bottom of window.

f	Find next character typed forward on current line.
F	Find next character typed backward on current line.
^F	Scroll forward one window.

g	Unused.
G	Go to specified line or end of file.
^G	Print information about file on status line.

h	Left arrow cursor key.
H	Move cursor to Home position.
^H	Left arrow cursor key; Backspace key in insert mode.

i	Insert text before cursor.
I	Insert text before first nonblank character on line.
^I	Unused in command mode; in insert mode, same as Tab key.

j	Down arrow cursor key.
J	Join two lines.
^J	Down arrow cursor key; in insert mode, move down a line.

k	Up arrow cursor key.
K	Unused.
^K	Unused.

l	Right arrow cursor key.
L	Move cursor to last position in window.
^L	Redraw screen.

m	Mark the current cursor position in register (a–z).
M	Move cursor to middle position in window.
^M	Carriage return.

n	Repeat the last search command.
N	Repeat the last search command in the reverse direction.

^N   Down arrow cursor key.

o   Open line below current line.
O   Open line above current line.
^O   Unused.

p   Put yanked or deleted text after or below cursor.
P   Put yanked or deleted text before or above cursor.
^P   Up arrow cursor key.

q   Unused.
Q   Quit vi and invoke ex.
^Q   Unused (on some terminals, resume data flow).

r   Replace character at cursor with the next character you type.
R   Replace characters.
^R   Redraw the screen.

s   Change the character under the cursor to typed characters.
S   Change entire line.
^S   Unused (on some terminals, stop data flow).

t   Move cursor forward to character before next character typed.
T   Move cursor backward to character after next character typed.
^T   Return to the previous location in the tag stack (Solaris vi command mode).
        If autoindent is set, indent another tab stop (insert mode).

u   Undo the last change made.
U   Restore current line, discarding changes.
^U   Scroll the screen upward half-window.

v   Unused.
V   Unused.
^V   Unused in command mode; in insert mode, quote next character.

w   Move to beginning of next word.
W   Move to beginning of next word, ignoring punctuation.
^W   Unused in command mode; in insert mode, back up to beginning of word.

x   Delete character under cursor.
X   Delete character before cursor.
^X   Unused.

y   Yank or copy operator.
Y   Make copy of current line.
^Y   Show one more line at top of window.

z   Reposition line containing cursor. z must be followed either by: Return (reposition line to top of screen), . (reposition line to middle of screen), or – (reposition line to bottom of screen).

ZZ   Exit the editor, saving changes.

^Z   Suspend vi (only works on systems that have job control).

Setting Up vi

This section describes the following:

- The :set command

- Options available with :set

- Example .exrc file

The :set Command

The :set command allows you to specify options that change characteristics of your editing environment. Options may be put in the ~/.exrc file or set during a vi session.

The colon should not be typed if the command is put in .exrc:

:set x	Enable option x.
:set nox	Disable option x.
:set x=val	Give *value* to option x.
:set	Show changed options.
:set all	Show all options.
:set x?	Show value of option x.

Options Used by :set

Table 8-1 contains brief descriptions of the important set command options. In the first column, options are listed in alphabetical order; if the option can be abbreviated, that abbreviation is shown in parentheses. The second column shows the default setting vi uses unless you issue an explicit set command (either manually or in the .exrc file). The last column describes what the option does, when enabled.

Table 8-1: :set Options

Option	Default	Description
autoindent (ai)	noai	In insert mode, indent each line to the same level as the line above or below. Use with the shiftwidth option.
autoprint (ap)	ap	Display changes after each editor command. (For global replacement, display last replacement.)

Table 8–1: :set Options (continued)

Option	Default	Description
autowrite (aw)	noaw	Automatically write (save) the file if changed before opening another file with :n or before giving Unix command with :!.
beautify (bf)	nobf	Ignore all control characters during input (except tab, newline, or formfeed).
directory (dir)	/tmp	Name directory in which ex/vi stores buffer files. (Directory must be writable.)
edcompatible	noedcompatible	Remember the flags used with the most recent substitute command (global, confirming) and use them for the next substitute command. Despite the name, no version of ed actually behaves this way.
errorbells (eb)	errorbells	Sound bell when an error occurs.
exrc (ex)	noexrc	Allow the execution of .exrc files that reside outside the user's home directory.
hardtabs (ht)	8	Define boundaries for terminal hardware tabs.
ignorecase (ic)	noic	Disregard case during a search.
lisp	nolisp	Insert indents in appropriate Lisp format. ( ), { }, [[, and]] are modified to have meaning for Lisp.
list	nolist	Print tabs as ^I; mark ends of lines with $. (Use list to tell if end character is a tab or a space.)
magic	magic	Wildcard characters . (dot), * (asterisk), and [ ] (brackets) have special meaning in patterns.
mesg	mesg	Permit system messages to display on terminal while editing in vi.
novice	nonovice	Require the use of long ex command names, such as copy or read.
number (nu)	nonu	Display line numbers on left of screen during editing session.

Table 8-1: :set Options (continued)

Option	Default	Description
open	open	Allow entry to *open* or *visual* mode from ex. Although not in Solaris vi, this option has traditionally been in vi, and may be in your Unix's version of vi.
optimize (opt)	noopt	Abolish carriage returns at the end of lines when printing multiple lines; speed output on dumb terminals when printing lines with leading whitespace (spaces or tabs).
paragraphs (para)	IPLPPPQP LIpplpipbp	Define paragraph delimiters for movement by { or }. The pairs of characters in the value are the names of troff macros that begin paragraphs.
prompt	prompt	Display the ex prompt (:) when vi's Q command is given.
readonly (ro)	noro	Any writes (saves) of a file fail unless you use ! after the write (works with w, ZZ, or autowrite).
redraw (re)		vi redraws the screen whenever edits are made (in other words, insert mode pushes over existing characters, and deleted lines immediately close up). Default depends on line speed and terminal type. noredraw is useful at slow speeds on a dumb terminal: deleted lines show up as @, and inserted text appears to overwrite existing text until you press Escape.
remap	remap	Allow nested map sequences.
report	5	Display a message on the status line whenever you make an edit that affects at least a certain number of lines. For example, 6dd reports the message "6 lines deleted."
scroll	[½ *window*]	Number of lines to scroll with ^D and ^U commands.

Table 8–1: :set Options (continued)

Option	Default	Description
sections (sect)	SHNHH HU	Define section delimiters for [[and]] movement. The pairs of characters in the value are the names of troff macros that begin sections.
shell (sh)	/bin/sh	Pathname of shell used for shell escape (:!) and shell command (:sh). Default value is derived from shell environment, which varies on different systems.
shiftwidth (sw)	8	Define number of spaces in backward (^D) tabs when using the autoindent option, and for the << and >> commands.
showmatch (sm)	nosm	In vi, when) or } is entered, cursor moves briefly to matching (or {. (If no match, rings the error message bell.) Very useful for programming.
showmode	noshowmode	In insert mode, display a message on the prompt line indicating the type of insert you are making. For example, "OPEN MODE" or "APPEND MODE."
slowopen (slow)		Hold off display during insert. Default depends on line speed and terminal type.
tabstop (ts)	8	Define number of spaces a tab indents during editing session. (Printer still uses system tab of 8.)
taglength (tl)	0	Define number of characters that are significant for tags. Default (zero) means that all characters are significant.
tags	*tags /usr/lib/tags*	Define pathname of files containing tags. (See the Unix ctags command.) (By default, vi searches the file tags in the current directory and /usr/lib/tags.)
tagstack	tagstack	Enable stacking of tag locations on a stack.

Table 8-1: :set Options (continued)

Option	Default	Description
term		Set terminal type.
terse	noterse	Display shorter error messages.
timeout (to)	timeout	Keyboard maps time out after 1 second.[a]
ttytype		Set terminal type. This is just another name for term.
warn	warn	Display the warning message, "No write since last change."
window (w)		Show a certain number of lines of the file on the screen. Default depends on line speed and terminal type.
wrapscan (ws)	ws	Searches wrap around either end of file.
wrapmargin (wm)	0	Define right margin. If greater than zero, automatically insert carriage returns to break lines.
writeany (wa)	nowa	Allow saving to any file.

[a] When you have mappings of several keys (for example, :map zzz 3dw), you probably want to use notimeout. Otherwise you need to type zzz within 1 second. When you have an insert mode mapping for a cursor key (for example, :map! ^[OB ^[ja), you should use timeout. Otherwise, vi won't react to Escape until you type another key.

Example .exrc File

```
set nowrapscan wrapmargin=7
set sections=SeAhBhChDh nomesg
map q :w^M:n^M
map v dwElp
ab ORA O'Reilly & Associates, Inc.
```

CHAPTER 9

The ex Editor

The ex line editor serves as the foundation for the screen editor vi. Commands in ex work on the current line or on a range of lines in a file. Most often, you use ex from within vi. In vi, ex commands are preceded by a colon and entered by pressing Return.

You can also invoke ex on its own—from the command line—just as you would invoke vi. (You could execute an ex script this way.) You can also use the vi command Q to quit the vi editor and enter ex.

This chapter presents the following topics:

- Syntax of ex commands

- Alphabetical summary of commands

For more information, see *Learning the vi Editor*, listed in the Bibliography.

Syntax of ex Commands

To enter an ex command from vi, type:

    :[address] command [options]

An initial : indicates an ex command. As you type the command, it is echoed on the status line. Enter the command by pressing the Return key. *address* is the line number or range of lines that are the object of *command. options* and *addresses* are described below. ex commands are described in the "Alphabetical Summary" section.

You can exit ex in several ways:

:x   Exit (save changes and quit).

:q! Quit without saving changes.

:vi Switch to the vi editor on the current file.

Addresses

If no address is given, the current line is the object of the command. If the address specifies a range of lines, the format is:

    x, y

where x and y are the first and last addressed lines (x must precede y in the buffer). x and y may each be a line number or a symbol. Using ; instead of , sets the current line to x before interpreting y. The notation 1,$ addresses all lines in the file, as does %.

Address Symbols

1,$	All lines in the file.
x, y	Lines x through y.
$x; y$	Lines x through y, with current line reset to x.
0	Top of file.
.	Current line.
n	Absolute line number n.
$	Last line.
%	All lines; same as 1,$.
$x-n$	n lines before x.
$x+n$	n lines after x.
-[n]	One or n lines previous.
+[n]	One or n lines ahead.
'x	Line marked with x.
' '	Previous mark.
/pattern/	Forward to line matching *pattern*.
?pattern?	Backward to line matching *pattern*.

See Chapter 6, *Pattern Matching*, for more information on using patterns.

Options

!   Indicates a variant form of the command, overriding the normal behavior.

count
> The number of times the command is to be repeated. Unlike in vi commands, *count* cannot precede the command, because a number preceding an

---

ex command is treated as a line address. For example, d3 deletes three lines beginning with the current line; 3d deletes line 3.

file The name of a file that is affected by the command. % stands for the current file; # stands for the previous file.

Alphabetical Summary of ex Commands

ex commands can be entered by specifying any unique abbreviation. In this listing, the full name appears in the margin, and the shortest possible abbreviation is used in the syntax line. Examples are assumed to be typed from vi, so they include the : prompt.

---

ab [*string text*]   abbrev

Define *string* when typed to be translated into *text*. If *string* and *text* are not specified, list all current abbreviations.

Examples

Note: ^M appears when you type ^V followed by Return.

```
:ab ora O'Reilly & Associates, Inc.
:ab id Name:^MRank:^MPhone:
```

[*address*] a[!]   append
text
.

Append *text* at specified *address*, or at present address if none is specified. Add a ! to toggle the autoindent setting that is used during input. That is, if autoindent was enabled, ! disables it.

---

ar   args

Print the members of the argument list (files named on the command line), with the current argument printed in brackets ([]).

[*address*] c[!]   change
text
.

Replace the specified lines with *text*. Add a ! to switch the autoindent setting during input of *text*.

---

copy	[*address*] co *destination*
	Copy the lines included in *address* to the specified *destination* address. The command t (short for "to") is a synonym for copy.
	Example
| | ```
:1,10 co 50
``` |
delete	[*address*] d [*buffer*]
	Delete the lines included in *address*. If *buffer* is specified, save or append the text to the named buffer. Buffer names are the lower-case letters a–z. Uppercase names append text to the buffer.
	Examples
| | ```
:/Part I/,/Part II/-1d
:/main/+d
:.,$d
``` *Delete to line above "Part II"*<br>*Delete line below "main"*<br>*Delete from this line to last line* |
edit	e[!] [+*n*] [*filename*]
	Begin editing on *filename*. If no *filename* is given, start over with a copy of the current file. Add a ! to edit the new file even if the current file has not been saved since the last change. With the +*n* argument, begin editing on line *n*. Or *n* may be a pattern, of the form /*pattern*.
	Examples
| | ```
:e file
:e#
:e!
``` |
file	f [*filename*]
	Change the name of the current file to *filename*, which is considered "not edited." If no *filename* is specified, print the current status of the file.
	Example
| | ```
:f %.new
``` |
| **global** | [*address*] g[!]/*pattern*/[*commands*] |
| | Execute *commands* on all lines which contain *pattern* or, if *address* is specified, on all lines within that range. If *commands* |

are not specified, print all such lines. Add a ! to execute *commands* on all lines *not* containing *pattern*. See also **v**.

Examples

```
:g/Unix/p
:g/Name:/s/tom/Tom/
```

[*address*] i[!]
text
.

Insert *text* at line before the specified *address*, or at present address if none is specified. Add a ! to switch the autoindent setting during input of *text*.

insert

[*address*] j[!] [*count*]

Place the text in the specified range on one line, with whitespace adjusted to provide two space characters after a period (.), no space characters after a), and one space character otherwise. Add a ! to prevent whitespace adjustment.

join

Example

```
:1,5j!                Join first five lines, preserving whitespace
```

[*address*] k *char*

Mark the given *address* with *char*, a single lowercase letter. Return later to the line with 'x. k is equivalent to mark.

k

[*address*] l [*count*]

Print the specified lines so that tabs display as ^I, and the ends of lines display as $. l is like a temporary version of :set list.

list

---

map[!] [*char commands*]

Define a keyboard macro named *char* as the specified sequence of *commands*. *char* is usually a single character, or the sequence #*n*, representing a function key on the keyboard. Use a ! to create a macro for input mode. With no arguments, list the currently defined macros.

map

$\rightarrow$

ex

map ←	**Examples** :map K dwwP *Transpose two words* :map q :w^M:n^M *Write current file; go to next* :map! + ^[bi(^[ea) *Enclose previous word in parentheses*
mark	[*address*] ma *char* Mark the specified line with *char*, a single lowercase letter. Return later to the line with 'x. Same as k.
move	[*address*] m *destination* Move the lines specified by *address* to the *destination* address. **Example** :.,/Note/m /END/ *Move text block after line containing "END"*
next	n[!] [[+n] *filelist*] Edit the next file from the command-line argument list. Use args to list these files. If *filelist* is provided, replace the current argument list with *filelist* and begin editing on the first file. With the +*n* argument, begin editing on line *n*. Or *n* may be a pattern, of the form /*pattern*. **Example** :n chap* *Start editing all "chapter" files*
number	[*address*] nu [*count*] Print each line specified by *address*, preceded by its buffer line number. Use # as an alternate abbreviation for number. *count* specifies the number of lines to show, starting with *address*.
open	[*address*] o [/*pattern*/] Enter open mode (vi) at the lines specified by *address*, or at the lines matching *pattern*. Exit open mode with Q. Open mode lets you use the regular vi commands, but only one line at a time. It

can be useful on slow dialup lines (or on very distant Internet telnet connections).

open

---

pre

preserve

Save the current editor buffer as though the system were about to crash.

[*address*] p [*count*]

print

Print the lines specified by *address*. *count* specifies the number of lines to print, starting with *address*. P is another abbreviation.

Example

```
:100;+5p            Show line 100 and the next five lines
```

[*address*] pu [*char*]

put

Restore previously deleted or yanked lines from named buffer specified by *char*, to the line specified by *address*. If *char* is not specified, the last deleted or yanked text is restored.

---

q[!]

quit

Terminate current editing session. Use ! to discard changes made since the last save. If the editing session includes additional files in the argument list that were never accessed, quit by typing q! or by typing q twice.

[*address*] r *filename*

read

Copy the text of *filename* after the line specified by *address*. If *filename* is not specified, the current filename is used.

Example

```
:0r $HOME/data      Read file in at top of current file
```

[*address*] r !*command*

read

Read the output of Unix *command* into the text after the line specified by *address*.

→

read ←	**Example** `:$r !cal` *Place a calendar at end of file*
recover	`rec [file]` Recover *file* from the system save area.
rewind	`rew[!]` Rewind argument list and begin editing the first file in the list. Add a `!` to rewind even if the current file has not been saved since the last change.

set	`se parameter1 parameter2 ...`
	
	Set a value to an option with each *parameter*, or, if no *parameter* is supplied, print all options that have been changed from their defaults. For toggle options, each *parameter* can be phrased as *option* or *nooption*; other options can be assigned with the syntax *option=value*. Specify all to list current settings. The form set *option*? displays the value of *option*. See the list of set options in Chapter 8, *The vi Editor*.
	
	Examples
	   `:set nows wm=10`
	   `:set all`

shell	`sh` Create a new shell. Resume editing when the shell terminates.

source	`so file`
	
	Read and execute ex commands from *file*.
	
	Examples
	   `:so $HOME/.exrc`

substitute	`[address] s [/pattern/replacement/] [options] [count]` Replace each instance of *pattern* on the specified lines with *replacement*. If *pattern* and *replacement* are omitted, repeat last substitution. *count* specifies the number of lines on which to

substitute, starting with *address*. See additional examples in Chapter 6. (Spelling out the command name does not work in Solaris vi.)

Options

c Prompt for confirmation before each change.
g Substitute all instances of *pattern* on each line (global).
p Print the last line on which a substitution was made.

Examples

```
:1,10s/yes/no/g      Substitute on first 10 lines
:%s/[Hh]ello/Hi/gc   Confirm global substitutions
:s/Fortran/\U&/ 3    Uppercase "Fortran" on next three lines
```

[*address*] t *destination*

Copy the lines included in *address* to the specified *destination* address. t is equivalent to copy.

Example

```
:%t$                 Copy the file and add it to the end
```

[*address*] ta *tag*

Switch the focus of editing to *tag*.

Example

Run ctags, then switch to the file containing *myfunction*:

```
:!ctags *.c
:tag myfunction
```

---

una *word*

Remove *word* from the list of abbreviations.

---

u

Reverse the changes made by the last editing command.

substitute

t

tag

unabbreviate

undo

ex

unmap	unm[!] *char*
	Remove *char* from the list of keyboard macros. Use ! to remove a macro for input mode.
v	[*address*] v/*pattern*/[*commands*]
	Execute *commands* on all lines *not* containing *pattern*. If *commands* are not specified, print all such lines. v is equivalent to g!.
	Example
	:v/#include/d *Delete all lines except "#include" lines*
version	ve
	Print the editor's current version number and date of last change.
visual	[*address*] vi [*type*] [*count*]
	Enter visual mode (vi) at the line specified by *address*. Exit with Q. *type* can be one of -, ^, or . (See the z command). *count* specifies an initial window size.
visual	vi [+ *n*] *file*
	Begin editing *file* in visual mode (vi), optionally at line *n*.
write	[*address*] w[!] [[>>] *file*]
	Write lines specified by *address* to *file*, or write full contents of buffer if *address* is not specified. If *file* is also omitted, save the contents of the buffer to the current filename. If >> *file* is used, write contents to the end of the specified *file*. Add a ! to force the editor to write over any current contents of *file*.
	Example
	:1,10w name_list *Copy first 10 lines to name_list*
	:50w >> name_list *Now append line 50*
write	[*address*] w !*command*
	Write lines specified by *address* to *command*.

> :1,66w !pr -h myfile | lp   *Print first page of file*

Write and quit the file in one movement. The file is always written. The ! flag forces the editor to write over any current contents of *file*.

Write the file if it was changed since the last write; then quit.

Place lines specified by *address* in named buffer *char*. If no *char* is given, place lines in general buffer. *count* specifies the number of lines to yank, starting with *address*.

Example

> :101,200 ya a

Print a window of text with the line specified by *address* at the top. *count* specifies the number of lines to be displayed.

Type

+   Place specified line at the top of the window (default).

–   Place specified line at the bottom of the window.

.   Place specified line in the center of the window.

^   Print the previous window.

=   Place specified line in the center of the window and leave the current line at this line.

Execute Unix *command* in a shell. If *address* is specified, apply the lines contained in *address* as standard input to *command*, and replace the lines with the output and error output. (This is called *filtering* the text through the *command*.)

$\rightarrow$

! ←	**Examples** `:!ls` — *List files in the current directory* `:11,20!sort -f` — *Sort lines 11–20 of current file*
=	[*address*] = Print the line number of the line indicated by *address*. Default is line number of the last line.
< >	[*address*] < [*count*] or [*address*] > [*count*] Shift lines specified by *address* either left (<) or right (>). Only leading spaces and tabs are added or removed when shifting lines. *count* specifies the number of lines to shift, starting with *address*. The shiftwidth option controls the number of columns that are shifted. Repeating the < or > increases the shift amount. For example, :>>> shifts three times as much as :>.
address	*address* Print the lines specified in *address*.
RETURN	Print the next line in the file.
&	[*address*] & [*options*] [*count*] Repeat the previous substitute (s) command. *count* specifies the number of lines on which to substitute, starting with *address*. *options* are the same as for the substitute command. **Examples** `:s/Overdue/Paid/` — *Substitute once on current line* `:g/Status/&` — *Redo substitution on all "Status" lines*
~	[*address*] ~ [*count*] Replace the last used regular expression (even if from a search, and not from an s command) with the replacement pattern from the most recent s (substitute) command. This is rather obscure; see Chapter 6 of *Learning the vi Editor* for details.

CHAPTER 10

The sed Editor

This chapter presents the following topics:

- Conceptual overview of sed
- Command-line syntax
- Syntax of sed commands
- Group summary of sed commands
- Alphabetical summary of sed commands

For more information, see *sed & awk*, listed in the Bibliography.

Conceptual Overview

sed is a noninteractive, or stream-oriented, editor. It interprets a script and performs the actions in the script. sed is stream-oriented because, like many Unix programs, input flows through the program and is directed to standard output. For example, sort is stream-oriented; vi is not. sed's input typically comes from a file or pipe but can be directed from the keyboard. Output goes to the screen by default but can be captured in a file or sent through a pipe instead.

Typical Uses of sed Include:

- Editing one or more files automatically.
- Simplifying repetitive edits to multiple files.
- Writing conversion programs.

sed Operates as Follows:

- Each line of input is copied into a "pattern space," an internal buffer where editing operations are performed.

- All editing commands in a sed script are applied, in order, to each line of input.

- Editing commands are applied to all lines (globally) unless line addressing restricts the lines affected.

- If a command changes the input, subsequent commands and address tests are applied to the current line in the pattern space, not the original input line.

- The original input file is unchanged because the editing commands modify a copy of each original input line. The copy is sent to standard output (but can be redirected to a file).

- sed also maintains the "hold space," a separate buffer that can be used to save data for later retrieval.

Command-Line Syntax

The syntax for invoking sed has two forms:

```
sed [-n] [-e] 'command' file(s)
sed [-n]  -f  scriptfile file(s)
```

The first form allows you to specify an editing command on the command line, surrounded by single quotes. The second form allows you to specify a *scriptfile*, a file containing sed commands. Both forms may be used together, and they may be used multiple times. If no *file(s)* are specified, sed reads from standard input.

The following *options* are recognized:

-n   Suppress the default output; sed displays only those lines specified with the p command or with the p flag of the s command.

-e *cmd*
    Next argument is an editing command. Useful if multiple scripts or commands are specified.

-f *file*
    Next argument is a file containing editing commands.

If the first line of the script is #n, sed behaves as if -n had been specified.

Syntax of sed Commands

sed commands have the general form:

    [*address*[, *address*]][!]*command* [*arguments*]

sed copies each line of input into the pattern space. sed instructions consist of *addresses* and editing *commands*. If the address of the command matches the line

---

in the pattern space, the command is applied to that line. If a command has no address, it is applied to each input line. If a command changes the contents of the pattern space, subsequent commands and addresses are applied to the current line in the pattern space, not the original input line.

commands consist of a single letter or symbol; they are described later, alphabetically and by group. *arguments* include the label supplied to b or t, the filename supplied to r or w, and the substitution flags for s. *addresses* are described below.

Pattern Addressing

A sed command can specify zero, one, or two addresses. An address can be a line number, the symbol $ (for last line), or a regular .expression enclosed in slashes (*/pattern/*). Regular expressions are described in Chapter 6, *Pattern Matching*. Additionally, \n matches any newline in the pattern space (resulting from the N command), but not the newline at the end of the pattern space.

If the Command Specifies:	Then the Command is Applied to:
No address	Each input line.
One address	Any line matching the address. Some commands accept only one address: a, i, r, q, and =.
Two comma-separated addresses	First matching line and all succeeding lines up to and including a line matching the second address.
An address followed by !	All lines that do *not* match the address.

Examples

s/xx/yy/g	Substitute on all lines (all occurrences).
/BSD/d	Delete lines containing BSD.
/^BEGIN/,/^END/p	Print between BEGIN and END, inclusive.
/SAVE/!d	Delete any line that doesn't contain SAVE.
/BEGIN/,/END/!s/xx/yy/g	Substitute on all lines, except between BEGIN and END.

Braces ({ }) are used in sed to nest one address inside another or to apply multiple commands at the same address.

```
[/pattern/[,/pattern/]]{
command1
command2
}
```

The opening curly brace must end its line, and the closing curly brace must be on a line by itself. Be sure there are no spaces after the braces.

Group Summary of sed Commands

In the lists below, the sed commands are grouped by function and are described tersely. Full descriptions, including syntax and examples, can be found afterward in the "Alphabetical Summary" section.

Basic Editing

a\   Append text after a line.
c\   Replace text (usually a text block).
i\   Insert text before a line.
d   Delete lines.
s   Make substitutions.
y   Translate characters (like Unix tr).

Line Information

=   Display line number of a line.
l   Display control characters in ASCII.
p   Display the line.

Input/Output Processing

n   Skip current line and go to line below.
r   Read another file's contents into the output stream.
w   Write input lines to another file.
q   Quit the sed script (no further output).

Yanking and Putting

h   Copy into hold space; wipe out what's there.
H   Copy into hold space; append to what's there.
g   Get the hold space back; wipe out the destination line.
G   Get the hold space back; append to the pattern space.
x   Exchange contents of hold space and pattern space.

Branching Commands

b   Branch to *label* or to end of script.
t   Same as b, but branch only after substitution.
:label   Label branched to by t or b.

Multiline Input Processing

N   Read another line of input (creates embedded newline).
D   Delete up to the embedded newline.
P   Print up to the embedded newline.

Alphabetical Summary of sed Commands

**#**

Begin a comment in a sed script. Valid only as the first character of the first line. (Some versions allow comments anywhere, but it is better not to rely on this.) If the first line of the script is #n, sed behaves as if -n had been specified.

:*label*   **:**

Label a line in the script for transfer of control by b or t. *label* may contain up to seven characters.

[/*pattern***/]=**   **=**

Write to standard output the line number of each line addressed by *pattern.*

[*address***]a**   **a**
text

Append *text* following each line matched by *address.* If *text* goes over more than one line, newlines must be "hidden" by preceding them with a backslash. The *text* is terminated by the first newline that is not hidden in this way. The *text* is not available in the pattern space, and subsequent commands cannot be applied to it. The results of this command are sent to standard output when the list of editing commands is finished, regardless of what happens to the current line in the pattern space.

Example

```
$a\
This goes after the last line in the file\
(marked by $).  This text is escaped at the\
end of each line, except for the last one.
```

b	[*address1*[,*address2*]]b[*label*]

Transfer control unconditionally to :*label* elsewhere in script. That is, the command following the *label* is the next command applied to the current line. If no *label* is specified, control falls through to the end of the script, so no more commands are applied to the current line.

Example

```
# Ignore tbl tables; resume script after TE:
/^\.TS/,/^\.TE/b
```

c	[*address1*[,*address2*]]c\
	text

Replace (change) the lines selected by the address(es) with *text*. (See **a** for details on *text*.) When a range of lines is specified, all lines as a group are replaced by a single copy of *text*. The contents of the pattern space are, in effect, deleted and no subsequent editing commands can be applied to the pattern space (or to *text*).

Example

```
# Replace first 100 lines in a file:
1,100c\
\
<First 100 names to be supplied>
```

d	[*address1*[,*address2*]]d

Delete the addressed line (or lines) from the pattern space. Thus, the line is not passed to standard output. A new line of input is read, and editing resumes with the first command in the script.

Example

```
# delete all blank lines:
/^$/d
```

D	[*address1*[,*address2*]]D

Delete first part (up to embedded newline) of multiline pattern space created by N command and resume editing with first command in script. If this command empties the pattern space, a new line of input is read, as if the d command had been executed.

```
# Strip multiple blank lines, leaving only one:
/^$/{
N
/^\n$/D
}
```

D

[*address1*[,*address2*]]g

g

Paste the contents of the hold space (see **h** and **H**) back into the pattern space, wiping out the previous contents of the pattern space. The Example shows a simple way to copy lines.

Example

This script collects all lines containing the word *Item:* and copies them to a place marker later in the file. The place marker is overwritten:

```
/Item:/H
/<Replace this line with the item list>/g
```

[*address1*[,*address2*]]G

G

Same as g, except that a newline and the the hold space are pasted to the end of the pattern space instead of overwriting it. The Example shows a simple way to "cut and paste" lines.

Example

This script collects all lines containing the word *Item:* and moves them after a place marker later in the file. The original *Item:* lines are deleted.

```
/Item:/{
H
d
}
/Summary of items:/G
```

[*address1*[,*address2*]]h

h

Copy the pattern space into the hold space, a special temporary buffer. The previous contents of the hold space are obliterated. You can use h to save a line before editing it.

Example

```
# Edit a line; print the change; replay the original
/Unix/{
h
s/.* Unix \(.*\) .*/\1:/
p
```

→

h
←
	``
	x
	}
	``

Sample input:

```
This describes the Unix ls command.
This describes the Unix cp command.
```

Sample output:

```
ls:
This describes the Unix ls command.
cp:
This describes the Unix cp command.
```

H [*address1*[,*address2*]]H

Append a newline and then the contents of the pattern space to the contents of the hold space. Even if the hold space is empty, H still appends a newline. H is like an incremental copy. See examples under **g** and **G**.

---

i [*address*]i\
text

Insert *text* before each line matched by *address*. (See **a** for details on *text*.)

Example

```
/Item 1/i\
The five items are listed below:
```

---

l [*address1*[,*address2*]]l

List the contents of the pattern space, showing nonprinting characters as ASCII codes. Long lines are wrapped.

---

n [*address1*[,*address2*]]n

Read next line of input into pattern space. The current line is sent to standard output, and the next line becomes the current line. Control passes to the command following n instead of resuming at the top of the script.

Example

In the *ms* macros, a section header occurs on the line below an .NH macro. To print all lines of header text, invoke this script with sed -n:

```
/^\.NH/{
n
p
}
```

[*address1*[,*address2*]]N

Append next input line to contents of pattern space; the new line is separated from the previous contents of the pattern space by a newline. (This
command is designed to allow pattern matches across two lines.) Using \n
to match the embedded newline, you can match patterns across multiple
lines. See Example under **D**.

Examples

Like the Example in **n**, but print .NH line as well as header title:

```
/^\.NH/{
N
p
}
```

Join two lines (replace newline with space):

```
/^\.NH/{
N
s/\n/ /
p
}
```

[*address1*[,*address2*]]p

Print the addressed line(s). Note that this can result in duplicate output
unless default output is suppressed using #n or the –n command-line
option. Typically used before commands that change flow control (d, n, b)
and might prevent the current line from being output. See Examples under
h, **n**, and **N**.

[*address1*[,*address2*]]P

Print first part (up to embedded newline) of multiline pattern space created by N command. Same as p if N has not been applied to a line.

Example

Suppose you have function references in two formats:

```
function(arg1, arg2)
function(arg1,
        arg2)
```

The following script changes argument arg2, regardless of whether it
appears on the same line as the function name:

```
s/function(arg1, arg2)/function(arg1, XX)/
/function(/{
N
s/arg2/XX/
```

→

P ←	P D }

---

q	**[address]q**
	
	Quit when *address* is encountered. The addressed line is first written to the output (if default output is not suppressed), along with any text appended to it by previous a or r commands.
	
	Examples
	
	Delete everything after the addressed line:
	
	`/Garbled text follows:/q`
	
	Print only the first 50 lines of a file:
	
	`50q`

---

r	**[address]r file** Read contents of *file* and append after the contents of the pattern space. There must be exactly one space between the r and the filename. **Example** `/The list of items follows:/r item_file`

---

s	**[address1[,address2]]s/pattern/replacement/[flags]** Substitute *replacement* for *pattern* on each addressed line. If pattern addresses are used, the pattern // represents the last pattern address specified. Any delimiter may be used. Use \ within *pattern* or *replacement* to escape the delimiter. The following flags can be specified: g Replace all instances of *pattern* on each addressed line, not just the first instance. p Print the line if a successful substitution is done. If several successful substitutions are done, sed prints multiple copies of the line. w *file* Write the line to *file* if a replacement was done. A maximum of 10 different *files* can be opened. *n* Replace *n*th instance of *pattern* on each addressed line. *n* is any number in the range 1 to 512, and the default is 1.

Examples

Here are some short, commented scripts:

```
# Change third and fourth quote to ( and ):
/function/{
s/"/(/3
s/"/)/4
}

# Remove all quotes on a given line:
/Title/s/"//g

# Remove first colon and all quotes; print resulting lines:
s/://p
s/"//gp

# Change first "if" but leave "ifdef" alone:
/ifdef/!s/if/   if/
```

[*address1*[,*address2*]]t [*label*]   t

Test if successful substitutions have been made on addressed lines, and if
so, branch to the line marked by : *label* (see **b** and :). If *label* is not specified, control branches to the bottom of the script. The t command is like a
case statement in the C programming language or the various shell programming languages. You test each case: when it's true, you exit the construct.

Example

Suppose you want to fill empty fields of a database. You have this:

```
ID: 1   Name: greg   Rate: 45
ID: 2   Name: dale
ID: 3
```

You want this:

```
ID: 1   Name: greg   Rate: 45   Phone: ??
ID: 2   Name: dale   Rate: ??   Phone: ??
ID: 3   Name: ????   Rate: ??   Phone: ??
```

You need to test the number of fields already there. Here's the script
(fields are tab-separated):

```
#n
/ID/{
s/ID: .* Name: .* Rate: .*/&   Phone: ??/p
t
s/ID: .* Name: .*/&   Rate: ??   Phone: ??/p
t
s/ID: .*/&   Name: ????   Rate: ??   Phone: ??/p
}
```

w	[*address1*[,*address2*]]w *file*

Append contents of pattern space to *file*. This action occurs when the command is encountered rather than when the pattern space is output. Exactly one space must separate the w and the filename. A maximum of 10 different files can be opened in a script. This command creates the file if it does not exist; if the file exists, its contents are overwritten each time the script is executed. Multiple write commands that direct output to the same file append to the end of the file.

Example

```
# Store tbl and eqn blocks in a file:
/^\.TS/,/^\.TE/w troff_stuff
/^\.EQ/,/^\.EN/w troff_stuff
```

x	[*address1*[,*address2*]]x

Exchange the contents of the pattern space with the contents of the hold space. See **h** for an example.

y	[*address1*[,*address2*]]y/*abc*/*xyz*/

Translate characters. Change every instance of *a* to *x*, *b* to *y*, *c* to *z*, etc.

Example

```
# Change item 1, 2, 3 to Item A, B, C ...
/^item [1-9]/y/i123456789/IABCDEFGHI/
```

CHAPTER 11

The awk Programming Language

This chapter presents the following topics:

- Conceptual overview
- Command-line syntax
- Patterns and procedures
- Built-in variables
- Operators
- Variables and array assignment
- User-defined functions
- Group listing of functions and commands
- Implementation limits
- Alphabetical summary of functions and commands

For more information, see *sed & awk*, listed in the Bibliography.

Conceptual Overview

awk is a pattern-matching program for processing files, especially when they are databases. The new version of awk, called nawk, provides additional capabilities.* Every modern Unix system comes with a version of new awk, and its use is recommended over old awk.

---

* It really isn't so new. The additional features were added in 1984, and it was first shipped with System V Release 3.1 in 1987. Nevertheless, the name was never changed on most systems.

Different systems vary in what the two versions are called. Some have oawk and awk, for the old and new versions, respectively. Others have awk and nawk. Still others only have awk, which is the new version. This example shows what happens if your awk is the old one:

```
$ awk 1 /dev/null
awk: syntax error near line 1
awk: bailing out near line 1
```

awk exits silently if it is the new version.

Source code for the latest version of awk, from Bell Labs, can be downloaded starting at Brian Kernighan's home page: *http://cm.bell-labs.com/~bwk*. Michael Brennan's mawk is available via anonymous FTP from *ftp://ftp.whidbey.net/pub/brennan/mawk1.3.3.tar.gz*. Finally, the Free Software Foundation has a version of awk called gawk, available from *ftp://gnudist.gnu.org/gnu/gawk/gawk-3.0.4.tar.gz*. All three programs implement "new" awk. Thus, references below such as "nawk only," apply to all three. gawk has additional features.

With original awk, you can:

- Think of a text file as made up of records and fields in a textual database.

- Perform arithmetic and string operations.

- Use programming constructs such as loops and conditionals.

- Produce formatted reports.

With nawk, you can also:

- Define your own functions.

- Execute Unix commands from a script.

- Process the results of Unix commands.

- Process command-line arguments more gracefully.

- Work more easily with multiple input streams.

- Flush open output files and pipes (latest Bell Labs awk).

In addition, with GNU awk (gawk), you can:

- Use regular expressions to separate records, as well as fields.

- Skip to the start of the next file, not just the next record.

- Perform more powerful string substitutions.

- Retrieve and format system time values.

Command-Line Syntax

The syntax for invoking awk has two forms:

```
awk [options] 'script' var=value file(s)
awk [options] -f scriptfile var=value file(s)
```

You can specify a *script* directly on the command line, or you can store a script in a *scriptfile* and specify it with -f. nawk allows multiple -f scripts. Variables can be assigned a value on the command line. The value can be a literal, a shell variable ($name), or a command substitution (`cmd`), but the value is available only after the BEGIN statement is executed.

awk operates on one or more *files*. If none are specified (or if - is specified), awk reads from the standard input.

The recognized *options* are:

-F*fs*

> Set the field separator to *fs*. This is the same as setting the system variable FS. Original awk allows the field separator to be only a single character. nawk allows *fs* to be a regular expression. Each input line, or record, is divided into fields by whitespace (blanks or tabs) or by some other user-definable record separator. Fields are referred to by the variables $1, $2,..., $*n*. $0 refers to the entire record.

-v *var=value*

> Assign a *value* to variable *var*. This allows assignment before the script begins execution (available in nawk only).

To print the first three (colon-separated) fields of each record on separate lines:

```
awk -F: '{ print $1; print $2; print $3 }' /etc/passwd
```

More examples are shown in the section "Simple Pattern-Procedure Examples."

Patterns and Procedures

awk scripts consist of patterns and procedures:

```
pattern { procedure }
```

Both are optional. If *pattern* is missing, { *procedure* } is applied to all lines; if { *procedure* } is missing, the matched line is printed.

Patterns

A pattern can be any of the following:

```
/regular expression/
relational expression
pattern-matching expression
BEGIN
END
```

- Expressions can be composed of quoted strings, numbers, operators, functions, defined variables, or any of the predefined variables described later in the section "Built-in Variables."

- Regular expressions use the extended set of metacharacters and are described in Chapter 6, *Pattern Matching*.

- ^ and $ refer to the beginning and end of a string (such as the fields), respectively, rather than the beginning and end of a line. In particular, these metacharacters will *not* match at a newline embedded in the middle of a string.

- Relational expressions use the relational operators listed in the section "Operators" later in this chapter. For example, $2 > $1 selects lines for which the second field is greater than the first. Comparisons can be either string or numeric. Thus, depending on the types of data in $1 and $2, awk does either a numeric or a string comparison. This can change from one record to the next.

- Pattern-matching expressions use the operators ~ (match) and !~ (don't match). See the section "Operators" later in this chapter.

- The BEGIN pattern lets you specify procedures that take place *before* the first input line is processed. (Generally, you set global variables here.)

- The END pattern lets you specify procedures that take place *after* the last input record is read.

- In nawk, BEGIN and END patterns may appear multiple times. The procedures are merged as if there had been one large procedure.

Except for BEGIN and END, patterns can be combined with the Boolean operators || (or), && (and), and ! (not). A range of lines can also be specified using comma-separated patterns:

```
pattern,pattern
```

Procedures

Procedures consist of one or more commands, functions, or variable assignments, separated by newlines or semicolons, and contained within curly braces. Commands fall into five groups:

- Variable or array assignments

- Printing commands

- Built-in functions

- Control-flow commands

- User-defined functions (nawk only)

Simple Pattern-Procedure Examples

- Print first field of each line:

    ```
    { print $1 }
    ```

- Print all lines that contain *pattern*:

    ```
    /pattern/
    ```

- Print first field of lines that contain *pattern*:

    ```
    /pattern/ { print $1 }
    ```

- Select records containing more than two fields:

    ```
    NF > 2
    ```

- Interpret input records as a group of lines up to a blank line. Each line is a single field:

    ```
    BEGIN { FS = "\n"; RS = "" }
    ```

- Print fields 2 and 3 in switched order, but only on lines whose first field matches the string "URGENT":

    ```
    $1 ~ /URGENT/ { print $3, $2 }
    ```

- Count and print the number of *pattern* found:

    ```
    /pattern/ { ++x }
    END { print x }
    ```

- Add numbers in second column and print total:

    ```
    { total += $2 }
    END { print "column total is", total}
    ```

- Print lines that contain less than 20 characters:

    ```
    length($0) < 20
    ```

- Print each line that begins with *Name:* and that contains exactly seven fields:

    ```
    NF == 7 && /^Name:/
    ```

- Print the fields of each input record in reverse order, one per line:

    ```
    {
            for (i = NF; i >= 1; i--)
                    print $i
    }
    ```

Built-in Variables

Version	Variable	Description
awk	FILENAME	Current filename
	FS	Field separator (a space)
	NF	Number of fields in current record
	NR	Number of the current record
	OFMT	Output format for numbers ("%.6g") and for conversion to string
	OFS	Output field separator (a space)
	ORS	Output record separator (a newline)
	RS	Record separator (a newline)
	$0	Entire input record
	$n	nth field in current record; fields are separated by FS
nawk	ARGC	Number of arguments on command line
	ARGV	An array containing the command-line arguments, indexed from 0 to ARGC - 1
	CONVFMT	String conversion format for numbers ("%.6g") (POSIX)
	ENVIRON	An associative array of environment variables
	FNR	Like NR, but relative to the current file
	RLENGTH	Length of the string matched by match() function
	RSTART	First position in the string matched by match() function
	SUBSEP	Separator character for array subscripts ("\034")
gawk	ARGIND	Index in ARGV of current input file
	ERRNO	A string indicating the error when a redirection fails for getline or if close() fails
	FIELDWIDTHS	A space-separated list of field widths to use for splitting up the record, instead of FS
	IGNORECASE	When true, all regular expression matches, string comparisons, and calls to index()s ignore case
	RT	The text matched by RS, which can be a regular expression in gawk

Operators

The following table lists the operators, in order of increasing precedence, that are available in awk. Note: while ** and **= are common extensions, they are not part of POSIX awk.

Symbol	Meaning
= += -= *= /= %= ^= **=	Assignment
?:	C conditional expression (nawk only)
||	Logical OR (short-circuit)
&&	Logical AND (short-circuit)

Symbol	Meaning
in	Array membership (nawk only)
~ !~	Match regular expression and negation
< <= > >= != ==	Relational operators
(blank)	Concatenation
+ -	Addition, subtraction
* / %	Multiplication, division, and modulus (remainder)
+ - !	Unary plus and minus, and logical negation
^ **	Exponentiation
++ --	Increment and decrement, either prefix or postfix
$	Field reference

Variables and Array Assignments

Variables can be assigned a value with an = sign. For example:

```
FS = ","
```

Expressions using the operators +, -, /, and % (modulo) can be assigned to variables.

Arrays can be created with the split() function (see below), or they can simply be named in an assignment statement. Array elements can be subscripted with numbers (*array*[1], ..., *array*[*n*]) or with strings. Arrays subscripted by strings are called *associative arrays*.* For example, to count the number of widgets you have, you could use the following script:

```
/widget/ { count["widget"]++ }          Count widgets
END      { print count["widget"] }       Print the count
```

You can use the special for loop to read all the elements of an associative array:

```
for (item in array)
        process array[item]
```

The index of the array is available as item, while the value of an element of the array can be referenced as array[item].

You can use the operator in to see if an element exists by testing to see if its index exists (nawk only):

```
if (index in array)
    ...
```

This sequence tests that array[index] exists, but you cannot use it to test the value of the element referenced by array[index].

You can also delete individual elements of the array using the delete statement (nawk only).

---

* In fact, all arrays in awk are associative; numeric subscripts are converted to strings before using them as array subscripts. Associative arrays are one of awk's most powerful features.

Escape Sequences

Within string and regular expression constants, the following escape sequences may be used. Note: The \x escape sequence is a common extension; it is not part of POSIX awk.

Sequence	Meaning	Sequence	Meaning
\a	Alert (bell)	\v	Vertical tab
\b	Backspace	\\	Literal backslash
\f	Form feed	\nnn	Octal value nnn
\n	Newline	\xnn	Hexadecimal value nn
\r	Carriage return	\"	Literal double quote (in strings)
\t	Tab	\/	Literal slash (in regular expressions)

User-Defined Functions

nawk allows you to define your own functions. This makes it easy to encapsulate sequences of steps that need to be repeated into a single place, and reuse the code from anywhere in your program. Note: for user-defined functions, no space is allowed between the function name and the left parenthesis when the function is called.

The following function capitalizes each word in a string. It has one parameter, named input, and five local variables, which are written as extra parameters.

```
# capitalize each word in a string
function capitalize(input,    result, words, n, i, w)
{
        result = ""
        n = split(input, words, " ")
        for (i = 1; i <= n; i++) {
                w = words[i]
                w = toupper(substr(w, 1, 1)) substr(w, 2)
                if (i > 1)
                        result = result " "
                result = result w
        }
        return result
}

# main program, for testing
{ print capitalize($0) }
```

With this input data:

```
A test line with words and numbers like 12 on it.
```

This program produces:

```
A Test Line With Words And Numbers Like 12 On It.
```

Group Listing of awk Functions and Commands

The following table classifies awk functions and commands.

Arithmetic Functions	String Functions	Control Flow Statements	I/O Processing	Time Functions	Program-ming
atan2[a]	gensub[b]	break	close[a]	strftime[b]	delete[a]
cos[a]	gsub[a]	continue	fflush[c]	systime[b]	function[a]
exp	index	do/while[a]	getline[a]		system[a]
int	length	exit	next		
log	match[a]	for	nextfile[c]		
rand[a]	split	if	print		
sin[a]	sprintf	return[a]	printf		
sqrt	sub[a]	while			
srand[a]	substr				
	tolower[a]				
	toupper[a]				

[a] Available in nawk.
[b] Available in gawk.
[c] Available in Bell Labs awk and gawk.

Implementation Limits

Many versions of awk have various implementation limits, on things such as:

- Number of fields per record
- Number of characters per input record
- Number of characters per output record
- Number of characters per field
- Number of characters per printf string
- Number of characters in literal string
- Number of characters in character class
- Number of files open
- Number of pipes open
- The ability to handle 8-bit characters and characters that are all zero (ASCII NUL)

gawk does not have limits on any of these items, other than those imposed by the machine architecture and/or the operating system.

Alphabetical Summary of Functions and Commands

The following alphabetical list of keywords and functions includes all that are available in awk, nawk, and gawk. nawk includes all old awk functions and keywords, plus some additional ones (marked as {N}). gawk includes all nawk functions and keywords, plus some additional ones (marked as {G}). Items marked with {B} are available in the Bell Labs awk. Items that aren't marked with a symbol are available in all versions.

atan2	atan2(*y*, *x*) Return the arctangent of y/x in radians. {N}
break	break Exit from a while, for, or do loop.
close	close(*filename-expr*) close(*command-expr*) In most implementations of awk, you can have only 10 files open simultaneously and one pipe. Therefore, nawk provides a close function that allows you to close a file or a pipe. It takes as an argument the same expression that opened the pipe or file. This expression must be identical, character by character, to the one that opened the file or pipe; even whitespace is significant. {N}
continue	continue Begin next iteration of while, for, or do loop.
cos	cos(*x*) Return the cosine of *x*, an angle in radians. {N}
delete	delete *array*[*element*] delete *array* Delete *element* from *array*. The brackets are typed literally. The second form is a common extension, which deletes *all* elements of the array at one shot. {N}

```
do
    statement
while (expr)
```

Looping statement. Execute *statement*, then evaluate *expr* and, if true, execute *statement* again. A series of statements must be put within braces. {N}

```
exit [expr]
```

Exit from script, reading no new input. The END procedure, if it exists, will be executed. An optional *expr* becomes awk's return value.

```
exp(x)
```

Return exponential of x (e^x).

```
fflush([output-expr])
```

Flush any buffers associated with open output file or pipe *output-expr*. {B}

gawk extends this function. If no *output-expr* is supplied, it flushes standard output. If *output-expr* is the null string (""), it flushes all open files and pipes. {G}

```
for (init-expr; test-expr; incr-expr)
    statement
```

C-style looping construct. *init-expr* assigns the initial value of a counter variable. *test-expr* is a relational expression that is evaluated each time before executing the *statement*. When *test-expr* is false, the loop is exited. *incr-expr* increments the counter variable after each pass. All the expressions are optional. A missing *test-expr* is considered to be true. A series of statements must be put within braces.

```
for (item in array)
    statement
```

Special loop designed for reading associative arrays. For each element of the array, the *statement* is executed; the element can be referenced by *array*[*item*]. A series of statements must be put within braces.

function	```
function name(parameter-list) {
    statements
}
```
Create *name* as a user-defined function consisting of awk *statements* that apply to the specified list of parameters. No space is allowed between *name* and the left paren when the function is called. {N} |
| **getline** | ```
getline [var] [< file]
    or
command | getline [var]
```
Read next line of input. Original awk doesn't support the syntax to open multiple input streams. The first form reads input from *file*; the second form reads the output of *command*. Both forms read one record at a time, and each time the statement is executed, it gets the next record of input. The record is assigned to $0 and is parsed into fields, setting NF, NR and FNR. If *var* is specified, the result is assigned to *var*, and $0 and NF aren't changed. Thus, if the result is assigned to a variable, the current record doesn't change. getline is actually a function and returns 1 if it reads a record successfully, 0 if end-of-file is encountered, and −1 if it's otherwise unsuccessful. {N} |
| **gensub** | ```
gensub(r, s, h [, t])
```
General substitution function. Substitute *s* for matches of the regular expression *r* in the string *t*. If *h* is a number, replace the *h*th match. If it is "g" or "G", substitute globally. If *t* is not supplied, $0 is used. Return the new string value. The original *t* is *not* modified. (Compare **gsub** and **sub**.) {G} |
| **gsub** | ```
gsub(r, s [, t])
```
Globally substitute *s* for each match of the regular expression *r* in the string *t*. If *t* is not supplied, defaults to $0. Return the number of substitutions. {N} |
| **if** | ```
if (condition)
    statement
[else
    statement]
```
If *condition* is true, do *statement(s)*; otherwise do *statement* in the optional else clause. The *condition* can be an expression using any of the relational operators <, <=, ==, !=, >=, or >, as well as the array membership operator in, and the pattern-matching operators ~ and !~ |
```

(e.g., if ($1 ~ /[Aa].*/)). A series of statements must be put within braces. Another if can directly follow an else in order to produce a chain of tests or decisions.

```
index(str, substr)
```

Return the position (starting at 1) of *substr* in *str*, or zero if *substr* is not present in *str*.

```
int(x)
```

Return integer value of *x* by truncating any fractional part.

```
length([arg])
```

Return length of *arg*, or the length of $0 if no argument.

```
log(x)
```

Return the natural logarithm (base *e*) of *x*.

```
match(s, r)
```

Function that matches the pattern, specified by the regular expression *r*, in the string *s*, and returns either the position in *s*, where the match begins, or 0 if no occurrences are found. Sets the values of RSTART and RLENGTH to the start and length of the match, respectively. {N}

```
next
```

Read next input line and start new cycle through pattern/procedures statements.

```
nextfile
```

Stop processing the current input file and start new cycle through pattern/procedures statements, beginning with the first record of the next file. {B} {G}

```
print [ output-expr[, ...]] [ dest-expr ]
```

Evaluate the *output-expr* and direct it to standard output, followed by the value of ORS. Each comma-separated *output-expr* is separated in the output by the value of OFS. With no *output-expr*, print $0.

→

---

print ←	**Output Redirections**

dest-expr is an optional expression that directs the output to a file or pipe.

> `> file`
>> Directs the output to a file, overwriting its previous contents.

> `>> file`
>> Appends the output to a file, preserving its previous contents. In both cases, the file is created if it does not already exist.

> `| command`
>> Directs the output as the input to a Unix command.

Be careful not to mix > and >> for the same file. Once a file has been opened with >, subsequent output statements continue to append to the file until it is closed.

Remember to call `close()` when you have finished with a file or pipe. If you don't, eventually you will hit the system limit on the number of simultaneously open files.

printf	`printf(format [, expr-list ]) [ dest-expr ]`

An alternative output statement borrowed from the C language. It can produce formatted output and also output data without automatically producing a newline. *format* is a string of format specifications and constants. *expr-list* is a list of arguments corresponding to format specifiers. See **print** for a description of *dest-expr*.

format follows the conventions of the C-language *printf*(3S) library function. Here are a few of the most common formats:

`%s`	A string.
`%d`	A decimal number.
`%n.mf`	A floating-point number; n = total number of digits. m = number of digits after decimal point.
`%[-]nc`	n specifies minimum field length for format type c, while - left-justifies value in field; otherwise, value is right-justified.

Like any string, *format* can also contain embedded escape sequences: \n (newline) or \t (tab) being the most common. Spaces and literal text can be placed in the *format* argument by quoting the entire argument. If there are multiple expressions to be printed, there should be multiple formats specified.

Example

Using the script:

```
{ printf("The sum on line %d is %.0f.\n", NR, $1+$2) }
```

The following input line:

```
5    5
```

produces this output, followed by a newline:

```
The sum on line 1 is 10.
```

`rand()`

Generate a random number between 0 and 1. This function returns the same series of numbers each time the script is executed, unless the random number generator is seeded using srand(). {N}

`return [expr]`

Used within a user-defined function to exit the function, returning value of *expr*. The return value of a function is undefined if *expr* is not provided. {N}

`sin(x)`

Return the sine of *x*, an angle in radians. {N}

`split(string, array [, sep])`

Split *string* into elements of array *array*[1],...,*array*[*n*]. The string is split at each occurrence of separator *sep*. If *sep* is not specified, FS is used. The number of array elements created is returned.

`sprintf(format [, expressions])`

Return the formatted value of one or more *expressions*, using the specified *format* (see **printf**). Data is formatted but not printed. {N}

`sqrt(arg)`

Return square root of *arg*.

srand	`srand([expr])` Use optional *expr* to set a new seed for the random number generator. Default is the time of day. Return value is the old seed. {N}
strftime	`strftime([format [,timestamp]])` Format *timestamp* according to *format*. Return the formatted string. The *timestamp* is a time-of-day value in seconds since midnight, January 1, 1970, UTC. The *format* string is similar to that of `sprintf`. (See the Example for **systime**.) If *timestamp* is omitted, it defaults to the current time. If *format* is omitted, it defaults to a value that produces output similar to that of `date`. {G}
sub	`sub(r, s [, t])` Substitute *s* for first match of the regular expression *r* in the string *t*. If *t* is not supplied, defaults to $0. Return 1 if successful; 0 otherwise. {N}
substr	`substr(string, beg [, len])` Return substring of *string* at beginning position *beg* and the characters that follow to maximum specified length *len*. If no length is given, use the rest of the string.
system	`system(command)` Function that executes the specified *command* and returns its status. The status of the executed command typically indicates success or failure. A value of 0 means that the command executed successfully. A nonzero value indicates a failure of some sort. The documentation for the command you're running will give you the details. The output of the command is *not* available for processing within the awk script. Use *command* | `getline` to read the output of a command into the script. {N}
systime	`systime()` Return a time-of-day value in seconds since midnight, January 1, 1970, UTC. {G} *Example* Log the start and end times of a data-processing program:

```
BEGIN {
        now = systime()
        mesg = strftime("Started at %m/%d/%Y %H:%M:%S", now)
        print mesg
}
process data ...
END {
        now = systime()
        mesg = strftime("Ended at %m/%d/%Y %H:%M:%S", now)
        print mesg
}
```

systime

`tolower(str)`

tolower

Translate all uppercase characters in *str* to lowercase and return the new string.* {N}

`toupper(str)`

toupper

Translate all lowercase characters in *str* to uppercase and return the new string. {N}

`while (condition)`
  `statement`

while

Do *statement* while *condition* is true (see if for a description of allowable conditions). A series of statements must be put within braces.

printf Formats

Format specifiers for printf and sprintf have the following form:

  `%[flag][width][.precision]letter`

The control letter is required. The format conversion control letters are as follows.

Character	Description
c	ASCII character
d	Decimal integer
i	Decimal integer (added in POSIX)
e	Floating-point format ([-]d.precisione[+-]dd)
E	Floating-point format ([-]d.precisionE[+-]dd)
f	Floating-point format ([-]ddd.precision)

---

* Very early versions of nawk don't support tolower() and toupper(). However, they are now part of the POSIX specification for awk, and are included in the SVR4 nawk.

Character	Description
g	e or f conversion, whichever is shortest, with trailing zeros removed
G	E or f conversion, whichever is shortest, with trailing zeros removed
o	Unsigned octal value
s	String
x	Unsigned hexadecimal number; uses a-f for 10 to 15
X	Unsigned hexadecimal number; uses A-F for 10 to 15
%	Literal %

The optional *flag* is one of the following.

Character	Description
-	Left-justify the formatted value within the field.
space	Prefix positive values with a space and negative values with a minus.
+	Always prefix numeric values with a sign, even if the value is positive.
#	Use an alternate form: %o has a preceding 0; %x and %X are prefixed with 0x and 0X, respectively; %e, %E, and %f always have a decimal point in the result; and %g and %G do not have trailing zeros removed.
0	Pad output with zeros, not spaces. This happens only when the field width is wider than the converted result.

The optional *width* is the minimum number of characters to output. The result will be padded to this size if it is smaller. The 0 flag causes padding with zeros; otherwise, padding is with spaces.

The *precision* is optional. Its meaning varies by control letter, as shown in this table.

Conversion	Precision Means
%d, %i, %o %u, %x, %X	The minimum number of digits to print
%e, %E, %f	The number of digits to the right of the decimal point
%g, %G	The maximum number of significant digits
%s	The maximum number of characters to print

PART III

Text Formatting

Part III describes the Unix tools for document formatting. These tools are no longer part of standard SVR4 but are provided in the BSD compatibility packages that come with SVR4. They do come as a standard part of Solaris (with the exception of pic).

Many Unix vendors supply an enhanced set of formatting tools—in some cases, as an extra cost option.

- Chapter 12, *nroff and troff*
- Chapter 13, *mm Macros*
- Chapter 14, *ms Macros*
- Chapter 15, *me Macros*
- Chapter 16, *man Macros*
- Chapter 17, *troff Preprocessors*

CHAPTER 12

nroff and troff

This chapter presents the following topics:

- Introduction

- Command-line invocation

- Conceptual overview

- Default operation of requests

- Group summary of requests

- Alphabetical summary of requests

- Escape sequences

- Predefined number registers

- Special characters

Introduction

nroff and troff are Unix programs for formatting text files. nroff is designed to format output for line printers and letter-quality printers; you can also display the output on your screen. troff is designed for typesetting and laser printers. The same commands work for both programs; nroff simply ignores commands it can't implement.

nroff and troff are not part of standard SVR4 but are included in the compatibility packages. It is this version that is documented here. In addition, we make references to ditroff, or device-independent troff, which is a later version of troff. For the most part, ditroff works the same as troff; where there are distinctions, the original troff is referred to as otroff. The Solaris troff is the device-independent version and is a standard part of the Solaris distribution.

Some Unix vendors include a vendor-specific version of nroff/troff. Others don't include them at all. Various enhanced packages are also available, such as sqtroff from SoftQuad or groff from the Free Software Foundation.* These packages include additional requests or escape sequences. For completely accurate information, you should consult the text-processing manuals that come with your specific version of Unix.

Finally, if the checknr program is available, you should use it on your troff documents. Note: the device-independent version of troff is 8-bit clean. You may not be so lucky if your system only supplies otroff.

Command-Line Invocation

nroff and troff are invoked from the command line as follows:

```
nroff [options] [files]
```

```
troff [options] [files]
```

Many of the options are the same for both formatters.

nroff/troff Options

-F*dir*
    Search for font tables in directory *dir*.

-i   Read standard input after *files* are processed.

-m*name*
    Prepend a macro file to input *files*. Historically, one of /usr/lib/tmac/ tmac.*name* or /usr/share/lib/tmac/tmac.*name* were the locations of the macros for *name*. Solaris uses /usr/share/lib/tmac/*name*. The actual location and filename(s) vary among different Unix systems.

-n*N* First output page has page number *N*.

-o*list*
    Print pages contained only in the comma-separated *list*. Page ranges can be specified as *n–m*, *-m* (first page through *m*), or *n-* (*n* through end of file).

-r*aN*
    Set register *a* to *N*. The register *a* is restricted to one-character names.

-s*N* Stop every *n* pages. This allows changing a paper cassette. Resume by pressing Return (in nroff) or by pressing the start button on the typesetter (in troff).

---

* groff in particular is worth noting; it has numerous useful extensions over standard troff and is very stable. (See *http://www.gnu.org*).

-T*name*
>Prepare output designed for printer or typesetter *name*. For device names, see your specific documentation or a local expert.

-u*N* The font in position 3 is overstruck *N* times. Typically used to adjust the weight of the bold font.

-z Discard output except messages generated by .tm request (otroff only).

nroff-Only Options

-e When justifying output lines, space words equally (using terminal resolution instead of full space increments).

-h Hasten output by replacing eight horizontal spaces with a tab.

-q Invoke simultaneous input/output of .rd requests.

troff-Only Options

-a Format a printable ASCII approximation. Useful for finding page counts without producing printed output.

-f Don't stop the typesetter when formatting is done (otroff only).

-N Run as nroff instead of as troff (recent versions of ditroff only).

Examples

Run chap1 through the tbl preprocessor, then format the result using the *mm* macros, with register N set to 5 (sets the page-numbering style), etc.:

```
tbl chap1 | troff -mm -rN5 | spooler &
```

Format chap2 using the *ms* macros; the first page is 7, but print only pages 8–10, 15, and 18 through the end of the file:

```
nroff -ms -n7 -o8-10,15,18- chap2 | col > chap2.txt &
```

Conceptual Overview

This sections provides a brief overview of how to prepare input for nroff and troff. It presents the following topics:

- Requests and macros

- Common requests

- Specifying measurements

- Requests that cause a line break

- Embedded formatting controls

Requests and Macros

Formatting is specified by embedding brief codes (called *requests*) into the text source file. These codes act as directives to nroff and troff when they run. For example, to center a line of text, type the following code in a file:

```
.ce
This text should be centered.
```

When formatted, the output appears centered:

This text should be centered.

There are two types of formatting codes:

- *Requests*, which provide the most elementary instructions

- *Macros*, which are predefined combinations of requests

Requests, also known as *primitives*, allow direct control of almost any feature of page layout and formatting. Macros combine requests to create a total effect. In a sense, requests are like atoms, and macros are like molecules.

All nroff/troff requests are two-letter lowercase names. Macros are usually upper- or mixed-case names.

See Chapter 13, *mm Macros*, Chapter 14, *ms Macros*, Chapter 15, *me Macros*, and Chapter 16, *man Macros*, for more information on the standard macro packages.

Common Requests

The most commonly used requests are:

```
.ad   .ds   .ll   .nr   .sp
.br   .fi   .na   .po   .ta
.bp   .ft   .ne   .ps   .ti
.ce   .in   .nf   .so   .vs
.de   .ls
```

For example, a simple macro could be written as follows:

```
.                 \" Ps macro - show literal text display
.de Ps            \" Define a macro named "Ps"
.sp .5            \" Space down half a line
.in 1i            \" Indent one inch
.ta 10n +10n      \" Set new tabstops
.ps 8             \" Use 8-point type
.vs 10            \" Use 10-point vertical spacing
.ft CW            \" Use constant width font
.br               \" Break line (.ne begins count on next line)
.ne 3             \" Keep 3 lines together
.nf               \" No-fill mode (output lines as is)
..                \" End macro definition
```

Specifying Measurements

With some requests, the numeric argument can be followed by a scale indicator that specifies a unit of measurement. The valid indicators and their meanings are listed in the following table. Note that all measurements are internally converted to basic units (this conversion is shown in the last column). A basic unit is the smallest possible size on the printer device. The device resolution (e.g., 600 dots per inch) determines the size of a basic unit. Also, T specifies the current point size, and R specifies the device resolution.

Scale Indicator	Meaning	Equivalent Unit	# of Basic Units
c	Centimeter	2.54 inches	$R / 2.54$
i	Inch	6 picas or 72 points	R
m	Em	T points	$R \times T / 72$
n	En	0.5 em	$R \times T / 144$
p	Point	1/72 inch	$R / 72$
P	Pica	1/6 inch	$R / 6$
u	Basic unit		1
v	Vertical line space		(Current value in basic units)
None	Default		

It is worth noting that *all* numbers in nroff/troff are stored internally using integers. This applies even to apparently fractional values in commands such as:

```
.sp .5
```

which spaces down one-half of the current vertical spacing.

An "em" is the width of the letter "m" in the current font and point size. An "en" is the width of the letter "n" in the current font and point size. Note that in nroff, an "em" and an "en" are the same—the width of one character.

You can specify a scale indicator for any of the requests in the following table, except for .ps, which always uses points. If no unit is given, the default unit is used. (The second column lists the scale indicators as described in the previous table.) For horizontally oriented requests, the default unit is ems. For vertically oriented requests, the default is usually vertical lines.

Request	Default Scale	Request	Default Scale
.ch	v	.pl	v
.dt	v	.po	v
.ie	u	.ps	p
.if	u	.rt	v
.in	m	.sp	v
.ll	m	.sv	v
.lt	m	.ta	m
.mc	m	.ti	m

Request	Default Scale		Request	Default Scale
.ne	v		.vs	p
.nr	u		.wh	v

Requests That Cause a Line Break

A *line break* occurs when nroff/troff writes the current output line, even if it is not completely filled. Most requests can be interspersed with text without causing a line break in the output. The following requests cause a break:

```
.bp   .ce   .fi   .in   .sp
.br   .cf   .fl   .nf   .ti
```

If you need to prevent these requests from causing a break, begin them with the "no break" control character (normally ′) instead of a dot (.). For example, .sp takes effect right away, but ′sp waits until the output line is completely filled. Only then does it add a line space.

Embedded Formatting Controls

In addition to requests and macros, which are written on their own separate lines, you may also have formatting controls embedded within your text lines. These typically provide the following capabilities:

General formatting
Considerable formatting control is available, such as switching fonts (\f), changing point sizes (\s), computing widths (\w), and many other things. For example:

```
This text is in \fIitalic\fR, but this is in roman.
This text is \s-2VERY SMALL\s0 but this text is not.
```

Special characters
Predefined special typesetting characters, such as the bullet symbol \(bu (•), the left hand \(lh (☜), and the right hand \(rh (☞).

Strings
User-defined sequences of characters, like macros, but usable inline. For example:

```
.\" define a shorthand for UNIX
.ds UX  the \s-1UNIX\s0 Operating System
...
Welcome to \*(UX.
While \*(UX may appear daunting at first,
it is immensely powerful. ...
```

Number registers
Like variables in programming languages, number registers store numeric values that can be printed in a range of formats (decimal, roman, etc.). They can be set to auto-increment or auto-decrement, and are particularly useful when writing macro packages, for managing automatic numbering of headings, footnotes, figures, and so on. For example:

```
.nr C1 0 1  \" Chapter Level
.de CH
.bp
\\n+(C1. \\$1 \\$2 \\$3
..
```

This creates a macro that uses register C1 as the "chapter level." The first three arguments to the macro become the chapter title. The extra backslashes are needed inside the macro definition.

Later sections in this chapter describe the predefined special characters, strings and number registers, and all of the escape sequences that are available.

Default Operation of Requests

nroff/troff initializes the formatting environment. For example, unless you reset the line length, nroff/troff uses 6.5 inches. Most requests can change the default environment, and those that can are listed in Table 12-1. The second column lists the initial or default value in effect before the request is used. If no initial value applies, a hyphen (–) is used. The third column shows the effect if a request's optional argument is not used. Here, a hyphen is used if the request doesn't accept an argument or if the argument is required.

Table 12–1: Requests That Affect the Default Environment

Request	Initial Value	If No Argument	Description
.ad	Justify	Justify	Adjust margins.
.af	Lowercase arabic	–	Assign a format to a register.
.am	–	End call with ..	Append to a macro.
.bd	Off	–	Embolden font.
.c2	'	'	Set no-break control character.
.cc	.	.	Set control character.
.ce	Off	Center one line	Center lines.
.ch	–	Turn off trap	Change trap position.
.cs	Off	–	Set constant-width spacing.
.cu	Off	One line	Continuous underline/italicize.
.da	–	End the diversion	Divert text and append to a macro.
.de	–	End macro with ..	Define a macro.
.di	–	End the diversion	Divert text to a macro.
.dt	–	Turn off trap	Set a diversion trap.
.ec	\	\	Set escape character.
.eo	On	–	Turn off escape character.

Table 12–1: Requests That Affect the Default Environment (continued)

Request	Initial Value	If No Argument	Description
.ev	0	Previous environment	Change environment (push down).
.fc	Off	Off	Set field delimiter and pad character.
.fi	Fill	–	Fill lines.
.fp	1=R	–	Mount font (on positions 1–4).
	2=I		
	3=B		
	4=S		
.ft	Roman	Previous font	Set font.
.hc	\%	\%	Set hyphenation character.
.hy	Mode 1	Mode 1	Set hyphenation mode.
.ig	–	End with ..	Suppress (ignore) text in output.
.in	0	Previous indent	Indent.
.it	–	Turn off trap	Set a trap for input line counting.
.lc	.	None	Set leader character.
.lg	Off (nroff)	On	Ligature mode.
	On (troff)		
.ll	6.5 inches	Previous line length	Set line length.
.ls	Single-space	Previous mode	Set line spacing.
.lt	6.5 inches	Previous title length	Set length of title.
.mc	–	Turn off	Set the margin character.
.mk	–	Internal	Mark vertical position.
.na	Adjust	–	Don't adjust margins.
.ne	–	One vertical line	Keep lines on same page if there's room.
.nf	Fill	–	Don't fill lines.
.nh	On	–	Turn off hyphenation.
.nm	Off	Off	Line-numbering mode.
.nn	–	One line	Don't number next N lines.
.ns	Space mode	–	Enable no-space mode.
.nx	–	End of file	Go to a file.

Table 12–1: Requests That Affect the Default Environment (continued)

Request	Initial Value	If No Argument	Description
.pc	%	Off	Set page character.
.pl	11 inches	11 inches	Set page length.
.pn	Page 1	–	Set page number.
.po	0 (nroff); 26/27 inch (otroff) 1 inch (ditroff)	Previous offset	Change page offset.
.ps	10	Previous point size	Set point size.
.rd	–	Ring bell	Read from the terminal.
.rt	–	Internal	Return to marked vertical place.
.sp	–	One vertical line	Output blank spacing.
.ss	12/36 em	Ignored	Set character spacing.
.sv	–	One vertical line	Save (store) spacing.
.ta	8 en (nroff); 1/2 inch (troff)	–	Define tab settings.
.tc	–	–	Set tab repetition character.
.ti	0	–	Indent next line.
.tm	–	Newline	Print a message, then continue.
.tr	–	–	Translate pairs of characters on output.
.uf	Italic	Italic	Set font for underlining.
.ul	0	One line	Underline/italicize.
.vs	1/6 inch (nroff); 12 points (troff)	Previous value	Set vertical spacing for lines.

Comments in nroff/troff begin with \". Lines beginning with . that contain an unknown request are ignored. In general, don't put leading whitespace on your text lines. This causes a break, and nroff and troff honors the leading whitespace literally.

Note: the canonical reference for nroff/troff is *Bell Labs Computing Science Technical Report #54, Troff User's Manual,* by J.F. Ossanna and B.W. Kernighan. It is available in PostScript from *http://cm.bell-labs.com/cm/cs/cstr/54.ps.gz.* You should read it if you plan to do any serious work in nroff/troff (such as writing or modifying macro packages). This document explains the ideas of diversions, environments, fields, registers, strings, and traps.

Group Summary of Requests

As an aid to finding the right request for a particular task, the 85 nroff/troff requests are listed below by subject.

Character Output

.cu	Continuous underline/italicize.
.lg	Ligature mode.
.tr	Translate characters.
.uf	Set font for underlining.
.ul	Underline/italicize.

Conditional Processing

.el	*Else* portion of *if-else*.
.ie	*If* portion of *if-else*.
.if	*If* statement.

Customizing n/troff Requests

.c2	Set no-break control character.
.cc	Set control character.
.ec	Set escape character.
.eo	Turn off escape character.
.hc	Set hyphenation character.
.pc	Set page character.

Diagnostic Output

.ab	Print a message, then abort.
.fl	Flush output buffer.
.ig	Suppress (ignore) text in output.
.lf	Set line number and filename.
.mc	Set the margin character.
.pm	Print name and size of macros.
.tm	Print a message, then continue.

Font and Character Size

.bd	Embolden font.
.cs	Set constant-width spacing.
.fp	Mount font (on positions 1–4).
.ft	Set font.
.ps	Set point size.
.ss	Set character spacing.

Horizontal Positioning

.in	Indent.
.ll	Set line length.
.lt	Set length of title.
.po	Change page offset.
.ti	Indent next line.
.tl	Specify three-part title.

Hyphenation

.hw	Set hard-coded hyphenation.
.hy	Set hyphenation mode.
.nh	Turn off hyphenation.

Input/Output Switching

.cf	Copy raw file to output.
.ex	Exit from nroff/troff.
.nx	Go to a file.
.pi	Pipe output to a Unix command.
.rd	Read from the terminal.
.so	Go to a file, then return.
.sy	Execute a Unix command.

Line Numbering

.nm   Line-numbering mode.
.nn   Don't number lines.

Macro and String Processing

.am   Append to a macro.
.as   Append to a string.
.ch   Change trap position.
.da   Divert text; append to a macro.
.de   Define a macro.
.di   Divert text to a macro.
.ds   Define a string.
.dt   Set a diversion trap.
.em   Set the ending macro.
.ev   Change environment.
.it   Set trap for input line counting.
.rm   Remove macro, request, or string.
.rn   Rename macro, request, or string.
.wh   Set a page trap.

Number Registers

.af   Assign a format to a register.
.nr   Define a number register.
.rr   Remove a number register.

Pagination

.bp   Begin a new page.
.mk   Mark vertical position.
.ne   Keep lines on same page if there's room.
.pl   Set page length.
.pn   Set page number.
.rt   Return to marked vertical place.

Tabs

.fc   Set a field delimiter and a pad character.
.lc   Set leader character.
.ta   Define tab settings.
.tc   Set tab character.

Text Adjustments

.ad   Adjust margins.
.br   Break the output line.
.ce   Center lines.
.fi   Fill lines.
.na   Don't adjust margins.
.nf   Don't fill lines.

Vertical Spacing

.ls   Line spacing (e.g., single-spaced).
.ns   Enable no-space mode.
.os   Output vertical space from .sv.
.rs   Restore spacing mode.
.sp   Output blank spacing.
.sv   Save (store) spacing.
.vs   Set vertical spacing for lines.

nroff/troff

Alphabetical Summary of Requests

.ab	.ab [*text*] Abort and print *text* as message. If *text* is not specified, the message User Abort is printed.
.ad	.ad [*c*] Adjust output lines according to format *c*. Fill mode must be on (see .fi). With no argument, same as .ad 1. The current adjustment mode is stored in register .j, with the following values: 0=l, 1=b, 3=c, 5=r (see .na). ***Values for c*** b Lines are justified. n Lines are justified. c Lines are centered. l Lines are flush left. r Lines are flush right.
.af	.af *r c* Assign format *c* to register *r*. ***Values for c*** 1 0, 1, 2, etc. 001 000, 001, 002, etc. i Lowercase roman numerals. I Uppercase roman numerals. a Lowercase alphabetic. A Uppercase alphabetic. ***Example*** Paginate front matter using the *ms* macros: .af PN i *Set page number register PN to i*

.am *xx* [*yy*]

Take the requests (etc.) that follow and append them to the definition of macro *xx*; end the append at call of *.yy* (or .., if *yy* is omitted).

.as *xx string*

Append *string* to string register *xx*. *string* may contain spaces and is terminated by a newline. An initial quote (") is ignored.

.bd [s] *f n*

Overstrike characters in font *f n* times. If s is specified, overstrike characters in special font *n* times when font *f* is in effect.

.bp [*n*]

Begin new page. Number next page *n*.

.br

Break to a newline (output partial line).

.c2 *c*

Use *c* (instead of ′) as the no-break control character.

.cc *c*

Use *c* (instead of .) as the control character to introduce requests and macros.

.ce [*n*]

Center next *n* lines (default is 1); if *n* is 0, stop centering. *n* applies only to lines containing output text. Blank lines don't count.

.cf *file*

Copy contents of *file* into output and don't interpret (ditroff only).

.ch	`.ch xx [n]`
	Change trap position for macro *xx* to *n*. If *n* is absent, remove the trap.
.cs	`.cs f n m`
	Use constant spacing for font *f.* Constant character width is *n*/36 ems. If *m* is given, the em is taken to be *m* points.
	Example
	`.cs CW 18` *squeeze spacing of constant-width font*
.cu	`.cu [n]`
	Continuous underline (including interword spaces) on next *n* lines. If *n* is 0, stop underlining. Use .ul to underline visible characters only. Underline font can be switched in troff with .uf request. In troff, .cu and .ul produce italics (you must use a macro to underline).
.da	`.da [xx]`
	Divert following text and append it to macro *xx.* If no argument, end the diversion.
.de	`.de xx [yy]`
	Define macro *xx.* End definition at call of .*yy* (or .., if *yy* is omitted).
.di	`.di [xx]`
	Divert following text into a newly defined macro *xx.* If no argument, end the diversion.
.ds	`.ds xx string`
	Define *xx* to contain *string.* An initial quote (") is ignored.
.dt	`.dt n xx`
	Install diversion trap at position *n*, within diversion, to invoke macro *xx.*

`.ec` [*c*]

Set escape character to *c*. Default is \.

`.el`

Else portion of *if-else* (see `.ie` below).

`.em` *xx*

Set end macro to be *xx*. *xx* is executed automatically when all other output complete.

`.eo`

Turn escape character mechanism off. All escape characters are printed literally.

`.ev` [*n*]

Change environment to *n*. For example, many requests that affect horizontal position, hyphenation, or text adjustment are stored in the current environment. If *n* is omitted, restore previous environment. The initial value of *n* is 0, and $0 \leq n \leq 2$. You must return to the previous environment by using `.ev` with no argument, or you will get a stack overflow. (ditroff simply ignores an invalid argument and issues a warning.)

`.ex`

Exit from the formatter and perform no further text processing. Typically used with `.nx` for form-letter generation.

`.fc` *a b*

Set field delimiter to *a* and pad character to *b*.

`.fi`

Turn on fill mode, the inverse of `.nf`. Default is on.

.fl	.fl
	Flush output buffer. Useful for interactive debugging.

.fp	.fp *n f*
	Assign font *f* to position *n*. *n* ranges from 1 to 4 in otroff and from 1 to 99 in ditroff.

Examples

```
.fp 7 CW    \" position 7 is constant width
.fp 8 CI    \" position 8 is constant italic
.fp 9 CB    \" position 9 is constant bold
```

.ft	.ft *f*
	Change font to *f*, where *f* is a one- or two-character font name, or a font position assigned with .fp. Similar to escape sequence \f.

.hc	.hc [*c*]
	Change input hyphenation-indication character to *c*. Default is \%.

.hw	.hw *words*
	Specify hyphenation points for *words* (e.g., .hw spe-ci-fy). There is a limit of around 128 total characters for the total list of *words*.

.hy	.hy *n*
	Turn hyphenation on (*n* ≥ 1) or off (*n* = 0). See also **.nh**.

Values for n

1	Hyphenate whenever necessary.
2	Don't hyphenate last word on page.
4	Don't split off first two characters.
8	Don't split off last two characters.
14	Use all three restrictions.

```
.ie [!]condition anything
.el anything
```

If portion of *if-else*. If *condition* is true, do *anything*. Otherwise do *anything* following .el request. .ie/.el pairs can be nested. Syntax for *condition* is described under .if.

Example

If first argument isn't 2, columns are 1.8 inches wide; otherwise, columns are 2.5 inches wide:

```
.ie !'\\$1'2' .MC 1.8i 0.2i
.el .MC 2.5i 0.25i
```

```
.if [!]condition anything
```

If *condition* is true, do *anything*. The presence of an ! negates the condition. If *anything* runs over more than one line, it must be delimited by \{ and \}.

Conditions

o	True if the page number is odd.
e	True if the page number is even.
n	True if the processor is nroff.
t	True if the processor is troff.
"str1"str2"	True if *str1* is identical to *str2*. Often used to test the value of arguments passed to a macro.
expr	True if the value of expression *expr* is greater than zero.

Expressions

Expressions typically contain number register interpolations and can use any of the following operators:

+ -	Addition, subtraction
/ *	Multiplication, division
%	Modulo
< >	Less than, greater than
<= >=	Less than or equal, greater than or equal
= ==	Equal
!	Logical negation
&	Logical AND
:	Logical OR

Note: expressions are evaluated left to right; there is no operator precedence. Parentheses may be supplied to force a particular evaluation order.

nroff/troff

.if ←	*Example* Inside a macro definition, set the spacing and print the second argument. (The extra backslashes are necessary in \\$2. One backslash is stripped off when the macro is first read, so the second one is needed for it to be evaluated correctly when the macro is executed.) ``` .if t .nr PD 0.5v \" Set spacing between ms paragraphs .if !"\\$2"" \{ \" If arg 2 is non null, print it in bold \fB\\$2\fP\} ```
.ig	`.ig [yy]` Ignore following text, up to line beginning with .*yy* (default is .., as with .de). Useful for commenting out large blocks of text or macro definitions.
.in	`.in [[±]n]` Set indent to *n* or increment indent by ±*n*. If no argument, restore previous indent. Current indent is stored in register .i. Default scale is ems.
.it	`.it n xx` Set trap for input-line count, so as to invoke macro *xx* after *n* lines of input text have been read.
.lc	`.lc c` Set leader repetition character (value for \a) to *c* instead of . (dot).
.lf	`.lf n filename` Set the line number and filename for subsequent error messages to *n* and *filename* (recent versions of ditroff only). Modifies registers .c and .F.
.lg	`.lg n` Turn ligature mode on if *n* is absent or nonzero.

.ll [[±]*n*]   .ll

Set line length to *n* or increment line length by ±*n*. If no argument, restore previous line length. Current line length is stored in register .l. Default value is 6.5 inches.

.ls [*n*]   .ls

Set line spacing to *n*. If no argument, restore previous line spacing. Initial value is 1.

Example

  .ls 2   *Produce double-spaced output*

.lt [*n*]   .lt

Set title length to *n* (default scale is ems). If no argument, restore previous value.

.mc [*c*] [*n*]   .mc

Set margin character to *c* and place it *n* spaces to the right of margin. If *c* is missing, turn margin character off. If *n* is missing, use previous value. Initial value for *n* is .2 inches in nroff and 1 em in troff.

This command is usually used for producing "change bars" in documents. See **diffmk** in Chapter 2, *Unix Commands*.

.mk [*r*]   .mk

Mark current vertical place in register *r*. Return to mark with .rt or .sp|\n*r*.

.na   .na

Do not adjust margins. Current adjustment mode is stored in register .j. See also .ad.

.ne *n*   .ne

If *n* lines do not remain on this page, start a new page.

.nf	`.nf` Do not fill or adjust output lines. See also **.ad** and **.fi**.
.nh	`.nh` Turn hyphenation off. See also **.hy**.
.nm	`.nm [n m s i]` Number output lines (if $n \geq 0$), or turn numbering off (if $n = 0$). $\pm n$ sets initial line number; m sets numbering interval; s sets separation of numbers and text; i sets indent of text. Useful for code segments, poetry, etc. See also **.nn**.
.nn	`.nn n` Do not number next n lines, but keep track of numbering sequence, which can be resumed with .nm +0. See also **.nm**.

.nr	`.nr r n [m]`
	
	Assign value n to number register r and optionally set auto-increment to m.
	
	Examples
	
	Set the "box width" register to line length minus indent:
	
	`    .nr BW \n(.l-\n(.i`
	
	Set page layout values for *ms* macros:
	
	`    .nr LL 6i                    `*Line length*
	`    .nr PO ((8.25i-\n(LLu)/2u)    `*Page offset*
	`    .nr VS \n(PS+2                `*Vertical spacing*
	
	In groff, auto-increment a footnote-counter register:
	
	`    .nr footcount 0 1        `*Reset to zero on each page*
	
	Note: inside a macro definition, \n should be \\n.

.ns

Turn on no-space mode. See also **.rs**.

.nx *file*

Switch to *file* and do not return to current file. See also .so.

.os

Output saved space specified in previous .sv request.

.pc *c*

Use *c* (instead of %) as the page number character within nroff/troff coding.

.pi *command*

Pipe the formatter output through a Unix *command*, instead of placing it on standard output (ditroff and nroff only). Request must occur before any output.

Example

```
.pi /usr/bin/col        Process nroff output with col
```

.pl [[±]*n*]

Set page length to *n* or increment page length by ±*n*. If no argument, restore default. Current page length is stored in register .p. Default is 11 inches.

.pm

Print names and sizes of all defined macros.

.pn [[±]*n*]

Set next page number to *n* or increment page number by ±*n*. Current page number is stored in register %.

.po	.po [[±]*n*] Offset text a distance of *n* from left edge of page or else increment the current offset by ±*n*. If no argument, return to previous offset. Current page offset is stored in register .o.
.ps	.ps *n* Set point size to *n* (troff only, accepted but ignored by nroff). Current point size is stored in register .s. Default is 10 points.
.rd	.rd [*prompt*] Read input from terminal, after printing optional *prompt*.
.rm	.rm *xx* Remove request macro or string *xx*.
.rn	.rn *xx yy* Rename request, macro, or string *xx* to *yy*.
.rr	.rr *r* Remove register *r*. See also **.nr**.
.rs	.rs Restore spacing (disable no-space mode). See **.ns**.
.rt	.rt [±*n*] Return (upward only) to marked vertical place, or to ±*n* from top of page or diversion. See also **.mk**.
.so	.so *file* Switch out to *file*, then return to current file; that is, read the contents of another *file* into the current file. See also **.nx**.

`.sp n`

Leave *n* blank lines. Default is 1. You may use any vertical value, with an appropriate unit specifier, for *n*.

`.ss n`

Set space-character size to *n*/36 em (no effect in `nroff`).

`.sv n`

Save *n* lines of space; output saved space with `.os`.

`.sy command [args]`

Execute Unix *command* with optional arguments (`ditroff` only).

Example

Search for the first argument; accumulate in a temp file:

```
.sy sed -n 's/\\$1/Note: &/p' list >> /tmp/notesfile
```

(Note the extra backslash in `\\$1`. This example occurs inside a macro definition. One backslash is stripped off when the macro is first read, so the second one is needed for it to be evaluated correctly when the macro is executed.)

`.ta n[t] [+]m[t] ...`

Set tab stops at positions *n*, *m*, etc. If *t* is not given, tab is left-adjusting. Use a + to move relative to the previous tab stop.

Values for t

L   Left adjust
R   Right adjust
C   Center

`.tc c`

Define tab repetition character as *c* (instead of whitespace). nroff/troff uses *c* when expanding tabs. For example, you might use `.tc .` when formatting a table of contents.

.ti	`.ti [[±]n]`
	Temporary indent. Indent the next output line by *n* or increment the current indent by ±*n* for the next output line. Default scale is ems.
	Example
	``
	.in 10
	.ti -5
	The first line of this paragraph sticks out by 5 ems ...
	.in -10
	``
.tl	`.tl 'l'c'r'`
	Specify *l*eft, *c*entered, or *r*ight title. Title length is specified by `.lt`, not `.ll`. Use `%` to get the page number, for example, `.tl ''- % -''`.
.tm	`.tm text`
	Terminal message. Print *text* on standard error. Useful for debugging, as well for producing indexes and cross references.
.tr	`.tr ab...`
	Translate character *a* (first of a pair) to *b* (second of pair).
	Example
	Produce uppercase and later restore. Useful for title macros:
	``
	.tr aAbBcCdDeEfFgGhHiIjJkKlLmM Et cetera
	.tr aabbccddeeffgghhiijjkkllmm Et cetera
	``
.uf	`.uf f`
	Set underline font to *f* (to be switched to by `.ul` or `.cu`); default is *italics*.
.ul	`.ul [n]`
	Underline (italicize in `troff`) next *n* input lines. Do not underline interword spaces. Use `.cu` for continuous underline. Underline font can be switched in `troff` with `.uf` request. However, you must use a macro to actually underline in `troff`.

.vs [*n*]	.vs

Set vertical line spacing to *n*. If no argument, restore previous spacing. Current vertical spacing is stored in register .v. Default is 1/6 inch.

.wh *n* [*xx*]	.wh

The "when" request. When position *n* is reached, execute macro *xx*; negative values are calculated with respect to the bottom of the page. If *xx* is not supplied, remove any trap(s) at that location. (A trap is the position on the page where a given macro is executed.) Two traps can be at the same location if one is moved over the other with .ch. They cannot be placed at the same location with .wh.

Escape Sequences

Sequence	Effect
\\	Prevent or delay the interpretation of \.
\e	Printable version of the current escape character (usually \).
\'	´ (acute accent); equivalent to \(aa.
\`	` (grave accent); equivalent to \(ga.
\-	– (minus sign in the current font).
\.	Period (dot).
\space	Unpaddable space-size space character.
\newline	Concealed (ignored) newline.
\0	Digit-width space.
|	1/6-em narrow space character (zero width in nroff).
\^	1/12-em half-narrow space character (zero width in nroff).
\&	Nonprinting, zero-width character.
\!	Transparent line indicator.
\"	Beginning of comment.
\$*n*	Interpolate macro argument $1 \leq n \leq 9$.
\%	Default optional hyphenation character.
\(*xx*	Character named *xx*. See the later section "Special Characters."
*x or *(*xx*	Interpolate string *x* or *xx*.
\a	Noninterpreted leader character.
\b'*abc*...'	Bracket-building function.
\c	Make next line continuous with current.
\C'*abcd*'	Character named *abcd* (ditroff only).
\d	Forward (down) 1/2-em vertical motion (1/2 line in nroff).

Sequence	Effect
\D'l *x,y'*	Draw a line from current position by deltas *x,y* (ditroff only).
\D'c *d'*	Draw circle of diameter *d* with left edge at current position (ditroff only).
\D'e *d1 d2'*	Draw ellipse with horizontal diameter *d1* and vertical diameter *d2*, with left edge at current position (ditroff only).
\D'a *x1 y1 x2 y2'*	Draw arc counterclockwise from current position, with center at *x1,y1* and endpoint at *x1+x2,y1+y2* (ditroff only).
\D'~ *x1 y1 x2 y2...'*	Draw spline from current position through the specified coordinates (ditroff only).
\f*x* or \f(*xx* or \f*n*	Change to font named *x* or *xx* or to position *n*. If *x* is P, return to the previous font.
\g*x* or \g(*xx*	Format of number register *x* or *xx*, suitable for use with .af
\h'*n'*	Local horizontal motion; move right *n* or, if *n* is negative, move left.
\H'*n'*	Set character height to *n* points, without changing width (ditroff only).
\k*x*	Mark horizontal *input* place in register *x*.
\l'*nc'*	Draw horizontal line of length *n* (optionally with *c*).
\L'*nc'*	Draw vertical line of length *n* (optionally with *c*).
\n*x*, \n(*xx*	Interpolate number register *x* or *xx*.
\n+*x*, \n+(*xx*	Interpolate number register *x* or *xx*, applying auto-increment.
\n-*x*, \n-(*xx*	Interpolate number register *x* or *xx*, applying auto-decrement.
\N'*n'*	Character number *n* in the current font (ditroff only).
\o'*abc...'*	Overstrike characters *a*, *b*, *c* ...
\p	Break and spread output line.
\r	Reverse 1-em vertical motion (reverse line in nroff).
\s*n*, \s±*n*	Change point size to *n* or increment by *n*. For example, \s0 returns to previous point size.
\s(*nn*, \s±(*nn*	Just like \s, but allow unambiguous two-character point sizes (recent ditroff only).
\S'*n'*	Slant output *n* degrees to the right. Negative values slant to the left. A value of zero turns off slanting (ditroff only).
\t	Noninterpreted horizontal tab.
\u	Reverse (up) 1/2-em vertical motion (1/2 line in nroff).
\v'*n'*	Local vertical motion; move down *n*, or, if *n* is negative, move up.
\w'*string'*	Interpolate width of *string*.
\x'*n'*	Extra line-space function (*n* negative provides space before, *n* positive provides after).

Sequence	Effect
\X' *text* '	Output *text* as a device control function (ditroff only).
\z*c*	Print *c* with zero width (without spacing).
\{	Begin multiline conditional input.
\}	End multiline conditional input.
x	*x*, any character not listed above.

Predefined Registers

There are two types of predefined registers: read-only and read-write. These are all accessed via the \n escape sequence, even though some of them actually return string values.

Read-Only Registers

.$ Number of arguments available at the current macro level.

$$ Process ID of troff process (ditroff only).

.A   Set to 1 in troff, if -a option used; always 1 in nroff.

.F   Name of the current input file (recent ditroff only).

.H   Available horizontal resolution in basic units.

.L   Current line spacing (set by .ls) value (recent ditroff only).

.R   Number of unused number registers (recent ditroff only).

.T   Set to 1 in nroff, if -T option used; always 0 in oroff; in ditroff, the string *(.T contains the value of -T.

.V   Available vertical resolution in basic units.

.a   Post-line extra line space most recently utilized using \x'*n*'.

.b   Emboldening level (recent ditroff only).

.c   Number of lines read from current input file.

.d   Current vertical place in current diversion; equal to register nl when there is no diversion.

.f   Current font as number (1 to 4 in otroff; 1 to 99 in ditroff).

.h   Text baseline high-water mark on current page or diversion.

.i   Current indent.

.j   Current adjustment mode.

.k   Current *output* horizontal position.

.l   Current line length.

.n   Length of text portion on previous output line.

.o   Current page offset.

.p   Current page length.

.s   Current point size.

.t   Distance to the next trap.

.u   Equal to 1 in fill mode and 0 in no-fill mode.

.v   Current vertical line spacing.

.w   Width of previous character.

.x	Reserved version-dependent register.
.y	Reserved version-dependent register.
.z	Name of current diversion.

Read-Write Registers

%	Current page number.
ct	Character type (set by \w function).
dl	Width (maximum) of last completed diversion.
dn	Height (vertical size) of last completed diversion.
dw	Current day of the week (1 to 7).
dy	Current day of the month (1 to 31).
hp	Current horizontal place on *input* line.
ln	Output line number.
mo	Current month (1 to 12).
nl	Vertical position of last printed text baseline.
sb	Depth of string below baseline (generated by \w function).
st	Height of string above baseline (generated by \w function).
yr	Years since 1900.[a]

[a] Yes, there's a potential Y2K problem here. This will be 100 in 2000.

Special Characters

This section lists the following special characters:

- Characters that reside on the standard fonts

- Miscellaneous characters

- Bracket-building symbols

- Mathematics symbols

- Greek characters

The characters in the first table below are available on the standard fonts. The characters in the remaining tables are available only on the special font.

Table 12–2: Characters on the Standard Fonts

Input	Char	Character Name
'	'	Close quote
`	'	Open quote
\(em	—	Em-dash (width of "m")
\(en	–	En-dash (width of "n")

Table 12–2: Characters on the Standard Fonts (continued)

Input	Char	Character Name
\-	–	Minus in current font
-	–	Hyphen
\(hy	–	Hyphen
\(bu	•	Bullet
\(sq	□	Square
\(ru	_	Rule
\(14	¼	1/4
\(12	½	1/2
\(34	¾	3/4
\(fi	fi	fi ligature
\(fl	fl	fl ligature
\(ff	ff	ff ligature
\(Fi	ffi	ffi ligature
\(Fl	ffl	ffl ligature
\(de	°	Degree
\(dg	†	Dagger
\(fm	′	Foot mark
\(ct	¢	Cent sign
\(rg	®	Registered
\(co	©	Copyright

Table 12–3: Miscellaneous Characters

Input	Char	Character Name
\(sc	§	Section
\(aa	´	Acute accent
\´	´	Acute accent
\(ga	`	Grave accent
\`	`	Grave accent
\(ul	_	Underrule
\(->	→	Right arrow
\(<-	←	Left arrow
\(ua	↑	Up arrow
\(da	↓	Down arrow
\(br			Box rule
\(dd	‡	Double dagger

Table 12–3: Miscellaneous Characters (continued)

Input	Char	Character Name
\(rh	☞	Right hand
\(lh	☜	Left hand
\(ci	○	Circle

Table 12–4: Bracket-Building Symbols

Input	Char	Character Name
\(lt	⌠	Left top of big curly bracket
\(lk	⎨	Left center of big curly bracket
\(lb	⌡	Left bottom of big curly bracket
\(rt	⌠	Right top of big curly bracket
\(rk	⎬	Right center of big curly bracket
\(rb	⌡	Right bottom of big curly bracket
\(lc	⌈	Left ceiling (left top) of big square bracket
\(bv	│	Bold vertical
\(lf	⌊	Left floor (left bottom) of big square bracket
\(rc	⌉	Right ceiling (right top) of big square bracket
\(rf	⌋	Right floor (right bottom) of big square bracket

Table 12–5: Mathematics Symbols

Input	Char	Character Name
\(pl	+	Math plus
\(mi	−	Math minus
\(eq	=	Math equals
\(**	*	Math star
\(sl	/	Slash (matching backslash)
\(sr	√	Square root
\(rn	‾	Root en extender
\(>=	≥	Greater than or equal to
\(<=	≤	Less than or equal to
\(==	≡	Identically equal
\(~~	≈	Approximately equal
\(ap	~	Approximates
\(!=	≠	Not equal
\(mu	×	Multiply
\(di	÷	Divide

Table 12-5: Mathematics Symbols (continued)

Input	Char	Character Name
\(+-	±	Plus-minus
\(cu	∪	Cup (union)
\(ca	∩	Cap (intersection)
\(sb	⊂	Subset of
\(sp	⊃	Superset of
\(ib	⊆	Improper subset
\(ip	⊇	Improper superset
\(if	∞	Infinity
\(pd	∂	Partial derivative
\(gr	∇	Gradient
\(no	¬	Not
\(is	∫	Integral sign
\(pt	∝	Proportional to
\(es	∅	Empty set
\(mo	∈	Member of
\(or	|	Or

Greek Characters

Characters with equivalents as uppercase English letters are available on the standard fonts; otherwise, the characters in Table 12-6 exist only on the special font.

Table 12-6: Greek Characters

Input	Char	Char Name	Input	Char	Char Name
\(*a	α	alpha	\(*A	A	ALPHA
\(*b	β	beta	\(*B	B	BETA
\(*g	γ	gamma	\(*G	Γ	GAMMA
\(*d	δ	delta	\(*D	δ	DELTA
\(*e	ε	epsilon	\(*E	E	EPSILON
\(*z	ζ	zeta	\(*Z	Z	ZETA
\(*y	η	eta	\(*Y	H	ETA
\(*h	θ	theta	\(*H	Θ	THETA
\(*i	ι	iota	\(*I	I	IOTA
\(*k	κ	kappa	\(*K	K	KAPPA
\(*l	λ	lambda	\(*L	Λ	LAMBDA
\(*m	µ	mu	\(*M	M	MU

nroff/troff

Table 12-6: Greek Characters (continued)

Input	Char	Char Name	Input	Char	Char Name
\(*n	ν	nu	\(*N	N	NU
\(*c	ξ	xi	\(*C	Ξ	XI
\(*o	o	omicron	\(*O	O	OMICRON
\(*p	π	pi	\(*P	Π	PI
\(*r	ρ	rho	\(*R	P	RHO
\(*s	σ	sigma	\(*S	Σ	SIGMA
\(ts	ς	terminal sigma			
\(*t	τ	tau	\(*T	T	TAU
\(*u	υ	upsilon	\(*U	Υ	UPSILON
\(*f	ϕ	phi	\(*F	Φ	PHI
\(*x	χ	chi	\(*X	X	CHI
\(*q	ψ	psi	\(*Q	Ψ	PSI
\(*w	ω	omega	\(*W	Ω	OMEGA

CHAPTER 13

mm Macros

This chapter presents the following topics:

- Alphabetical summary of the *mm* macros
- Predefined string names
- Number registers
- Other reserved names
- Sample document

Alphabetical Summary of mm Macros

.1C	.1C
Return to single-column format.	
.2C	.2C
Start two-column format.	
.AE	.AE
End abstract (see **.AS**).	

.AF	.AF [*company name*]
	Alternate format for first page. Change first-page "Subject/Date/From" format. If argument is given, other headings are not affected. No argument suppresses company name and headings.
.AL	.AL [*type*] [*indent*] [1]
	Initialize numbered or alphabetized list. Specify list *type*, and *indent* of text. If third argument is 1, spacing between items is suppressed. Mark each item in list with .LI; end list with .LE. Default is numbered listing. Default text indent is specified in register Li.
	Type
	1 Arabic numbers
	A Uppercase letters
	a Lowercase letters
	I Roman numerals, uppercase
	i Roman numerals, lowercase
.AS	.AS [*type*] [*n*]
	Start abstract of specified *type*, indenting *n* spaces. Used with .TM and .RP only. End with .AE.
	Type
	1 Abstract on cover sheet and first page
	2 Abstract only on cover sheet
	3 Abstract only on Memorandum for File cover sheet
.AT	.AT *title*
	Author's *title* appears after author's name in formal memoranda.
.AU	.AU *name* [*init*] [*loc*] [*dept*] [*ext*] [*room*]
	Author's *name* and other information (up to nine arguments) supplied at beginning of formal memoranda.

.AV *name*   .AV

Approval signature line for *name*. Closing macro in formal memoranda.

.B [*barg*] [*parg*] ...   .B

Set *barg* in bold (underline or overstruck in `nroff`) and *parg* in previous font; up to six arguments.

.BE   .BE

End bottom block and print after footnotes (if any), but before footer. See .BS.

.BI [*barg*] [*iarg*]   .BI

Set *barg* in bold (underline or overstruck in `nroff`) and *iarg* in italics; up to six arguments.

.BL [*indent*] [1]   .BL

Initialize bullet list. Specify *indent* of text. Default indent is 3 and is specified in register Pi. If second argument is 1, suppress blank line between items.

.BR [*barg*] [*rarg*]   .BR

Set *barg* in bold (underline or overstruck in `nroff`) and *rarg* in roman; up to six arguments.

.BS   .BS

Begin block of text to be printed at bottom of page, after footnotes (if any), but before footer. End with .BE.

.CS [*pgs*] [*other*] [*tot*] [*figs*] [*tbls*] [*ref*]   .CS

Cover-sheet information supplied for formal memoranda. The arguments represent the counts of the respective items that are normally automatically computed. You may provide a value to override the computed one.

mm
Macros

.DE	.DE End static display started with .DS or floating display started with .DF.
.DF	.DF [type] [mode] [rindent] Start floating display. That is, if the amount of space required to output text exceeds the space remaining on the current page, the display is saved for the next page, while text following the display is used to fill the current page. (See also registers De and Df.) Default *type* is no indent; default *mode* is no-fill. *rindent* is the amount by which to shorten the line length in order to bring text in from the right margin. End display with .DE. **Type** L or 0 No indent (default). I or 1 Indent standard amount. C or 2 Center each line individually. CB or 3 Center as a block. **Mode** N or 0 No-fill mode (default). F or 0 Fill mode.
.DL	.DL [indent] [1] Initialize dashed list. Specify *indent* of text. Default indent is 3 and is specified in register Pi. If second argument is 1, suppress blank line between items.
.DS	.DS [type] [mode] [rindent] Start static display. That is, if the display doesn't fit in the remaining space on the page, a page break occurs, placing the display at the top of the next page. See .DF about *type*, *mode*, and *rindent*. End display with .DE.
.EC	.EC [caption] [n] [flag] Equation *caption*. Arguments optionally override default numbering, where *flag* determines use of number *n*. See .EQ.

Flag

0   *n* is a prefix to number (the default).
1   *n* is a suffix.
2   *n* replaces number.

.EF ['*left*'*center*'*right*']

Print three-part string as even page footer; parts are left-justified, centered, and right-justified at bottom of every even page.

.EH ['*left*'*center*'*right*']

Print three-part string as even page header; parts are left-justified, centered, and right-justified at top of every even page.

.EN

End equation display. See .EQ.

.EQ [*text*]

Start equation display to be processed by eqn, using *text* as label (see .EC). End with .EN. See Chapter 17, *troff Preprocessors*, for more information on eqn.

.EX [*caption*] [*n*] [*flag*]

Exhibit *caption*. Arguments optionally override default numbering, where *flag* determines use of number *n*.

Flag

0   *n* is a prefix to number (the default).
1   *n* is a suffix.
2   *n* replaces number.

.FC [*text*]

Use *text* for formal closing.

mm
Macros

.FD	.FD [n] [1]

Set default footnote format to *n*, as described in the next table. With a second argument of 1, footnote numbering starts over at 1 each time a first-level heading is encountered.

Value	Hyphenation	Adjust	Text Indent	Label Justification
0	Off	On	On	Left
1	On	On	On	Left
2	Off	Off	On	Left
3	On	Off	On	Left
4	Off	On	Off	Left
5	On	On	Off	Left
6	Off	Off	Off	Left
7	On	Off	Off	Left
8	Off	On	On	Right
9	On	On	On	Right
10	Off	Off	On	Right
11	On	Off	On	Right

.FE	.FE

End footnote. See .**FS**.

.FG	.FG [title] [n] [flag]

Figure *title* follows. Arguments optionally override default numbering, where *flag* determines use of number *n*.

Flag

0   *n* is a prefix to number (the default).
1   *n* is a suffix.
2   *n* replaces number.

.FS	.FS [c]

Start footnote using *c* as indicator. Default is numbered footnote. End with .FE.

.H	.H n [heading] [suffix]

Print a numbered *heading* at level *n*, where *n* is from 1 to 7. The optional *suffix* is appended to the heading, and may be used for footnote marks or other text that should not appear in the Table of Contents. See any of the following sections for more information.

.H

Number Registers

Ej	Page eject.
Hb	Break after heading.
Hc	Centered heading.
Hi	Type of first paragraph after heading.
Hs	Space after heading.
Hu	Unnumbered headings.

Strings

HF	Font control.
HP	Point size.

Macros

.HM	Heading mark.
.HU	Unnumbered headings.
.HX, .HY, .HZ	User-supplied macros invoked during output of header.

.HC [*c*]

.HC

Use character *c* as hyphenation indicator.

.HM [*H1*] ... [*H7*]

.HM

Set the heading mark style for the seven levels of headings. Each heading can be arabic (1 or 001), roman (i or I), or alphabetic (a or A).

.HU *heading*

.HU

Unnumbered *heading* follows. Same as .H except that no heading mark is printed (see number register Hu).

.HX *dlevel rlevel text*

.HX

User-supplied exit macro executed before printing the heading.

→

.HX ←	The derived level *dlevel* is equal to the real level *rlevel* if .H is invoked by the user. If .HU is used, *dlevel* is equal to the value of the Hu register, and *rlevel* is zero. In both cases, *text* is the actual heading text.
.HY	.HY *dlevel rlevel text* User-supplied exit macro executed in middle of printing the heading. See .HX for information about *dlevel*, *rlevel*, and *text*.
.HZ	.HZ *dlevel rlevel text* User-supplied macro executed after printing the heading. See .HX for information about *dlevel*, *rlevel*, and *text*.
.I	.I [*iarg*] [*parg*] Set *iarg* in italics (underline in nroff) and *parg* in previous font. Up to six arguments.
.IB	.IB [*iarg*] [*barg*] Set *iarg* in italics (underline in nroff) and *barg* in bold. Up to six arguments.
.IR	.IR [*iarg*] [*rarg*] Set *iarg* in italics (underline in nroff) and *rarg* in roman. Up to six arguments.

.LB	.LB *n m pad type* [*mark*] [*LI-space*] [*LB-space*]
	
	List beginning. Allows complete control over list format. Begin each list item in the list with .LI; end the list with .LE:
	
	n Text indent.
	
	m Mark indent.
	
	pad
	    Padding associated with mark.
	
	type
	    If 0, use the specified *mark*. If nonzero, and *mark* is 1, A, a, I, or i, the list is automatically numbered or alphabetically sequenced. In this case, *type* controls how *mark* is displayed. For example, if *mark* is currently 1, *type* has the following results.

Type	Result
1	1.
2	1)
3	(1)
4	[1]
5	<1>
6	{1}

mark
> Symbol or text to label each list entry. *mark* can be null (creates hanging indent); a text string; or 1, A, a, I, or i to create an automatically numbered or lettered list. See **.AL**.

LI-space
> Number of blank lines to output between each following .LI macro. Default is 1.

LB-space
> Number of blank lines to output by .LB macro itself. Default is 0.

.LC [*n*]

.LC

Clear list level up to *n*.

.LE [1]

.LE

End item list started by .AL, .BL, .DL, .LB, .ML, or .VL. An argument of 1 produces a line of whitespace (.5v) after the list.

.LI [*mark*] [1]
text

.LI

Item in list. List must be initialized (see **.AL**, **.BL**, **.DL**, **.LB**, **.ML**, and **.VL**) and then closed using .LE. If *mark* is specified, it replaces the mark set by the list-initialization macro. If *mark* is specified along with second argument of 1, the mark is prefixed to the current mark.

.ML *mark* [*indent*] [1]

.ML

Initialize list with specified *mark*, which can be one or more characters. Specify *indent* of text (default is one space wider than *mark*). If third argument is 1, omit space between items in list.

Alphabetical Summary of mm Macros — .ML   421

.MT	.MT [type] [title] Specify memorandum *type* and *title*. Controls format of formal memoranda and must be specified after other elements, such as .TL, .AF, .AU, .AS, and .AE. User-supplied *title* is prefixed to page number. *Type* 0 No type. 1 Memorandum for file (default). 2 Programmer's notes. 3 Engineer's notes. 4 Released paper. 5 External letter. *string* *string* is printed.
.ND	.ND *date* New date. Change date that appears in formal memoranda.
.NE	.NE Notation end. See .NS.
.nP	.nP Numbered paragraphs with double-line indent at start of paragraph. See also .P.
.NS	.NS [type] Notation start. Used with .MT 1 and .AS 2/.AE (memorandum for file) to specify note for cover sheet. Otherwise used at end of formal memoranda. Specify notation *type*. *Type* 0 Copy to (the default). 1 Copy (with attention) to. 2 Copy (without att.) to. 3 Att. 4 Atts. 5 Enc. 6 Encs. 7 Under Separate Cover.

8	Letter to.	.NS
9	Memorandum to.	
10	Copy (with atts.) to.	
11	Copy (without atts.) to.	
12	Abstract Only to.	
13	Complete Memorandum to.	
string	Copy *string* to.	

.OF ['*left*'*center*'*right*']

Print three-part string as odd page footer; parts are left-justified, centered, and right-justified at bottom of every odd page.

.OH ['*left*'*center*'*right*']

Print three-part string as odd page header; parts are left-justified, centered, and right-justified at top of every odd page.

.OK [*topic*]

Other keywords. Specify *topic* to appear on cover sheet of formal memoranda. Up to nine arguments.

.OP

Force an odd page.

.P [*type*]

Start new paragraph. A paragraph *type* can be specified, overriding default. Various registers can be set to control default formats:

Pt   Paragraph type for document (default is 0).
Pi   Amount of indent (default is 3n).
Ps   Spacing between paragraphs (default is one line of white space).
Np   Set this to 1 to produce numbered paragraphs.

Type

0   Left-justified (the default).
1   Indented.
2   Indented except after displays (.DE), lists (.LE), and
     headings (.H).

.PF	`.PF ['left'center'right']`
	Print three-part string as page footer; parts are left-justified, centered, and right-justified at bottom of every page. Use \\\\nP in string to obtain page number. See also **.EF** and **.OF**.
.PH	`.PH ['left'center'right']`
	Print three-part string as page header; parts are left-justified, centered, and right-justified at top of every page. Use \\\\nP in string to obtain page number. See also **.EH** and **.OH**.
.PM	`.PM [type]`
	Proprietary marking on each page.
	Type
	P Private.
	N Notice.
.PX	`.PX`
	Page-heading user exit. Invoked after restoration of default environment. See **.TP**.
.R	`.R`
	Return to roman font (end underlining or overstriking in nroff).
.RB	`.RB [rarg] [barg]`
	Set *rarg* in roman and *barg* in bold. Up to six arguments.
.RD	`.RD [prompt]`
	Read input from terminal, supplying optional *prompt*.
.RF	`.RF`
	End of reference text. See also **.RS**.

.RI [*rarg*] [*barg*]   **.RI**

Set *rarg* in roman and *barg* in italics. Up to six arguments.

.RL [*indent*] [1]   **.RL**

Initialize reference list, essentially a numbered list with number set within
brackets ([ ]). Specify *indent* of text; the default is set through register
Li. If second argument is 1, omit space between list items.

.RP [*counter*] [*skip*]   **.RP**

Produce reference page.

Counter

0   Reset the reference counter (default).
1   Do not reset the reference counter.

Skip

0   Put on a separate page (default).
1   Do not issue a following .SK.
2   Do not issue a preceding .SK.
3   Do not issue either a preceding or following .SK.

.RS [*strname*]   **.RS**

Start automatically numbered reference. End with .RF. If provided, use
strname as a troff string in which to save the reference number surrounded by brackets and appropriate line motions. This allows referring
to the reference again from text further on in the document.

Example

```
J. Programmer\*(Rf
.RS W1
.I "Whizprog \- The Be All and End All Program,"
J. Programmer, Wizard Corp, April 1, 1999.
.RF
describes the design of
.IR whizprog .
The second chapter\*(W1
presents

an especially insightful analysis.  ...
```

.S	`.S [[±]n] [[±]m]`
	Set point size to *n* and vertical spacing to *m* (`troff` only). Alternatively, either argument can be specified by incrementing or decrementing the current value (C), default value (D), or previous value (P). Default point size is 10; default vertical spacing is 12.
.SA	`.SA [n]`
	Set right margin justification to *n*. Defaults are no justification for `nroff`, justification for `troff`.
	Values for n
	0 No justification.
	1 Justification.
.SG	`.SG [typist] [1]`
	Add *typist* to Author's name on the signature line. (The Author's name is obtained from the `.AU` macro.) With a second argument of 1, the author's location, department etc. are placed on the same line as the name of the first author, instead of on the line with the last author's name.
.SK	`.SK n`
	Skip *n* pages. Similar to a `.bp` request.
.SM	`.SM x [y] [z]`
	Reduce a string by one point. Multiple arguments are concatenated, with one of them reduced in size, as described in this table.

# of Arguments	Action
One	Reduce size of first string by one point.
Two	Reduce size of first string by one point.
Three	Reduce size of middle string by one point.

.SP [*n*]	.SP

Output *n* blank vertical spaces. The spacing requests of two consecutive .SP macros do not accumulate.

.TB [*title*] [*n*] [*flag*]	.TB

Supply table *title*. Arguments optionally override default numbering, where *flag* determines use of number *n*.

Flag

0   *n* is a prefix to number (default).
1   *n* is a suffix.
2   *n* replaces number.

.TC [*slevel*] [*spacing*] [*tlevel*] [*tab*] [*head1*] ...	.TC

Generate table of contents in format specified by arguments. The levels of headings that are saved for table of contents are determined by setting the Cl register.

slevel sets the levels of headings that have spacing before them. *spacing* sets the amount of spacing. Default is 1; first-level headings have a blank line before them.

tlevel and *tab* affect the location of the page number. Heading levels less than or equal to *tlevel* are output with page numbers at the right margin; otherwise, the heading and page number are separated by two spaces. If page numbers are at the right margin, and if *tab* is 0, a leader is output using dots; otherwise, spaces are used.

.TE	.TE

End table. See .TS.

.TH [N]	.TH

End table header. Must be used with a preceding .TS H. Use N to suppress table headers until a new page.

.TL	.TL [*charge* [*file*]] *text* Supply title for formal memoranda. *charge* and *file* are the "charging case" and "filing case" for the memorandum; not too useful outside the Bell System.
.TM	.TM [*n*] Supply number *n* for technical memoranda.
.TP	.TP Page top macro, invoked automatically at the beginning of a new page. Executed in environment in which heading is output. See also .PH.
.TS	.TS [H] Start table to be processed by tbl. Use H to put a table header on all pages. End table header with .TH. End table with .TE. See Chapter 17 for more information on tbl.
.TX	.TX User-supplied macro executed before table-of-contents titles.
.TY	.TY User-supplied macro executed before table-of-contents header.
.VL	.VL *n* [*m*] [1] Initialize variable item list. Used to produce indented or labeled paragraphs. Indent text *n* spaces and indent mark *m* spaces. If third argument is 1, omit space between list items. Begin each item with .LI, specifying a label for each item; end list with .LE.
.VM	.VM [*n*] [*m*] Vertical margin. Add *n* lines to top margin and *m* lines to bottom.

.WC [x]

Change column or footnote width to *x.*

Values for x

FF	All footnotes same as first.
-FF	Turn off FF mode. Normal default mode.
WD	Wide displays.
-WD	Use default column mode.
WF	Wide footnotes.
-WF	Turn off WF mode.

Predefined String Names

BU	Bullet; same as \(bu.
Ci	List of indents for table-of-contents levels.
DT	Current date, unless overridden. Month, day, year (e.g., January 1, 2000).
EM	Em dash string (em dash in troff and a double hyphen in nroff).
F	Footnote number generator.
HF	Fonts used for each level of heading (1 = roman, 2 = italic, 3 = bold).
HP	Point size used for each level of heading.
Le	Title set for "LIST OF EQUATIONS."
Lf	Title set for "LIST OF FIGURES."
Lt	Title set for "LIST OF TABLES."
Lx	Title set for "LIST OF EXHIBITS."
RE	SCCS release and level of *mm.*
Rf	Reference number generator.
Rp	Title for "REFERENCES."
Tm	Trademark string. Places the letters "TM" in a smaller point size, one-half line above the text it follows.

Number Registers Used in mm

Table 13-1 lists *mm*'s number registers. A dagger (†) next to a register name indicates that the register can be set only from the command line or before the *mm* macro definitions are read by the formatter. Any register having a single-character name can be set from the command line with the -r option.

Table 13-1: mm Number Registers

Register	Description
At	If set to 1, omit technical memorandum headings and provide spaces appropriate for letterhead (see **.AF** macro).
Au	Omit author information on first page (see **.AU** macro).
Ct	Flag indicating type of copy (original, draft, etc.).
Cl	Level of headings saved for table of contents (see **.TC** macro). Default is 2.
Cp	If set to 1 (default), list of figures and tables appear on same page as table of contents. Otherwise, they start on a new page.
Dt	If set to 1, use debug mode (*mm* continues even after encountering normally fatal errors). Default is 0.
De	If set to 1, eject page after each floating display. Default is 0.
Df	Set format of floating displays (see **.DF** macro).
Ds	Set space used before and after static displays.
Et	Font for Subject/Date/From. 0 (bold, the default) or 1 (roman).
Ec	Equation counter, incremented for each `.EC` macro.
Ej	Heading level for page eject before headings. Default is 0 and no eject.
Eq	If set to 1, place equation label at left margin. Default is 0.
Ex	Exhibit counter, incremented for each `.EX` macro.
Fg	Figure counter, incremented for each `.FG` macro.
Fs	Vertical spacing between footnotes.
H1 ... H7	Heading counters for levels 1 to 7, incremented by `.H` macro of corresponding level or by `.HU` macro if at level given by register Hu. Registers H2 to H7 are reset to 0 by any `.H` (or `.HU`) macro at a lower-numbered level.
Hb	Level of heading for which break occurs before output of body text. Default is 2.
Hc	Level of heading for which centering occurs. Default is 0.
Hi	Type of indent after heading. Values are 0 (left-justified), 1 (indented, the default), 2 (indented except after `.H`, `.LC`, `.DE`).
Hs	Level of heading for which space after heading occurs. Default is 2.
Ht	Numbering type of heading: 1 (single) or 0 (concatenated, the default).
Hu	Set level of heading at which unnumbered headings occur. Default is 2.
Hy	If set to 1, enable hyphenation. Default is 0.
Lt	Set length of page. Default is 66v.

Table 13–1: mm Number Registers (continued)

Register	Description
Le	Flag to print list of equations after table of contents: 0 (don't print, the default) or 1 (print).
Lf	Like Le, but for list of figures.
Li	Default indent of lists. Default is 6n for nroff and 5n for troff.
Ls	Set spacing between items in nested lists. Default is 6 (spacing between all levels of list).
Lt	Like Le, but for list of tables.
Lx	Like Le, but for list of exhibits.
Nt	Set page-numbering style:
	0 All pages get header (the default)
	1 Header printed as footer on page 1
	2 No header on page 1
	3 Section-page as footer
	4 No header unless .PH has been invoked
	5 Section-page and section-figure as footer
Np	Set numbering style for paragraphs: 0 (unnumbered, the default) or 1 (numbered).
O	Offset of page. For nroff, value is unscaled number representing character positions; default is 9 (.75i). For troff, value is scaled; default is .5i.
Oc	Set numbering style for pages in table of contents: 0 (lowercase roman, the default) or 1 (arabic).
Of	Set separator for figure number in captions. 0 (use period, the default); 1 (use hyphen).
P	Current page number.
Pi	Amount of indent for paragraph. Default is 5n for nroff and 3n for troff.
Ps	Amount of spacing between paragraphs. Default is 3v.
Pt	Paragraph type. Values are 0 (left-justified, the default), 1 (indented), 2 (indented except after .H, .LC, .DE).
Pv	Suppress "PRIVATE" header by setting to 0 (default).
Rf	Reference counter, incremented for each .RS.
St	Default point size for troff. Default is 10. Vertical spacing is \nS+2.
Si	Standard indent for displays. Default is 5n for nroff and 3n for troff.
Tt	Type of nroff output device. Sets registers for specific devices.
Tb	Table counter, incremented for each .TB.

mm
Macros

Table 13-1: mm Number Registers (continued)

Register	Description
Ut	Style of nroff underlining for .H and .HU. If not set, use continuous underline; if set, don't underline punctuation and whitespace. Default is 0.
Wt	Width of page (line and title length). Default is 6i.

Other Reserved Macro and String Names

In *mm*, the only macro and string names you can safely use are names consisting of a single lowercase letter, or two-character names whose first character is a lowercase letter and whose second character is anything but a lowercase letter. Of these, only c2 and nP are already used.

Sample Document

```
.ND "April 1, 1999"
.TL
Whizprog \- The Be All and End All Program
.AF "Wizard Corp."
.ds XX "012 Binary Road, Programmer's Park, NJ 98765-4321"
.AU "J. Programmer" "" XX
.AT "Coder, Extraordinaire"
.\" Abstract
.AS 1
This memorandum discusses the design and
implementation of
.I whizprog ,
the next generation of really
.B cool
do-it-all programs.
.AE
.\" Released paper
.MT 4
.H 1 Requirements
.P
The following requirements were identified. ...
.H 1 Analysis
.P
Here is what we determined. ...
.H 1 Design
.P
After much popcorn, we arrived at the
following design. ...
.H 1 Implementation
.P
```

```
After more popcorn and lots of Jolt Cola, we
implemented
.I whizprog
using ...
.H 1 Conclusions
.P
We're ready to blow the socks off the market!
.SG
.CS
```

CHAPTER 14

ms Macros

This chapter presents the following topics:

- Alphabetical summary of *ms* macros
- Number registers for page layout
- Reserved macro and string names
- Reserved number register names
- Sample document

Alphabetical Summary of ms Macros

.1C	.1C
	Return to single-column format after .2C or .MC. The .1C macro causes a page break.
.2C	.2C
	Start two-column format. Return to single-column with .1C.
.AB	.AB
	Begin abstract in cover sheet. End abstract with .AE.

.AE

End abstract begun with .AB.

.AI
name
address

Print name, address, etc. of author's institution. Generally follows .AU in a cover sheet sequence; may be repeated up to nine times for multiple author/institution pairs.

.AU
name

Print author's name. Generally follows .TL and precedes .AI in a cover sheet sequence; may be repeated up to nine times for multiple authors.

.B [*text*] [*text2*]

Print *text* in boldface. If *text2* is provided, concatenate it with *text*, but in the previous font. If no arguments are supplied, equivalent to .ft 3 or .ft B.

.B1

Enclose following text in a box. End box with .B2.

.B2

End boxed text (started with .B1).

.BD

Start block display. Text is output exactly as it appears in the source file, centered around the longest line. Same as .DS B. End with .DE.

.BX *word*

Surround *word* in a box. Usually doesn't work for more than one word at a time, due to problems with filling. To box more than one word, separate each with an unpaddable space (*space*).

ms Macros

.CD	`.CD` Start centered display. Each line in the display is individually centered. Same as `.DS C`. End with `.DE`.
.DA	`.DA` Print today's date as the center footer of each page.
.DE	`.DE` End displayed text started with `.DS`.
.DS	`.DS [type]` Start displayed text. End with `.DE`. *Type* B Left-justified block, centered; see **.BD**. C Centered display; see **.CD**. I Indented display (the default); see **.ID**. L Left-centered display; see **.LD**.
.EN	`.EN` End equation display started with `.EQ`.
.EQ	`.EQ` Start equation display to be processed by eqn. End with `.EN`. See Chapter 17, *troff Preprocessors*, for more information on eqn.
.FS	`.FS` Start footnote. Text of footnote follows on succeeding lines. End with `.FE`.
.FE	`.FE` End footnote started with `.FS`.

.I [*text*] [*text2*]	**.I**
Print *text* in italics. If *text2* is provided, concatenate it with *text*, but in the previous font. If no arguments are supplied, equivalent to .ft 2 or .ft I.	
.ID	**.ID**
Start indented display. Text is output exactly as it is in the source file, but indented 8 ens. Same as .DS I. End with .DE.	
.IP *label n*	**.IP**
Indent paragraph *n* spaces with hanging *label*. .RS and .RE can be used for nested indents.	
.KE	**.KE**
End static keep started with .KS or floating keep started with .KF.	
.KF	**.KF**
Begin floating keep. End with .KE. That is, if the amount of space required to output the text exceeds the space remaining on the current page, the keep is saved for the next page, while text following the display is used to fill the current page.	
.KS	**.KS**
Start keep. End with .KE. Enclosed text stays on same page. If text won't fit on current page, a page break occurs.	
.LD	**.LD**
Start left-justified display. Block is centered, but individual lines are left justified in the block. Same as .DS L. End with .DE.	
.LG	**.LG**
Increase type size by two points (troff only). Restore normal type with .NL.	

.LP	`.LP` Start block paragraph. Interparagraph spacing is determined by register `PD`. Default is .5v in `troff` and 1 line in `nroff`.
.MC	`.MC` *cw gw* Start multicolumn mode, with column-width *cw* and gutter width *gw*. The macro generates as many columns as can fit in the current line length. Return to single-column mode with `.1c`.
.ND	`.ND` *date* Supply the date, instead of using the current date. See also **.DA**.
.NH	`.NH` *[n]* *heading text* Numbered section heading; level *n* of the section number is automatically incremented.
.NL	`.NL` Restore default type size (`troff` only). Used after `.LG` or `.SM`.
.PP	`.PP` Start standard indented paragraph. Size of paragraph indent is stored in register `PI` (default is 5 ens).
.QE	`.QE` End quoted paragraph started by `.QS`. `.QS`/`.QE` is similar to `.QP`.
.QP	`.QP` Begin quoted paragraph: indented on both sides, with blank lines above and below, and (in `troff`) with the type size reduced by 1 point.

.QS

Begin quoted paragraph, retaining current point size and vertical spacing. End with `.QE`.

.R

Return to the roman font; essentially equivalent to `.ft R`.

.RE

End one level of relative indent started with `.RS`.

.RP

Initiate title page for a "released paper."

.RS

Right shift. Increase relative indent one level. End with `.RE`. Often used with `.IP`.

.SG

Print a signature line.

.SH
heading text

Unnumbered section heading. See also **.NH**.

.SM

Change to smaller type size (`troff` only). Restore normal type with `.NL`.

.TE

End table to be processed by `tbl`. See **.TS**.

.TH	.TH
	End of table header. Must be used with a preceding .TS H.
.TL	.TL *multiline title*
	Title line(s) for cover sheet. A multiline title can be specified, ended by the next macro (usually .AU in the cover sheet sequence).
.TS	.TS [H]
	Start table to be processed by tbl. Use H to put a table header on all pages (end table header with .TH). End table with .TE. See Chapter 17 for more information on tbl.
.UL	.UL
	Underline following text, even in troff.

Number Registers for Page Layout

Name	Meaning	Default
CW	Column width	7/15 of line length
FL	Footnote length	11/12 of line length
FM	Bottom margin	1 inch
GW	Intercolumn gap	1/15 of line length
HM	Top margin	1 inch
LL	Line length	6 inches
LT	Title length	6 inches
PD	Paragraph spacing	.3v
PI	Paragraph indent	5 ens
PO	Page offset	1 inch
PS	Point size	10 points
QI	Quotation indent	5 ens
VS	Vertical line spacing	12 points

Reserved Macro and String Names

The following macro and string names are used by the *ms* package. Avoid using these names for compatibility with the existing macros. An italicized *n* means that the name contains a numeral (generally the interpolated value of a number register).

,	.]	:	[.	[c	[o	^	`	~
1C	2C	AB	AE	AI	A*n*	AT	AU	AX
B	B1	B2	BB	BG	BT	BX	C	C1
C2	CA	CC	CF	CH	CM	CT	DA	DW
DY	EE	EG	EL	EM	EN	E*n*	EQ	EZ
FA	FE	FF	FG	FJ	FK	FL	FN	FO
FS	FV	FX	FY	HO	I	IE	IH	IM
I*n*	IP	IZ	KD	KF	KJ	KS	LB	LG
LP	LT	MC	ME	MF	MH	MN	MO	MR
ND	NH	NL	NP	OD	OK	PP	PT	PY
QE	QF	QP	QS	R	R3	RA	RC	RE
R*n*	RP	RS	RT	S0	S2	S3	SG	SH
SM	SN	SY	TA	TC	TD	TE	TH	TL
TM	TQ	TR	TS	TT	TX	UL	US	UX
WB	WH	WT	XF	XK	XP			

Reserved Number Register Names

The following number register names are used by the *ms* package. An italicized *n* means that the name contains a numeral (generally the interpolated value of another number register).

*n*T	AJ	AV	BC	BD	BE	BH	BQ	BW
CW	EF	FC	FL	FM	FP	GA	GW	H1
H2	H3	H4	H5	HM	HT	I0	IF	IK
IM	IP	IR	IS	IT	IX	I*n*	J*n*	KG
KI	KM	L1	LE	LL	LT	MC	MF	MG
ML	MM	MN	NA	NC	ND	NQ	NS	NX
OJ	PD	PE	PF	PI	PN	PO	PQ	PS
PX	QI	QP	RO	SJ	ST	T.	TB	TC
TD	TK	TN	TQ	TV	TY	TZ	VS	WF
XX	YE	YY	ZN					

When you're writing your own macros, the safest bet is to use mixed-case letters for macro names. (Using uppercase letters could conflict with reserved *ms* names, and using lowercase letters could conflict with troff requests.)

Sample Document

```
.ND April 1, 1999
.\" Released paper
.RP
.TL
Whizprog \- The Be All and End All Program
.AU
J. Programmer
.AI
```

```
Wizard Corp.
012 Binary Road
Programmer's Park, NJ 98765-4321
USA
.\" Abstract
.AB
This memorandum discusses the design and
implementation of
.I whizprog ,
the next generation of really
.B cool
do-it-all programs.
.AE
.NH
Requirements
.PP
The following requirements were identified. ...
.NH
Analysis
.PP
Here is what we determined. ...
.NH
Design
.PP
After much popcorn, we arrived at the
following design. ...
.NH
Implementation
.PP
After more popcorn and lots of Jolt Cola,
we implemented
.I whizprog
using ...
.NH
Conclusions
.PP
We're ready to blow the socks off the market!
.SG
```

CHAPTER 15

me Macros

This chapter presents the following topics:

- Alphabetical summary of *me* macros
- Predefined strings
- Predefined number registers
- Sample document

Alphabetical Summary of me Macros

.1c	.1c
Return to single-column format. See .2c.	
.2c	.2c
Enter two-column format. Force a new column with .bc; end two-column mode with .1c.	
.ar	.ar
Set page number in arabic.	

.b	.b w x
	Set w in bold and x in previous font.

.(b	.(b *type*
	Begin block keep. End with .)b.
	Type
	c Centered block keep.
	F Filled block keep.
	L Left-justified block keep.

.)b	.)b
	End block keep started with .(b.

.ba	.ba n
	Set the base indent to n.

.bc	.bc
	Begin column; used after .2c.

.bi	.bi w x
	Set w in bold italics and x in previous font.

.bl	.bl n
	Leave n lines of whitespace. Equivalent to .sp n inside a block.

.bu	.bu
	Begin paragraph marked by a bullet.

`.bx w x`	**.bx**
Set *w* in a box and *x* immediately outside the box.	
`.+c title`	**.+c**
Begin chapter with *title*.	
`.$c title`	**.$c**
Begin numbered chapter with *title*.	
`.$C keyword n title`	**.$C**
User-definable macro. Called by `.$c`, supplying *keyword* (e.g., "Chapter" or "Appendix"), chapter or appendix number (*n*), and *title*.	
`.(c`	**.(c**
Begin centered block. End with `.)c`.	
`.)c`	**.)c**
End centered block started with `.(c`.	
`.(d`	**.(d**
Begin delayed text. End with `.)d`.	
`.)d`	**.)d**
End delayed text. Print text with `.pd`.	
`.ef 'l'c'r'`	**.ef**
Print three-part footer on all even pages. Parts are left-justified, centered, and right-justified at bottom of every even page.	

.eh	`.eh 'l'c'r'`
	Print three-part header on all even pages. Parts are left-justified, centered, and right-justified at top of every even page.
.EN	`.EN`
	End equation display started with `.EQ`.
.ep	`.ep`
	End this page and print footnotes.
.EQ	`.EQ` *format title*
	Start equation display to be processed by eqn, using output *format* and having *title* printed on the right margin next to the equation. End with `.EN`. See Chapter 17, *troff Preprocessors*, for more information on eqn.
	Format
	C Centered.
	I Indented.
	L Left-justified.
.$f	`.$f`
	Call to print footer.
.(f	`.(f`
	Begin text for footnote. End with `.)f`.
.)f	`.)f`
	End footnote text started with `.(f`.
.fo	`.fo 'l'c'r'`
	Print three-part footer on all pages. Parts are left-justified, centered, and right-justified at bottom of every page.

.GE

End a picture created by gremlin. Must be used with a preceding .GS. Recent versions of *me* only.

.GE

.GF

End a picture created by gremlin, and "flyback" to the initial vertical position. Must be used with a preceding .GS. Recent versions of *me* only.

.GF

.GS [*flag*]

Start a picture created by gremlin. Must be used with a following .GE or .GF. Recent versions of *me* only. (gremlin is a picture-drawing tool similar to pic that was developed at UCB.) The default action is to center the picture.

Values for flag

L   Place the picture next to the left margin.
R   Place the picture next to the right margin.

.GS

.$H

Normally undefined macro, called immediately before printing text on a page. Can be used for column headings, etc.

.$H

.$h

Call to print header.

.$h

.he '*l*'*c*'*r*'

Print three-part heading on all pages. Parts are left-justified, centered, and right-justified at top of every page.

.he

.hl

Draw a horizontal line equal to the width of page.

.hl

.hx

Don't print headings and footers on next page.

.hx

.i	.i *w x*
	Set *w* in italics (underline in nroff) and *x* in previous font.
.IE	.IE
	End a picture created by ideal. Must be used with a preceding .IS. Recent versions of *me* only.
.IF	.IF
	End a picture created by ideal, and "flyback" to the initial vertical position. Must be used with a preceding .IS. Recent versions of *me* only.
.IS	.IS
	Start a picture created by ideal. Must be used with a following .IE or .IF. Recent versions of *me* only. (ideal is a picture-drawing tool similar to pic that was developed at Bell Labs.)
.ip	.ip *label n*
	Indent paragraph *n* spaces with hanging *label*.
.ix	.ix [±*n*]
	Indent but don't break the line. Equivalent to 'in *n*.
.(l	.(l *type*
	Begin list. End with .)l.
	Type
	C Centered list
	F Filled list
	L Left-justified list
.)l	.)l
	End list started with .(l.

.11 +*n*	.ll

Set line length to +*n* (all environments). This is a macro, not the nroff/troff .11 request.

.lo	.lo

Load a locally defined set of macros (usually /usr/lib/me/local.me). (Not in recent versions.)

.lp	.lp

Begin block paragraph (left-justified).

.m1 *n*	.m1

Set *n* spaces between top of page and heading.

.m2 *n*	.m2

Set *n* spaces between heading and first line of text.

.m3 *n*	.m3

Set *n* spaces between footer and text.

.m4 *n*	.m4

Set *n* spaces between footer and bottom of page.

.n1	.n1

Number lines in margin beginning with 1.

.n2 *n*	.n2

Number lines in margin beginning with *n*; stop numbering if *n* is 0.

me Macros

.np	.np Begin a numbered paragraph. Current number is accessed via \n($p.
.of	.of '*l*'*c*'*r*' Print three-part footer on all odd pages. Parts are left-justified, centered, and right-justified at bottom of every odd page.
.oh	.oh '*l*'*c*'*r*' Print three-part header on all odd pages. Parts are left-justified, centered, and right-justified at top of every odd page.
.$p	.$p *title n d* Print section heading with specified *title*, section number *n*, and depth of section *d*.
.$0	.$0 *title n d* Called automatically after every call to .$p. Normally undefined, but may be used to put every section title automatically into table of contents, or for some similar function.
.$*n*	.$*n* These are traps called just before printing a section of depth *n* (*n* is 1–6). Called from .$p.
.pa	.pa [±*n*] Equivalent to .bp.
.pd	.pd Print delayed text, indicated by .(d and .)d.

.PE

End a picture created by pic. Must be used with a preceding .PS. Recent versions of *me* only.

.PS *vert indent*

Start a picture created by pic. Must be used with a following .PE. Recent versions of *me* only.

vert is the amount of vertical space to provide for the picture, and *indent* is how far from the left margin to place the picture.

.pp

Begin indented paragraph.

.q *w x*

Surround *w* with double quotes and *x* immediately outside the quotes.

.(q

Begin major quote. End with .)q.

.)q

End major quote started with .(q.

.r *w x*

Set *w* in roman font and *x* in previous font.

.rb *w x*

Set *w* in bold and *x* in previous font.

.re

Reset tabs to every 0.5 inch (in troff) or to every 0.8 inch (in nroff).

.ro	`.ro` Set page number in roman numerals.
.$s	`.$s` Separate footnotes with a 1.5-inch horizontal line.
.sh	`.sh` Begin numbered section heading.
.sk	`.sk` Leave next page blank. Like the troff `.bp` request.
.sm	`.sm small reg` Concatenate *small* and *reg*, with *small* set one point smaller in size. Recent versions of *me* only.
.sx	`.sx +n` Begin a paragraph at level *n*.
.sz	`.sz n` Set character point size to *n*, with line spacing set proportionally.
.TE	`.TE` End table. See .**TS**.
.TH	`.TH` End table header. Must be used with a preceding `.TS H`.

`.th`	.th

Initialize for a thesis. (Not in recent versions.)

`.tp`	.tp

Initialize for a title page.

`.TS [H]`	.TS

Start table to be processed by tbl. Use H to put a table header on all pages (end table header with .TH). End table with .TE. See Chapter 17 for more information on tbl.

`.u w x`	.u

Underline *w* and set *x* in previous font.

`.uh title`	.uh

Begin unnumbered section heading using *title*.

`.(x`	.(x

Begin index entry. End with .)x.

`.)x [page] [author]`	.)x

End index entry started with .(x. Print index with .xp.

The arguments are optional. If *page* is "_" (an underscore), the page number for this index entry is omitted. Otherwise, *page* is the page number to use instead of the one that is automatically calculated.

The second argument is printed right-justified at the end of the entry; it might be used for the author's name, for example. If *author* is specified, *page* must be too: use \n% to get the current page number.

`.xl n`	.xl

Set the line length to *n* (current environment only). (This is actually the nroff/troff internal .ll request.)

.xp	`.xp` Print index. See also .(x and .)x.
.(z	`.(z` Begin floating keep.
.)z	`.)z` End floating keep.
.++	`.++ type header` Define the section of the paper being entered. Specify a *type* with a *header* title string. *Type* `A` Appendix. `AB` Abstract. `B` Bibliography. `C` Chapter. `P` Preliminary section (table of contents, etc.). `RA` Appendix, with page numbers reset to 1. `RC` Chapter, with page numbers reset to 1.

Predefined Strings

Items marked with a dagger (†) appear in more recent versions of the *me* macros. You will need to double-check them on your system.

`*`	Footnote number, incremented by .)f macro
`#`	Delayed text number
`[`	Superscript; move up and shrink type size
`]`	Undo superscript
`<`	Subscript; move down and shrink type size
`>`	Undo subscript
`−`	3/4 em dash
`dw`	Day of week, as a word
`mo`	Month, as a word
`td`	Today's date, in the form January 20, 1999.
`lq`	Left quote mark

rq	Right quote mark
$n†	Section name
'†	Acute accent
`†	Grave accent
qa†	For all
qe†	There exists
,†	Cedilla
:†	Umlaut
^†	Caret
o†	Circle (e.g., for Scandinavian Å). Usage is A*o.
v†	Inverted "v" for Czech ě. Usage is e*v.
{†	Begin superscript
}†	End superscript
~†	Tilde

Predefined Number Registers

Items marked with a dagger (†) appear in more recent versions of the *me* macros. You will need to double-check them on your system.

$0†	Section depth
$1†	First section number
$2†	Second section number
$3†	Third section number
$4†	Fourth section number
$5†	Fifth section number
$6†	Sixth section number
$v†	Relative vertical spacing in displays
$c	Current column number
$d	Delayed text number
$f	Footnote number
$i†	Paragraph base indent
$l	Column width
$m	Number of columns in effect
$p	Numbered paragraph number
$s	Column indent
$v†	Relative vertical spacing in text
bi	Display (block) indent
bm	Bottom title margin
bs	Display (block) pre/post spacing
bt†	Block keep threshold
ch	Current chapter number
df†	Display font
es†	Equation pre/post space

ff†	Footnote font
fi†	Footnote indent (first line only)
fm	Footer margin
fp†	Footnote point size
fs	Footnote prespace
fu†	Footnote undent (from right margin)
hm	Header margin
ii	Indented paragraph indent
pf	Paragraph font
pi	Paragraph indent
po†	Simulated page offset
pp	Paragraph point size
ps	Paragraph prespace
qi	Quote indent (also shortens line)
qp	Quote point size
qs	Quote pre/post space
sf†	Section title font
si†	Relative base indent per section depth
so†	Additional section title offset
sp†	Section title point size
ss†	Section prespace
tf	Title font
tm	Top title margin
tp	Title point size
xs	Index entry prespace
xu†	Index undent (from right margin)
zs	Floating keep pre/post space

Sample Document

```
.tp
.(l C
Whizprog \- The Be All and End All Program
.sp
by
.sp
.ce 2
J. Programmer
Wizard Corp.
.)l
.+c Abstract
This memorandum discusses the design and
implementation of
.i whizprog ,
the next generation of really
.b cool
do-it-all programs.
.+c "The Whole Story"
.sh 1 Requirements
```

```
.pp
The following requirements were identified. ...
.sh 1 Analysis
.pp
Here is what we determined. ...
.sh 1 Design
.pp
After much popcorn, we arrived at the
following design. ...
.sh 1 Implementation
.pp
After more popcorn and lots of Jolt Cola, we
implemented
.i whizprog
using ...
.+c "Conclusion"
.pp
We're ready to blow the socks off the market!
```

CHAPTER 16

man Macros

This chapter presents the following topics:

- Alphabetical summary of the *man* macros
- Predefined strings
- Names used internally by the *man* macros
- Sample document

Alphabetical Summary of man Macros

As many as six arguments may be given for all the macros that change fonts or produce a heading. Use double quotes around multiple words to get longer headings.

The .TS, .TE, .EQ, and .EN macros are not defined by the *man* macros. But because nroff and troff ignore unknown requests, you can still use them in your manpages; tbl and eqn work with no problems.

.B	.B [*text* ...]
	Set the arguments in the bold font, with a space between each argument. If no arguments are supplied, the next input line is set in bold.
.BI	.BI *barg iarg* ...
	Set alternating *barg* in bold and *iarg* in italic, with no intervening spaces.

.BR *barg rarg* ...

Set alternating *barg* in bold and *rarg* in roman, with no intervening spaces.

.BR

.DT

Reset the tab stops to their defaults, every 1/2 inch.

.DT

.HP [*indent*]
tag text

Start a paragraph with a "hanging" indent, one where a tag sits out to the left side. The optional *indent* is how far to indent the paragraph. The tag text follows on the next line. See the example under .TP.

.HP

.I [*text* ...]

Set the arguments in the italic font, with a space between each argument. If no arguments are supplied, the next input line is set in italic.

.I

.IB *iarg barg* ...

Set alternating *iarg* in italic and *barg* in bold, with no intervening spaces.

.IB

.IP *tag* [*indent*]

Start a paragraph with a hanging indent, one where a tag sits out to the left side. Unlike .HP and .TP, the *tag* is supplied as an argument to the macro. The optional *indent* is how far to indent the paragraph.

Example

```
.IP 1.
The first point is ...
.IP 2.
The second point is ...
```

.IP

.IR *iarg rarg* ...

Set alternating *iarg* in italic and *rarg* in roman, with no intervening spaces.

.IR

.IX	`.IX` *text*
	Index macro. Solaris only; intended for SunSoft internal use.
.LP	`.LP`
	Start a new paragraph. Just like `.PP`.
.P	`.P`
	Start a new paragraph. Just like `.PP`.
.PD	`.PD` [*distance*]
	Set the interparagraph spacing to *distance*. With no argument, reset it to the default. Most useful to get multiple tags for a paragraph.

Example

Show that two options do the same thing.

```
.PP
.I Whizprog
accepts the following options.
.TP \w'\fB\-\^\-help\fP'u+3n
.PD 0
.B \-h
.TP
.PD
.B \-\^\-help
Print a helpful message and exit.
```

.PP	`.PP`
	Start a new paragraph. This macro resets all the defaults, such as point size, font, and spacing.
.RB	`.RB` *rarg barg* ...
	Set alternating *rarg* in roman and *barg* in bold, with no intervening spaces.

.RE

End a relative indent. Each .RE should match a preceding .RS. See **.RS** for an example.

.RI *rarg iarg* ...

Set alternating *rarg* in roman and *iarg* in italic, with no intervening spaces.

.RS [*indent*]

Start a relative indent. Each successive .RS increases the indent. The optional *indent* is how far to indent the following text. Each .RS should have an accompanying .RE.

Example

```
.PP
There are a number of important points to remember.
.RS
.IP 1.
The first point is ...
.IP 2.
The second point is ...
...
.RE
Forget these at your own risk!
```

.SB *arg* ...

Set arguments in bold, using a smaller point size, separated by spaces.

.SH *arg* ...

Section header. Start a new section, such as NAME or SYNOPSIS. Use double quotes around multiple words for longer headings.

.SM *arg* ...

Set arguments in roman, using a smaller point size, separated by spaces.

.SS *arg* ...

Subsection header. Start a new subsection. Use double quotes around multiple words for longer headings.

man
Macros

.TH	.TH *title section date* ...

Title heading. This is the first macro of a manpage, and sets the header and footer lines. The *title* is the name of the manpage. The *section* is the section the manpage should be in (a number, possibly followed by a letter). The *date* is the date the manpage was last updated. Different systems have different conventions for the remaining arguments to this macro. For Solaris, the fourth and fifth arguments are the left-page footer and the main (center) header.

Example

```
.TH WHIZPROG 1L "April 1, 1999"
.SH NAME
whizprog \- do amazing things
...
```

.TP	.TP [*indent*] tag text

Start a paragraph with a hanging indent, one where a tag sits out to the left side. The optional *indent* is how far to indent the paragraph. The tag text follows on the next line. See also the example under **.PD**.

Example

```
.TP .2i
1.
The first point is ...
.TP .2i
2.
The second point is ...
```

Predefined Strings

The following strings are predefined; of these, only R and S are documented.

String	Effect in troff	Effect in nroff
*(lq	`` (")	"
*(rq	'' (")	"
*(PN	Current page number	Current page number
*(R	\(rg (®)	(Reg.)
*(S	Restore default point size	Restore default point size

Internal Names

The Solaris *man* macros use a number of macro, string, and number register names that begin with], }, and). Such names should be avoided in your own files.

The number registers D, IN, LL, P, X, d, m, and x are used internally by the Solaris *man* macros. Using .nr D 1 before calling the .TH macro generates pages with different even and odd footers.*

Sample Document

```
.TH WHIZPROG 1 "April 1, 1999"
.SH NAME
whizprog \- do amazing things
.SH SYNOPSIS
.B whizprog
[
.I options
] [
.I files
\&... ]
.SH DESCRIPTION
.I Whizprog
is the next generation of really
.B cool
do-it-all programs. ...
.SH OPTIONS
.PP
.I Whizprog
accepts the following options.
.TP \w'\fB\-\^\-level\fP'u+3n
.PD 0
.B \-h
.TP
.PD
.B \-\^\-help
Print a helpful message and exit.
.TP
.BI \-\^\-level " level"
Set the level for the
.B \-\^\-stun
option.
.TP
.B \-\^\-stun
Stun the competition, or other beings, as needed. ...
.SH SEE ALSO
.IR "Whizprog \- The Be All and End All Program" ,
by J. Programmer.
.PP
.IR wimpprog (1)
.SH FILES
.B /dev/phaser
.br
```

---

* This information was gleaned by examining the actual macros. It is not documented, so Your Mileage May Vary.

```
.B /dev/telepath
.SH CAVEATS
.PP
There are a number of important points to remember.
.RS
.IP 1.
Use
.B \-\^\-help
to get help.
.IP 2.
Use
.B \-\^\-stun
with care.  ...
.RE
Forget these at your own risk!
.SH BUGS
The
.B \-\^\-stun
option currently always uses
.BR "\-\^\-level 10" ,
making it rather dangerous.
.SH AUTHOR
J. Programmer,
.B jp@wizard-corp.com
```

CHAPTER 17

troff Preprocessors

This chapter is divided into the following four sections, each covering a different preprocessor of the nroff/troff formatting system:

- The tbl preprocessor

- The eqn preprocessor

- The pic graphics language preprocessor

- The refer preprocessor

Each of these preprocessors translates code into nroff/troff requests and escape sequences. They process information only between delimiting macros: other input text is left alone. Usually, one or more of these preprocessors are invoked as part of a command pipeline to format a file:

```
$ pic file | tbl | eqn | troff options | spooler
```

On multiuser systems, it is typical to have a general-purpose shell script for formatting. You would then select various command-line options to specify which (if any) preprocessors to include in your particular format command. However, you can also invoke the preprocessors individually. This is useful for confirming that syntax is correct or for determining where it fails. For example, the command:

```
$ tbl file
```

takes input between each .TS/.TE macro pair and converts it to tbl code. All other input is passed through to the output unchanged.

In SVR4, these commands are part of the BSD compatibility package and are found in /usr/ucb. On Solaris, with the exception of pic, they are a standard part of the system and are found in /usr/bin. The GNU version of troff (groff, see *http://www.gnu.org*) comes with versions of tbl, eqn, pic, and refer.

tbl

tbl is a preprocessor for formatting tables in nroff/troff. When used in a command pipeline, tbl should precede eqn. This makes output processing more efficient. tbl has the following command-line syntax:

```
tbl [options] [files]
```

The canonical reference for tbl is *Tbl—A Program to Format Tables*, by L.L. Cherry and M.E. Lesk, in *UNIX Programmer's Manual, Tenth Edition*, Volume 2, AT&T Bell Laboratories, M.D. McIlroy and A.G. Hume editors, Holt Rinehart & Winston, 1990. This paper may be downloaded from *http://cm.bell-labs.com/cm/cs/doc/76/tbl.ps.gz*.

Options

-me Prepend the *me* macros to the front of *files*.

-mm Prepend the *mm* macros to the front of *files*.

-ms Prepend the *ms* macros to the front of *files*.

-TX Produce output using only full vertical line motions. This is useful when formatting with nroff or when printing to a device that does not support fractional line motion. (This option is not on Solaris tbl.)

General Coding Scheme

In a text file, coding for tbl might look like this:

```
.TS H
options;
format1
format2.
Column Titles
.TH
Item1     Item2     Item3
Item1     Item2     Item3 ...
.TE
```

Successful processing of a table by tbl depends largely on the header lines, which consist of one line listing the options and one or more format lines. Each field of the table input must be separated by a tab or the designated tab symbol, with each row typed entirely on a single line unless a field is enclosed by the text block symbols T{ and T}.

tbl Macros

.TS   Start table.

.TE   End table.

.TS H   Used when the table continues onto more than one page. Used with .TH
        to define a header that prints on every page.

.TH	With .TS H, end the header portion of the table.
.T&	Continue table with new format line(s).

Options

Options affect the entire table. Options can be separated by commas or spaces, but the line must end with a semicolon.

center	Center with current margins.
expand	Flush with current right and left margins.
(leave *blank*)	Flush with current left margin (the default).
box	Enclose table in a box.
doublebox	Enclose table in two boxes.
allbox	Enclose each table entry in a box.
tab(x)	Define the tab symbol to be *x* instead of a tab.
linesize *n*	Set type size of lines or rules (e.g., from box) to *n* points.
delim *xy*	Recognize *x* and *y* as the eqn delimiters.

Format

The format line affects the layout of individual columns and rows of the table. Each line contains a key letter for each column of the table. The column entries should be separated by spaces, and the format section must end with a period. Each line of format corresponds to one line of the table, except for the last, which corresponds to all following lines up to the next .T&, if any.

Key letters

c	Center.
l	Flush left.
r	Flush right.
n	Align numerical entries.
a	Align alphabetic subcolumns.
s	Horizontally span previous column entry across this column.
^	Vertically span (center) entry from previous row down through this row.

Key modifiers

These must follow a key letter.

b	Boldface.
i	Italics.
f*x*	Font *x*.
p*n*	Point size *n*.
v*n*	Vertical line spacing, in points. Applies only to text blocks.

t	Begin any corresponding vertically spanned table entry (i.e., from ^) at the top line of its range.
e	Equal-width columns.
w(*n*)	Minimum column width. Also used with text blocks. *n* can be given in any acceptable troff units.
n	Amount of separation (in ens) between columns (default is 3).
|	Separate columns with a single vertical line. Typed between key letters.
||	Separate columns with a double vertical line. Typed between key letters.
_	Separate rows with a single horizontal line. Used in place of a key letter.
=	Separate rows with a double horizontal line. Used in place of a key letter.

Data

The data portion includes both the heading and text of the table. Each table entry must be separated by a tab character. In the description below, → represents the tab character.

.xx	troff requests may be used (such as .sp *n*, .na, etc.).
\	As last character in a line, combine following line with current line (hide newline).
\^	Span table entry that is above this row, bringing it down to be vertically centered.
_ or =	As the only character in a line, extend a single or double horizontal line the full width of the table.
\$_ or \$=	Extend a single or double horizontal line the full width of the column.
_	Extend a single horizontal line the width of the column's contents.
\R*x*	Print *x*s as wide as the column's contents.
...→T{	Start text block as a table entry. Must end a line. Necessary when a line of text is input over more than one line, or it will span more than one line of output.
T}→...	End text block. Must begin a line.

A tbl Example

Input:

```
.TS
center box linesize(6) tab(@);
cb s s.
Horizontal Local Motions
_
.T&
ci | ci s
ci | ci s
ci | ci | ci
c | l s.
Function@Effect in
\^@_
```

```
\^@troff@nroff

\eh'n'@Move distance N
\e(space)@Unpaddable space-size space
\e0@Digit-size space

.T&
c | l | l.
\e|@1/6 em space@ignored
\e^@1/12 em space@ignored
.TE
```

Result:

Horizontal Local Motions		
Function	*Effect in*	
	troff	*nroff*
\h'n'	Move distance N	
\(space)	Unpaddable space-size space	
\0	Digit-size space	
|	1/6 em space	ignored
\^	1/12 em space	ignored

eqn

eqn is a preprocessor designed to facilitate the typesetting of mathematical equations. Use neqn with nroff. eqn has the following command-line syntax:

```
eqn [options] [files]
```

The canonical reference for eqn is *Typesetting Mathematics—User's Guide*, by L.L. Cherry and B.W. Kernighan, in *UNIX Programmer's Manual, Tenth Edition*, Volume 2, AT&T Bell Laboratories, M.D. McIlroy and A.G. Hume editors, Holt Rinehart & Winston, 1990. This paper may be downloaded from *http://cm.bell-labs.com/cm/cs/doc/74/eqn.ps.gz*.

Options

-d*xy*

Use x and y as start and stop delimiters; same as specifying the eqn directive delim *xy*.

-f*n* Change to font *n*; same as the gfont directive.

-p*n* Reduce size of superscripts and subscripts by *n* points. If -p is not specified, the default reduction is 3 points.

-s*n* Reduce the point size by *n* points; same as the gsize directive.

-T*dev*

Format output to device *dev*. The default value comes from the TYPESETTER environment variable. Not available with neqn. (This option is not on Solaris eqn.)

eqn Macros

`.EQ`   Start typesetting mathematics.

`.EN`   End typesetting mathematics.

Use the `checkeq` command to check for unmatched macro pairs. (Not all systems have it, though.)

Mathematical Characters

The character sequences below are recognized and translated as shown:

Character	Translation	Character	Translation
>=	≥	approx	≈
<=	≤	nothing	
==	≡	cdot	·
!=	≠	times	×
+-	±	del	∇
->	→	grad	∇
<-	←	. . .	...
<<	≪	, . . . ,	,....,
>>	≫	sum	Σ
inf	∞	int	∫
partial	∂	prod	Π
half	½	union	∪
prime	′	inter	∩

Mathematical Text

Digits, parentheses, brackets, punctuation marks, and the following mathematical words are printed out in roman font:

```
sin    cos    tan    arc
sinh   cosh   tanh
and    if     for    det
max    min    lim
log    ln     exp
Re     Im
```

Greek Characters

Greek letters can be printed in uppercase or lowercase. To obtain Greek letters, simply spell them out. Some uppercase Greek letters are not supported because they can be specified by a roman equivalent (e.g, A for alpha, B for beta).

Name	Character	Name	Character
alpha	α	tau	τ
beta	β	upsilon	υ
gamma	γ	phi	π
delta	δ	chi	χ
epsilon	ε	psi	ψ
zeta	ζ	omega	ω
eta	η	GAMMA	Γ
theta	θ	DELTA	Δ
iota	ι	THETA	Θ
kappa	κ	LAMBDA	Λ
lambda	λ	XI	Ξ
mu	μ	PI	Π
nu	ν	SIGMA	Σ
xi	ξ	UPSILON	Υ
omicron	o	PHI	Φ
pi	π	PSI	Ψ
rho	ρ	OMEGA	Ω
sigma	σ		

Diacritical Marks

Several keywords are available to mark the tops of characters. eqn centers a mark at the correct height. bar and under span the necessary length.

Character	Translation
x dot	$\dot{x}$
x dotdot	$\ddot{x}$
x hat	$\hat{x}$
x tilde	$\tilde{x}$
x vec	$\vec{x}$
x dyad	$\overleftrightarrow{x}$
x bar	$\bar{x}$
x under	$\underline{x}$

Keywords Recognized by eqn

In addition to character names and diacritical marks, eqn recognizes the following keywords.

above   Separate the pieces of a pile or matrix column.
back n Move backwards horizontally n 1/100s of an em.
bold   Change to bold font.
ccol   Center-align a column of a matrix.

cpile	Make a centered pile (same as `pile`).
define	Create a name for a frequently used string.
delim *xy*	Define two characters to mark the left and right ends of an `eqn` equation to be printed inline. Use `delim off` to turn off delimiters.
down *n*	Move down *n* 1/100s of an em.
fat	Widen the current font by overstriking it.
font *x*	Change to font *x*, where *x* is the name or number of a font.
from	Used in summations, integrals, and similar constructions to signify the lower limit.
fwd *n*	Move forward horizontally *n* 1/100s of an em.
gfont *x*	Set a global font *x* for all equations.
gsize *n*	Set a global size for all equations.
italic	Change to italic font.
lcol	Left-justify a column of a matrix.
left	Create big brackets, big braces, big bars, etc.
lineup	Line up marks in equations on different lines.
lpile	Left-justify the elements of a pile.
mark	Remember the horizontal position in an equation. Used with `lineup`.
matrix	Create a matrix.
ndefine	Create a definition that takes effect only when `neqn` is running.
over	Make a fraction.
pile	Make a vertical pile with elements centered above each other.
rcol	Right-adjust a column of a matrix.
right	Create big brackets, big braces, big bars, etc. Must have a matching `left`.
roman	Set following constant in roman.
rpile	Right-justify the elements of a pile.
size *n*	Change the size of the font to *n*.
sqrt	Take the square root of the following equation element.
sub	Start a subscript.
sup	Start a superscript.
tdefine	Make a definition that applies only to `eqn`.
to	Used in summations, integrals, and similar constructions to signify the upper limit.
up *n*	Move up *n* 1/100s of an em.
~	Force extra space into the output.
^	Force a space one-half the size of the space forced by ~.
{ }	Force `eqn` to treat an element as a unit.
"..."	A string within quotes is not subject to alterations by `eqn`.

Precedence

If you don't use braces, `eqn` performs operations in the order shown in this list, reading from left to right.

dyad	vec	under	bar
tilde	hat	dot	dotdot
fwd	back	down	up
fat	roman	italic	bold
size	sub	sup	sqrt
over	from	to	

These operations group to the left:

over	sqrt	left	right

All others group to the right.

eqn defines a language for writing mathematics. Thus, there is a grammar with rules about how to group and order items within the equation. See the Bell Labs memorandum for the full story.

eqn Examples

Input:

```
.EQ
delim %%
.EN
%sum from i=0 to inf c sup i~=~lim from {m -> inf}
sum from i=0 to m c sup i%
.EQ
delim off
.EN
```

Result:

$$\sum_{i=0}^{\infty} c^i = \lim_{m \to \infty} \sum_{i=0}^{m} c^i$$

Input:

```
.EQ
x ~=~ left [ { -b ~+-~ sqrt {b sup 2 - ~4ac} }
over 2a right ]
.EN
```

Result:

$$x = \left[\frac{-b \pm \sqrt{b^2 - 4ac}}{2a} \right]$$

pic

pic is a graphics language program that facilitates the drawing of simple flowcharts and diagrams. pic offers dozens of ways to draw a picture, not only because of the many abbreviations it allows, but because pic tries to combine the language of geometry with English. For example, you can specify a line by its direction, magnitude, and starting point, yet you can often achieve the same effect by simply stating, "from *there* to *there*."

pic has the following command-line syntax:

```
pic [files]
```

Full descriptions of primitive objects in pic can be ended by starting another line, or with the semicolon character (;). A single primitive description can be continued on the next line, however, by ending the first with a backslash character (\). Comments may be placed on lines beginning with the pound sign (#).

Solaris does not have pic.

The canonical reference for pic is *Bell Labs Computing Science Technical Report #116*, by B.W. Kernighan. This paper may be downloaded from *http://cm.bell-labs.com/cm/cs/cstr/116.ps.gz*. That document describes a newer version of pic with more features than what is described here, but such features may not be universally available. You should read it if you plan to do any serious work in pic.

pic Macros

.PS [*h* [*w*]]	Start pic description. *h* and *w*, if specified, are the desired height and width of the picture; the full picture can expand or contract to fill this space.
.PS < *file*	Read contents of *file* in place of current line.
.PE	End pic description.
.PF	End pic description and return to vertical position before matching .PS.

troff requests or macros embedded in the body of a picture description are passed through unchanged. They are assumed to make sense at that point. Be careful not to use requests or macros that generate any horizontal or vertical motion.

Declarations

At the beginning of a pic description, you may declare a new scale, and declare any number of variables. pic assumes you want a 1-to-1 scale, where units are inches by default. You can declare a different scale, i.e., centimeters, by declaring:

```
scale = 2.54
```

You may use variables instead of numbers in a description; pic substitutes the variable's value. Instead of:

```
line right n
```

you may use a variable, for example, a, by declaring at the top of the description:

```
a = n
```

You may then write:

```
line right a
```

Variable names must begin with a lowercase letter. The rest of the name may consist of uppercase or lowercase letters, digits, and underscores. Variables retain their values from picture to picture.

Primitives

pic recognizes several basic graphical objects, or primitives. These primitives are specified by the following keywords:

arc	circle	move
arrow	ellipse	spline
box	line	"text"

Syntax

Primitives may be followed by relevant options. Options are discussed later in this section.

arc [cw] [options]	A fraction of a circle (default is 1/4 of a circle). The cw option specifies a clockwise arc; default is counter-clockwise.
arrow [options]	Draw an arrow. Essentially the same as line ->.
box [options]	Draw a box.
circle [options]	Draw a circle.
ellipse [options]	Draw an ellipse.
line [options]	Draw a line.
move [options]	A change of position in the drawing. Essentially, an invisible line.
spline [options]	A smooth curve, with the feature that a then option results in a gradual (sloped) change in direction. In other words, when drawing a path using line, you get sharp corners each time the path changes direction. With a spline, you instead get a smooth curve.
"text"	Text centered at current point.

Options

The options below are grouped by function. Note that at, with, and from specify points. Points may be expressed as Cartesian coordinates or with respect to previous objects.

right [n]	The direction of the primitive; default is the direction
left [n]	in which the previous description had been heading.
up [n]	Create diagonal motion by using two directions on the
down [n]	option line. Each direction can be followed by a specified length n.

rad *n* diam *n*	Create the primitive using radius or diameter *n*.
ht *n* wid *n*	Create the primitive using height or width *n*. For an arrow, line, or spline, height and width refer to arrow-head size.
same	Create the primitive using the same dimensions specified for the most recent matching primitive.
at *point*	Center the primitive at *point*.
with .*part* at *point*	Designate the *part* of the primitive to be at *point* (e.g., top, or a corner).
from *point1* to *point2* -> <- <->	Draw the primitive from *point1* to *point2*. Direct the arrowhead forward. Direct the arrowhead backward. Direct the arrowhead both ways.
chop *n m*	Chop *n* from beginning of primitive and *m* from end. With only one argument, the same value is chopped from both ends. With no arguments, chop a default amount (usually `circlerad`).
dotted dashed invis	Draw the primitive using lines that are dotted, dashed, or invisible. (An invisible object still occupies space in the output.) Default is solid lines.
then ...	Continue primitive in a new direction. Relevant only to lines, splines, moves, and arrows. Can be placed before or after any text.
"*text*"	Center the text over the center point of the object. The options for text described in the next section may also be used.

Text

Text must be placed within quotes. To break the line, break into two (or more) sets of quotes. Text always appears centered within the object, unless given one of the following arguments:

ljust	Text appears flush left, vertically centered.
rjust	Text appears flush right, vertically centered.
above	Text appears above the center.
below	Text appears below the center.

Object Blocks

Several primitives can be combined to make a complex object (for example, an octagon). This complex object can be treated as a single object by declaring it as a block:

```
Object: [
        description
        .
        .
        .
    ]
```

Brackets are used as delimiters. Note that the object is declared as the name of a place, and hence it must begin with a capital letter.

Macros

The same sequence of commands can be repeated by using macros. The syntax is:

```
define sequence %
        description
        .
        .
    %
```

Here the percent sign (%) is the delimiter, but you can use any character that isn't in the description.

Macros can take parameters, expressed in the definition as $1 through $9. Invoke the macro with the syntax:

```
sequence(value1,value2,...)
```

Positioning

In a pic description, the first action begins at (0,0) unless otherwise specified with coordinates. Thus, as objects are placed above and left of the first object, the point (0,0) moves down and right on the drawing.

All points are ultimately translated by the formatter into x- and y-coordinates. You may therefore refer to a specific point in the picture by incrementing or decrementing the coordinates. For example:

```
2nd ellipse + (.5,0)
```

This refers to the position 1/2 inch to the right of the center of the second ellipse.

The x- and y-coordinates of an object are the point where the center of the object is placed. You may refer to the x- and y-coordinates of an object by placing .x or .y at the end. For example:

```
last box.x
```

troff
Preprocessors

refs to the x-coordinate of the most recent box drawn. You can refer to some of the object's physical attributes in a similar way:

.x	x-coordinate of object's center.
.y	y-coordinate of object's center.
.ht	Height of object.
.wid	Width of object.
.rad	Radius of object.
.corner	One of the object's corners. Corners are described below.

Unless otherwise positioned, each object begins at the point where the last object left off. However, if a command (or sequence of commands) is set off by curly braces ({ }), pic then returns to the position before the first brace.

Positioning between objects

There are two ways to refer to a previous object.

- Refer to it by order. For example:

  ```
  1st box
  3rd box
  last box
  2nd last box
  ```

- Declare it with a name, in initial caps, on its declaration line. For example:

  ```
  Line1: line 1.5 right from last box.sw
  ```

To refer to a point between two objects, or between two points on the same object, you may write:

```
fraction of the way between first.position and second.position
```

or (abbreviated):

```
fraction <first.position, second.position>
```

Corners

When you refer to a previous object, pic assumes you mean the object's center unless you specify a corner. To specify a corner, use either of these forms:

```
.corner of object
object.corner
```

For example:

```
.sw of last box
last box.sw
```

Valid corners can be specified as any of the following:

n	North
s	South
e	East
w	West
ne	Northeast
nw	Northwest
se	Southeast
sw	Southwest
t	Top (same as n)
b	Bottom (same as s)
r	Right (same as e)
l	Left (same as w)
start	Point where drawing of object began
end	Point where drawing of object ended

You may also refer to the following parts of an object:

upper right	lower right
upper left	lower left

Expressions

Expressions may be used anywhere pic needs a numeric value (such as when specifying coordinates or amounts of motion). Expressions consist of numeric constants, variables, and operators.

pic recognizes the following operators.

+	Addition
−	Subtraction
*	Multiplication
/	Division
%	Modulus (remainder after division)
^	Exponentiation

Default Values

Various system variables control the default dimensions of objects. You can change these defaults by typing a description line of the form:

```
variable = value
```

Variable	Default	Variable	Default
arcrad	0.25	ellipsewid	0.75
arrowwid	0.05	linewid	0.5
arrowht	0.1	lineht	0.5
boxwid	0.75	movewid	0.5
boxht	0.5	moveht	0.5
circlerad	0.25	scale	1
dashwid	0.05	textht	0
ellipseht	0.5	textwid	0

pic Examples

Input:

```
.PS
define smile %
a = $1
circle radius a at 0,0
arc cw radius a*.75 from a*.5,-a*.25 to -a*.5,-a*.25
"\(bu" at a*.33,a*.25
"\(bu" at a*-.33,a*.25
%
smile(.5)
.PE
```

Result:

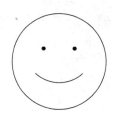

Input (from CSTR #116):

```
.PS
ellipse "document"
arrow
box "PIC"
arrow
box "TBL/EQN" "(optional)" dashed
arrow
box "TROFF"
arrow
ellipse "typesetter"
.PE
```

Result:

refer

Along with several associated commands, `refer` is a preprocessor for managing a database of bibliographic references. The database is kept in a separate file, and short references within a document are replaced by an expanded formal version.

The alphabetical command summary at the end of this section lists the usage and options for `refer` and the other commands that work with bibliographic databases.

`refer` is not supplied with SVR4, but it is a standard part of Solaris.

Bibliographic Entries

Bibliographic databases are text files, with each entry separated from the next by one or more blank lines. Within an entry, each field consists of a key letter (given as %*letter*) and associated value. Values may continue onto subsequent lines, ending at the next line that starts with a %. For example:

```
%T 5-by-5 Palindromic Word Squares
%A M.D. McIlroy
%J Word Ways
%V 9
%P 199-202
%D 1976
```

.Except for %A (the author), fields should only be supplied once. Irrelevant or inapplicable fields should not be provided.

Key	Meaning
%A	Author's name
%B	Book containing article
%C	City (place where published)
%D	Date of publication
%E	Editor of book containing article
%F	Footnote number or label (supplied by `refer`)
%G	Government order number
%H	Header commentary, printed before reference
%I	Issuer (publisher)
%J	Journal containing article
%K	Keywords to use in locating reference
%L	Label field used by `refer -k`
%M	Bell Labs Memorandum

Key	Meaning
%N	Number within volume
%O	Other commentary, printed at end of reference
%P	Page number(s)
%Q	Corporate or Foreign Author (unreversed)
%R	Report, paper, or thesis (unpublished)
%S	Series title
%T	Title of article or book
%V	Volume number
%X	Abstract (used by roffbib, not refer)
%Y, %Z	Ignored by refer

General Coding Scheme

In a document, use of refer might look like this:

```
Palindromes are fun.
Very large ones can be used to impress your friends.
Palindromic word squares
.[
%A McIlroy
.]
are even more amazing,
and should be reserved for impressing your boss.
...
.SH REFERENCES
.[
$LIST$
.]
```

The document shown here uses refer's collection mode (-e), where all the references are printed at the end of the document, instead of at each place they are referenced.

Alphabetical Summary of Commands

addbib	addbib [*options*] *database*
	Interactively add bibliography records to *database*.
	Options
	-a Don't prompt for an abstract.
	-p *file* Use *file* as the prompting "skeleton." Each line should be a prompt, a tab, and then the key letter to write.

indxbib *files*

Create an inverted index for refer bibliographic database files. These
are then used by lookbib and refer.

Generated files

For each original file *x*, indxbib creates four new files.

x.ia   The entry file
x.ib   The posting file
x.ic   The tag file
x.ig   The reference file

---

lookbib *database*

Search a bibliographic database created by indxbib. lookbib prompts
with a > sign for keywords and prints all records matching the keyword. If none are found, only another > prompt appears. While lookbib works without the inverted index files created by indxbib, such
operation is slower. See also **addbib** and **indxbib**.

---

refer [*options*] *files*

Process files for bibliographic references. Input is passed through to
the output unchanged, except for lines bracketed by .[and .]. Such
lines are taken to be references to citations kept in a separate
database. Based on the keywords provided between the brackets,
refer generates troff .ds commands that define strings containing
the relevant pieces of information. It then generates calls to macros
that can format the references appropriately. The *ms* and *me* macro
packages contain macro definitions for use with refer. The line right
before the call to .[will have a suitable string appended to its end to
indicate the use of a reference. Using the -e option, references can be
gathered for placement at the end as a group.

Options

-a[*n*]
> Reverse the first *n* author names (i.e., last name first). With no
> *n*, all names are reversed.

-b   Bare mode. Do not add inline references to the text.

-c*list*
> Capitalize, with SMALL CAPS, those fields whose letters are given
> in *list*.

→

-e   Collect references for output at the end. References to the same source are only printed once. The references are printed when these lines are encountered:

```
.[
$LIST$
.]
```

-kc Instead of numbered references, use labeled references, where the data supplied is from field %c in the database. The default is %L.

-l[m[,n]]
    Instead of numbered references, use labeled references, where the label is generated based on the senior (first) author's last name, and the year of publication. If supplied, *m* and *n* indicate how many letters from the author's last name and the last *n* digits of the year. Otherwise, the full name and year are used.

-n   Do not search the default file (found in /usr/lib/refer/papers).

-p *refsfile*
    Use *refsfile* as a list of references.

-s*keylist*
    Sort references based on the fields listed in *keylist*. This implies -e. Each letter may be followed by a number, indicating how many of that field is to be used. A + is equivalent to infinity. The default is -sAD, which sorts on the senior author and date.

Example

Sort on all authors, and then the date; use mybib for references.

```
refer -sA+D -p mybib thesis.ms | tbl | eqn | troff -ms - | lp
```

---

roffbib [*options*] [*files*]

Print a bibliographic database. roffbib is a shell script that processes the named *files* (or standard input if no *files*) through refer and prints the results as a bibliography. By default, the bibliography is formatted using nroff, use the -Q option to use troff instead.

roffbib accepts the following nroff/troff options and simply passes them to the formatter: -e, -h, -m, -n, -o, -q, -r, -s, and -T. See Chapter 12, *nroff and troff*, for more details.

Options

-H *header*
    Set the "header" (title) to *header*. The default is BIBLIOGRAPHY. (This option is in the script, but is not documented.)

-Q Use troff instead of nroff. The page offset is set to one inch.

-v Typeset for Versatec printer/plotter. While documented in the manpage, this option is not in the script.

-x Format abstracts or comments in the %X field of a bibliographic reference. Useful for annotated bibliographies. refer does not use the %X field.

Example

Sort a database and print it to a PostScript printer:

```
sortbib refs | roffbib -Q -x | /usr/lib/lp/postscript/dpost | lp
```

---

sortbib [*option*] *files*

Sort one or more bibliographic databases. Typically used for printing with roffbib. Up to 16 databases may be sorted. Records may not exceed 4096 bytes in length.

Option

-s *keys*
   Sort on the given *keys*. The first four keys influence the sort; the rest are ignored. Letters in *keys* correspond to the key letters in bibliography entries. Append a + to a letter to sort completely by that key before moving to the next.

Examples

Sort by authors first, then by date:

```
sortbib -sA+D myrefs | ...
```

Sort by author, title, and date:

```
sortbib -sATD myrefs | ...
```

PART IV

Software Development

The Unix operating system earned its reputation by providing an unexcelled environment for software development. SCCS, RCS, and make are major contributors to the efficiency of this environment. SCCS and RCS allow multiple versions of a source file to be stored in a single archival file. make automatically updates a group of interrelated programs.

- Chapter 18, *The Source Code Control System*
- Chapter 19, *The Revision Control System*
- Chapter 20, *The make Utility*

CHAPTER 18

The Source Code Control System

This chapter presents the following topics:

- Introduction

- Overview of commands

- Basic operation

- Identification keywords

- Data keywords

- Alphabetical summary of commands

- sccs and pseudo-commands

Note: SCCS users who are more familiar with RCS may benefit from the "Conversion Guide for SCCS Users" in Chapter 19, *The Revision Control System*, which lists SCCS commands and their RCS equivalents.

For more information, see *Applying RCS and SCCS*, listed in the Bibliography.

Introduction

The Source Code Control System (SCCS) lets you keep track of each revision of a document, avoiding the confusion that often arises from having several versions of one file online. SCCS is particularly useful when programs are enhanced, but the original version is still needed.

All changes to a file are stored in a file named s.*file*, which is called an SCCS file. Each time a file is "entered" into SCCS, SCCS notes which lines have been changed or deleted since the most recent version. From that information, SCCS can regenerate the file on demand. Each set of changes depends on all previous sets of changes.

Each set of changes is called a *delta* and is assigned an SCCS identification string (*sid*). The *sid* consists of either two components: release and level numbers (in the form *a.b*) or of four components: the release, level, branch, and sequence numbers (in the form *a.b.c.d*). The branches and sequences are for situations when two on-running versions of the same file are recorded in SCCS. For example, *delta 3.2.1.1* refers to release 3, level 2, branch 1, sequence 1.

Overview of Commands

SCCS commands fall into several categories.

Basic Setup and Editing

admin   Create new SCCS files and change their parameters.
get   Retrieve versions of SCCS files.
delta   Create a new version of an SCCS file (i.e., append a new *delta*).
unget   Cancel a get operation; don't create a new delta.

Fixing Deltas

cdc   Change the comment associated with a delta.
comb   Combine consecutive deltas into a single delta.
rmdel   Remove an accidental delta from an SCCS file.

Information

help   Print a command synopsis or clarify diagnostic messages.
prs   Print portions of SCCS files in a specified format.
prt   Format and print the contents of one or more SCCS files. Solaris only.
sact   Show editing activity on SCCS files.
what   Search for all occurrences of the pattern get substitutes for %Z%, and print the following text.

Comparing Files

sccsdiff   Show the differences between any two SCCS files.
val   Validate an SCCS file.

Basic Operation

This section outlines the steps to follow when using SCCS:

- Creating an SCCS file

- Retrieving a file

- Creating new releases and branches

- Recording changes

- Caveats

Creating an SCCS File

The `admin` command with the `-i` option creates and initializes SCCS files. For example:

```
admin -ich01 s.ch01
```

creates a new SCCS file and initializes it with the contents of ch01, which becomes *delta 1.1*. The message "No id keywords (cm7)" appears if you do not specify any keywords. In general, "id keywords" refer to variables in the files that are replaced with appropriate values by `get`, identifying the date and time of creation, the version retrieved, etc. A listing of identification keywords occurs later in this chapter.

Once the s.ch01 file is created, the original ch01 file can be removed, since it can be easily regenerated with the `get` command.

Retrieving a File

The `get` command can retrieve any version of a file from SCCS. Using the example above, you can retrieve ch01 by entering:

```
get -e s.ch01
```

and the messages:

```
1.1
new delta 1.2
272 lines
```

may appear. This indicates that you are "getting" *delta 1.1*, and the resulting file has 272 lines of text. When the file is reentered into the SCCS file s.ch01 with the `delta` command, its changes are *delta 1.2*.

The `-e` option indicates to SCCS that you intend to make more changes to the file and then reenter it into SCCS. Without this option, you will receive the file with read-only permissions. The `-e` option, besides releasing the file with read-write permissions, also creates a file p.ch01, which records information that is used by SCCS when the file is returned.

Creating New Releases and Branches

The `-r` option to `get` tells SCCS what release and level number you want, but if no level is specified, it defaults to the highest level available. With the command:

```
get -r3.2 ch01
```

delta 3.2 is the release. However, the command:

```
get -r3 ch01
```

returns the highest-numbered level in release 3, for example, 3.8. With the -r option omitted, get defaults to the highest release, highest level—in other words, the latest version.

When major changes are in store for a file, you may want to begin a new release of the file by "getting" the file with the next highest release number. For example, if the latest release of a file is 3.2, and you want to start release 4, enter:

```
get -e -r4 ch01
```

You receive the message:

```
3.2
new delta 4.1
53 lines
```

If you want to make a change to an older version of the same file, you can enter:

```
get -e -r2.2 ch01
```

and receive the message:

```
2.2
new delta 2.2.1.1
121 lines
```

You have now created a new branch from the trunk, stemming from version 2.2. Changes in this delta will not affect those in the trunk deltas, i.e., 2.3, 3.1, etc.

Recording Changes

Once changes have been made to the SCCS file, return it to SCCS with:

```
delta s.ch01
```

You are prompted for comments on the changes. The delta command then does its own get and uses diff to compare the new version of the file with the most recent version. It then prints messages giving the new release number and the number of lines that were inserted, deleted, and unchanged.

Caveats

Here are some things to bear in mind when using SCCS:

- You can't store binary data in an SCCS file. Solaris SCCS allows it by encoding the file using uuencode.

- SCCS doesn't preserve the execute bit from the file permissions of files checked into it. This is important particularly for shell scripts: you have to explicitly make them executable after retrieving them from SCCS. This should be automated using make.

- Using ID keywords (see the next section) in your *printf*(3S) format strings can lead to disaster. Find some indirect way to generate these strings for printing.

Identification Keywords

The following keywords may be used in an SCCS file. A get command expands these keywords to the value described.

%A%   Shorthand for providing what strings for program files:
      %A% = %Z%%Y% %M% %I%%Z%
%B%   Branch number
%C%   Current line number, intended for identifying where error occurred
%D%   Current date (YY/MM/DD)
%E%   Date newest applied delta was created (YY/MM/DD)
%F%   SCCS filename
%G%   Date newest applied delta was created (MM/DD/YY)
%H%   Current date (MM/DD/YY)
%I%   *sid* of the retrieved text (%R%.%L%.%B%.%S%)
%L%   Level number
%M%   Module name (filename without s. prefix)
%P%   Fully qualified SCCS filename
%Q%   Value of *string*, as defined by admin -fq *string*
%R%   Release number
%S%   Sequence number
%T%   Current time (HH:MM:SS)
%U%   Time newest applied delta was created (HH:MM:SS)
%W%   Another shorthand like %A%; %W% = %Z%%M% *tab* %I%
%Y%   Module type, as defined by admin -ft *type*
%Z%   String recognized by what; that is, @(#)

Data Keywords

Data keywords specify which parts of an SCCS file are to be retrieved and output using the -d option of the prs command.

:A: Form of what string
:B: Branch number
:BD: Body
:BF: Branch flag
:C: Comments for delta
:CB: Ceiling boundary
:D: Date delta created (:Dy:/:Dm:/:Dd:)
:Dd: Day delta created
:Dg: Deltas ignored (sequence number)
:DI: Sequence number of deltas (:Dn:/:Dx:/:Dg:)
:DL: Delta line statistics (:Li:/:Ld:/:Lu:)

:Dm:	Month delta created
:Dn:	Deltas included (sequence number)
:DP:	Predecessor delta sequence number
:Ds:	Default sid
:DS:	Delta sequence number
:Dt:	Delta information
:DT:	Delta type
:Dx:	Deltas excluded (sequence number)
:Dy:	Year delta created
:F:	SCCS filename
:FB:	Floor boundary
:FD:	File descriptive text
:FL:	Flag list
:GB:	Gotten body
:I:	SCCS ID string (sid) (:R:.:L:.:B:.:S:)
:J:	Joint edit flag
:KF:	Keyword error/warning flag
:KV:	Keyword validation string (not on Solaris.)
:L:	Level number
:Ld:	Lines deleted by delta
:Li:	Lines inserted by delta
:LK:	Locked releases
:Lu:	Lines unchanged by delta
:M:	Module name
:MF:	Modification Request validation flag
:MP:	Modification Request validation program name
:MR:	Modification Request numbers for delta
:ND:	Null delta flag
:P:	Username of programmer who created delta
:PN:	SCCS file pathname
:Q:	User-defined keyword
:R:	Release number
:S:	Sequence number
:T:	Time delta created (:Th:::Tm:::Ts:)
:Th:	Hour delta created
:Tm:	Minutes delta created
:Ts:	Seconds delta created
:UN:	Usernames
:W:	A form of what string (:Z::M:\t:I:)
:Y:	Module type flag
:Z:	what string delimiter (@(#))

Alphabetical Summary of SCCS Commands

File arguments to SCCS commands can be either filenames or directory names. Naming a directory processes all the files in that directory, with nonapplicable and unreadable files ignored. (Unreadable files produce an error message.) If in place of a file argument a dash (–) is entered, the command reads the names of files to process from standard input, one on each line.

Use the form *yy[mm[dd[hh[mm[ss]]]]]* for commands that accept times and dates. Values left out default to the highest valid value. Furthermore, Solaris treats years from 69 to 99 as being in the 20th century, while years between zero and 68 are in the 21st.

On Solaris, all SCCS commands reside in /usr/ccs/bin. To use these commands, be sure to add this directory to your PATH environment variable.

---

admin [*options*] files   **admin**

Add *files* to SCCS or change *options* of SCCS *files.*

Options

-a[*user | groupid*]
 Assign *user* or *groupid* permission to make deltas; a ! before *user* or *groupid* denies permission. If no list is given, anyone has permission.

-b Encode the file contents as binary data. Files that contain ASCII NUL or other control characters, or that do not end in a newline, are automatically treated as binary files and encoded. This option is typically used together with -i. Solaris only.

-d*flag*
 Delete *flag* previously set with -f. Applicable *flags* are:

b	Enable the –b option in a get command; this allows branch deltas.
c*n*	Set highest release to *n* (default is 9999).
d*n*	Set get's default delta number to *n.*
f*n*	Set lowest release to *n* (default is 1).
i[*string*]	Treat "No id keywords (ge6)" as a fatal error. *string*, if present, forces a fatal error if keywords do not exactly match *string*. Solaris does not allow you to supply a *string*.
j	Allow multiple concurrent gets.
l*list*	Releases in *list* cannot accept changes; use the letter a to specify all releases.
m*name*	Substitute %M% keyword with module *name*.
n	Create a null delta from which to branch.
q*string*	Substitute %Q% keyword with *string*.
t*type*	Substitute %Y% keyword with module *type*.

→

admin
←

v[*prog*]   Force delta command to prompt for modification request numbers as the reason for creating a delta. Run program *prog* to check for valid numbers.

-e[*user* | *groupid*]
Permission to make deltas is denied to each *user* or *groupid*.

-f*flag*
Set *flag* (see -d above).

-h   Check an existing SCCS file for possible corruption.

-i[*file*]
Create a new SCCS file using the contents of *file* as the initial delta. If *file* is omitted, use standard input. This option implies the -n option.

-m[*list*]
Insert *list* of modification request numbers as the reason for creating the file.

-n   Create a new SCCS file that is empty.

-r*n.n*
Set initial delta to release number *n.n*. Default is 1.1. Can only be used with -i.

-t[*file*]
Replace SCCS file description with contents of *file*. If *file* is missing, the existing description is deleted.

-y[*text*]
Insert *text* as comment for initial delta (valid only with -i or -n).

-z   Recompute the SCCS file checksum and store in first line. The file should be verified first; see **val**.

---

cdc

cdc -r*sid* [*options*] *files*

Change the delta comments of the specified *sid* (SCCS ID) of one or more SCCS *files*.

Options

-m[*list*]
Add the *list* of modification request numbers (use a ! before any number to delete it). -m is useful only when admin has set the v flag for *file*. If -m is omitted, the terminal displays MRs? as an input prompt.

-y[*string*]

    Add *string* to the comments for the specified delta. If -y is omitted, the terminal displays comments? as an input prompt.

Example

For delta 1.3 of file s.prog.c, add modification numbers x01-5 and x02-8, and then add comments:

```
$ cdc -r1.3 s.prog.c
MRs? x01-5 x02-8
comments? this went out to review
```

---

comb [*options*] `files`

Reduce the size of the specified SCCS *files*. This is done by pruning selected deltas and combining those that remain, thereby reconstructing the SCCS file. The default behavior prunes all but the most recent delta in a particular branch and keeps only those ancestors needed to preserve the tree structure. comb produces a shell script on standard output. Actual reconstruction of the SCCS files is done by running the script.

Options

-c*list*

    Preserve only those deltas whose SCCS IDs are specified in the comma-separated *list*. Use a hyphen (–) to supply a range; e.g., 1.3,2.1-2.5.

-o Access the reconstructed *file* at the release number of the delta that is created, instead of at the most recent ancestor. This option may change the tree structure.

-p*sid*

    In reconstructing *file*, discard all deltas whose SCCS identification string is older than *sid*.

-s Generate a shell script that calculates how much the file will be reduced in size. -s is useful as a preview of what comb does when actually run.

---

delta [*options*] `files`

Incorporate changes (add a delta) to one or more SCCS *files*. delta stores changes made to a text file retrieved by get -e and then edited. delta normally removes the text file.

$\rightarrow$

delta
←

Options

-d Use `diff` instead of `bdiff` to find the changes. Solaris only.

-g*list*
> Ignore deltas whose SCCS IDs (version numbers) are specified in the comma-separated *list*. Use – to supply a range; e.g., 1.3,2.1-2.5.

-m[*list*]
> Supply a *list* of modification request numbers as reasons for creating new deltas. -m is useful only when `admin` has set the v flag for *file*. If -m is omitted, the terminal displays MRs? as an input prompt.

-n Do not remove the edited file (extracted by `get` -e) after execution of `delta`.

-p Print a `diff`-style listing of delta changes to *file*.

-r*SID*
> Delta version number that identifies *file*. -r is needed only when more than one version of an SCCS file is being edited simultaneously.

-s Suppress printing of new SID and other delta information.

-y[*string*]
> Insert *string* as a comment describing why the delta was made. If -y is omitted, the terminal displays comments? as an input prompt.

---

get

get [*options*] *files*

Retrieve a text version of an SCCS *file*. The retrieved text file (also called the g-file) has the same name as the SCCS file but drops the s. prefix. For each SCCS *file*, `get` prints its version number and the number of lines retrieved. See the previous section, "Identification Keywords", for a list of keywords that can be placed in text files.

Options

-a*n* Retrieve delta sequence number *n*; not very useful (used by `comb`).

-b Create new branch (use with -e).

-c*date*
> Retrieve a version that includes only those changes made before *date*. *date* is a series of two-digit numbers indicating the year, followed by an optional month, day, hour, minute, and second. Nonnumeric characters can be used as field separators; they are essentially ignored.

-e   Retrieve a text file for editing; this is the most commonly used option. Implies -k.

-g   Suppress the text and just retrieve the SCCS ID (version number), typically to check it.

-G*name*

    Save retrieved text in file *name* (default is to drop the s. prefix). Solaris only.

-i*list*

    Incorporate into the retrieved text file any deltas whose SCCS IDs (version numbers) are specified in the comma-separated *list*. Use a hyphen (–) to supply a range (e.g., 1.3,2.1-2.5).

-k   Do not expand ID keywords to their values; use in place of -e to regenerate (overwrite) a text file that was ruined during editing.

-l[p]

    Create a delta summary (saved to a file or, with -lp, displayed on standard output).

-m   Precede each text line with the SCCS ID of the delta it relates to.

-n   Precede each text line with the %M% keyword (typically the name of the text file).

-p   Write retrieved text to standard output instead of to a file.

-r[*sid*]

    Retrieve SCCS ID (version number) *sid*. With no *sid*, retrieve the latest version or the version specified by the d flag in the SCCS file.

-s   Suppress normal output (show error messages only).

-t   Retrieve the top (most recent) version of a release.

-w*string*

    Replace the %W% keyword with *string*; %W% is the header label used by what.

-x*list*

    Exclude the *list* of deltas from the retrieved text file; the inverse of -i.

Examples

Retrieve file prog.c for editing; a subsequent delta creates a branch at version 1.3:

```
get -e -b -r1.3 s.prog.c
```

Retrieve file prog.c; contents will exclude changes made after 2:30 p.m. on June 1, 1990 (except for deltas 2.6 and 2.7, which are included):

$\rightarrow$

get ←	``` get -c'90/06/01 14:30:00' -i'2.6,2.7' s.prog.c ``` Display the contents of s.text.c (all revisions except 1.1 – 1.7): ``` get -p -x1.1-1.7 s.text.c ```

help	`help [commands	error_codes]`
		
		Online help facility to explain SCCS commands or error messages. With no arguments, help prompts for a command name or an error code. To display a brief syntax, supply the SCCS command name. To display an explanation of an error message, supply the code that appears after an SCCS error message. The help files usually reside in /usr/ccs/lib.
		
		Error messages produced by aborted SCCS commands are of the form:
		
		`ERROR filename: message (code)`
		
		The *code* is useful for finding out the nature of your error. To do this, type:
		
		`help code`
		
		Example
		
		When everything else fails, try this:
		
		`help stuck`

prs	`prs [options] files`
	
	Print formatted information for one or more SCCS *files*.
	
	Options
	
	-a Include information for all deltas, including removed ones.
	
	-c*date*
	    Cutoff *date* used with -e or -l (see **get** for format of *date*).
	
	-d[*format*]
	    Specify output *format* by supplying text and/or SCCS keywords. See the previous section, "Data Keywords," for a list of valid keywords. Use \t and \n in the *format* to create a tab and newline, respectively.
	
	-e With -r, list data for deltas earlier than or including *sid*; with -c, list data for deltas not newer than *date*.

-l   Like -e, but later than or including *sid* or *date*.

-r[*sid*]

Specify SCCS ID *sid*; default is the most recent delta.

Example

The following command:

```
prs -d"program :M: version :I: by :P:" -r s.yes.c
```

might produce this output:

```
program yes.c version 2.4.6 by daniel
```

---

prt [*options*] *files*

Solaris only. Format and print the contents of one or more SCCS files.
By default, prt prints the delta table (i.e., the version log). The
sccsfile(4) manpage describes the contents of SCCS files in detail.

Options

-a   Display entries for all deltas, including removed ones.

-b   Print the body of the SCCS file.

-c*date*

Exclude entries that are prior to *date*. Each entry is printed as a
single line, preceded by the name of the file. This makes it possible to easily sort multiple version logs.

-d   Print delta table entries. This is the default action.

-e   Print everything. This option implies -d, -i, -f, -t, and -u.

-f   Print the flags for each SCCS file.

-i   Print the SIDs of included, excluded, and ignored deltas.

-r*date*

Exclude deltas that are newer than *date*.

-s   Print only the first line (the statistics) of each delta table.

-t   Print the SCCS file's descriptive text.

-u   Print the usernames and/or numerical group IDs of users that are
allowed to make changes.

-y[*sid*]

Exclude deltas that are older than *sid*. If no delta in the table
matches *sid*, print the entire table. With no *sid*, print information
for the current delta.

rmdel	`rmdel -r sid files`
	Remove a delta from one or more SCCS *files*, where *sid* is the SCCS ID. The delta must be the most recent in its branch, and it cannot be checked out for editing.
sact	`sact files`
	For the specified SCCS *files*, report which deltas are about to change (i.e., which files are currently being edited via `get -e` but haven't yet been updated via `delta`). `sact` lists output in five fields: SCCS ID of the current delta being edited, SCCS ID of the new delta to create, user who issued the `get -e`, and the date and time it was issued.
sccsdiff	`sccsdiff -rsid1 -rsid2 [options] files`
	Report differences between two versions of an SCCS *file*. *sid1* and *sid2* identify the deltas to be compared. This command invokes `bdiff`, which in turn calls `diff`. Solaris `sccsdiff` calls `diff`, not `bdiff`.
	Options
	`-p` Pipe output through `pr`.
	`-sn` Use file segment size *n* (*n* is passed to `bdiff`).
unget	`unget [options] files`
	Cancel a previous `get -e` for one or more SCCS *files*. If a file is being edited via `get -e`, issuing `delta` processes the edits (creating a new delta), whereas `unget` deletes the edited version (preventing a new delta from being made).
	Options
	`-n` Do not remove file retrieved with `get -e`.
	`-rsid`
	The SCCS ID of the delta to cancel; needed only if `get -e` is issued more than once for the same SCCS file.
	`-s` Suppress display of the intended delta's *sid*.
val	`val [options] files`
	Validate that the SCCS *files* meet the characteristics specified in the options. `val` produces messages on the standard output for each file and returns an 8-bit code upon exit. The codes are described in

"Return Value Bits"; bits are counted left to right.

Options

– Read standard input and interpret each line as a `val` command-line argument. Exit with an *EOF*. This option is used by itself.

`-mname`
> Compare *name* with `%M%` keyword in *file*.

`-rsid` .
> Check whether the SCCS ID is ambiguous or invalid.

`-s` Silence any error message.

`-ytype`
> Compare *type* with `%Y%` keyword in *file*.

Return Value Bits

Bit	Meaning
0	Missing file argument.
1	Unknown or duplicate option.
2	Corrupted SCCS file.
3	Cannot open file, or file is not an SCCS file.
4	SID is invalid or ambiguous.
5	Nonexistent SID.
6	Mismatch between type and -y argument.
7	Mismatch between filename and -m argument.

`what [option] files`

Search *files* for the pattern `@(#)` and print the text that follows it. (Typically, *files* are binary executables.) Actually, the pattern searched for is the value of `%Z%`, but the `get` command expands this keyword to `@(#)`. The main purpose of `what` is to print identification strings.

Option

`-s` Quit after finding the first occurrence of a pattern.

---

sccs and Pseudo-Commands

The compatibility packages include `sccs`, a front-end to the SCCS utility. This command provides a more user-friendly interface to SCCS and has the following command-line syntax:

```
sccs [options] command [SCCS_flags] [files]
```

In addition to providing all the regular SCCS commands, sccs offers pseudo-commands. These are easy-to-use, prebuilt combinations of the regular SCCS commands. *options* apply only to the sccs interface. *command* is the SCCS command or pseudo-command to run, and *SCCS_flags* are specific options passed to the SCCS command being run.

sccs makes it easier to specify files because it automatically prepends SCCS/s. to any filename arguments. For example:

```
sccs get -e file.c
```

would be interpreted as:

```
get -e SCCS/s.file.c
```

Thus, when using sccs, you would first make a directory named SCCS to hold all the s. SCCS files.

Options

-d*prepath*
> Locate files in *prepath* rather than in current directory. For example:
>
> ```
> sccs -d/home get file.c
> ```
>
> is interpreted as:
>
> ```
> get /home/SCCS/s.file.c
> ```

-p*endpath*
> Access files from directory *endpath* instead of SCCS. For example:
>
> ```
> sccs -pVERSIONS get file.c
> ```
>
> is interpreted as:
>
> ```
> get VERSIONS/s.file.c
> ```

-r Invoke sccs as the real user instead of as the effective user.

Pseudo-Commands

Equivalent SCCS actions are indicated in parentheses.

check
> Like info, but return nonzero exit codes instead of filenames.

clean
> Remove from current directory any files that aren't being edited under SCCS (via get -e, for example).

create
> Create SCCS files (admin -i followed by get).

deledit
Same as delta followed by get -e.

delget
Same as delta followed by get.

diffs
Compare file's current version and SCCS version (like sccsdiff).

edit
Get a file to edit (get -e).

enter
Like create, but without the subsequent get (admin -i).

fix Same as rmdel (must be followed by -r).

info
List files being edited (similar to sact).

print
Print information (like prs -e followed by get -p -m).

tell
Like info, but list one filename per line.

unedit
Same as unget.

Solaris Notes

- SCCS is not available unless you have done at least a developer-system install.

- The environment variable PROJECTDIR specifies a location where sccs searches for SCCS files. There are two possible kinds of values you can use.

    An absolute pathname
    sccs searches for SCCS files in the directory named by $PROJECTDIR.

    A username
    sccs looks in the src or source subdirectory of the given user's home directory.

CHAPTER 19

The Revision Control System

This chapter presents the following topics:

- Overview of commands

- Basic operation

- General RCS specifications

- Conversion guide for SCCS users

- Alphabetical summary of commands

As with SCCS in the preceding chapter, the Revision Control System (RCS) is designed to keep track of multiple file revisions, thereby reducing the amount of storage space needed. With RCS you can automatically store and retrieve revisions, merge or compare revisions, keep a complete history (or log) of changes, and identify revisions using symbolic keywords. RCS is believed to be more efficient than SCCS. Unlike SCCS, RCS preserves execute permission on the files it manages, and you can store binary data in RCS files.

RCS is not part of standard SVR4 or Solaris. It can be obtained from the Free Software Foundation (see *http://www.gnu.org*). This chapter describes RCS Version 5.7.

For more information, see *Applying RCS and SCCS*, listed in the Bibliography.

Overview of Commands

The three most important RCS commands are:

ci   Check in revisions (put a file under RCS control).
co   Check out revisions.
rcs   Set up or change attributes of RCS files.

Two commands provide information about RCS files:

ident   Extract keyword values from an RCS file.

rlog   Display a summary (log) about the revisions in an RCS file.

You can compare RCS files with these commands:

merge   Incorporate changes from two files into a third file.

rcsdiff   Report differences between revisions.

rcsmerge   Incorporate changes from two RCS files into a third RCS file.

The following commands help with configuration management. However, they are considered optional, so they are not always installed.

rcsclean   Remove working files that have not been changed.

rcsfreeze Label the files that make up a configuration.

Basic Operation

Normally, you maintain RCS files in a subdirectory called RCS, so the first step in using RCS should be:

mkdir RCS

Next, you place an existing file (or files) under RCS control by running the check-in command:

ci *file*

This creates a file called *file,*v in the RCS directory. *file,*v is called an RCS file, and it stores all future revisions of *file.* When you run ci on a file for the first time, you are prompted to describe the contents. ci then deposits *file* into the RCS file as revision 1.1.

To edit a new revision, check out a copy:

co -l *file*

This causes RCS to extract a copy of *file* from the RCS file. You must lock the file with -l to make it writable by you. This copy is called a working file. When you're done editing, you can record the changes by checking the working file back in again:

ci *file*

This time, you are prompted to enter a log of the changes made, and the file is deposited as revision 1.2. Note that a check-in normally removes the working file. To retrieve a read-only copy, do a check-out without a lock:

co *file*

This is useful when you need to keep a copy on hand for compiling or searching. As a shortcut to the previous ci/co, you could type:

```
ci -u file
```

This checks in the file but immediately checks out a read-only ("unlocked") copy. In practice, you would probably make a "checkpoint" of your working version and then keep going, like this:

```
ci -l file
```

This checks in the file, and then checks it back out again, locked, for continued work. To compare changes between a working file and its latest revision, you can type:

```
rcsdiff file
```

Another useful command is rlog, which shows a summary of log messages. System administrators can use the rcs command to set up default behavior of RCS.

General RCS Specifications

This section discusses:

- Keyword substitution
- Keywords
- Example values
- Revision numbering
- Specifying the date
- Specifying states
- Standard options and environment variables

Keyword Substitution

RCS lets you place keyword variables in your working files. These variables are later expanded into revision notes. You can then use the notes either as embedded comments in the input file or as text strings that appear when the output is printed. To create revision notes via keyword substitution, follow this procedure:

1. In your working file, type any of the keywords listed below.
2. Check the file in.
3. Check the file out again. Upon checkout, the co command expands each keyword to include its value. That is, co replaces instances of:

    ```
    $keyword$
    ```

    with:

    ```
    $keyword: value $.
    ```

4. Subsequent check-in and check-out of a file updates any existing keyword values. Unless otherwise noted below, existing values are replaced by new values.

Many commands have a -k option that provides considerable flexibility during keyword substitution.

Keywords

$Author$	Username of person who checked in the revision.
$Date$	Date and time of check-in.
$Header$	A title that includes the RCS file's full pathname, revision number, date, author, state, and (if locked) the person who locked the file.
Id	Same as $Header$, but exclude the full pathname of the RCS file.
$Locker$	Username of person who locked the revision. If the file isn't locked, this value is empty.
Log	The message that was typed during check-in to describe the file, preceded by the RCS filename, revision number, author, and date. Log messages accumulate rather than being overwritten.
	RCS uses the "comment leader" of the Log line for the log messages left in the file. The comment leader stored in the RCS file is useful only for exchanging files with older versions of RCS.
$Name$	The symbolic name used to check in the revision, if any.
$RCSfile$	The RCS filename, without its pathname.
$Revision$	The assigned revision number.
$Source$	The RCS filename, including its pathname.
$State$	The state assigned by the -s option of ci or rcs.

Example Values

Let's assume that the file /projects/new/chapter3 has been checked in and out by a user named daniel. Here's what keyword substitution produces for each keyword, for the second revision of the file:

```
$Author: daniel $

$Date: 1992/03/18 17:51:36 $

$Header: /projects/new/chapter3,v 1.2 92/03/18 17:51:36 daniel \
    Exp Locker: daniel $

$Id: chapter3,v 1.2 1992/03/18 17:51:35 daniel Exp Locker: daniel $

$Locker: daniel $

$Log:      chapter3,v $
# Revision 1.2  92/03/18  17:51:36  daniel
# Added section on error-handling
#
# Revision 1.1  92/03/18  16:49:59  daniel
```

```
# Initial revision
#

$Name: Alpha2 $

$RCSfile: chapter3,v $

$Revision: 1.2 $

$Source: /projects/new/chapter3,v $

$State: Exp $
```

Revision Numbering

Unless told otherwise, RCS commands typically operate on the latest revision.
Some commands have an -r option that specifies a revision number. In addition,
many options accept a revision number as an optional argument. (In the command
summary, this argument is shown as [R].) Revision numbers consist of up to four
fields: release, level, branch, and sequence; but most revisions consist of only the
release and level. For example, you can check out revision 1.4 as follows:

```
co -l -r1.4 ch01
```

When you check it in again, the new revision will be marked as 1.5. Now suppose
the edited copy needs to be checked in as the next release. You would type:

```
ci -r2 ch01
```

This creates revision 2.1. You can also create a branch from an earlier revision.
The following command creates revision 1.4.1.1:

```
ci -r1.4.1 ch01
```

Numbers that begin with a period are considered to be relative to the default
branch of the RCS file. Normally, this is the "trunk" of the revision tree.

Numbers are not the only way to specify revisions, though. You can assign a text
label as a revision name, using the -n option of ci or rcs. You can also specify
this name in any option that accepts a revision number for an argument. For
example, you could check in each of your C files, using the same label regardless
of the current revision number:

```
ci -u -nPrototype *.c
```

In addition, you may specify a $, which means the revision number extracted from
the keywords of a working file. For example:

```
rcsdiff -r$ ch01
```

compares ch01 to the revision that is checked in. You can also combine names and
symbols. The command:

```
rcs -nDraft:$ ch*
```

assigns a name to the revision numbers associated with several chapter files.

Specifying the Date

Revisions are timestamped by time and date of check-in. Several keyword strings include the date in their values. Dates can be supplied in options to ci, co, and rlog. RCS uses the following date format as its default:

    2000/01/10 02:00:00 Year/month/day time

The default time zone is Greenwich Mean Time (GMT), which is also referred to as Coordinated Universal Time (UTC). Dates can be supplied in free format. This lets you specify many different styles. Here are some of the more common ones, which show the same time as in the previous example:

    6:00 pm lt   Assuming today is Jan. 10, 2000
    2:00 AM, Jan. 10, 2000
    Mon Jan 10 18:00:00 2000 LT
    Mon Jan 10 18:00:00 PST 2000

The uppercase or lowercase "lt" indicates local time (here, Pacific Standard Time). The third line shows ctime format (plus the "LT"); the fourth line is the date command format.

Specifying States

In some situations, particularly programming environments, you want to know the status of a set of revisions. RCS files are marked by a text string that describes their *state*. The default state is Exp (experimental). Other common choices include Stab (stable) or Rel (released). These words are user-defined and have no special internal meaning. Several keyword strings include the state in their values. In addition, states can be supplied in options to ci, co, rcs, and rlog.

Standard Options and Environment Variables

RCS defines an environment variable, RCSINIT, which sets up default options for RCS commands. If you set RCSINIT to a space-separated list of options, they will be prepended to the command-line options you supply to any RCS command.

Six options are useful to include in RCSINIT: -q, -V, -Vn, -T, -x, and -z. They can be thought of as standard options because most RCS commands accept them.

-q[R]
: Quiet mode; don't show diagnostic output. R specifies a file revision.

-T
: If the file with the new revision has a later modification time than that of the RCS file, update the RCS file's modification time. Otherwise, preserve the RCS file's modification time. This option should be used with care; see the discussion in the ci manpage for more detail.

-V
: Print the RCS version number.

-Vn
: Emulate version n of RCS; useful when trading files between systems that run different versions. n can be 3, 4, or 5.

-xsuffixes

Specify an alternate list of *suffixes* for RCS files. Each suffix is separated by a
/. On Unix systems, RCS files normally end with the characters ,v. The -x
option provides a workaround for systems that don't allow a comma character
in filenames.

-ztimezone

timezone controls the output format for dates in keyword substitution. *timezone* should have one of the following values:

Value	Effect
empty	Default format: UTC with no time zone and slashes separating the parts of the date.
LT	The local time and date, in ISO-8601 format, with time-zone indication (*YYYY-MM-DD HH:MM:SS-ZZ*).
±hh:mm	With a numeric offset from UTC, the output is in ISO-8601 format.

For example, when depositing a working file into an RCS file, the command:

```
ci -x,v/ ch01        Second suffix is blank
```

searches in order for the RCS filenames:

```
RCS/ch01,v
ch01,v
RCS/ch01
```

RCS allows you to specify a location for temporary files. It checks the environment
variables TMPDIR, TMP, and TEMP, in that order. If none of those exist, it uses a
default location, such as /tmp.

Conversion Guide for SCCS Users

SCCS commands have functional equivalents to RCS commands. The following
table provides a very general guide for SCCS users.

SCCS	RCS
admin	rcs
admin -i	ci
cdc	rcs -m
delta	ci
get	co
prs	ident or rlog
rmdel	rcs -o
sact	rlog
sccsdiff	rcsdiff
unget	co (with overwrite), or ci with rcs -o
what	ident

Alphabetical Summary of Commands

For details on the syntax of keywords, revision numbers, dates, states, and standard options, refer to the previous discussions.

---

ci [*options*] *files*

Check in revisions. ci stores the contents of the specified working *files* into their corresponding RCS files. Normally, ci deletes the working file after storing it. If no RCS file exists, the working file is an initial revision. In this case, the RCS file is created, and you are prompted to enter a description of the file. If an RCS file exists, ci increments the revision number and prompts you to enter a message that logs the changes made. If a working file is checked in without changes, the file reverts to the previous revision.

The two mutually exclusive options -u and -l, along with -r, are the most common. Use -u to keep a read-only copy of the working file (for example, so the file can be compiled or searched). Use -l to update a revision and then immediately check it out again with a lock. This allows you to save intermediate changes but continue editing (for example, during a long editing session). Use -r to check in a file with a different release number. ci accepts the standard options -q, -V, -V*n*, -T, -x, and -z.

Options

-d[*date*]
> Check the file in with a timestamp of *date* or, if no date is specified, with the time of last modification.

-f[*R*]
> Force a check-in even if there are no differences.

-i[*R*]
> Initial check-in, report an error if the RCS file already exists.

-I[*R*]
> Interactive mode; prompt user even when standard input is not a terminal (e.g., when ci is part of a command pipeline).

-j[*R*]
> Just check in and do not initialize. Report an error if the RCS file does not already exist.

-k[*R*]
> Assign a revision number, creation date, state, and author from keyword values that were placed in the working file, instead of computing the revision information from the local environment. -k is useful for software distribution: the preset keywords serve as a timestamp shared by all distribution sites.

→

−1[*R*]

Do a co −1 after checking in. This leaves a locked copy of the next revision.

−m*msg*

Use the *msg* string as the log message for all files checked in. When checking in multiple files, ci normally prompts whether to reuse the log message of the previous file. −m bypasses this prompting.

−M[*R*]

Set the working file's modification time to that of the retrieved version. Use of −M can confuse make and should be used with care.

−n*name*

Associate a text *name* with the new revision number.

−N*name*

Same as −n, but override a previous *name*.

−r*R* Check the file in as revision *R*.

−r Without a revision number, −r restores the default behavior of releasing a lock and removing the working file. It is intended to override any default −1 or −u set up by aliases or scripts. The behavior of −r in ci is different from most other RCS commands.

−s*state*

Set the *state* of the checked-in revision.

−t*file*

Replace RCS file description with contents of *file*. This works only for initial check-in.

−t−*string*

Replace RCS file description with *string*. This works only for initial check-in.

−u[*R*]

Do a co −u after checking in. This leaves a read-only copy.

−w*user*

Set the author field to *user* in the checked-in revision.

Examples

Check in chapter files using the same log message:

```
ci -m'First round edits' chap*
```

Check in edits to prog.c, leaving a read-only copy:

```
ci -u prog.c
```

Start revision level 2; refer to revision 2.1 as "Prototype":

```
ci -r2 -nPrototype prog.c
```

co [*options*] *files*

Retrieve (check out) a previously checked-in revision and place it in the corresponding working file (or print to standard output if -p is specified). If you intend to edit the working file and check it in again, specify -l to lock the file. co accepts the standard options -q, -V, -V*n*, -T, -x, and -z.

Options

-d*date*

Retrieve latest revision whose check-in timestamp is on or before *date*.

-f[*R*]

Force the working file to be overwritten.

-I[*R*]

Interactive mode; prompt user even when standard input is not a terminal.

-j*R2*:*R3*[, ...]

This works like rcsmerge. *R2* and *R3* specify two revisions whose changes are merged into a third file: either the corresponding working file or a third revision (any *R* specified by other co options). Multiple comma-separated pairs may be provided; the output of the first join becomes the input of the next. See the co manpage for more details.

-k*c* Expand keyword symbols according to flag *c*. *c* can be:

b   Like -ko, but uses binary I/O. This is most useful on non-Unix systems.

kv   Expand symbols to keyword and value (the default). Insert the locker's name only during a ci -l or co -l.

kvl Like kv, but always insert the locker's name.

k   Expand symbols to keywords only (no values). This is useful for ignoring trivial differences during file comparison.

o   Expand symbols to keyword and value present in previous revision. This is useful for binary files that don't allow substring changes.

v   Expand symbols to values only (no keywords). This prevents further keyword substitution and is not recommended.

→

co	
←	**-l[R]**

-l[R]

> Same as -r, but also lock the retrieved revision.

-M[R]

> Set the working file's modification time to that of the retrieved version. Use of -M can confuse make and should be used with care.

-p[R]

> Send retrieved revision to standard output instead of to a working file. Useful for output redirection or filtering.

-r[R]

> Retrieve the latest revision or, if R is given, retrieve the latest revision that is equal to or lower than R. If R is $, retrieve the version specified by the keywords in the working file.

-sstate

> Retrieve the latest revision having the given *state*.

-u[R]

> Same as -r, but also unlock the retrieved revision if you locked it previously.

-w[user]

> Retrieve the latest revision that was checked in either by the invoking user or by the specified *user*.

Examples

Sort the latest stored version of *file*:

```
co -p file | sort
```

Check out (and lock) all uppercase filenames for editing:

```
co -l [A-Z]*
```

Note that filename expansion fails unless a working copy resides in the current directory. Therefore, this example works only if the files were previously checked in via ci -u. Finally, here are some different ways to extract the working files for a set of RCS files (in the current directory):

`co -r3 *,v`	*Latest revisions of release 3*
`co -r3 -wjim *,v`	*Same, but only if checked in by jim*
`co -d'May 5, 2 pm LT' *,v`	*Latest revisions that were*
	modified on or before the date
`co -rPrototype *,v`	*Latest revisions named Prototype*

ident	
	`ident [options] [files]`

Extract keyword/value symbols from *files*. *files* can be text files, object files, or dumps. ident accepts the standard option -v.

Options

-q Suppress warning message when no keyword patterns are found.

-V Print the version number of ident.

Examples

If file prog.c is compiled, and it contains this line of code:

```
char rcsID[] = "$Author: arnold $";
```

the following output is produced:

```
$ ident prog.c prog.o
prog.c:
        $Author: arnold $
prog.o:
        $Author: arnold $
```

Show keywords for all RCS files (suppress warnings):

```
co -p RCS/*,v | ident -q
```

---

merge [*options*] [*diff3 options*] *file1 file2 file3*

Perform a three-way merge of files (via diff3) and place changes in *file1. file2* is the original file. *file1* is the "good" modification of *file2. file3* is another, conflicting modification of *file2.* merge finds the differences between *file2* and *file3*, and then incorporates those changes into *file1*. If both *file1* and *file3* have changes to common lines, merge warns about overlapping lines and inserts both choices in *file1*. The insertion appears as follows:

```
<<<<<<< file1
lines from file1</>
=======
lines from file3
>>>>>>> file3
```

You'll need to edit *file1* by deleting one of the choices. merge exits with a status of 0 (no overlaps), 1 (some overlaps), or 2 (unknown problem). See also **rcsmerge**.

merge accepts the -A, -e, and -E options for diff3, and simply passes them on, causing diff3 to perform the corresponding kind of merge. See the entry for **diff3** in Chapter 2, *Unix Commands*, for details. (The -A option is for the GNU version of diff3.)

$\rightarrow$

merge
←
	Options
	
	-L *label*
	    This option may be provided up to three times, providing differ-
	    ent labels in place of the filenames *file1*, *file2*, and *file3*, respec-
	    tively.
	
	-p Send merged version to standard output instead of to *file1*.
	
	-q Produce overlap insertions but don't warn about them.

rcs	**rcs [*options*] *files***

An administrative command for setting up or changing the default attributes of RCS files. rcs requires you to supply at least one option. (This is for "future expansion.")

Among other things, rcs lets you set strict locking (-L), delete revisions (-o), and override locks set by co (-1 and -u). RCS files have an access list (created via -a); anyone whose username is on the list can run rcs. The access list is often empty, meaning that rcs is available to everyone. In addition, you can always invoke rcs if you own the file, if you're a privileged user, or if you run rcs with -i. rcs accepts the standard options -q, -V, -V*n*, -T, -x, and -z.

Options

-a*users*
    Append the comma-separated list of *users* to the access list.

-A*otherfile*
    Append *otherfile*'s access list to the access list of *files*.

-b[*R*]
    Set the default branch to *R* or, if *R* is omitted, to the highest branch on the trunk.

-c'*s*'
    The comment leader for Log keywords is set to string *s*. You could, for example, set *s* to .\" for troff files or set *s* to * for C programs. (You would need to manually insert an enclosing /* and */ before and after Log.)

    -c is obsolescent; RCS uses the character(s) preceding Log in the file as the comment leader for log messages. You may wish to set this, though, if you are accessing the RCS file with older versions of RCS.

-e[*users*]
    Erase everyone (or only the specified *users*) from the access list.

-i   Create (initialize) an RCS file, but don't deposit a revision.

-I   Interactive mode; prompt user even when standard input is not a terminal.

-kc Use *c* as the default style for keyword substitution. (See **co** for values of *c*.) -kkv restores the default substitution style.

-l[*R*]

    Lock revision *R* or the latest revision. -l "retroactively locks" a file and is useful if you checked out a file incorrectly by typing co instead of co -l. **rcs** will ask you if it should break the lock if someone else has the file locked.

-L   Turn on strict locking (the default). This means that everyone, including the owner of the RCS file, must use co -l to edit files. Strict locking is recommended when files are to be shared. (See -U.)

-m*R*:*msg*

    Use the *msg* string to replace the log message of revision *R*.

-M   Do not send mail when breaking a lock. This is intended for use by RCS frontends, not for direct use by users!

-n*flags*

    Add or delete an association between a revision and a name. *flags* can be:

    name:*R*   Associate *name* with revision *R*.

    name: Associate *name* with latest revision.

    name   Remove association of *name*.

-N*flags*

    Same as -n, but overwrite existing *names*.

-o*R_list*

    Delete (outdate) revisions listed in *R_list*. *R_list* can be specified as: *R1*, *R1*:*R2*, *R1*:, or :*R2*. When a branch is given, -o deletes only the latest revision on it. The - range separator character from RCS versions prior to 5.6 is still valid.

-s*state*[:*R*]

    Set the state of revision *R* (or the latest revision) to the word *state*.

-t[*file*]

    Replace RCS file description with contents of *file* or, if no file is given, with standard input.

→

-t-*string*
> Replace RCS file description with *string*.

-u[R]
> The complement of -l: unlock a revision that was previously checked out via co -l. If someone else did the check-out, you are prompted to state the reason for breaking the lock. This message is mailed to the original locker.

-U Turn on nonstrict locking. Everyone except the file owner must use co -l to edit files. (See -L.)

Examples

Associate the label *To_customer* with the latest revision of all RCS files:

```
rcs -nTo_customer: RCS/*
```

Add three users to the access list of file beatle_deals:

```
rcs -ageorge,paul,ringo beatle_deals
```

Delete revisions 1.2 through 1.5:

```
rcs -o1.2:1.5 doc
```

Replace an RCS file description with the contents of a variable:

```
echo "$description" | rcs -t file
```

---

rcsclean

rcsclean [*options*] [*files*]

Although included with RCS, this command is optional and might not be installed on your system. rcsclean compares checked-out files against the corresponding latest revision or revision *R* (as given by the options). If no differences are found, the working file is removed. (Use rcsdiff to find differences.) rcsclean is useful in makefiles; for example, you could specify a "clean-up" target to update your directories. rcsclean is also useful prior to running rcsfreeze. rcsclean accepts the standard options -q, -V, -V*n*, -T, -x, and -z.

Options

-k*c* When comparing revisions, expand keywords using style *c*. (See co for values of *c*.)

-n[R]
> Show what would happen but don't actually execute.

-r[R]
> Compare against revision *R*. *R* can be supplied as arguments to other options, so -r is redundant.

–u[*R*]   **rcsclean**

    Unlock the revision if it's the same as the working file.

Example

Remove unchanged copies of program and header files:

```
rcsclean *.c *.h
```

---

rcsdiff [*options*] [*diff_options*] *files*   **rcsdiff**

Compare revisions via diff. Specify revisions using –r as follows:

# of Revisions	Comparison Made
None	Working file against latest revision.
One	Working file against specified revision.
Two	One revision against the other.

rcsdiff accepts the standard options -q, -V, -V*n*, -T, -x, and -z, as well as *diff_options*, which can be any valid diff option. rcsdiff exits with a status of 0 (no differences), 1 (some differences), or 2 (unknown problem). The -c option to diff can be very useful with rcsdiff.

rcsdiff prints "retrieving revision ..." messages to standard error, as well as a line of equals signs for separating multiple files. It is often useful to redirect standard error and standard output to the same file.

Options

-k*c* When comparing revisions, expand keywords using style *c*. (See co for values of *c*.)

-r*R1*

    Use revision *R1* in the comparison.

-r*R2*

    Use revision *R2* in the comparison. (-r*R1* must also be specified.)

Examples

Compare the current working file against the last checked-in version:

```
rcsdiff -c ch19.sgm 2>&1 | more
```

Compare the current working file against the very first version:

```
rcsdiff -c -r1.1 ch19.sgm 2>&1 | more
```

→

rcsdiff ←	Compare two earlier versions of a file against each other: `rcsdiff -c -r1.3 -r1.4 ch19.sgm 2>&1	more`
rcsfreeze	rcsfreeze [*name*] Although included with RCS, this shell script is optional and might not be installed on your system. rcsfreeze assigns a name to an entire set of RCS files, which must already be checked in. This is useful for marking a group of files as a single configuration. The default *name* is C_*n*, where *n* is incremented each time you run rcsfreeze.

rcsmerge	rcsmerge [*options*] [*diff3 options*] *file*
	
	Perform a three-way merge of file revisions, taking two differing versions and incorporating the changes into the working *file*. You must provide either one or two revisions to merge (typically with -r). Overlaps are handled the same as with merge, by placing warnings in the resulting file. rcsmerge accepts the standard options -q, -V, -V*n*, -T, -x, and -z. rcsmerge exits with a status of 0 (no overlaps), 1 (some overlaps), or 2 (unknown problem).
	
	rcsmerge accepts the -A, -e, and -E options for diff3 and simply passes them on, causing diff3 to perform the corresponding kind of merge. See **merge**, and also see the entry for **diff3** in Chapter 2 for details. (The -A option is for the GNU version of diff3.)
	
	Options
	
	-k*c* When comparing revisions, expand keywords using style *c*. (See co for values of *c*.)
	
	-p[*R*]
	    Send merged version to standard output instead of overwriting *file*.
	
	-r[*R*]
	    Merge revision *R* or, if no *R* is given, merge the latest revision.
	
	Examples
	
	Suppose you need to add updates to an old revision (1.3) of prog.c, but the current file is already at revision 1.6. To incorporate the changes:
	
	    `co -l prog.c` *Get latest revision*
	    (Edit latest revision by adding updates for revision 1.3, then:)
	    `rcsmerge -p -r1.3 -r1.6 prog.c > prog.updated.c`

Undo changes between revisions 3.5 and 3.2, and overwrite the working file:	rcsmerge

```
rcsmerge -r3.5 -r3.2 chap08
```

rlog [*options*] *files*   rlog

Display identification information for RCS *files*, including the log message associated with each revision, the number of lines added or removed, date of last check-in, etc. With no options, rlog displays all information. Use options to display specific items. rlog accepts the standard options -q, -V, -V*n*, -T, -x, and -z.

Options

-b Prune the display; print only about the default branch.

-d*dates*
    Display information for revisions whose check-in timestamp falls in the range of *dates* (a list separated by semicolons). Be sure to use quotes. Each date can be specified as:

    d1 < *d2*
        Select revisions between date *d1* and *d2*, inclusive.

    d1 <
        Select revisions made on or after *date1*.

    d1 >
        Select revisions made on or before *date1*.

        Timestamp comparisons are strict. If two files have exactly the same time, < and > won't work. Use <= and >= instead.

-h Display the beginning of the normal rlog listing.

-l[*users*]
    Display information only about locked revisions or, if *users* is specified, only about revisions locked by the list of *users*.

-L Skip files that aren't locked.

-N Don't print symbolic names.

-r[*list*]
    Display information for revisions in the comma-separated *list* of revision numbers. If no *list* is given, the latest revision is used.

→

Items can be specified as:

R1   Select revision *R1*. If *R1* is a branch, select all revisions on it.

R1.   If *R1* is a branch, select its latest revision.

R1:*R2*   Select revisions *R1* through *R2*.

:*R1*   Select revisions from beginning of branch through *R1*.

R1:   Select revisions from *R1* through end of branch.

The – range separator character from RCS versions prior to 5.6 is still valid.

-R Display only the name of the RCS file.

-s*states*
    Display information for revisions whose state matches one from the comma-separated list of *states*.

-t Same as -h, but also display the file's description.

-w[*users*]
    Display information for revisions checked in by anyone in the comma-separated list of *users*. If no *users* are supplied, assume the name of the invoking user.

Examples

Display the revision histories of all your RCS files:

```
rlog RCS/*,v | more
```

Display names of RCS files that are locked by user daniel.

```
rlog -R -L -ldaniel RCS/*
```

Display the "title" portion (no revision history) of a working file:

```
rlog -t calc.c
```

CHAPTER 20

The make Utility

This chapter presents the following topics:

- Conceptual overview
- Command-line syntax
- Description file lines
- Macros
- Special target names
- Writing command lines
- Sample default macros, suffixes, and rules

For more information, see *Managing Projects with make*, listed in the Bibliography.

Conceptual Overview

The make program generates a sequence of commands for execution by the Unix shell. It uses a table of file dependencies provided by the programmer, and, with this information, can perform updating tasks automatically for the user. It can keep track of the sequence of commands that create certain files, and the list of files or programs that require other files to be current before they can operate efficiently. When a program is changed, make can create the proper files with a minimum of effort.

Each statement of a dependency is called a *rule*. Rules define one or more *targets*, which are the files to be generated, and the files they depend upon, the *prerequisites* or *dependencies*. For example, prog.o would be a target that depends upon prog.c; each time you update prog.c, prog.o must be regenerated. It is this task that make automates, and it is a critical one for large programs that have many pieces.

This chapter covers the SVR4 make. Many Unix vendors have enhanced make in different, and often incompatible, ways. Check your local documentation for the final word.

On Solaris, /usr/lib/svr4.make is the generic SVR4 version of make. If you set USE_SVR4_MAKE in the environment, /usr/ccs/bin/make or /usr/xpg4/bin/make runs this version.

Command-Line Syntax

    make [options] [targets] [macro definitions]

Options, targets, and macro definitions can appear in any order. Macro definitions are typed as:

    name=string

If no makefile or Makefile exists, make will attempt to extract the most recent version of one from an SCCS file, if one exists. (Some versions also know about RCS.)

Options

-e   Environment variables override any macros defined in description files.

-f *file*
     Use *file* as the description file; a filename of - denotes standard input. -f can be used more than once to concatenate multiple description files. With no -f option, make first looks for a file named makefile, and then one named Makefile.

-i   Ignore error codes from commands (same as .IGNORE).

-k   Abandon the current target when it fails, but keep working with unrelated targets.

-n   Print commands but don't execute (used for testing). -n prints commands even if they begin with @ in the description file.

     Lines that begin with $(MAKE) are an exception. Such lines *are* executed. However, since the -n is passed to the subsequent make in the MAKEFLAGS environment variable, that make also just prints the commands it executes. This allows you to test out all the makefile files in a whole software hierarchy without actually doing anything.

-p   Print macro definitions, suffixes, and target descriptions.

-q   Query; return 0 if file is up to date; nonzero otherwise.

-r   Do not use the default rules.

-s   Do not display command lines (same as .SILENT).

-t   Touch the target files, causing them to be updated.

Description File Lines

Instructions in the description file are interpreted as single lines. If an instruction must span more than one input line, use a backslash (\) at the end of the line so that the next line is considered a continuation. The description file may contain any of the following types of lines:

Blank lines
Blank lines are ignored.

Comment lines
A pound sign (#) can be used at the beginning of a line or anywhere in the middle. make ignores everything after the #.

Dependency lines
Depending on one or more targets, certain commands that follow are executed. Possible formats include:

```
targets : prerequisites
targets :: prerequisites
```

In the first form, subsequent commands are executed if the prerequisites are met. The second form is a variant that lets you specify the same targets on more than one dependency line. In both forms, if no prerequisites are supplied, subsequent commands are always executed (whenever any of the targets are specified). No tab should precede any *targets*. (At the end of a dependency line, you can specify a command, preceded by a semicolon; however, commands are typically entered on their own lines, preceded by a tab.)

Targets of the form *library*(*member*) represent members of archive libraries, e.g., libguide.a(dontpanic.o).

Suffix rules
These specify that files ending with the first suffix can be prerequisites for files ending with the second suffix (assuming the root filenames are the same). Either of these formats can be used:

```
.suffix.suffix:
.suffix:
```

The second form means that the root filename depends on the filename with the corresponding suffix.

Macro definitions
These have the following form:

```
name = string
```

Blank space is optional around the =.

Include statements
Similar to the C include directive, these have the form:

```
include file
```

make processes the value of *file* for macro expansions before attempting to open the file.

Command lines

These lines are where you give the commands to actually rebuild those files that are out of date. Commands are grouped below the dependency line and are typed on lines that begin with a tab. If a command is preceded by a hyphen (–), make ignores any error returned. If a command is preceded by an at sign (@), the command line won't echo on the display (unless make is called with -n). Further advice on command lines is given below.

Macros

This section summarizes internal macros, modifiers, string substitution, and special macros.

Internal Macros

$?   The list of prerequisites that have been changed more recently than the current target. Can be used only in normal description file entries—not suffix rules.

$@   The name of the current target, except in description file entries for making libraries, where it becomes the library name. Can be used both in normal description file entries and in suffix rules.

$$@   The name of the current target. Can be used only to the right of the colon in dependency lines. (May not work on all versions of make.)

$<   The name of the current prerequisite that has been modified more recently than the current target. Can be used only in suffix rules and in the .DEFAULT: entry.

$*   The name—without the suffix—of the current prerequisite that has been modified more recently than the current target. Can be used only in suffix rules.

$%   The name of the corresponding .o file when the current target is a library module. Can be used both in normal description file entries and in suffix rules.

Macro Modifiers

Macro modifiers are not available in all variants of make.

D   The directory portion of any internal macro name except $?. Valid uses are:

        $(*D) $$(@D)
        $(<D) $(%D)
        $(@D)

F   The file portion of any internal macro name except $?. Valid uses are:

        $(*F) $$(@F)
        $(<F) $(%F)
        $(@F)

Macro String Substitution

String substitution is not available in all variants of make.

$(macro:s1=s2)
Evaluates to the current definition of $(macro), after substituting the string s2
for every occurrence of s1 that occurs either immediately before a blank or
tab, or at the end of the macro definition.

Macros with Special Handling

MAKEFLAGS Contains the flags inherited in the environment variable MAKEFLAGS,
plus any command-line options. Used to pass the flags to subsequent
invocations of make, usually via command lines in a makefile that
contain $(MAKE).

SHELL Sets the shell that interprets commands. If this macro isn't defined in
the description file, the value depends on your system. Some Unix
implementations use the shell from the user's environment (as with
other macros). Other implementations (including SVR4) set the
default SHELL to /bin/sh.

VPATH (Not available in all variants of make.) Specifies a list of directories to
search for prerequisites when not found in the current directory.

Special Target Names

.DEFAULT: Commands associated with this target are executed if make can't find
any description file entries or suffix rules with which to build a
requested target.

.IGNORE: Ignore error codes. Same as the -i option.

.PRECIOUS: Files you specify for this target are not removed when you send a signal (such as interrupt) that aborts make, or when a command line in
your description file returns an error.

.SILENT: Execute commands but do not echo them. Same as the -s option.

.SUFFIXES: Suffixes associated with this target are meaningful in suffix rules. If no
suffixes are listed, the existing list of suffix rules are effectively
"turned off."

Writing Command Lines

Writing good, portable Makefile files is a bit of an art. Skill comes with practice
and experience. Here are some tips to get you started:

- Naming your file Makefile instead of makefile usually causes it to be listed
first with ls. This makes it easier to find in a directory with many files.

- Remember that command lines must start with a leading tab character. You
cannot just indent the line with spaces, even eight spaces. If you use spaces,
make exits with an unhelpful message about "missing separator characters."

- Remember that $ is special to make. To get a literal $ into your command lines, use $$. This is particularly important if you want to access an environment variable that isn't a make macro. Also, if you wish to use the shell's $$ for the current process ID, you have to type it as $$$$.

- Write multiline shell statements, such as shell conditionals and loops, with trailing semicolons and a trailing backslash:

```
if [ -f specfile ] ; then \
... ; \
else \
... ; \
fi
```

  Note that the shell keywords then and else don't need the semicolon. (What happens is that make passes the backslashes and the newlines to the shell. The escaped newlines are not syntactically important, so the semicolons are needed to separate the different parts of the command. This can be confusing. If you use a semicolon where you would normally put a newline in a shell script, things should work correctly.)

- Remember that each line is run in a separate shell. This means that commands that change the shell's environment (such as cd) are ineffective across multiple lines. The correct way to write such commands is to separate commands on the same line with a semicolon:

```
cd subdir; $(MAKE)
```

- For guaranteed portability, always set SHELL to /bin/sh. Some versions of make use whatever value is in the environment for SHELL, unless it is explicitly set in the Makefile.

- Use macros for standard commands. make already helps out with this, providing macros such as $(CC), $(YACC), and so on.

- When removing files, start your command line with -$(RM) instead of $($RM). (The − causes make to ignore the exit status of the command.) This way, if the file you were trying to remove doesn't exist, and rm exits with an error, make can keep going.

- When running subsidiary invocations of make, typically in subdirectories of your main program tree, always use $(MAKE), and not make. Lines that contain $(MAKE) are always executed, even if -n has been provided, allowing you to test out a whole hierarchy of Makefile files. This does not happen for lines that invoke make directly.

- Often, it is convenient to organize a large software project into subprojects, with each one having a subdirectory. The top-level Makefile then just invokes make in each subdirectory. Here's the way to do it:

```
SUBDIRS = proj1 proj2 proj3
...
projects: $(SUBDIRS)
        for i in $(SUBDIRS); \
        do \
                echo ====== Making in $$i ; \
```

```
                    ( cd $$i ; $(MAKE) $(MAKEFLAGS) $@ ) ; \
        done
```

Sample Default Macros, Suffixes, and Rules

```
.SUFFIXES: .o .c .c~ .y .y~ .l .l~ .s .s~ .sh .sh~ .h .h~ .f .f~ \
.C .C~ .Y .Y~ .L .L~

MAKE=make
BUILD=build
AR=ar
ARFLAGS=rv
AS=as
ASFLAGS=
CC=cc
CFLAGS=-O
F77=f77
FFLAGS=-O
GET=get
GFLAGS=
LD=ld
LDFLAGS=
LEX=lex
LFLAGS=
YACC=yacc
YFLAGS=
C++C=CC
C++FLAGS=-O


.c:
        $(CC) $(CFLAGS) $< -o $@ $(LDFLAGS)
.c~:
        $(GET) $(GFLAGS) $<
        $(CC) $(CFLAGS) $*.c -o $@ $(LDFLAGS)
        -rm -f $*.c
.f:
        $(F77) $(FFLAGS) $< -o $@ $(LDFLAGS)
.f~:
        $(GET) $(GFLAGS) $<
        $(F77) $(FFLAGS) $*.f -o $@ $(LDFLAGS)
        -rm -f $*.f
.s:
        $(AS) $(ASFLAGS) $< -o $@ $(LDFLAGS)
.s~:
        $(GET) $(GFLAGS) $<
        $(AS) $(ASFLAGS) $*.s -o $* $(LDFLAGS)
        -rm -f $*.s
.sh:
        cp $< $@; chmod 0777 $@
.sh~:
        $(GET) $(GFLAGS) $<
        cp $*.sh $*; chmod 0777 $@
        -rm -f $*.sh
.C:
        $(C++C) $(C++FLAGS) $< -o $@ $(LDFLAGS)
.C~:
        $(GET) $(GFLAGS) $<
        $(C++C) $(C++FLAGS) $*.C -o $@ $(LDFLAGS)
        -rm -f $*.C
```

```
.c.a:
          $(CC) $(CFLAGS) -c $<
          $(AR) $(ARFLAGS) $@ $*.o
          -rm -f $*.o
.c.o:
          $(CC) $(CFLAGS) -c $<
.c~.a:
          $(GET) $(GFLAGS) $<
          $(CC) $(CFLAGS) -c $*.c
          $(AR) $(ARFLAGS) $@ $*.o
          -rm -f $*.[co]
.c~.c:
          $(GET) $(GFLAGS) $<
.c~.o:
          $(GET) $(GFLAGS) $<
          $(CC) $(CFLAGS) -c $*.c
          -rm -f $*.c
.f.a:
          $(F77) $(FFLAGS) -c $*.f
          $(AR) $(ARFLAGS) $@ $*.o
          -rm -f $*.o
.f.o:
          $(F77) $(FFLAGS) -c $*.f
.f~.a:
          $(GET) $(GFLAGS) $<
          $(F77) $(FFLAGS) -c $*.f
          $(AR) $(ARFLAGS) $@ $*.o
          -rm -f $*.[fo]
.f~.f:
          $(GET) $(GFLAGS) $<
.f~.o:
          $(GET) $(GFLAGS) $<
          $(F77) $(FFLAGS) -c $*.f
          -rm -f $*.f
.h~.h:
          $(GET) $(GFLAGS) $<
.l.c:
          $(LEX) $(LFLAGS) $<
          mv lex.yy.c $@
.l.o:
          $(LEX) $(LFLAGS) $<
          $(CC) $(CFLAGS) -c lex.yy.c
          -rm lex.yy.c; mv lex.yy.o $@
.l~.c:
          $(GET) $(GFLAGS) $<
          $(LEX) $(LFLAGS) $*.l
          mv lex.yy.c $@
          -rm -f $*.l
.l~.l:
          $(GET) $(GFLAGS) $<
.l~.o:
          $(GET) $(GFLAGS) $<
          $(LEX) $(LFLAGS) $*.l
          $(CC) $(CFLAGS) -c lex.yy.c
          -rm -f lex.yy.c $*.l
          mv lex.yy.o $@
.s.a:
          $(AS) $(ASFLAGS) -o $*.o $*.s
          $(AR) $(ARFLAGS) $@ $*.o
```

```
.s.o:
        $(AS) $(ASFLAGS) -o $@ $<
.s~.a:
        $(GET) $(GFLAGS) $<
        $(AS) $(ASFLAGS) -o $*.o $*.s
        $(AR) $(ARFLAGS) $@ $*.o
        -rm -f $*.[so]
.s~.o:
        $(GET) $(GFLAGS) $<
        $(AS) $(ASFLAGS) -o $*.o $*.s
        -rm -f $*.s
.s~.s:
        $(GET) $(GFLAGS) $<
.sh~.sh:
        $(GET) $(GFLAGS) $<
.y.c:
        $(YACC) $(YFLAGS) $<
        mv y.tab.c $@
.y.o:
        $(YACC) $(YFLAGS) $<
        $(CC) $(CFLAGS) -c y.tab.c
        -rm y.tab.c
        mv y.tab.o $@
.y~.c:
        $(GET) $(GFLAGS) $<
        $(YACC) $(YFLAGS) $*.y
        mv y.tab.c $*.c
        -rm -f $*.y
.y~.o:
        $(GET) $(GFLAGS) $<
        $(YACC) $(YFLAGS) $*.y
        $(CC) $(CFLAGS) -c y.tab.c
        -rm -f y.tab.c $*.y
        mv y.tab.o $*.o
.y~.y :
        $(GET) $(GFLAGS) $<
.C.a:
        $(C++C) $(C++FLAGS) -c $<
        $(AR) $(ARFLAGS) $@ $*.o
        -rm -f $*.o
.C.o:
        $(C++C) $(C++FLAGS) -c $<
.C~.a:
        $(GET) $(GFLAGS) $<
        $(C++C) $(C++FLAGS) -c $*.C
        $(AR) $(ARFLAGS) $@ $*.o
        -rm -f $*.[Co]
.C~.C:
        $(GET) $(GFLAGS) $<
.C~.o:
        $(GET) $(GFLAGS) $<
        $(C++C) $(C++FLAGS) -c $*.C
        -rm -f $*.C
.L.C:
        $(LEX) $(LFLAGS) $<
        mv lex.yy.c $@
.L.o:
        $(LEX) $(LFLAGS) $<
        $(C++C) $(C++FLAGS) -c lex.yy.c
        -rm lex.yy.c; mv lex.yy.o $@
```

```
.L~.C:
        $(GET) $(GFLAGS) $<
        $(LEX) $(LFLAGS) $*.L
        mv lex.yy.c $@
        -rm -f $*.L
.L~.L:
        $(GET) $(GFLAGS) $<
.L~.o:
        $(GET) $(GFLAGS) $<
        $(LEX) $(LFLAGS) $*.L
        $(C++C) $(C++FLAGS) -c lex.yy.c
        -rm -f lex.yy.c $*.L
        mv lex.yy.c $@
.Y.C:
        $(YACC) $(YFLAGS) $<
        mv y.tab.c $@
.Y.o:
        $(YACC) $(YFLAGS) $<
        $(C++C) $(C++FLAGS) -c y.tab.c
        -rm y.tab.c
        mv y.tab.o $@
.Y~.C:
        $(GET) $(GFLAGS) $<
        $(YACC) $(YFLAGS) $*.Y
        mv y.tab.c $*.C
        -rm -f $*.Y
.Y~.o:
        $(GET) $(GFLAGS) $<
        $(YACC) $(YFLAGS) $*.Y
        $(C++C) $(C++FLAGS) -c y.tab.c
        -rm -f y.tab.c $*.Y
        mv y.tab.o $*.o
.Y~.Y :
        $(GET) $(GFLAGS) $<

markfile.o:        markfile
        echo "static char _sccsid[] = \"`grep @'(#)' markfile`\";" > markfile.c
        $(CC) -c markfile.c
        -rm -f markfile.c

.SCCS_GET:
        $(GET) $(GFLAGS) s.$@
```

PART V

Appendixes

Part V contains an appendix of ASCII characters, an appendix describing obsolete commands, and a Unix bibliography.

- Appendix A, *ASCII Character Set*
- Appendix B, *Obsolete Commands*
- *Bibliography*

APPENDIX A

ASCII Character Set

This appendix presents the set of ASCII characters, along with their equivalent values in decimal, octal, and hexadecimal. The first table shows nonprinting characters; it's useful when you need to represent nonprinting characters in some printed form, such as octal. For example, the echo and tr commands let you specify characters using octal values of the form *nnn*. Also, the od command can display nonprinting characters in a variety of forms.

The second table shows printing characters. This table is useful when using the previous commands, but also when specifying a range of characters in a pattern-matching construct.

Table A–1: Nonprinting Characters

Decimal	Octal	Hex	Character	Remark
0	000	00	CTRL-@	NUL (Null prompt)
1	001	01	CTRL-A	SOH (Start of heading)
2	002	02	CTRL-B	STX (Start of text)
3	003	03	CTRL-C	ETX (End of text)
4	004	04	CTRL-D	EOT (End of transmission)
5	005	05	CTRL-E	ENQ (Enquiry)
6	006	06	CTRL-F	ACK (Acknowledge)
7	007	07	CTRL-G	BEL (Bell)
8	010	08	CTRL-H	BS (Backspace)
9	011	09	CTRL-I	HT (Horizontal tab)
10	012	0A	CTRL-J	LF (Linefeed)
11	013	0B	CTRL-K	VT (Vertical tab)
12	014	0C	CTRL-L	FF (Formfeed)

Table A–1: Nonprinting Characters (continued)

Decimal	Octal	Hex	Character	Remark
13	015	0D	CTRL-M	CR (Carriage return)
14	016	0E	CTRL-N	SO (Shift out)
15	017	0F	CTRL-O	SI (Shift in)
16	020	10	CTRL-P	DLE (Data link escape)
17	021	11	CTRL-Q	DC1 (XON)
18	022	12	CTRL-R	DC2
19	023	13	CTRL-S	DC3 (XOFF)
20	024	14	CTRL-T	DC4
21	025	15	CTRL-U	NAK (Negative acknowledge)
22	026	16	CTRL-V	SYN (Synchronous idle)
23	027	17	CTRL-W	ETB (End transmission blocks)
24	030	18	CTRL-X	CAN (Cancel)
25	031	19	CTRL-Y	EM (End of medium)
26	032	1A	CTRL-Z	SUB (Substitute)
27	033	1B	CTRL-[	ESC (Escape)
28	034	1C	CTRL-\	FS (File separator)
29	035	1D	CTRL-]	GS (Group separator)
30	036	1E	CTRL-^	RS (Record separator)
31	037	1F	CTRL-_	US (Unit separator)
127	177	7F		DEL (Delete or rubout)

Table A–2: Printing Characters

Decimal	Octal	Hex	Character	Remark
32	040	20		Space
33	041	21	!	Exclamation point
34	042	22	"	Double quote
35	043	23	#	Pound sign
36	044	24	$	Dollar sign
37	045	25	%	Percent sign
38	046	26	&	Ampersand
39	047	27	'	Apostrophe
40	050	28	(	Left parenthesis
41	051	29	)	Right parenthesis
42	052	2A	*	Asterisk
43	053	2B	+	Plus sign

Table A-2: Printing Characters (continued)

Decimal	Octal	Hex	Character	Remark
44	054	2C	,	Comma
45	055	2D	–	Hyphen
46	056	2E	.	Period
47	057	2F	/	Slash
48	060	30	0	
49	061	31	1	
50	062	32	2	
51	063	33	3	
52	064	34	4	
53	065	35	5	
54	066	36	6	
55	067	37	7	
56	070	38	8	
57	071	39	9	
58	072	3A	:	Colon
59	073	3B	;	Semicolon
60	074	3C	<	Left angle bracket
61	075	3D	=	Equal sign
62	076	3E	>	Right angle bracket
63	077	3F	?	Question mark
64	100	40	@	At sign
65	101	41	A	
66	102	42	B	
67	103	43	C	
68	104	44	D	
69	105	45	E	
70	106	46	F	
71	107	47	G	
72	110	48	H	
73	111	49	I	
74	112	4A	J	
75	113	4B	K	
76	114	4C	L	
77	115	4D	M	
78	116	4E	N	
79	117	4F	O	

ASCII
Set

Decimal	Octal	Hex	Character	Remark
80	120	50	P	
81	121	51	Q	
82	122	52	R	
83	123	53	S	
84	124	54	T	
85	125	55	U	
86	126	56	V	
87	127	57	W	
88	130	58	X	
89	131	59	Y	
90	132	5A	Z	
91	133	5B	[	Left square bracket
92	134	5C	\	Backslash
93	135	5D	]	Right square bracket
94	136	5E	^	Caret
95	137	5F	_	Underscore
96	140	60	`	Back quote
97	141	61	a	
98	142	62	b	
99	143	63	c	
100	144	64	d	
101	145	65	e	
102	146	66	f	
103	147	67	g	
104	150	68	h	
105	151	69	i	
106	152	6A	j	
107	153	6B	k	
108	154	6C	l	
109	155	6D	m	
110	156	6E	n	
111	157	6F	o	
112	160	70	p	
113	161	71	q	
114	162	72	r	
115	163	73	s	

Table A–2: Printing Characters (continued)

Decimal	Octal	Hex	Character	Remark
116	164	74	t	
117	165	75	u	
118	166	76	v	
119	167	77	w	
120	170	78	x	
121	171	79	y	
122	172	7A	z	
123	173	7B	{	Left curly brace
124	174	7C	I	Vertical bar
125	175	7D	}	Right curly brace
126	176	7E	~	Tilde

ASCII
Set

APPENDIX B

Obsolete Commands

This appendix contains entries for commands that are still shipped with SVR4 and/or Solaris, but which have been superseded in their functions by other commands or technologies. Here you will find:

- Introduction

- Alphabetical summary of commands

Introduction

The commands in this appendix fall into several categories. This list describes the commands and why they are obsolete.

Archive maintenance

lorder and tsort were used to order the placement of object files in a library archive. Modern versions of ar maintain a symbol table, allowing the loader ld to find object files as needed.

Communications

cu, uucp, uuglist, uulog, uuname, uupick, uustat, uuto, uux, and write.

These commands were used for dial-up interactive or system-to-system communications. Widely available Internet connectivity has generally made them obsolete. talk is a better alternative to write.

Compression

pack, pcat, and unpack have been made obsolete by compress/uncompress, and by gzip/gunzip.

File processing

- bfs was intended for processing large files, up to one megabyte. vi on modern systems easily handles files that are considerably larger.

- crypt provided file encryption. However, its algorithm is considered weak, and better tools are available today.

- newform was intended for data-reformatting. This is much more easily handled with sed or awk.

- red is a restricted version of ed. In practice, the restricted versions of various commands were never very useful. They were hard to set up and use correctly. ed itself is rarely used today.

- sum apparently just adds up the bytes in a file, making its checksum of questionable value. cksum should be used instead.

- tabs controlled setting tab stops on reprogrammable terminals. However, Unix systems are rarely, if ever, used for writing in the programming languages it handles.

- vc provided a very simple-minded form of version control. RCS and SCCS are much better alternatives.

Layers

ismpx, jterm, jwin, layers, relogin, and shl.

All but shl are specific to the now obsolete AT&T Teletype 5620 DMD windowing terminal. The X Window system provides windowing functionality on modern Unix systems. shl was an attempt to provide functionality similar to BSD job control that never caught on.

Network status

ruptime, rwho, whois.

The first two programs use daemons that often overloaded local area networks. The whois registry has been outgrown by the Internet, which is now much too large for centrally tracking everyone who might use it.

Simple menus

face and fmli provided a simple way to create menu-driven programs for CRT terminals. They simply never caught on, particularly with the increase in popularity of systems based on the X Window system.

UPAS

mailalias, notify, and vacation are used with the UPAS mailing system, which was standard with SVR4. Modern Unix systems use sendmail.

Windowing systems

OpenWindows (started by the openwin command) was the default windowing system on SunOS and Solaris for many years. CDE (the Common Desktop Environment) is now Sun's preferred windowing environment for Solaris. OpenWindows will not be supported past Solaris 7.

- cof2elf converts object files and archives in COFF format to ELF format. As ELF format is now at least 10 years old, this program is not likely to still be necessary.

- fmtmsg was intended to provide a standardized way of generating error messages from shell scripts. It was never widely used.

- fold wraps lines to fit in a specific width. fmt generally does a better job.

- lptest generates a ripple pattern for line printers. Today, laser printers and ink-jet printers are more common.

- newgrp dates from when Unix systems allowed a user to be in only one group at a time. Modern Unix systems allow users to be in multiple groups simultaneously.

- news provides items of interest to system users. It is per-machine. Usenet news software is a much better alternative.

- pg is a simple pager. Use more instead.

Alphabetical Summary of Commands

bfs	bfs [*option*] *file*
	Big file scanner. Read a large *file*, using ed-like syntax. This command is more efficient than ed for scanning very large files because the file is not read into a buffer. Files can be up to 1024K bytes. bfs can be used to view a large file and identify sections to be divided with csplit. Not too useful.
	Option
	- Do not print the file size.
cof2elf	cof2elf [*options*] *files*
	Convert one or more COFF *files* to ELF format, overwriting the original contents. Input can be object files or archives.
	Options
	-i Ignore unrecognized data; do the conversion anyway.
	-q Quiet mode; suppress messages while running.

-Qc Print information about cof2elf in output (if *c* = y) or suppress information (if *c* = n, the default).

-s*dir*
    Save the original files to an existing directory *dir*.

-V Print the version of cof2elf on standard error.

cof2elf

---

crypt [*password*] < *file* > *encryptedfile*

crypt

Encrypt a *file* to prevent unauthorized access. *password* is either a string of characters you choose or the option -k, which assigns the value of the environment variable CRYPTKEY (Solaris: CrYpTkEy) as the password. The same *password* encrypts a file or decrypts an encrypted file. If no password is given, crypt prompts for one. crypt is available only in the United States (due to export restrictions).

The algorithm used is considered weak, and this command should not be used for serious encryption. See *PGP: Pretty Good Privacy*, listed in the Bibliography.

---

cu [*options*] [*destination*] [*command*]

cu

Call up another Unix system or a terminal via a direct line or a modem. A non-Unix system can also be called.

Options

-b*n* Process lines using *n*-bit characters (7 or 8).

-c*name*
    Search UUCP's Devices file and select the local area network that matches *name* (this assumes connection to a system).

-C Instead of entering interactive mode, run the *command* from the command line with standard input and standard output connected to the remote system. Solaris only.

-d Print diagnostics.

-e Send even-parity data to remote system.

-h Emulate local echo and support calls to other systems expecting terminals to use half duplex mode.

-H Ignore one hangup. Useful when calling a remote system that will disconnect and call you back with a login prompt. Solaris only.

$\rightarrow$

Obsolete Commands

-l*line*
> Communicate on device named *line* (e.g., /dev/tty001).

-L   Use the chat sequence specified in /etc/uucp/Systems. Solaris only.

-n   Prompt user for a telephone number.

-o   Use odd parity (opposite of -e).

-s*n* Set transmission rate to *n* (e.g., 1200, 2400, 9600 bps). Default is Any.

-t   Dial an ASCII terminal that has auto-answer set.

Destination

telno   The telephone number of the modem to connect to.

system   Call the *system* known to uucp (run uuname to list valid system names).

addr   An address specific to your local area network.

cu runs as two processes: transmit and receive. Transmit reads from standard input and passes characters to the remote system; receive reads data from the remote system and passes lines to standard output. Lines that begin with a tilde (~) are treated as commands and not passed.

Transmit Options

~.   Terminate the conversation.

~!   Escape to an interactive shell on the local system.

~!*cmd* ...
> Run command on local system (via sh -c).

~$*cmd* ...
> Run command locally; send output to remote system.

~%cd
> Change directory on the local system.

~%take *file* [*target*]
> Copy *file* from remote system to *target* on the local system. If *target* is omitted, *file* is used in both places. The remote system must be running Unix for this command to work. No checksumming of the transmitted data is provided.

~%put *file* [*target*]
> Copy *file* from the local system to *target* on the remote system. If *target* is omitted, *file* is used in both places. The remote system must be running Unix for this command to work. No checksumming of the transmitted data is provided.

~~ ...

Use two tildes when you want to pass a line that begins with a tilde. This lets you issue commands to more than one system in a cu chain. For example, use ~~. to terminate the conversation on a second system cud to from the first.

~%b   Send a BREAK sequence to the remote system.

~%d   Turn debug mode on or off.

~t   Print termio structure for local terminal. (Intended for debugging.)

~l   Print termio structure for communication line. (Intended for debugging.)

~%ifc
    Turn on/off the DC3/DC1 XOFF/XON control protocol (characters ^S, ^Q) for the remainder of the session (formerly ~%nostop, which is still valid).

~%ofc
    Set output flow control either on or off.

~%divert
    Allow/prevent diversions not specified by ~%take.

~%old
    Allow/prevent old-style syntax for diversions received.

Examples

Connect to terminal line /dev/ttya at 9600 baud:

    cu -s9600 -l/dev/ttya

Connect to modem with phone number 555-9876:

    cu 5559876

Connect to system named usenix:

    cu usenix

---

face [*options*] [*files*]

Invoke the Framed Access Command Environment Interface and open *files*. By convention, each filename must be of the form Menu. *string*, Form. *string*, or Text. *string*, depending on the type of object being opened. If no *files* are specified, face opens the FACE menu along with the default objects specified by the environment variable LOGINWIN.

→

face ←	*Options* -a `afile` 　　Load the list of pathname aliases specified in the file *afile*. Entries have the form *alias=pathname*. Once this file is loaded, you can use the shorthand notation $*alias* to refer to a long pathname. -c `cfile` 　　Load the list of command aliases specified in the file *cfile*. This file allows you to modify the default behavior of FACE commands or create new commands. -i `ifile` 　　Load file *ifile*, which specifies startup features such as the introductory frame, banner information, screen colors, and labels.
fmli	fmli [*options*] `files` Invoke the Form and Menu Language Interpreter and open *files*. By convention, each filename must be of the form Menu.*string*, Form.*string*, or Text.*string*, depending on the type of object being opened. *Options* -a `afile` 　　Load the list of pathname aliases specified in the file *afile*. Entries have the form *alias=pathname*. Once this file is loaded, you can use the shorthand notation $*alias* to refer to a long pathname. -c `cfile` 　　Load the list of command aliases specified in the file *cfile*. This file allows you to modify the default behavior of FMLI commands or create new commands. -i `ifile` 　　Load file *ifile*, which specifies startup features such as the introductory frame, banner information, screen colors, and labels.
fmtmsg	fmtmsg [*options*] `text` Print *text* as part of a formatted error message on standard error (or on the system console). *text* must be quoted as a single argument. fmtmsg is used in shell scripts to print messages in a standard format.

Messages display as follows:

```
label:    severity:        text
TO FIX:   action           tag
```

You can define the MSGVERB variable to select which parts of the message to print. Each part is described with the options below.

The SEV_LEVEL environment variable allows you to add additional severities and associated strings to be printed when those severities are provided.

Options

-a action

A string describing the first action to take in recovering the error. The string "TO FIX:" precedes the *action* string.

-c source

The source of the problem, where *source* is one of hard (hardware), soft (software), or firm (firmware).

-l label

Identify the message source with a text *label*, often of the form *file*: *command*.

-s severity

How serious the condition is. *severity* is one of halt, error, warn, or info.

-t tag

Another string identifier for the message.

-u types

Classify the message as one or more *types* (separated by commas). *types* can be one of the keywords appl, util, or opsys (meaning that the problem comes respectively from an application, utility, or the kernel), either of the keywords recov or nrecov (application will or won't recover), print (message displays on standard error), and console (message displays on system console).

---

fold [*options*] [*files*]

Break the lines of the named *files* so that they are no wider than the specified width. fold breaks lines exactly at the specified width, even in the middle of a word.

$\rightarrow$

fold ←	**Options** -b The line width specifies bytes, not characters. Solaris only. -s Break lines after the last whitespace character within the first *width* characters. Solaris only. -w *n* Create lines having width *n* (default is 80). (Can also be invoked as -*n* for compatibility with BSD.)

ismpx	`ismpx [option]`
	
	Test whether standard input is running under layers. (Command name comes from "Is the multiplexor running?") Output is either yes (exit status 0) or no (exit status 1). Useful for shell scripts that download programs to a layers windowing terminal or that depend on screen size.
	
	Option
	
	-s Suppress output and return exit status only.
	
	Example
	
	<pre>if ismpx -s
	then jwin
	fi</pre>

jterm	`jterm` Reset layer of windowing terminal after a program changes the terminal attributes of the layer. Used only under layers. Returns 0 on success, 1 otherwise.
jwin	`jwin` Print size of current window in bytes. Used only under layers.
layers	`layers [options] [layers_program]` A layer multiplexor for DMD windowing terminals. layers manages asynchronous windows on a windowing terminal. *layers_program* is a file containing a firmware patch that layers downloads to the terminal (before layers are created or startup commands are executed).

Options

-d   Print sizes of the text, data, and bss portions of a downloaded firmware patch on standard error.

-D   Print debugging messages on standard error.

-f *file*
    Initialize layers with a configuration given by *file*. Each line of *file* is a layer to be created and has the format *x1 y1 x2 y2 commands*, specifying the origin, the opposite corner, and start-up commands. For example:

```
10 10 800 240 date; who; exec $SHELL
```

-h *list*
    Supply a comma-separated *list* of STREAMS modules to push onto a layer.

-m *size*
    Set data part of xt packets to maximum *size* (32–252).

-p   Print downloading protocol statistics and a trace of a downloaded firmware patch on standard error.

-s   Report protocol statistics on standard error after exiting layers.

-t   Turn on xt driver packet tracing and produce a trace dump on standard error after exiting layers.

`/usr/ccs/bin/lorder objfiles`

Take object filenames (e.g., files with .o suffix) and output a list of related pairs. The first file listed includes references to external identifiers that are defined in the second. lorder output can be sent to tsort to make the ordering of files in an archive more efficient for loading.

Example

To produce an ordered list of object files and replace them in the library libmyprog.a (provided they are newer):

```
ar cru libmyprog.a `lorder *.o | tsort`
```

`/usr/ucb/lptest [length [n]]`

Display all 96 printable ASCII characters on the standard output. Characters are printed in each position, forming a "ripple pattern." You can specify the output line *length* (default is 79) and display *n*

$\rightarrow$

lptest ←	lines of output (default is 200). `lptest` is useful for testing printers and terminals or for running shell scripts with dummy input.
mailalias	`mailalias [options] names` Display the email addresses associated with one or more alias *names*. `mailalias` displays addresses that are listed in the files /var/mail/*name*, $HOME/lib/names, and in the files pointed to by the list in /etc/mail/namefiles. `mailalias` is called by `mail`. Note: this command is part of the UPAS mailing system software. Commercial Unix systems all use `sendmail`, thus this command isn't applicable. *Options* -s Suppress *names*; show only corresponding mail address. -v Verbose mode; show debugging information.

newform	`newform [options] files`
	
	Format *files* according to the options specified. `newform` resembles `cut` and `paste` and can be used to filter text output. Options can appear more than once and can be interspersed between *files* (except for -s, which must appear first).
	
	Options
	
	-a[*n*]
	    Append *n* characters to the end of each line or, if *n* isn't specified, append characters until each line has the length specified by -l.
	
	-b[*n*]
	    Delete *n* characters from beginning of each line or, if *n* isn't specified, delete characters until each line has the length specified by -l.
	
	-c*m* Use character *m* (instead of a space) when padding lines with -a or -p; -c must precede -a or -p.
	
	-e[*n*]
	    Same as -b, but delete from the end.
	
	-f Display *tabspec* format used by last -o option.
	
	-i'*tabspec*'
	    Expand tabs to spaces using *tabspec* conversion (default is 8 spaces); *tabspec* is one of the options listed under **tabs**.

-l[*n*]
> Use line length *n* (default is 72). If -l is not specified, default line length is 80. -l usually precedes other options that modify line length (-a, -b, -c, -e, or -p).

-o'*tabspec*'
> Turn spaces into tabs using *tabspec* conversion.

-p[*n*]
> Same as -a, but pad beginning of line.

-s   Strip leading characters from each line (up to and including first tab); the first seven characters are moved to the end of the line (without the tab). All lines must contain at least one tab.

Example

Remove sequence numbers from a COBOL program:

```
newform -11 -b7 file
```

---

newgrp [-] [*group*]

Log in to *group*. If *group* name is not specified, your original group is reinstated. If - is given, log in using the same environment as when logging in as *group*. Solaris allows -l as well as -.

This command is also built in to the Bourne and Korn shells. On modern Unix systems that allow users to simultaneously be in multiple groups, this command is obsolete.

---

news [*options*] [*item_files*]

Consult the news directory for information on current events. With no arguments, news prints all current *item_files*. Items usually reside in /usr/news or /var/news.

Note: this command is not related to Usenet news.

Options

-a   Print all news items, whether current or not.

-n   Print names of news items, but not their contents.

-s   Report the number of current news items.

---

notify [*options*]

Inform user when new mail arrives. With no options, indicate whether automatic notification is enabled or disabled.

→

notify ←	Note: this command is part of the UPAS mailing system software. Commercial Unix systems all use sendmail, thus, this command isn't applicable.

Options

-m *file*
> Save mail messages to *file* (default is $HOME/.mailfile). Applies only when automatic notification is enabled (-y option).

-n   Disable mail notification. -n is used alone.

-y   Enable mail notification.

---

openwin	/usr/openwin/bin/openwin [*options*]

Start the OpenWindows graphical user interface environment. This environment is now considered obsolete; the preferred environment is CDE (the Common Desktop Environment), and OpenWindows will not be supported past Solaris 7. See also **cde** in Chapter 2, *Unix Commands*.

Useful OpenWindows Commands

The following OpenWindows commands may be of interest. Look at the manpages for more information:

calctool	On-screen scientific calculator
clock	Clock
cm	Calendar manager
cmdtool	Terminal emulator
iconedit	Icon editor
mailtool	Mail reader
oclock	A round clock
pageview	PostScript viewer
perfmeter	System-performance meter
printtool	Print manager
shelltool	Another terminal emulator (respects stty settings)
snapshot	Saves portions of X display
textedit	Simple text editor
xbiff	Graphical mail arrival watchdog program
xcalc	Simple on-screen calculator
xditview	Device-independent troff output viewer
xedit	Simple text editor
xhost	Controls permissions for who can connect to display
xload	System load monitor
xlock	Screen saver/locker

xmag	Magnifies portions of the display	**openwin**
xman	Viewer for manpages	
xterm	Standard X Window system terminal emulator	

---

pack [*options*] *files* **pack**

Compact each *file* and place the result in *file*.z. The original file is replaced. To restore packed *files* to their original form, see **pcat** and **unpack**.

The compress and gzip commands give much better compression. Their use is recommended. (See **compress** and **gzip** in Chapter 2.)

Options

- Print number of times each byte is used, relative frequency, and byte code.

-f Force the pack even when disk space isn't saved.

---

pcat *files* **pcat**

Display (as with cat) one or more packed *files*. See also **pack** and **unpack**.

---

pg [*options*] [*files*] **pg**

Display the named *files* on a terminal, one page at a time. After each screen is displayed, you are prompted to display the next page by pressing the Return key. Press h for help with additional commands; press q to quit. See also **more** in Chapter 2.

Options

-c Clear screen (same as -c of more).

-e Do not pause between files.

-f Do not split long lines.

-n Issue a pg command at the prompt without waiting for a carriage return (more works this way).

-p*str*
    Use string *str* for the command prompt. The special variable %d displays the page number.

$\rightarrow$

pg
←
	-r Restricted mode; shell escapes aren't allowed.
	
	-s Display messages in standout mode (reverse video).
	
	-n Use *n* lines for each window (default is a full screen).
	
	+*num*
	      Begin displaying at line number *num*.
	
	+/*pat*
	      Begin displaying at first line containing pattern *pat.*
	
	Example
	
	    pg -p 'Page %d :' *file*

red	red [*options*] [*file*] Restricted version of ed. With red, only files in the current working directory can be edited. Shell commands using ! are not allowed.
relogin	relogin [*option*] [*terminal*] Change the login entry to reflect the current window running under layers. This ensures that commands like who and write use the correct login information. layers calls relogin automatically, but you may sometimes want to use relogin to change the destination window for write messages. *terminal* is the filename of the terminal to change; e.g., ttyp0. *Option* -s Don't print error messages.
ruptime	ruptime [*options*] Show the status of local networked machines (similar to uptime). This command is generally no longer used because the supporting daemon generates an inordinate amount of unnecessary network traffic. *Options* -a Include users even if they've been idle for more than one hour. Normally such users are not counted. -l Sort by load average.

-r   Reverse the sort order.

-t   Sort by up time.

-u   Sort by number of users.

ruptime

---

rwho [*option*]

Report who is logged on for all machines on the local network (similar to who).

This command is generally no longer used because the supporting daemon generates an inordinate amount of unnecessary network traffic.

Option

-a   List users even if they've been idle for more than one hour.

rwho

---

shl

Control more than one shell (layer) from a single terminal. From the shl prompt level, you can issue the commands listed below (abbreviating them to any unique prefix if desired). The *name* text string should not exceed eight characters. See also layers.

block *name* [*name2* ...]
    Block the output for each layer *name* (same as stty loblk).

create [*name*]
    Create the layer *name* (no more than seven total).

delete *name* [*name2* ...]
    Delete the layer *name*.

help or ?
    Provide shl command syntax.

layers [-l] [*name* ...]
    Print information about layers. -l provides a ps-like display.

name
    Make layer *name* be the current level.

quit
    Exit shl and kill all the layers.

resume [*name*]
    Return to latest layer or to layer *name*.

shl

Obsolete Commands

$\rightarrow$

shl
←
	toggle
	    Flip back to the previous layer.
	
	unblock *name* [*name2* ...]
	    Do not block output for each layer *name* (same as stty
	    -loblk).

sum	sum [*option*] *file* Calculate and print a checksum and the number of (512-byte) blocks for *file*. Possibly useful for verifying data transmission. See also **cksum** in Chapter 2. Note: /usr/ucb/sum reports sizes in kilobytes, while /usr/bin/sum reports sizes in 512-byte blocks, even with the -r option. *Option* -r Use an alternate checksum algorithm; this produces the same results as the BSD version of sum.
tabs	tabs [*tabspec*] [*options*] Set terminal tab stops according to *tabspec*. The default *tabspec*, -8, gives the standard Unix tab settings. Specify *tabspec* as a predefined set of tab stops for particular languages, for example: a (IBM assembler), c (COBOL), f (FORTRAN), p (PL/1), s (SNOBOL), and u (UNIVAC assembler). *tabspec* can also be a repeated number, arbitrary numbers, or called from a file. *Tabspec* -n Repeat tab every *n* columns (e.g., 1+*n*, 1+2*n, etc.). *n1,n2,...* Arbitrary ascending values. If *n* is preceded by +, it is added (i.e., tab is relative to previous position). -a 1, 10, 16, 36, 72. -a2 1, 10, 16, 40, 72. -c 1, 8, 12, 16, 20, 55. -c2 1, 6, 10, 14, 49. -c3 1, 6, 10, 14, 18, 22, 26, 30, 34, 38, 42, 46, 50, 54, 58, 62, 67. -f 1, 7, 11, 15, 19, 23.

-p   1, 5, 9, 13, 17, 21, 25, 29, 33, 37, 41, 45, 49, 53, 57, 61.

-s   1, 10, 55.

-u   1, 12, 20, 44.

--file
   Read first line of *file* for tabs.

Options

+m*n* Set left margin to *n* (default is 10).

-Ttype
   Set terminal *type* (default is $TERM).

/usr/ccs/bin/tsort [*file*]

Perform a topological sort on *file*. Typically used with lorder to reorganize an archive library for more efficient handling by ar or ld. Not very useful. See also **lorder**.

Example

Find the ordering relationship of all object files, and sort them for access by ld:

```
ld -o myprog `lorder *.o | tsort`
```

---

unpack *files*

Expand one or more *files*, created with pack, to their original form. See **pcat** and **pack**.

---

uucp [*options*] [*source!*]*file* [*destination!*]*file*

Copy a file (or group of files) from the source to the destination. The *source* and *destination* can be remote systems. The destination file can be a directory.

Options

-c   Do not copy files to the spool directory (the default).

-C   Copy files to the spool directory for transfer.

-d   Make directories for the copy when they don't exist (the default).

$\rightarrow$

uucp
←
	-f Do not make directories when they don't exist.
	
	-g*x* Set grade (priority) of job. *x* is typically a single letter or digit, where a and 1 give the highest transfer priority. Use uuglist to show values for *x*.
	
	-j Print the uucp job number.
	
	-m When copy is complete, send mail to person who issued uucp command.
	
	-n*user*
	      When copy is complete, send mail to (notify) *user*.
	
	-r Queue job, but don't start transfer program (uucico).
	
	-s*file*
	      Send transfer status to *file* (a full pathname); overrides -m. Solaris accepts but ignores this option for security reasons.
	
	-x*n* Debug at level *n* (0–9); higher numbers give more output.
	
	Example
	
	This shell script sends a compressed file to system orca:
	
	<pre>$ cat send_it
	#! /bin/sh
	compress $1
	uucp -C -n$2 -m $1.Z orca!/var/spool/uucppublic
	uncompress $1</pre>
	With -C, the transfer is made from a copy in the spool directory. (Normally, uucp gets the file from its original location, so you can't rename it or uncompress it until the call goes through.) The script also notifies the sender and the recipient when the transfer finishes. Here's a sample run:
	
	<pre>send_it chapter1 bob</pre>

uuglist	uuglist [*option*] List all service grades available for use with the -g option of uux and uucp. Service grades define the priority of data transferral; they are typically expressed as single characters or as a string. ***Option*** -u List grades available to the current user.

uulog [*options*]   uulog

Print information from the uucp or uuxqt log files, which reside in
/var/uucp/.Log (down subdirectories uucico or uuxqt). See also **tail**
in Chapter 2.

Options

-f*sys*
    Issue a tail -f to print the most recent actions for a given sys-
    tem.

-s*sys*
    Print all actions for the given system.

-x Check the uuxqt log file for the given system (used with -f or
    -s).

-n Execute a tail command of *n* lines (used with -f).

---

uuname [*options*]   uuname

Print the names of systems uucp knows about.

Options

-c Print system names known to cu (usually the same).

-1 Print the local system's node name.

---

uupick [*option*]   uupick

Query the status of files sent to the user with uuto.

Option

-s*system*
    Search only for files sent from *system*.

Interactive Responses

a[*dir*]
    Move all files sent from *system* to the named *dir*.

d   Delete the entry.

m[*dir*]
    Move the file to the directory *dir*.

→

uupick ←	p Print the file.
	q Quit uupick.
	* Print a command summary.
	! *cmd* Execute the shell command *cmd*.
	EOF Quit uupick.
	RETURN Move to next entry.

uustat	uustat [*options*]

Provide information about uucp requests. This command can also be used to cancel uucp requests. Options -a, -j, -k, -m, -p, -q, and -r cannot be used with each other.

Options

-a   Report all queued jobs.

-c   When used with -t, report average time spent on queue instead of average transfer rate.

-d*n* When used with -t, report averages for past *n* minutes instead of past hour.

-j   Report the total number of jobs displayed (use only with -a or -s).

-k*n* Kill job request *n*; you must own it.

-m Report accessibility of other systems.

-n Suppress standard output but not standard error.

-p   Execute a ps -flp on active UUCP processes.

-q   Report the jobs queued for all systems.

-r*n* Renew job *n* by issuing a touch on its associated files.

-s*system*
     Report the status of jobs for *system*.

-S*x* Report status for jobs of type *x*:

     c   Completed jobs.
     i   Interrupted jobs.
     q   Queued jobs.
     r   Running jobs.

-t*system*

 Report *system*'s average transfer rate (in bytes per second) over
 the past hour.

-u*user*

 Report the status of jobs for *user*.

uuto [*options*] *sourcefiles destination*

Send source files to a destination, where *destination* is of the form
system! user. The user on the destination system can pick up the files
with uupick.

Options

-m Send mail when the copy is complete.

-p Copy files to the spool directory.

uux [*options*] [[*sys*]! *command*]

Gather files from various systems and execute *command* on the
specified machine *sys*. uux also recognizes the uucp options -c, -C,
-g, -r, -s, and -x.

Options

- Same as -p (pass standard input to *command*).

-a*user*

 Notify *user* upon completion (see -z).

-b Print the standard input when the exit status indicates an error.

-j Print the uux job number.

-n Do not send mail if *command* fails.

-p Pass the standard input to *command*.

-z Notify invoking user upon successful completion.

vacation [*options*]

SVR4 version for UPAS. (See also **vacation** in Chapter 2.) Automatically return a mail message to the sender announcing that you are
on vacation. To disable this feature, type mail -F " ".

→

vacation ←	**Options**
	-d Append the date to *logfile* (see -1).
	-F *user*
	Forward mail to *user* when unable to send mail to *mailfile* (see -m).
	-1 *logfile*
	Record in *logfile* the names of senders who received an automated reply (default is $HOME/.maillog).
	-m *mailfile*
	Save received messages in *mailfile* (default is $HOME/.mailfile).
	-M *msg_file*
	Use *msg_file* as the automatic reply to mail (default is /usr/lib/mail/std_vac_msg).

vc	/usr/ccs/bin/vc [*options*] [*keyword=value* ...]
	"Version control." Copy lines from standard input to standard output under control of the vc keywords and arguments within the standard input.
	This command is completely unrelated to RCS and to SCCS; it is essentially useless.
	Options
	-a Replace control keywords in all lines, including text lines.
	-c*k* Use *k* instead of : as the control character.
	-s Suppress warning messages.
	-t If any control characters are found before the first tab in the file, remove all characters up to the first tab.

whois	whois [*option*] *name*
	Search an Internet directory for the person, login, handle, or organization specified by *name*. Precede *name* with the modifiers !, ., or *, alone or in combination, to limit the search to either (1) the name of a person or of a username, (2) a handle, or (3) an organization.

Option	**whois**
-h *host* Search on host machine *host*.	

`write` *user* [*tty*] *message* *EOF*	**write**
Initiate or respond to an interactive conversation with *user*. A write session is terminated with *EOF*. If the user is logged in to more than one terminal, specify a *tty*. See also **talk** in Chapter 2.	

Bibliography

Many books have been written about Unix and related topics. It would be impossible to list them all, nor would that be very helpful. In this chapter, we present the "classics"—those books that the true Unix wizard has on his or her shelf. (Alas, some of these are now out-of-print; thus only the older Unix wizard has them. ☺)

Because Unix has affected many aspects of computing over its history, you will find books listed here on things besides just the Unix operating system itself.

This chapter presents:

- Unix descriptions and programmer's manuals
- Unix internals
- Programming with the Unix mindset
- Programming languages
- TCP/IP networking
- Typesetting
- Emacs
- Standards
- O'Reilly books

Unix Descriptions and Programmer's Manuals

1. *The Bell System Technical Journal*, Volume 57 Number 6, Part 2, July-August 1978. AT&T Bell Laboratories, Murray Hill, NJ, USA. ISSN 0005-8580. A special issue devoted to Unix, by the creators of the system.

2. *AT&T Bell Laboratories Technical Journal*, Volume 63 Number 8, Part 2, October 1984. AT&T Bell Laboratories, Murray Hill, NJ, USA. Another special issue devoted to Unix.

These two volumes were republished as:

3. *UNIX System Readings and Applications*, Volume 1, Prentice-Hall, Englewood Cliffs, NJ, USA, 1987. ISBN 0-13-938532-0.

4. *UNIX System Readings and Applications*, Volume 2, Prentice-Hall, Englewood Cliffs, NJ, USA, 1987. ISBN 0-13-939845-7.

5. *UNIX Time-sharing System: UNIX Programmers Manual*, Seventh Edition, Volumes 1, 2A, 2B. Bell Telephone Laboratories, Inc., January 1979.

These are the reference manuals (Volume 1), and descriptive papers (Volumes 2A and 2B) for the landmark Seventh Edition Unix system, the direct ancestor of all current commercial Unix systems.

They were reprinted by Holt Rinehart & Winston, but are now long out-of-print. However, they are available online from Bell Labs in troff source, PDF, and PostScript formats. See *http://plan9.bell-labs.com/7thEdMan*.

6. *UNIX Research System: Programmer's Manual, Tenth Edition*, Volume 1, AT&T Bell Laboratories, M.D. McIlroy and A.G. Hume editors, Holt Rinehart & Winston, New York, NY, USA, 1990. ISBN 0-03-047532-5.

7. *UNIX Research System: Papers, Tenth Edition*, Volume 2, AT&T Bell Laboratories, M.D. McIlroy and A.G. Hume editors, Holt Rinehart & Winston, New York, NY, USA, 1990. ISBN 0-03-047529-5.

These are the manuals and papers for the Tenth Edition Unix system. Although this system was not used much outside of Bell Labs, many of the ideas from it and its predecessors were incorporated into various versions of System V. And the manuals make interesting reading, in any case.

8. *4.4BSD Manuals*, Computing Systems Research Group, University of California at Berkeley. O'Reilly & Associates, Sebastopol, CA, USA, 1994. ISBN: 1-56592-082-1. Out of print.

The manuals for 4.4BSD.

9. Your Unix programmer's manual. One of the most instructive things you can do is read your manual from front to back.* (This is harder than it used to be, as Unix systems have grown.) It is easier to do if your Unix vendor makes

---

* One summer, while working as a contract programmer, I spent my lunchtimes reading the manual for System III (yes, that long ago), from cover to cover. I don't know that I ever learned so much in so little time.

printed copies of their documentation available. Otherwise, start with the Seventh Edition manual, and then read your local documentation as needed.

10. *A Quarter Century of Unix*, Peter H. Salus, Addison Wesley, Reading, MA, USA, 1994. ISBN: 0-201-54777-5.

A delightful book that tells the history of Unix, from its inception up to the time the book was written. It reads like a good novel, except that it's all true!

11. *The Unix Philosophy*, Mike Gancarz, Digital Equipment Corp, USA, 1996. ISBN: 1-55558-123-4.

12. *Plan 9: The Manuals, The Documents, The System*, AT&T Bell Laboratories, Harcourt Brace and Company, Boston, MA, USA, 1995. ISBN: 0-03-017143-1 for the full set. ISBN: 0-03-01742-3 for just the manuals. See *http://plan9.bell-labs.com/plan9/distrib.html*.

These volumes document and provide the system and source code for "Plan 9 From Bell Labs," the next-generation system done by the same people at Bell Labs who created Unix. It contains many interesting and exciting ideas. The set comes with a CD-ROM including full source code, or you can purchase just the manuals.

Unix Internals

The dedicated Unix wizard knows not only how to use his or her system, but how it works.

1. *Lions' Commentary on UNIX 6th Edition, with Source Code*, John Lions, Peer-to-Peer Communications, San Jose, CA, USA, 1996. ISBN: 1-57398-013-7. See *http://www.peer-to-peer.com/catalog/opsrc/lions.html*.

This classic work provides a look at the internals of the Sixth Edition Unix system.

2. *The Design of the UNIX Operating System*, Maurice J. Bach, Prentice-Hall, Englewood Cliffs, NJ, USA, 1986. ISBN: 0-13-201799-7.

This book very lucidly describes the design of System V Release 2, with some discussion of important features in System V Release 3, such as STREAMS and the filesystem switch.

3. *The Magic Garden Explained: The Internals of Unix System V Release 4: An Open Systems Design*, Berny Goodheart, James Cox, John R. Mashey, Prentice-Hall, Englewood Cliffs, NJ, USA, 1994. ISBN: 0-13-098138-9.

4. *Unix Internals: The New Frontiers*, Uresh Vahalia, Prentice-Hall, Englewood Cliffs, NJ, USA, 1996. ISBN: 0-13-101908-2.

5. *Unix Internals: A Practical Approach*, Steve D. Pate, Addison Wesley, Reading, MA, USA, 1996. ISBN: 0-201-87721-X.

6. *The Design and Implementation of the 4.3BSD UNIX Operating System*, Samuel J. Leffler, Marshall Kirk McKusick, Michael J. Karels and John S. Quarterman, Addison Wesley, Reading, MA, USA, 1989. ISBN: 0-201-06196-1.

This book describes the 4.3BSD version of Unix. Many important features found in commercial Unix systems first originated in the BSD Unix systems, such as long filenames, job control, and networking.

7. *The Design and Implementation of the 4.4 BSD Operating System*, Marshall Kirk McKusick, Keith Bostic, Michael J. Karels, John S. Quarterman, Addison Wesley Longman, Reading, MA, USA, 1996. ISBN 0-201-54979-4.

   This book is an update of the previous one, for 4.4BSD, the last Unix system released from UCB. To quote from the publisher's description, the book "details the major changes in process and memory management, describes the new extensible and stackable filesystem interface, includes an invaluable chapter on the new network filesystem, and updates information on networking and interprocess communication."

Programming with the Unix Mindset

Any book written by Brian Kernighan deserves careful reading, usually several times. The first two books present the Unix "toolbox" programming methodology. They will help you learn how to "think Unix." The third book continues the process, with a more explicit Unix focus. The fourth and fifth are about programming in general, and also very worthwhile.

1. *Software Tools*, Brian W. Kernighan and P. J. Plauger, Addison Wesley, Reading, MA, USA, 1976. ISBN: 0-201-03669-X.

   A wonderful book* that presents the design and code for programs equivalent to Unix's grep, sort, ed, and others. The programs use RATFOR (Rational FORTRAN), a preprocessor for FORTRAN with C-like control structures.

2. *Software Tools in Pascal*, Brian W. Kernighan and P. J. Plauger, Addison Wesley, Reading, MA, USA, 1981. ISBN: 0-201-10342-7.

   A translation of the previous book into Pascal. Still worth reading; Pascal provides many things that FORTRAN does not.

3. *The Unix Programming Environment*, Brian W. Kernighan and Rob Pike, Prentice-Hall, Englewood Cliffs, NJ, USA, 1984. ISBN:0-13-937699-2 (hardcover), 0-13-937681-X (paperback).

   This books focuses explicitly on Unix, using the tools in that environment. In particular, it adds important material on the shell, awk, and the use of lex and yacc. See *http://cm.bell-labs.com/cm/cs/upe*.

4. *The Elements of Programming Style*, Second Edition. Brian W. Kernighan and P. J. Plauger, McGraw-Hill, New York, NY, USA, 1978. ISBN: 0-07-034207-5.

   Modeled after Strunk & White's famous *The Elements of Style*, this book describes good programming practices that can be used in any environment.

---

* One that changed my life forever.

5. *The Practice of Programming*, Brian W. Kernighan and Rob Pike, Addison Wesley Longman, Reading, MA, USA, 1999. ISBN: 0-201-61586-X.

    Similar to the previous book, with a somewhat stronger technical focus. See *http://cm.bell-labs.com/cm/cs/tpop*.

6. *Writing Efficient Programs*, Jon Louis Bentley, Prentice-Hall, Englewood Cliffs, NJ, USA, 1982. ISBN: 0-13-970251-2 (hardcover), 0-13-970244-X (paperback).

    Although not related to Unix, this is an excellent book for anyone interested in programming efficiently.

7. *Programming Pearls*, Jon Louis Bentley, Addison Wesley, Reading, MA, USA, 1986. ISBN: 0-201-10331-1.

8. *More Programming Pearls: Confessions of a Coder*, Jon Louis Bentley, Addison Wesley, Reading, MA, USA, 1988. ISBN: 0-201-11889-0.

    These two excellent books, to quote Nelson H. F. Beebe, "epitomize the Unix mindset, and are wonderful examples of little languages, algorithm design, and much more." These should be on every serious programmer's bookshelf.

9. *Advanced Programming in the Unix Environment*, W. Richard Stevens, Addison Wesley, Reading, MA, USA, 1992. ISBN: 0-201-56317-7.

    A thick but excellent work on how to use the wealth of system calls in modern Unix systems.

Programming Languages

A number of important programming languages were first developed under Unix. Note again the books written by Brian Kernighan.

1. *The C Programming Language*, Brian W. Kernighan and Dennis M. Ritchie, Prentice-Hall, Englewood Cliffs, NJ, USA, 1978. ISBN: 0-13-110163-3.

    The original "bible" on C. Dennis Ritchie invented C and is one of the two "fathers" of Unix. This edition is out-of-print.

2. *The C Programming Language*, Second Edition. Brian W. Kernighan and Dennis M. Ritchie, Prentice-Hall, Englewood Cliffs, NJ, USA, 1988. ISBN: 0-13-110362-8.

    This revision of the original covers ANSI C. It retains and improves upon the high qualities of the first edition. See *http://cm.bell-labs.com/cm/cs/cbook*.

3. *C: A Reference Manual*, Fourth Edition, Samuel P. Harbison and Guy L. Steele, Prentice-Hall, Englewood Cliffs, NJ, USA, 1994. ISBN: 0-13-326224-3.

    An excellent discussion of the details for those who need to know.

4. *The C++ Programming Language*, Third Edition, Bjarne Stroustrup, Addison Wesley, Reading, MA, USA, 1997. ISBN: 0-201-88954-4.

    The definitive statement on C++ by the language's inventor and the ANSI C++ committee chair. See *http://www.awl.com/cseng/titles/0-201-88954-4/*.

5. *C++ Primer*, Third Edition, Stanley B. Lippman and Josée Lajoie. Addison Wesley Longman, Reading, MA, USA, 1998. ISBN: 0-201-82470-1.

   An excellent introduction to C++. See *http://www.awl.com/cseng/titles/0-201-82470-1/*.

6. *The Java Programming Language*, Ken Arnold and James Gosling. Addison Wesley, Reading, MA, USA, 1997. ISBN: 0-201-31006-6.

   This book is intended for learning Java, by two of the designers of the language.

7. *The Java Language Specification*, James Gosling, Bill Joy, Guy L. Steele Jr. Addison Wesley, Reading, MA, USA, 1996. ISBN: 0-201-63451-1.

8. *The AWK Programming Language*, Alfred V. Aho and Brian W. Kernighan and Peter J. Weinberger, Addison Wesley, Reading, MA, USA, 1987. ISBN: 0-201-07981-X.

   The original definition for the awk programming language. Extremely worthwhile. See *http://cm.bell-labs.com/cm/cs/awkbook*.

9. *Effective AWK Programming*, Arnold Robbins, Specialized Systems Consultants, Seattle, WA, USA, 1997. ISBN: 1-57831-000-8.

   A more tutorial treatment of awk that covers the POSIX standard for awk. It also serves as the user's guide for gawk. See *http://www.ssc.com/ssc/eap/*.

10. *Tcl and the Tk Toolkit*, John K. Ousterhout. Addison Wesley, Reading, MA, USA, 1994. ISBN: 0-201-63337-X.

11. *Practical Programming in Tcl & Tk*, Brent B. Welch. Prentice-Hall, Englewood Cliffs, NJ, USA, 1997. ISBN: 0-13-616830-2.

12. *Effective Tcl/Tk Programming: Writing Better Programs in Tcl and Tk*, Mark Harrison and Michael J. McLennan. Addison Wesley, Reading, MA, USA, 1997. ISBN: 0-201-63474-0.

13. *The New Kornshell Command and Programming Language*, Morris I. Bolsky and David G. Korn, Prentice-Hall, Englewood Cliffs, NJ, USA, 1995. ISBN: 0-13-182700-6.

   The definitive work on the Korn shell, by its author.

14. *Hands-On KornShell 93 Programming*, Barry Rosenberg, Addison Wesley Longman, Reading, MA, USA, 1998. ISBN: 0-201-31018-X.

15. *Compilers—Principles, Techniques, and Tools*, Alfred V. Aho and Ravi Sethi and Jeffrey D. Ullman, Addison Wesley Longman, Reading, MA, USA, 1986. ISBN: 0-201-10088-6.

   This is the famous "dragon book" on compiler construction. It provides much of the theory behind the operation of lex and yacc.

Bibliography

TCP/IP Networking

The books by Comer are well-written; they are the standard descriptions of the TCP/IP protocols. The books by Stevens are also very highly regarded.

1. *Internetworking with TCP/IP: Principles, Protocols, and Architecture*, Third Edition, Douglas E. Comer, Prentice-Hall, Englewood Cliffs, NJ, USA, 1995. ISBN: 0-13-216987-8.

2. *Internetworking With TCP/IP: Design, Implementation, and Internals*, Third Edition, Douglas E. Comer and David L. Stevens, Prentice-Hall, Englewood Cliffs, NJ, USA, 1998. ISBN: 0-13-973843-6.

3. *Internetworking With TCP/IP: Client-Server Programming and Applications: BSD Socket Version*, Second Edition, Douglas E. Comer and David L. Stevens, Prentice-Hall, Englewood Cliffs, NJ, USA, 1996. ISBN: 0-13-260969-X.

4. *Internetworking With TCP/IP: Client-Server Programming and Applications: AT&T TLI Version*, Douglas E. Comer and David L. Stevens, Prentice-Hall, Englewood Cliffs, NJ, USA, 1993. ISBN: 0-13-474230-3.

5. *TCP/IP Illustrated, Volume 1: The Protocols*, W. Richard Stevens, Addison Wesley Longman, Reading, MA, USA, 1994. ISBN: 0-201-63346-9.

6. *TCP/IP Illustrated, Volume 2: The Implementation*, W. Richard Stevens and Gary R. Wright, Addison Wesley Longman, Reading, MA, USA, 1995. ISBN: 0-201-63354-X.

7. *TCP/IP Illustrated, Volume 3: TCP for Transactions, HTTP, NNTP, and the Unix Domain Protocols*, W. Richard Stevens, Addison Wesley Longman, Reading, MA, USA, 1996. ISBN: 0-201-63495-3.

8. *Unix Network Programming, Volume 1: Networking APIs: Sockets and XTI*, W. Richard Stevens, Prentice-Hall, Englewood Cliffs, NJ, USA, 1997. ISBN: 0-13-490012-X.

9. *Unix Network Programming, Volume 2: Interprocess Communications*, W. Richard Stevens, Prentice-Hall, Englewood Cliffs, NJ, USA, 1998. ISBN: 0-13-081081-9.

   This volume and the previous one are revisions of the first edition that was the standard book on Unix network programming for many years.

10. *Unix System V Network Programming*, Steven A. Rago, Addison Wesley Longman, Reading, MA, USA, 1993. ISBN: 0-201-56318-5.

Typesetting

1. *Document Formatting and Typesetting on the Unix System*, Second Edition, Narain Gehani, Silicon Press, Summit, NJ, USA, 1987. ISBN: 0-13-938325-5.

2. *Typesetting Tables on the Unix System*, Henry McGilton and Mary McNabb, Trilithon Press, Los Altos, CA, USA, 1990. ISBN: 0-9626289-0-5.

This book tells you everything you might ever want to know, and then some, about using tbl to format tables.

Emacs

1. *GNU Emacs Manual, for Version 20.1*, Thirteenth Edition, The Free Software Foundation, Cambridge, MA, USA, 1998. ISBN: 1882114 06X.

2. *GNU Emacs Lisp Reference Manual, for Emacs Version 20*, Edition 2.4, The Free Software Foundation, Cambridge, MA, USA, 1998. ISBN: 1882114 728.

3. *Writing GNU Emacs Extensions*, Bob Glickstein, O'Reilly & Associates, Sebastopol, CA, USA, 1997. ISBN: 1-56592-261-1.

See also the reference to *Learning GNU Emacs* in the O'Reilly section.

Standards

There are a number of "official" standards for the behavior of portable applications among Unix and Unix-like systems. The first two entries are the standards themselves, the next one is a guide for using the first standard. The final two entries are the formal standards for the C and C++ programming languages.

1. *ISO/IEC Standard 9945-1: 1996 [IEEE/ANSI Std 1003.1, 1996 Edition] Information Technology—Portable Operating System Interface (POSIX)—Part 1: System Application: Program Interface (API) [C Language]*. IEEE, 1996. ISBN: 1-55937-573-6.

   This edition incorporates extensions for real-time applications (1003.1b-1993, 1003.1i-1995) and threads (1003.1c-1995). Electronic versions are available via subscription, see *http://www.standards.ieee.org*.

   This book describes the interface to the operating system as seen by the C or C++ programmer.

2. *ISO/IEC Standard 9945-2: 1993 [IEEE/ANSI Std 1003.2-1992 & IEEE/ANSI 1003.2a-1992] Information Technology—Portable Operating System Interface (POSIX)—Part 2: Shell and Utilities* IEEE, 1996. ISBN: 1-55937-406-3. Includes and shipped with 1003.2d-1994.

   This standard is more relevant for readers of this book: it describes the operating system at the level of the shell and utilities.

3. *Posix Programmer's Guide: Writing Portable Unix Programs*, Donald A. Lewine. O'Reilly & Associates, Sebastopol, CA, USA, 1991. ISBN: 0-937175-73-0.

4. X3 Secretariat: *Standard—The C Language*. X3J11/90-013. ISO Standard ISO/IEC 9899. Computer and Business Equipment Manufacturers Association. Washington DC, USA, 1990.

5. X3 Secretariat: *International Standard—The C++ Language*. X3J16-14882. Information Technology Council (NSITC). Washington DC, USA, 1998.

O'Reilly Books

Here is a list of O'Reilly & Associates books cited throughout this book. There are, of course, many other O'Reilly books relating to Unix. See *http://www.oreilly.com/catalog*.

1. *Advanced Perl Programming*, Sriram Srinivasan, O'Reilly & Associates, Sebastopol, CA, USA, 1997. ISBN: 1-56592-220-4.

2. *Applying RCS and SCCS*. Don Bolinger and Tan Bronson, O'Reilly & Associates, Sebastopol, CA, USA, 1995. ISBN: 1-56592-117-8.

3. *Checking C Programs with lint*. Ian F. Darwin, O'Reilly & Associates, Sebastopol, CA, USA, 1988. ISBN: 0-937175-30-7.

4. *Learning GNU Emacs*, Second Edition, Debra Cameron, Bill Rosenblatt, and Eric Raymond, O'Reilly & Associates, Sebastopol, CA, USA, 1996. ISBN: 1-56592-152-6.

5. *Learning Perl*, Second Edition, Randal L. Schwartz and Tom Christiansen, O'Reilly & Associates, Sebastopol, CA, USA, 1997. ISBN: 1-56592-284-0.

6. *Learning the Korn Shell*, Bill Rosenblatt, O'Reilly & Associates, Sebastopol, CA, USA, 1993. ISBN: 1-56592-054-6.

7. *Learning the Unix Operating System*, Fourth Edition, Jerry Peek, Grace Todino, and John Strang, O'Reilly & Associates, Sebastopol, CA, USA, 1997. ISBN: 1-56592-390-1.

8. *Learning the vi Editor*, Sixth Edition, Linda Lamb and Arnold Robbins, O'Reilly & Associates, Sebastopol, CA, USA, 1998. ISBN: 1-56592-426-6.

9. *lex & yacc*, Second Edition, John Levine, Tony Mason, and Doug Brown, O'Reilly & Associates, Sebastopol, CA, USA, 1992. ISBN: 1-56592-000-7.

10. *Managing Projects with make*, Second Edition, Andrew Oram and Steve Talbott, O'Reilly & Associates, Sebastopol, CA, USA, 1991. ISBN: 0-937175-90-0.

11. *Mastering Regular Expressions*, Jeffrey E. F. Friedl, O'Reilly & Associates, Sebastopol, CA, USA, 1997. ISBN: 1-56592-257-3.

12. *PGP: Pretty Good Privacy*, Simson Garfinkel, O'Reilly & Associates, Sebastopol, CA, USA, 1994. ISBN: 1-56592-098-8.

13. *Programming Perl*, Second Edition, Larry Wall, Tom Christiansen, and Randal L. Schwartz, O'Reilly & Associates, Sebastopol, CA, USA, 1996. ISBN: 1-56592-149-6.

14. *sed & awk*, Second Edition, Dale Dougherty and Arnold Robbins, O'Reilly & Associates, Sebastopol, CA, USA, 1997. ISBN: 1-56592-225-5.

15. *termcap & terminfo.* Third Edition, John Strang, Linda Mui, and Tim O'Reilly, O'Reilly & Associates, Sebastopol, CA, USA, 1988. ISBN: 0-937175-22-6.

16. *Using csh & tcsh*, Paul DuBois, O'Reilly & Associates, Sebastopol, CA, USA, 1995. ISBN: 1-56592-132-1.

Index

bundling commands, 193
bundling software packages, 4

C

c command (sed), 354
C and C++ languages
  call-graph profile data, 78
  compilers, 5
  compiling source files, 24
  debugging, 41
  detecting bugs and errors, 104
  extracting messages from, 195
  extracting strings for localization, 65
  formatting files in, 24
  symbol cross references, 42
C- commands (emacs), 311–313
C shell (see csh)
cal command, 22
calculator commands
  bc command, 18
  dc command, 46
calendar command, 22
calendars, 22
call-graph profile data, 78
calling out (cu command), 545
cancel command, 23
canceling commands (emacs), 306
capitalization (see case)
case
  converting, 46
  emacs commands for, 307
case command, 230, 279
cat command, 23
cb command, 24
cc command, 24
cd command, 25, 231, 279
cdc command (SCCS), 496
CDE (Common Desktop Environment), 26
CDPATH shell variable, 218
cdpath shell variable, 268
CD-ROM, ejecting, 59
centering (see alignment/positioning), 309
cflow command, 27
change command (ex), 339
changing directory, 25
character classes, 209, 298

character sets, converting, 83
characters, 46
  ASCII character set, 537–541
  buffer block size, 46
  converting DOS to ISO, 53
  converting ISO to DOS, 182
  counting in files, 191
  Greek (eqn preprocessor), 470
  mathematical (eqn preprocessor), 470
  nroff/troff requests for, 390
  (see also text)
chdir command, 279
check pseudo-command (sccs), 504
checkeq command, 27
checking in files, 491, 497, 507, 513
checking out files, 498, 507, 515
checknr command, 27
checksum
  cksum command, 31
checksum, calculating, 558
chgrp command, 28
chkey command, 28
  (see also keylogin command; keylogout command)
chmod command, 28
chown command, 30
ci command (RCS), 507, 513
cksum command, 31
class files (Java), disassembling, 93
classes, character, 209, 298
classifying files by data type, 69
CLASSPATH environment variable, 93
clean pseudo-command (sccs), 504
clear command, 31
clearing terminal display, 31
clock modes, setting, 163
close function (awk), 370
cmp command, 31
cntrl character class, 210
co command (RCS), 507, 515
cof2elf command, 544
COFF files, converting to ELF, 544
col command, 32
columns
  merging file lines into, 131
  selecting from files, 42
COLUMNS shell variable, 218
comb command (SCCS), 497
combination modes, setting, 162

T

t command (sed), 359
t command (ex), 345
tab characters
    converting spaces to, 180
    expanding to spaces, 62
tab stops, setting, 558
tables
    converting files into, 196
    formatting in nroff/troff, 466–469
    symbol tables, printing, 127
tabs command, 558
tabs, nroff/troff requests for, 391
tag command (ex), 345
tail command, 164
talk command, 165
tape files, copying/restoring, 34, 166
tar command, 166
targets, updating, 118
tbl preprocessor (nroff/troff), 466–469
tee command, 169
tell pseudo-command (sccs), 505
telnet command, 170
telnet modes, 170
TERM environment variable, 219, 270
term shell variable, 268
terminals
    capability of, 172
    clearing displays, 31
    clearing settings, 145
    device name, printing, 178
    resetting window layers, 550
    setting modes, 177
    setting options, 157–164
    testing, 551
terminating process IDs, 98
termination status for background processes, 191
test command, 171, 249
text, 46
    ASCII character set, 537–541
    converting spaces into tabs, 180
    expanding tabs into spaces, 62
    line formatting, 74
    pattern matching, 295–301
    searching for (see searching)
    (see also characters)

text editors
    ed, 57
    edit, 58
    emacs (see emacs editor)
    ex, 61
    pattern-matching metacharacters
        for, 296
    recovering files after crash, 189
    screen-oriented, 189
    vedit editor, 187
    vi editor (see vi)
text formatting
    man macros, 458–464
        internal names, 463
        predefined strings, 462
    me macros, 443–457
        number registers, 455
        predefined strings, 454
    mm macros, 413–433
        number registers, 429
        predefined string names, 429
        reserved macro and string
            names, 432
    ms macros, 434–442
        number registers, 440–441
        reserved macro and string
            names, 440
    nroff and troff programs, 381–391
        command-line invocation, 382
        conceptual overview, 383
        default request operation, 387
        eqn processor, 469–473
        escape sequences, 405
        pic processor, 473–481
        predefined registers, 407
        refer processor, 481–485
        requests (by group), 390
        requests (by name), 392
        special characters, 408
        tbl processor, 466–469
    nroff/troff preprocessors, 187,
        465–485
TEXTDOMAIN environment variable,
    78
time command, 171, 252, 290
time shell variable, 268
times command (ksh93), 253
times command (sh, ksh), 253
timestamps, RCS, 511
timestamps, SCCS, 502

About the Author

Arnold Robbins, an Atlanta native, is a professional programmer and technical author. He is also a happy husband, the father of four very cute children, and an amateur Talmudist (Babylonian and Jerusalem). Since late 1997, he and his family have been living happily in Israel.

Arnold has been working with Unix systems since 1980, when he was introduced to a PDP-11 running a version of Sixth Edition Unix. He has been a heavy *awk* user since 1987, when he became involved with *gawk*, the GNU project's version of *awk*. As a member of the POSIX 1003.2 balloting group, he helped shape the POSIX standard for *awk*. He is currently the maintainer of *gawk* and its documentation. The documentation is available from the Free Software Foundation (*http://www.gnu.org*) and has also been published by SSC (*http://www.ssc.com*) as *Effective AWK Programming*.

O'Reilly has been keeping him busy: he is coauthor of the second edition of *sed & awk*, and coauthor of the sixth edition of *Learning the vi Editor*.

Colophon

Our look is the result of reader comments, our own experimentation, and feedback from distribution channels. Distinctive covers complement our distinctive approach to technical topics, breathing personality and life into potentially dry subjects.

The animal featured on the cover of *Unix in a Nutshell* is a tarsier, a nocturnal mammal related to the lemur. Its generic name, Tarsius, is derived from the animal's very long ankle bone, the tarsus. The tarsier is a native of the East Indies jungles from Sumatra to the Philippines and Sulawesi, where it lives in the trees, leaping from branch to branch with extreme agility and speed.

A small animal, the tarsier's body is only six inches long, followed by a ten-inch tufted tail. It is covered in soft brown or grey silky fur, has a round face, and huge eyes. Its arms and legs are long and slender, as are its digits, which are tipped with rounded, fleshy pads to improve the tarsier's grip on trees. Tarsiers are active only at night, hiding during the day in tangles of vines or in the tops of tall trees. They subsist mainly on insects, and though very curious animals, tend to be loners.

Mary Anne Weeks Mayo was the production editor and copyeditor for *Unix in a Nutshell, Third Edition*; Ellie Maden, Ellie Cutler, and Jane Ellin provided quality control. Maureen Dempsey, Colleen Gorman, and Kimo Carter provided production assistance. Lenny Muellner provided SGML support. Seth Maislin wrote the index.

Edie Freedman designed the cover of this book, using a 19th-century engraving from the Dover Pictorial Archive. The cover layout was produced by Kathleen Wilson with Quark XPress 3.32 using the ITC Garamond font. Whenever possible, our books use RepKover™, a durable and flexible lay-flat binding. If the page count exceeds RepKover's limit, perfect binding is used.

The inside layout was designed by Alicia Cech, based on a series design by Nancy Priest, and implemented in *gtroff* by Lenny Muellner. The text and heading fonts are ITC Garamond Light and Garamond Book. This colophon was written by Michael Kalantarian.

Linux

Using Samba

By Peter Kelly, Perry Donham &
David Collier-Brown
1st Edition October 1999 (est.)
420 pages (est.), Includes CD-ROM
ISBN 1-56592-449-5

Samba turns a UNIX or Linux system
into a file and print server for Microsoft
Windows network clients. This complete
guide to Samba administration covers basic 2.0 configuration,
security, logging, and troubleshooting. Whether you're playing
on one note or a full three-octave range, this book will help you
maintain an efficient and secure server. Includes a CD-ROM of
sources and ready-to-install binaries.

Learning Red Hat Linux

By Bill McCarty
1st Edition September 1999
394 pages, Includes CD-ROM
ISBN 1-56592-627-7

Learning Red Hat Linux will guide any
new Linux user through the installation
and use of the free operating system that
is shaking up the world of commercial
software. It demystifies Linux in terms familiar to Windows
users and gives readers only what they need to start being
successful users of this operating system.

MySQL & mSQL

By Randy Jay Yarger,
George Reese & Tim King
1st Edition July 1999
506 pages, ISBN 1-56592-434-7

This book teaches you how to use
MySQL and mSQL, two popular and
robust database products that support
key subsets of SQL on both Linux and
UNIX systems. Anyone who knows basic C, Java, Perl, or
Python can write a program to interact with a database, either
as a stand-alone application or through a Web page. This
book takes you through the whole process, from installation
and configuration to programming interfaces and basic
administration. Includes ample tutorial material.

Programming with Qt

By Matthias Kalle Dalheimer
1st Edition April 1999
384 pages, ISBN 1-56592-588-2

This indispensable guide teaches you
how to take full advantage of Qt, a
powerful, easy-to-use, cross-platform
GUI toolkit, and guides you through
the steps of writing your first Qt
application. It describes all of the GUI elements in Qt, along
with advice about when and how to use them. It also contains
material on advanced topics like 2D transformations,
drag-and-drop, and custom image file filters.

Open Sources:
Voices from the Open Source Revolution

Edited by Chris DiBona,
Sam Ockman & Mark Stone
1st Edition January 1999
280 pages, ISBN 1-56592-582-3

In Open Sources, leaders of Open
Source come together in print for the
first time to discuss the new vision of
the software industry they have created,
through essays that explain how the movement works, why it
succeeds, and where it is going. A powerful vision from the
movement's spiritual leaders, this book reveals the mysteries
of how open development builds better software and how
businesses can leverage freely available software for a
competitive business advantage.

Programming with GNU Software

By Mike Loukides & Andy Oram
1st Edition December 1996
260 pages, Includes CD-ROM
ISBN 1-56592-112-7

This book and CD combination is a
complete package for programmers
who are new to UNIX or who would like
to make better use of the system. The
tools come from Cygnus Support, Inc., and Cyclic Software,
companies that provide support for free software. Contents
include GNU Emacs, gcc, C and C++ libraries, gdb, RCS, and
make. The book provides an introduction to all these tools for
a C programmer.

Linux

The Cathedral & the Bazaar

By Eric S. Raymond
1st Edition October 1999
288 pages, ISBN 1-56592-724-9

After Red Hat's stunning IPO, even people outside the computer industry have now heard of Linux and open-source software. This book contains the essays, originally published online, that led to Netscape's decision to release their browser as open source, put Linus Torvalds on the cover of Forbes Magazine and Microsoft on the defensive, and helped Linux to rock the world of commercial software. These essays have been expanded and revised for this edition, and are in print for the first time.

UNIX Basics

Learning the vi Editor, 6th Edition

By Linda Lamb & Arnold Robbins
6th Edition October 1998
348 pages, ISBN 1-56592-426-6

This completely updated guide to editing with vi, the editor available on nearly every UNIX system, now covers four popular vi clones and includes command summaries for easy reference. It starts with the basics, followed by more advanced editing tools, such as ex commands, global search and replacement, and a new feature, multi-screen editing.

Learning GNU Emacs, 2nd Edition

By Debra Cameron, Bill Rosenblatt & Eric Raymond
2nd Edition September 1996
560 pages, ISBN 1-56592-152-6

Learning GNU Emacs is an introduction to Version 19.30 of the GNU Emacs editor, one of the most widely used and powerful editors available under UNIX. It provides a solid introduction to basic editing, a look at several important "editing modes" (special Emacs features for editing specific types of documents, including email, Usenet News, and the World Wide Web), and a brief introduction to customization and Emacs LISP programming. The book is aimed at new Emacs users, whether or not they are programmers. Includes quick-reference card.

UNIX Basics

Learning the Korn Shell

By Bill Rosenblatt
1st Edition June 1993
360 pages, ISBN 1-56592-054-6

A thorough introduction to the Korn shell, both as a user interface and as a programming language. This book provides a clear explanation of the Korn shell's features, including ksh string operations, co-processes, signals and signal handling, and command-line interpretation. Learning the Korn Shell also includes real-life programming examples and a Korn shell debugger (kshdb).

Using csh and tcsh

By Paul DuBois
1st Edition August 1995
242 pages, ISBN 1-56592-132-1

Using csh and tcsh describes from the beginning how to use these shells interactively to get your work done faster with less typing. You'll learn how to make your prompt tell you where you are (no more pwd); use what you've typed before (history); type long command lines with few keystrokes (command and filename completion); remind yourself of filenames when in the middle of typing a command; and edit a botched command without retyping it.

Volume 3M: X Window System User's Guide, Motif Edition, 2nd Edition

By Valerie Quercia & Tim O'Reilly
2nd Edition January 1993
956 pages, ISBN 1-56592-015-5

The X Window System User's Guide, Motif Edition orients the new user to window system concepts and provides detailed tutorials for many client programs, including the xtermterminal emulator and the twm, uwm, and mwmwindow managers. Later chapters explain how to customize the X environment. Revised for Motif 1.2 and X11 Release 5.

UNIX Basics

Learning the UNIX Operating System, 4th Edition

By Jerry Peek, Grace Todino & John Strang
4th Edition December 1997
106 pages, ISBN 1-56592-390-1

If you are new to UNIX, this concise introduction will tell you just what you need to get started and no more. The new fourth edition covers the Linux operating system and is an ideal primer for someone just starting with UNIX or Linux, as well as for Mac and PC users who encounter a UNIX system on the Internet. This classic book, still the most effective introduction to UNIX in print, now includes a quick-reference card.

Web Server Administration

Web Performance Tuning

By Patrick Killelea
1st Edition October 1998
374 pages, ISBN 1-56592-379-0

Web Performance Tuning hits the ground running and gives concrete advice for improving crippled Web performance right away. For anyone who has waited too long for a Web page to display or watched servers slow to a crawl, this book includes tips on tuning the server software, operating system, network, and the Web browser itself.

Web Security & Commerce

By Simson Garfinkel with Gene Spafford
1st Edition June 1997
506 pages, ISBN 1-56592-269-7

Learn how to minimize the risks of the Web with this comprehensive guide. It covers browser vulnerabilities, privacy concerns, issues with Java, JavaScript, ActiveX, and plug-ins, digital certificates, cryptography, Web server security, blocking software, censorship technology, and relevant civil and criminal issues.

Web Server Administration

Writing Apache Modules with Perl and C

By Lincoln Stein & Doug MacEachern
1st Edition March 1999
746 pages, ISBN 1-56592-567-X

This guide to Web programming teaches you how to extend the capabilities of the Apache Web server. It explains the design of Apache, mod_perl, and the Apache API, then demonstrates how to use them to rewrite CGI scripts, filter HTML documents on the server-side, enhance server log functionality, convert file formats on the fly, and more.

Apache: The Definitive Guide, 2nd Edition

By Ben Laurie & Peter Laurie
2nd Edition February 1999
388 pages, Includes CD-ROM
ISBN 1-56592-528-9

Written and reviewed by key members of the Apache group, this book is the only complete guide on the market that describes how to obtain, set up, and secure the Apache software on both UNIX and Windows systems. The second edition fully describes Windows support and all the other Apache 1.3 features. Includes CD-ROM with Apache sources and demo sites discussed in the book.

Practical Internet Groupware

By Jon Udell
1st Edition October 1999 (est.)
384 pages (est.), ISBN 1-56592-537-8

This revolutionary book tells users, programmers, IS managers, and system administrators how to build Internet groupware applications that organize the casual and chaotic transmission of online information into useful, disciplined, and documented data.

Web Server Administration

Stopping Spam

By Alan Schwartz & Simson Garfinkel
1st Edition October 1998
204 pages, ISBN 1-56592-388-X

This book describes spam – unwanted email messages and inappropriate news articles – and explains what you and your Internet service providers and administrators can do to prevent it, trace it, stop it, and even outlaw it. Contains a wealth of advice, technical tools, and additional technical and community resources.

sendmail, 2nd Edition

By Bryan Costales & Eric Allman
2nd Edition January 1997
1050 pages, ISBN 1-56592-222-0

sendmail, 2nd Edition, covers sendmail Version 8.8 from Berkeley and the standard versions available on most systems. This cross-referenced edition offers an expanded tutorial and solution-oriented examples, plus topics such as the #error delivery agent, sendmail's exit values, MIME headers, and how to set up and use the user database, mailertable, and smrsh.

How to stay in touch with O'Reilly

1. Visit Our Award-Winning Site

http://www.oreilly.com/

★ "Top 100 Sites on the Web" —*PC Magazine*
★ "Top 5% Web sites" —*Point Communications*
★ "3-Star site" —*The McKinley Group*

Our web site contains a library of comprehensive product information (including book excerpts and tables of contents), downloadable software, background articles, interviews with technology leaders, links to relevant sites, book cover art, and more. File us in your Bookmarks or Hotlist!

2. Join Our Email Mailing Lists

New Product Releases

To receive automatic email with brief descriptions of all new O'Reilly products as they are released, send email to:
listproc@online.oreilly.com
Put the following information in the first line of your message (*not* in the Subject field):
subscribe oreilly-news

O'Reilly Events

If you'd also like us to send information about trade show events, special promotions, and other O'Reilly events, send email to:
listproc@online.oreilly.com
Put the following information in the first line of your message (*not* in the Subject field):
subscribe oreilly-events

3. Get Examples from Our Books via FTP

There are two ways to access an archive of example files from our books:

Regular FTP

- ftp to:
  ftp.oreilly.com
  (login: anonymous
  password: your email address)
- Point your web browser to:
  ftp://ftp.oreilly.com/

FTPMAIL

- Send an email message to:
  ftpmail@online.oreilly.com
  (Write "help" in the message body)

4. Contact Us via Email

order@oreilly.com
To place a book or software order online. Good for North American and international customers.

subscriptions@oreilly.com
To place an order for any of our newsletters or periodicals.

books@oreilly.com
General questions about any of our books.

software@oreilly.com
For general questions and product information about our software. Check out O'Reilly Software Online at **http://software.oreilly.com/** for software and technical support information. Registered O'Reilly software users send your questions to:
website-support@oreilly.com

cs@oreilly.com
For answers to problems regarding your order or our products.

booktech@oreilly.com
For book content technical questions or corrections.

proposals@oreilly.com
To submit new book or software proposals to our editors and product managers.

international@oreilly.com
For information about our international distributors or translation queries. For a list of our distributors outside of North America check out:
http://www.oreilly.com/www/order/country.html

O'Reilly & Associates, Inc.
101 Morris Street, Sebastopol, CA 95472 USA
TEL   707-829-0515 or 800-998-9938
         (6am to 5pm PST)
FAX   707-829-0104

O'REILLY®

Titles from O'Reilly

O'REILLY®

International Distributors

UK, EUROPE, MIDDLE EAST AND AFRICA (EXCEPT FRANCE, GERMANY, AUSTRIA, SWITZERLAND, LUXEMBOURG, LIECHTENSTEIN, AND EASTERN EUROPE)

INQUIRIES

O'Reilly UK Limited
4 Castle Street
Farnham
Surrey, GU9 7HS
United Kingdom
Telephone: 44-1252-711776
Fax: 44-1252-734211
Email: josette@oreilly.com

ORDERS

Wiley Distribution Services Ltd.
1 Oldlands Way
Bognor Regis
West Sussex PO22 9SA
United Kingdom
Telephone: 44-1243-779777
Fax: 44-1243-820250
Email: cs-books@wiley.co.uk

FRANCE

ORDERS

GEODIF
61, Bd Saint-Germain
75240 Paris Cedex 05, France
Tel: 33-1-44-41-46-16 (French books)
Tel: 33-1-44-41-11-87 (English books)
Fax: 33-1-44-41-11-44
Email: distribution@eyrolles.com

INQUIRIES

Éditions O'Reilly
18 rue Séguier
75006 Paris, France
Tel: 33-1-40-51-52-30
Fax: 33-1-40-51-52-31
Email: france@editions-oreilly.fr

GERMANY, SWITZERLAND, AUSTRIA, EASTERN EUROPE, LUXEMBOURG, AND LIECHTENSTEIN

INQUIRIES & ORDERS

O'Reilly Verlag
Balthasarstr. 81
D-50670 Köln
Germany
Telephone: 49-221-973160-91
Fax: 49-221-973160-8
Email: anfragen@oreilly.de (inquiries)
Email: order@oreilly.de (orders)

CANADA (FRENCH LANGUAGE BOOKS)

Les Éditions Flammarion ltée
375, Avenue Laurier Ouest
Montréal (Québec) H2V 2K3
Tel: 00-1-514-277-8807
Fax: 00-1-514-278-2085
Email: info@flammarion.qc.ca

HONG KONG

City Discount Subscription Service, Ltd.
Unit D, 3rd Floor, Yan's Tower
27 Wong Chuk Hang Road
Aberdeen, Hong Kong
Tel: 852-2580-3539
Fax: 852-2580-6463
Email: citydis@ppn.com.hk

KOREA

Hanbit Media, Inc.
Sonyoung Bldg. 202
Yeksam-dong 736-36
Kangnam-ku
Seoul, Korea
Tel: 822-554-9610
Fax: 822-556-0363
Email: hant93@chollian.dacom.co.kr

PHILIPPINES

Mutual Books, Inc.
429-D Shaw Boulevard
Mandaluyong City, Metro
Manila, Philippines
Tel: 632-725-7538
Fax: 632-721-3056
Email: mbikikog@mnl.sequel.net

TAIWAN

O'Reilly Taiwan
No. 3, Lane 131
Hang-Chow South Road
Section 1, Taipei, Taiwan
Tel: 886-2-23968990
Fax: 886-2-23968916
Email: taiwan@oreilly.com

CHINA

O'Reilly Beijing
Room 2410
160, FuXingMenNeiDaJie
XiCheng District
Beijing
China PR 100031
Tel: 86-10-86631006
Fax: 86-10-86631007
Email: beijing@oreilly.com

INDIA

Computer Bookshop (India) Pvt. Ltd.
190 Dr. D.N. Road, Fort
Bombay 400 001 India
Tel: 91-22-207-0989
Fax: 91-22-262-3551
Email: cbsbom@giasbm01.vsnl.net.in

JAPAN

O'Reilly Japan, Inc.
Kiyoshige Building 2F
12-Bancho, Sanei-cho
Shinjuku-ku
Tokyo 160-0008 Japan
Tel: 81-3-3356-5227
Fax: 81-3-3356-5261
Email: japan@oreilly.com

ALL OTHER ASIAN COUNTRIES

O'Reilly & Associates, Inc.
101 Morris Street
Sebastopol, CA 95472 USA
Tel: 707-829-0515
Fax: 707-829-0104
Email: order@oreilly.com

AUSTRALIA

WoodsLane Pty., Ltd.
7/5 Vuko Place
Warriewood NSW 2102
Australia
Tel: 61-2-9970-5111
Fax: 61-2-9970-5002
Email: info@woodslane.com.au

NEW ZEALAND

Woodslane New Zealand, Ltd.
21 Cooks Street (P.O. Box 575)
Waganui, New Zealand
Tel: 64-6-347-6543
Fax: 64-6-345-4840
Email: info@woodslane.com.au

LATIN AMERICA

McGraw-Hill Interamericana
Editores, S.A. de C.V.
Cedro No. 512
Col. Atlampa
06450, Mexico, D.F.
Tel: 52-5-547-6777
Fax: 52-5-547-3336
Email: mcgraw-hill@infosel.net.mx

O'REILLY®